BROTHER BILL

Brother Bill

PRESIDENT CLINTON

AND THE POLITICS

OF RACE AND CLASS

DARYL A. CARTER

The University of Arkansas Press
Fayetteville
2016

Copyright © 2016 by The University of Arkansas Press
All rights reserved
Manufactured in the United States of America
ISBN: 978-1-55728-699-4 (paper)
ISBN: 978-1-68226-002-9 (cloth)
e-ISBN: 978-1-61075-585-6

20   19   18   17   16   5   4   3   2   1

Designed by Liz Lester

⊗ The paper used in this publication meets the minimum requirements
of the American National Standard for Permanence of Paper
for Printed Library Materials Z39.48-1984.

Library of Congress Control Number: 2015960127

To Crystal, Gracie, and Maxwell

CONTENTS

Acknowledgments

ix

INTRODUCTION

"The First Black President?"

1

CHAPTER 1

The Democratic Leadership Council
and African Americans

21

CHAPTER 2

Race and Class in the 1990s

53

CHAPTER 3

The Politics of Racial Appointments

67

CHAPTER 4

Responsibility and Accountability

95

CHAPTER 5

"Mend It, Don't End It"

135

CHAPTER 6

Welfare Reform

169

CHAPTER 7

A Missed Opportunity

203

CHAPTER 8
The Clinton Legacy
225

Conclusion
245

Notes
253

Bibliography
287

Index
301

CONTENTS

ACKNOWLEDGMENTS

This book has been a labor of love. I began my research in the fall of 2006 as a PhD student at the University of Memphis. I believed then, and I do now, that President Bill Clinton was and is an important political figure during the last third of the twentieth century. Clinton's relationship with African Americans uncovers the nuances of race in the United States. Further, Clinton represented the increasingly complex, intertwined relationship with America's most closely guarded secret: class. Engaging middle- and upper-class African Americans while ignoring the plight of the most vulnerable allowed Clinton to win the presidency in 1992 and 1996. It greatly assisted in maintaining a critical element of the Democratic Party's political base, white working- and middle-class voters. The effects of Clinton's reign as head of the Democratic Party and the United States paved the way for the inclusive presidency of George W. Bush and, most historically, the election of the first African American president of the United States, Barack Obama.

It is commonly believed that historians work alone. Many talk of the proverbial scholar sitting alone in front of a computer or typewriter with his or her notes and documents. The work of a historian is, contrary to this myth, collaboration between the historian and many others who educate, elucidate, and support the work. For this reason I have many to thank for their help in making this work possible.

First, I would like to thank the archivists and staff at the William J. Clinton Presidential Library in Little Rock, Arkansas. Their able and expert assistance was a godsend as I conducted the research for this book. I am forever grateful to them. Also, I wish to thank the staff of the Special Collections Library at Duke University. The research grant from the John Hope Franklin Center was very important to my work. Second, I wish to thank the following people: John Hope Franklin, William Winter, Tom Kean, and other members of the President's Initiative on Race for speaking with me about the important work they eagerly pursued. Peter Edelman was very helpful in explaining the atmosphere within the Clinton administration and in Washington,

D.C., during the tense debates over welfare reform. Moreover, I wish to thank Beverly Bond, Arwin Smallwood, Janann Sherman, Daniel Unowsky, Charles Crawford, and Karen Bradley at the University of Memphis. These fine individuals were instrumental in making me the historian I am today. The University of Memphis Department of History provided wonderful support in the form of a grant to support my research. While I may be biased, I believe the University of Memphis is the finest research institution in the United States. The tremendous work done by the faculty and staff and the expert leadership of Shirley Raines, president emeritus, makes the institution a wonderful and intellectually stimulating place in which to work and study.

There is one person, however, that I wish to thank most for making me the historian I am today, Dr. Aram Goudsouzian. Aram is one of the most important individuals in my professional life. He was tough! He was blunt! But he was always fair and constructive and encouraging. He disabused me of journalistic notions and forced me to think like and write like a historian. Also, Aram was key in getting my manuscript to the right people. I cannot thank him enough for all the work he did for me and the professional relationship we enjoy today. Thank you, Aram!

When I began looking for a publisher for my work, Aram directed me to the University of Arkansas Press. There, Larry Malley, then director and editor-in-chief, encouraged me and took great interest in my book. In essence he took me under his wing. I will forever be grateful to him for all the encouragement, support, and advice he gave me. This includes our wonderful discussions about American and Arkansas politics, the Clintons, and our shared love of sport. Equally important, I cannot say enough about the expert and wonderful support I have received from Larry's successor, Mike Bieker, and the wonderful staff at the University of Arkansas Press. They made this easy for me. As a first-time author, with tremendous professional and personal pressures, they treated with me respect and tender support, especially at very difficult moments in my life. I thank you all!

For the last eight years East Tennessee State University has been my intellectual home. This book would not have been possible without the following people: Dr. Dale Schmitt, Dr. Elwood Watson, Dr. Dorothy Drinkard-Hawkshawe, Dr. Dinah Mayo-Bobee, Ms. Mary

Jordan, Vice Provost Bill Duncan, and the late Dr. Ronnie Day. I especially would like to recognize my mentor and longtime friend Dr. Paul Stanton, president emeritus of ETSU. He is a gentleman who is always willing to listen to me and support my ambitions. Without Paul I would not be where I am today. Paul gave me an opportunity and I seized it. As someone with many friends in the historical profession, I am acutely aware of the paucity of tenure track jobs. To have the opportunity to complete my doctoral work at the University of Memphis and come back to my beloved alma mater, ETSU, was a dream come true. Needless to say, Paul is a member of the Carter family and will have my unyielding respect, love, and admiration.

Finally, I wish to acknowledge and thank the most important people in my life. My parents, Joseph and Deborah, raised me to love history. Also, they have supported me in all my pursuits and encourage my ambitions. They always sacrificed for me and my sisters, Stephanie and Lisa. I love you all!

I especially want to thank the three most important people in my life: my wife, Crystal, and our children, Gracie and Maxwell. It is not easy living with a mercurial, sometimes moody academic. My wife has been doing it for more than fifteen years. She has always supported and loved me. This book could not have been written without her support, whether encouraging me or taking the kids to give me time to research and write, she did it all. Gracie has been a wonderful daughter. She is full of spunk and sassiness, which I love. Thank you, Gracie! Maxwell is the sweet, happy-go-lucky, full-of-life little boy I always wanted. Thank you, Maxwell! His interest in my work and history has been very important to me and my life. I hope my children, as they grow up, will one day read this book and appreciate the various ways in which they contributed to it. Thank you, Gracie and Maxwell! I wish to recognize the most important of all, God and my savior, Jesus Christ. My faith has grown exponentially during my adulthood. Sometimes a man really has nowhere left to turn and must fall on his knees in deference to the Lord. My life and work has only been possible because of the Almighty.

All errors in this book are mine and mine alone.

DARYL A. CARTER
November 2015

"The First Black President?"

IN 1998, AS President Bill Clinton faced the most serious crisis of his presidency—the Monica Lewinsky affair and the possibility of impeachment—his most loyal constituency, African Americans, seethed with anger. Hounding this man for a private betrayal of his wife seemed like so many unjust investigations into the lives of African Americans. Nobel Laureate Toni Morrison disseminated for the world what many African Americans already thought:

> African-American men seemed to understand it right away. Years ago, in the middle of the Whitewater investigation, one heard the first murmurs: white skin notwithstanding, this is our first black president. Blacker than any actual black person who could ever be elected in our children's lifetime. After all, Clinton displays almost every trope of blackness: single-parent household, born poor, working-class, saxophone-playing, McDonald's-and-junk-food-loving boy from Arkansas. And when virtually all the African-American Clinton appointees began, one by one, to disappear, when the President's body, his privacy, his unpoliced sexuality became the focus of the persecution, when he was metaphorically seized and bodysearched, who could gainsay these black men who knew whereof they spoke? The message was clear, "No matter how smart you are, how hard you work, how much coin you earn for us, we will put you in your place or put you out of the place you have somehow, albeit with our

permission, achieved. You will be fired from your job, sent away in disgrace, and—who knows?—maybe sentenced and jailed to boot. In short, unless you do as we say (i.e., assimilate at once), your expletives belong to us."[1]

The notion of the "first black president" took hold in the public's imagination. Morrison's epistle captured much of the public's sentiment, both black and white, toward Clinton. However, despite the fervent support of African Americans, Clinton's share of the black vote in 1992 and 1996 was less than Al Gore's share in 2000. In 1992, Clinton received 83 percent of the African American vote. In 1996, Clinton was reelected with 84 percent of the African American vote. While those polling numbers were strong and conclusive in terms of the community's support of President Clinton, these numbers mask serious questions among African Americans about Clinton, generally, and his policies, specifically.

A great deal of the African American community's support for the forty-second president appeared to ignore more substantive policy issues. Clinton frustrated African Americans with his propensity to take both sides of an issue and hash out compromises that African American politicians believed had a negative impact on their community. On a whole host of issues such as the Racial Justice Act of the 1994 crime bill, Clinton's pro-business economic and tax policies, and endorsement of "workfare" over welfare, many saw Clinton's political behavior as opportunistic. What Clinton's position reflected was the deeply nuanced and very sophisticated philosophy of the Democratic Leadership Council. This philosophy gave the appearance, to African Americans, that white, middle-class Americans were the largest beneficiaries of Clinton's policies. Economic data from the US Department of Commerce demonstrates that between 1990 and 2000, blacks' median household income rose from $18,676 to $29,667. Whites' median household income rose from $31,231 to $43,916.[2] As the numbers demonstrate, economic gains of African Americans were matched by those of white Americans, thereby maintaining much of the disparity between the races. Further, Clinton's insistence on deregulation and pro-business policies struck some as disrespectful and condescending. The president's actions and rhetoric, many African

Americans believed, were an abandonment of traditional Democratic values that protected the poor, the vulnerable, and minorities. African Americans were also frustrated by the new ferocity of Republican opposition in the US Congress. While the New Democratic philosophy was problematic, Clinton's hands were often tied by those on the other side of the aisle.

The 1994 midterm elections changed the political calculus in Washington. Now Clinton was facing a Republican speaker in Newt Gingrich and Senate majority leaders, first, Robert Dole and, subsequently, Trent Lott, that were trying to force their legislative agenda through Congress. Their priorities included the end of welfare, the abolishment of affirmative action, and massive cuts in Social Security and Medicare/Medicaid funding. The politics of the era dictated compromise and negotiation. So did the basic philosophy of the New Democrats. As a result, Clinton and the Republicans worked well together, the investigations and impeachment of Clinton notwithstanding. Years after Clinton left office, it was revealed by historian Steve Gillon that Speaker Gingrich and President Clinton had secretly been planning to reform Social Security. In *The Pact: Bill Clinton, Newt Gingrich, and the Rivalry That Defined a Generation*, Gillon notes, "They [Clinton and Gingrich] both believed that any effort to update Social Security would require government to incorporate some measure of choice, and that meant some form of privately managed account."[3] It was this type of cooperation between Clinton and Republicans, grounded in the push/pull of the New Democratic philosophy, that so frustrated his liberal and African Americans supporters.

For New Democrats, 1994 was a watershed moment. President Clinton was forced back to the political center, forced to confront his failures and the mood of the electorate. All of his energy, enthusiasm, and intellectual prowess failed to galvanize a country struggling to come to grips with the postwar era, globalization, and a president who appeared more liberal and ethically compromised than they previously thought. *Washington Post* journalist John F. Harris noted, "There was something nuanced—and more fundamental—going on with Clinton during this period. As the 1994 election reached its end, he was asking himself basic questions about his leadership style and values. In the search for answers, he was reorienting himself intellectually and emotionally."[4] This search brought Clinton back to the centrist, poll-tested strategy that had served him so well in the past. In a January 1995 issue of *New Democrat*, a magazine published by the Democratic Leadership Council, an editorial argued in stringent language: "For Democrats, there's no turning back. If faced with a choice between old liberal programs and the Republicans' new Contract With America, today's disgruntled voters will choose the more radical alternative, even though they may have qualms about the details. The challenge for New Democrats is to offer the country a third choice."[5] Bill Clinton mostly followed that advice over the remaining six years of his presidency, sometimes to the great consternation of his African American base. In the wake of the election debacle of 1994, Clinton moved forcefully toward the New Democrat position on numerous issues. In spite of this, African Americans still believed that he was one of them because of the often-perceived reactionary zeal of the Republican Party and Clinton's support for many things that appealed to the black middle class. Their perceptions, in the face of Republican agenda proposals that often were perceived as antagonistic to black interests, proved accurate.

In the spring of 1992, social, political, and economic unrest roiled the American landscape. The United States was in the midst of a recession after twelve years of economic policies that threw the economy into a massive deficit. Reagan-era tax cuts, without accompanying spending cuts, and dramatic increases in defense spending had taken their toll. Many Americans were frightened as they encountered a move toward globalization, originating at the end of the 1960s, for which they had not been prepared. Deindustrialization wreaked havoc on US industries as jobs shifted to the Third World, where corporations found it easier and more profitable to produce their wares. Moreover, the economy had experienced a deep slowdown and recession from 1990 to 1991. The decline of the economy and the anxiety it produced rifled through middle-class America. Historian James T. Patterson notes, "4.5 million Americans lost their jobs, including many who had been members of the middle classes. Contemporaries spoke of a 'white-collar recession.' Unemployment jumped from 5.9 percent in 1989 to a peak of 7.8 percent in mid-1991. This was the highest rate in ten years."[6] Economic woes provided the spark that Clinton and the Democrats needed to mount a successful campaign to retake the presidency.

It was a time in which serious internal issues—race, class, economics, and society—could no longer be ignored in favor of a Cold War that had ceased to exist. Haynes Johnson noted in the early 1990s that Americans "discovered that the end of the Cold War removed the threat of a common enemy around which national consensus and unity of purpose could be achieved. In the absence of a Hitler, a Stalin, the Bomb, or communism and its 'evil empire,' Americans were left to ponder the wisdom of Walt Kelly's Pogo: the enemy is us."[7] After forty-five years of research and development, war, both hot and cold, and upward social and financial mobility, the United States was in the throes of acute economic, social, and political anxiety. Further, Johnson notes, "More and more, Americans are affixing responsibility for the nation's troubles on the country and its leaders—*and* on themselves."[8] As Jon Voight's character in the 1998 blockbuster hit, *Enemy of the State*, told Gene Hackman's character after Hackman complains about the domestic activity of the National Security Agency, "We're fighting the peace now; it's a lot more volatile."

Just months before the Soviet Union dissolved following decades of mismanagement, corruption, and pressure from the West to allow freedom behind the Iron Curtain, the United States stood atop the world as the only superpower. Its military prowess, clearly on display in the Persian Gulf in 1990–91, frightened other nations as much as its economic might. The loss of the Soviet Union as an adversary directed America's energies, both positive and negative, inward toward social issues, economics, and the culture wars emanating from the 1960s. Jean Bethke Elshtain pointed out, "Foreign policy was dead last on the list of voter concerns."[9] As the spring of 1992 dawned, the issues of race, class, gender, and morality began to capture America's attention.

Several political incidents also contributed to this underlying unrest. In New Hampshire and Iowa, former Nixon and Reagan administration official Patrick J. Buchanan pounded incumbent President George H. W. Bush for his tax increases and lack of conservative bona fides. Buchanan captured many people's imagination with his talk of values, morality, and limited government, as well as his scouring of gays, liberals, and activists that forced major changes in American society since the 1960s. As Ross K. Baker points out, Buchanan expanded attacks "to the areas of morals and values when he ran commercials accusing the National Endowment for the Arts of funding pornographic and blasphemous art. (The implication was that the Endowment, a federal agency directed by a Bush appointee, was supporting pornography with the president's approval.)"[10] Reactionary and defiant, Buchanan came to symbolize the rage and anger of Americans who rejected the growing secularization of American society.

On the political left, former California governor Jerry Brown campaigned for the Democratic nomination for the presidency. Like many conservatives, liberals were also upset over changes in American society that influenced the way that average Americans and the dispossessed lived. Brown's populist rhetoric, at times, brought to the imagination the ghostly image of William Jennings Bryan, with his rejection of the "cross of gold." This was especially true as it related to campaign finance. Money had flooded the political system for decades, but it seemed to have an outsized influence since the Nixon era. After all, central to the series of scandals that comprised Watergate and, subsequently, the savings and loan debacle of the 1980s, money and campaign finance were the common denominators in the corruption of America's political system. As Baker remarked, "He made campaign finance reform a centerpiece of his campaign and characterized excessive political spending as 'the root of all political evil.'"[11] Yet Governor "Moonbeam," as many in the media had taken to calling him years before, struggled to keep pace with Bill Clinton, the Democratic front-runner.

Still another political sensation contributed to the fluidity of the 1992 electoral season: Ross Perot. A businessman from Texas, Perot was short, shrewd, tough, accomplished, and very much "square" in appearance. He founded an electronics company decades before that made him a billionaire. Long a supporter of conservative causes, he also had a progressive streak. Perot supported gun control, protectionist tariff and economic policies, and pro-choice policies. His diatribes about the balancing the budget, not paying him if the economy did not improve, and restoring America's competitive edge appealed to an electorate weary of traditional politicians and the mainstream parties.

Baker notes, "Perot tapped into national discontent over the economy, such scandals as the 'Keating Five,' and revelations of numerous overdrafts on the House bank by members of Congress."[12]

Patrick Buchanan, Jerry Brown, and Ross Perot, however, could not capture the nation's interest as much Arkansas governor Bill Clinton. On October 3, 1991, on the front steps of the Old State House in Little Rock, Arkansas, Clinton announced his candidacy for president. A longtime governor of one of America's smallest and poorest states, Clinton appeared to be the epitome of the colorful, rogue southern politico: smooth, attractive, and wickedly smart. Initially, few in the political media gave Clinton any chance of capturing the Democratic nomination. For one thing, he was too unknown. Arkansas did not have very many electoral votes. Further, the darling of both liberals and the media, New York governor Mario Cuomo, known for his beautiful oratory and thoughtful positions on various issues, had been playing a cat-and-mouse game with the race for months. It seemed as though the nomination was his for the asking. By December 1991, however, Cuomo ended speculation and announced that he was out of the race. Clinton, therefore, had a real opportunity heading into the pivotal New Hampshire primary in late January.

Before he could make a move, just as Clinton's campaign was gaining serious traction, allegations surfaced of adultery and illicit drug use. Gennifer Flowers, a lounge singer in Little Rock, claimed to have had a twelve-year affair with the married governor. *Newsweek* reported "that audiotapes indicate Clinton did have an affair of some kind with Flowers—nonetheless [this] kicked off another of those now classic media sex carnivals, with Clinton as a more compromised Clarence Thomas and Flowers as a less credible Anita Hill."[13] Charges that Clinton had used marijuana also hit the campaign. In a February 8, 1992, article, the *Wall Street Journal* questioned whether or not Clinton had dodged service in the Vietnam War.[14] Lastly, and most seriously, a retired colonel who had served at the University of Arkansas ROTC program, publicly accused Clinton of dodging the draft during the Vietnam War. Struggling to come to grips with his fears and a war he did not support, Clinton used his political connections to secure a spot on the University of Arkansas's ROTC program and attend its law school. David Maraniss, Clinton's biographer, noted, "He fretted and planned every move, he got help from others when needed, he resorted to some deception or manipulation when necessary, and he was ultimately lucky."[15] When the federal government changed the manner in which it drafted young Americans, and Clinton received a high number in the draft lottery, he sent the now-famous letter to Col. Eugene Holmes announcing he decided to go to Yale instead. While not impressive in political terms, Clinton's vacillation reflected the inner qualms of many young men. Maraniss notes that Clinton felt "torn between two worlds," at once patriotic and full of vigor and yet deeply disturbed by the goings-on in Southeast Asia, the increasingly weak justifications from the White House, and the discontent filling the minds of America's young people.[16] During that tumultuous time, Col. Holmes even presented a letter from Clinton notifying the colonel that he would not be joining the ROTC program and that he intended to attend Yale Law School.

As a result of the shocking news that he had an affair with a lounge singer from Little Rock, Clinton and his wife appeared on *60 Minutes* to rebut the charges and proclaim their marriage strong. Clinton ended up coming in a close second in the New Hampshire primary and proclaimed himself "the Comeback Kid." The media coverage of the various scandals demonstrated a growing need for sensationalism by both the media and the public. As Jonathan Alter wrote in a sarcastic *Newsweek* article, "Politics ain't bean curd. In the reporters' bars beyond New Hampshire, the beast will never go hungry for long."[17]

While most journalists and casual observers viewed the turmoil with fascination, the events of 1992 revealed something much deeper, more important, and equally revealing: the Clinton persona. The son of a widowed mother, Virginia Blythe, William Jefferson Blythe was the favorite son and grandson of a working-class Arkansas family. His earlier years were spent with his maternal grandparents, who lavished affection on the lad. However, by the 1950s, Virginia Blythe had married Roger Clinton, a car salesman, alcoholic, and violent man. The trait Clinton has been most known for has always been his empathy. His ability to relate to the average American was a product of his chaotic upbringing. As the stepchild of an alcoholic, Clinton learned early to compromise in order to bring and preserve peace. Moreover, Clinton developed a desire to please people. As a way of preventing confrontation and engendering consensus, Clinton used unique powers to charm and cajole to win over adversaries and friends alike. Stephen J. Wayne of Georgetown University notes, "For his whole life, getting along for Bill Clinton has meant trying to please as many diverse and often conflicting interests as possible."[18] This was arguably the most important aspect of the Clinton political persona because it greatly helps to explain why Clinton was so frustrating to both his supporters and enemies.

Clinton's need to please, perhaps, is the reason he was so determined to make the media the villains during the 1992 campaign. As early as January 1992, with the allegations of infidelity, draft dodging, and drug use, his campaign's "War Room" designed itself to respond immediately to any negative story about the governor. The perception of media bias compelled the campaign to portray itself as a victim, while also imploring that the country needed to move beyond rather stale debates. Scholar William Schneider notes that it was "an interesting combination—a president who is responsive to public sentiment, but one who wants to minimize the impact of the press rather than win them over."[19] Equally important, "Clinton used the voters to defy the press and force them into submission." Schneider thus argues that the "1992 campaign continued a long-term trend toward a more direct, personal relationship between political leaders and the people."[20] The ghosts of the long-dead father and the alcoholic stepfather, as well as the need to please friends, colleagues, and the women in his life, gave Clinton an instinctive understanding of the populace in 1992 and, subsequently, throughout his years and in the White House.

Clinton's younger brother, Roger Jr., also had struggled with drugs and alcohol. In fact, Governor Clinton had been informed by authorities that Roger was going to be arrested for cocaine use and possession in 1985. The chaos brought on by Roger's drug use and incarceration, as well as Bill and Hillary's marital problems, forced all the Clintons into therapy. It was the therapy, along with Clinton's highly acute natural instincts, that made him so devastatingly effective on the campaign trail. Joe Klein reveals that "his mastery of the therapeutic vocabulary and *trompe l'oeil* sense of intimacy it provided" was an important "subtext for Clinton's success as a politician in the 1990s."[21] Contributing to his polarizing effect on the electorate, Clinton had embraced not only the 1960s but the yuppie ethos of the 1980s. The language of empathy, along with a populist streak that appealed to many of the working class, enhanced Clinton's political power. Even before Clinton won the Democratic nomination in July 1992, President Bush increasingly looked impotent and outdated in comparison to the urbane, highly intelligent, and pop culturally literate Bill Clinton. Pennsylvania governor Robert Casey summed up in April 1992 how many felt when he said, "The guy's a tough cadet. He is smart as hell. He is tough. He's resilient. He's all of these things."[22] But Clinton needed to convince a broad swath of middle-class voters of these qualities. There was no better place to start than confronting "radical" elements within his own party.

On June 13, 1992, in Los Angeles, California, Governor Bill Clinton was preparing to deliver his remarks before a gathering of the Rainbow Coalition. Racial tension abounded as the nation struggled to cope in the aftermath of the April riots in Los Angeles. On April 29, Los Angeles had erupted in violence after four Los Angeles police officers who had stopped and beaten motorist Rodney King were acquitted by a jury. The entire episode had been captured on a camcorder by a nearby resident, George Holliday. The riots lasted for several days, until the National Guard restored order. Yet a new problem arose as a young, unknown rap artist delivered a blistering critique on race, violence, and political neglect in an interview in the *Washington Post* a month before. Sister Souljah was a rapper, social satirist, and commentator, popular in many urban African American circles. In the interview with *Post* reporter David Mills, Sister Souljah said:

> I mean, if black people kill black people every day, why not have a week and kill white people? You understand what I'm saying? In other words, white people, this government and that mayor were well aware of the fact that black people were dying every day in Los Angeles under gang violence. So if you're a gang member and you would normally be killing somebody, why not kill a white person? Do you think that somebody thinks that white people are better, or above dying, when they would kill their own kind?[23]

These remarks, in a politically divisive period, were a powder keg set to explode. White people were scared of the violence. African Americans were both frightened and angry. They had complained of police brutality in their communities for decades. The Los Angeles Police Department was well known for its brutal mistreatment of the African American community. The King beating was noteworthy only because it was videotaped and disseminated worldwide. Everyone saw with their own eyes what many in the African American community had been alleging for decades: wanton violence and brutal mistreatment of African Americans at the hands of law enforcement. It was not just in Los Angeles but in places such as New Orleans, New York, Boston, Chicago, Oakland, and Washington, D.C. Sister Souljah's remarks were both a response to the violence and a manifestation of the black nationalism that had simmered in the urban black community since Marcus Garvey had begun promoting his United Negro Improvement Association during World War I. Sister Souljah's comments sparked a backlash that in routine, non-election years would not have provoked as much of a reaction. In an election year, it presented serious questions that the soon-to-be Democratic nominee would have to answer.

Pressure built on Bill Clinton to condemn her comments. This was a test of Clinton's political viability—whether he possessed the political manhood to deal with the African American community as well as middle-class white voters. In a display of audacity, Clinton told the crowd that if you were to reverse the words black and white, then it could have been David Duke delivering that speech. He chastised those supportive of her remarks. Clinton did not even tell the event's organizer, Jesse Jackson, that he was going to condemn her remarks. For the African Americans in attendance that day, it had the effect of a cold, wet slap of a towel. According to those who witnessed the event, Clinton had deliberately orchestrated the spectacle to appease white voters. Gwen Ifill of the *New York Times* noted, "Gov. Bill Clinton, reaching for a symbol that would demonstrate his desire not to be held captive by special interests, used a conference sponsored by the multiracial Rainbow Coalition to attack statements made by a popular rap artist."[24] Ronald Walters noted that the Sister Souljah moment "had been a deliberate strategy designed by campaign operative Paul Begala to help Clinton's appeal with the white Reagan Democrats."[25] Walters noted "that Clinton, by being willing to publicly criticize a well-known figure in the Black community, was not beholden to Jackson or the Black community."[26] Joe Klein of *Newsweek* wondered "whether Clinton was sufficiently worried about holding the Democrats' liberal base that he would be lured into Rainbow obeisance—or stick with the original plan and run a more mainstream campaign. Clinton not only stuck to his guns, he sent a quiet, but firm message to Jackson, that he wasn't in the mood to mess around this year."[27] Clinton and his surrogates' reply to such charges was that Clinton was only speaking out against racism and violence, as he always had done. *Time* magazine noted that by attacking Sister Souljah, Clinton achieved a "key political objective: refocusing the media spotlight on his message to moderate voters that he is unafraid to deliver unpopular messages to important Democratic constituencies, including blacks."[28] Further, it was legitimate to condemn Souljah's remarks because he had done the same thing in front of white audiences around the country about white racism. Thus, if he abrogated his opportunity to condemn the Sister Souljah interview, then he would have sacrificed his own credibility. Sister Souljah had a different opinion. As the *Los Angeles Times* reported, Sister Souljah believed, "Bill Clinton is using me as a political football, the Democratic version of [Willie Horton]."[29] The perception of a Democrat engaging in race baiting damaged Clinton's reputation among many African Americans, confirming suspicions about the New Democrat.

There is a grain of truth in both sides' arguments. Right or wrong, if Clinton did not speak out against Sister Souljah, then the media and the Republicans, in the fall campaign, would have used it against him. However, the manner in which Clinton went after her—without notice to organizers or the media—was troubling to many African Americans. It was seen as disrespectful to Jesse Jackson. It was interpreted as a direct insult to African Americans who were supporting Clinton's bid for the presidency. In the *New York Times*, Roger Wilkins remarked, "I do not defend Sister Souljah's comments [but] Clinton didn't know what had gone on at the Rainbow meeting. And he didn't ask Jesse Jackson, didn't give him any warning of what he was going to do."[30] Jesse Jackson said that Sister Souljah "represents the feelings and hopes of an entire generation of people." Sister Souljah called Clinton a hypocrite for dodging the draft, using pot, and mistreating his former paramour Gennifer Flowers. In *Time* Sister Souljah said,

"I think he is like a lot of white politicians—they eat soul food, they party with black women, they play the saxophone, but when it comes to domestic and foreign policy, they make the same decisions that are destruction, destructive to African people."[31] These comments reinforced suspicions of many African Americans about white politicians. In *Newsweek*, advisers to the Clinton campaign "privately acknowledged they had been out to appeal to suburban whites."[32] This was part of an internal strategy called "counterscheduling," meaning scheduling events around the country to say "unpopular things to certain groups to prove his independence."[33] And there was no better place for a white, national politician to demonstrate his toughness in the face of "extremists" than an African American crowd. In essence, Clinton may have been right on the particulars, but in violating protocols considered sacrosanct within the African American community, Clinton delivered an unmistakable warning to African Americans: I'm with you until I need to be against you.

Bill Clinton was also demonstrating his New Democrat credentials. He did not want to be too closely associated with the Reverend Jesse Jackson. As Marshall Frady noted, "In his determination to define himself as a new edition of Democrat free of the party's past liberal sentimentalisms, Clinton also applied himself with much more vigor than had Walter Mondale and Michael Dukakis to the presumed imperative of separating himself from Jackson, and he did it in some conclusive public way."[34] Jackson possessed stature as a leader of African Americans after his successful campaigns for president in 1984 and 1988. One of the results of these campaigns was that Jackson was named the shadow senator for the District of Columbia; thus Jackson was at the height of his political powers. He had accrued so much political capital through his success and through the millions of minority and poor voters he had registered to vote that the Clinton campaign understood that it had to deal with the so-called Jesse factor while not overly alienating the African American base of the Democratic Party. Basically, Clinton studied the political calculus and determined that the temporary blowback from the African American community was worth the price. Besides, would African Americans really vote for four more years of George H. W. Bush? Not likely. The damage was done.

The Sister Souljah moment's importance lies in the way it foreshadowed other issues concerning African Americans during the Clinton era. These episodes include, but are not limited to, the dismissals and forced resignations of Agriculture secretary Mike Espy, Surgeon General Jocelyn Elders, Housing and Urban Development secretary Henry Cisneros, and the investigation of Commerce secretary Ron Brown before his death in 1996 in Croatia. The failed nomination of Lani Guinier and Clinton's decision not to grant clemency to Rickey Ray Rector in 1992, thus allowing him to be executed by lethal injection, symbolized the New Democratic philosophy: conciliation, toughness, and sympathy to white moderates' concerns about racial and social progress. It was a difficult balancing act within a broad philosophical framework that sought to understand, explain, cajole, persuade, and push the American citizenry toward progressive gains of prosperity, productivity, and community in increasingly perplexing and confounding times. Some of the events left a bad taste in the mouths of liberals and African Americans. Other events—such as crime initiatives, welfare reform, and racial reconciliation—created mixed policy and political results. What Clinton's work and actions during the 1990s demonstrated were the complexity, fluidity, and nuance of race and politics at the end of the twentieth century. W.E.B. DuBois wrote, in the classic *Souls of Black Folk* in 1903, that the problem of the twentieth century would be the color line. As the last administration of the twentieth century and the first in the next, the Clinton years revealed that the problem of the twenty-first century concerned both the color line and the class line.

In order to grapple with the meaning of the Clinton years, we must first examine the philosophical framework within which President Clinton worked. The New Deal/liberal consensus, which dominated the Democratic Party from 1932 to 1988, had disappeared as Ronald Reagan, conservatives, and social and economic problems made liberal policies seem increasingly stale and even un-American. Those policies, which had contributed so greatly to the post–World War II economic boom, seemed incompatible in the era of globalization, social unrest, and growing distrust of so-called big government solutions to America's problems. Taxation, economic policy, and racial animus created a perfect storm for the modern conservative movement. Conservatives sought myriad strategies and tactics to recapture American electoral dominance.

It was a grassroots movement based in the Sunbelt and South that precipitated the rise of direct-mailing campaign tactics, the Christian Right, televangelists, anti-feminist women's groups, neighborhood activists, and conservative political clubs determined to take control of the White House, Congress, and the state houses around the nation. These activists who constituted the Modern Conservative movement finally had a candidate in 1980 that would espouse their views and, in the process, create what political scientists refer to as a realignment election. The *Age of Reagan*, as Sean Wilentz called it, changed the Democratic Party.[35] While the mainstream Democratic Party was slow to respond to the changing political environment, a new faction of the Democratic Party was strategizing on how to recapture what historian Arthur Schlesinger called "the vital center."[36]

In *From the New Deal to the New Right*, political scientist Joseph E. Lowndes argues, "The rightward shift in American politics since the 1960s has gone hand in hand with stubborn forms of racial stratification including starkly disproportionate rates of poverty, unemployment, infant mortality, [and] poor health."[37] Conservatives, who heavily influenced the New Democrats, reorganized their traditional interests in limited government and the sanctity of private property to include concerns about racial liberalism and militancy. Historian Patrick Allitt, for instance, notes that beginning in the 1960s, "conservative opponents of radical activism declared themselves the guardians of law and order and argued for a heavy-handed government policy that, in calmer times, they would have deplored."[38] Fostering such conservative opinions were groups dedicated to anticommunism. In *Suburban Warriors: The Origins of the New American Right*, Lisa McGirr explained how middle-class Americans, disturbed with the social upheaval of the 1960s and concerned with the increasingly dovish stance of the Democratic Party, turned to conservative groups to find solutions to these public problems.[39] The literature of modern conservatism has become voluminous in recent years, demonstrating the varying ways in which conservatives repudiated New Deal and Great Society liberalism. Paul Pierson and Theda Skocpol, among the most prominent scholars of American politics in the post–World War

II era, clearly demonstrate the influence of conservative activism in government during the so-called Age of Reagan.[40] The proliferation of conservative interest groups—churches, associations, business groups, anti-busing mobs, anticommunist organizations, and think tanks—had a great impact on American political life. These were major factors that shaped the belief that the Democratic Party must change in platform and rhetoric.

The Democratic Leadership Council, founded in the dreary months after the Democrats' disastrous performance in the 1984 presidential election, represented a new political and ideological force in American politics. As the 1990s dawned, the DLC was a growing and increasingly influential force in Democratic circles. Nowhere was this more apparent than in the initially quixotic campaign of Bill Clinton. A southern governor, Clinton understood the changed political environment and had embraced "centrism" as both prudent and politically sustainable. In order to understand Clinton's presidency, chapter 1 examines the formation of this controversial organization, its policy positions, its political appeal, and how it impacted debates and policies regarding African Americans.

Chapter 2 analyzes the intersection of race and class in the 1990s. The rising class disparities in the African American community contributed to the embrace of centrist politics by middle- and upper-class African Americans, often at the expense of poorer, more vulnerable blacks in the inner cities. In addition, it investigates how the civil rights movement's successes and failures contributed to the growing fragmentation of Black America along class lines, thus, in part, refuting dated arguments that downplay the role of race in the post civil rights era.

Chapter 3 concerns the first major racial incident of the Clinton presidency, the failed nomination of Lani Guinier. Nominated by Clinton for the position of assistant attorney general for the Civil Rights Division of the Department of Justice, Guinier was a poster child for the legacy of the civil rights movement: smart, liberated, highly educated, and a powerful proponent of equality for minorities, women, and those ignored by white, mainstream society. Despite the New Democratic agenda, Clinton plunged headfirst into a racial cauldron with the nomination of a person steeped in both the civil rights legal establishment and the liberal wing of academia. Her positions promoted an agenda that openly took notice of racial inequality, stirring media attention and conservative dissent. An examination of the media's coverage of the nomination will show how race, class, and politics intersected in the wake of the Reagan/Bush years. This incident demonstrates the forces against which Clinton was operating. Lastly, this incident reveals that Clinton did not "abandon" Guinier in a display of political weakness and opportunism; instead, it shows how open displays of racial liberalism became taboo in the era of colorblindness.

Chapter 4 turns to the first major policy event of the Clinton presidency, the 1994 crime bill. The common popular perception is that crime rates were out of control as the 1990s dawned. Gang violence, drugs, crack-cocaine use, and social breakdown led to a skyrocketing crime rate and a crisis in urban America. Despite the perception that the crime bill of 1994 cut violent crime rates and restored order to the troubled urban landscape, the landmark legislation had a serious unintentional consequence: compounding the crisis in Black America. More African Americans were sent to prison than any other racial group. In addition, one trip to prison usually turned into a revolving experience for those incarcerated, each time on more serious charges of criminal behavior. It contributed to the breakdown of the family, caused significant stress on those left behind, and circumscribed the life chances of millions of African Americans. Clinton's endorsement of this legislation gave credence to conservative ideas that argued prison was the only answer to social problems. The prison-industrial complex grew exponentially as a result of the crime bill of 1994.

Chapter 5 examines how the affirmative action review of 1995, as well as subsequent administration actions, buttressed the vulnerable policy. Since 1978 in *Bakke v. University of California*, conservatives had sought to destroy affirmative action. By 1995, the programs that constituted affirmative action in the federal government came under attack by the US Supreme Court. Ballot measures in California and talk of ballot measures elsewhere sought to eliminate the program. A crisis brewed for a program considered sacrosanct by many African Americans. Anticipating the court's decision in *Adarand v. Pena* and realizing the growing pressure of conservatives, Clinton ordered

George Stephanopoulos and Christopher Edley, two White House staffers, to review affirmative action programs within the federal government.[41] At the National Archives, in July 1995, Clinton delivered the most unequivocal defense of affirmative action since Lyndon Baines Johnson in 1965. This chapter examines why Clinton so vociferously defended affirmative action and the actions the administration took in defense of it.

Chapter 6 looks at one of the most controversial issues of the Clinton presidency: welfare reform. Originally put into law by the 1935 Social Security Act, the program was designed, in part, after the mother's pension programs of the Progressive era. In the decades after it was enacted, it became a favorite target of racists, social conservatives, and fiscal conservatives who broadly viewed the program as antithetical to American notions of work and fairness. In the liberal era, starting with the New Deal, politicians increased the size of welfare and included more people on the dole. As Reagan reached the White House, frustration boiled over at taxpayers' money being spent on those considered undeserving. Race inflected every debate concerning the controversial program. Liberal Democrats recoiled at the thought of repealing welfare. Conservatives salivated at the possibility to end a program they considered unfair to the American taxpayer. Yet, such easily defined positions masked deeper, more complex issues regarding welfare. Class, race, and changing political ideology, by the 1990s, made the welfare issue more complex. Repeal it? And replace it with what? Keep it? Can it be modified to be more efficient? Is work simply the answer? These questions were on display as President Clinton engaged in the volatile debate. Clinton had promised to "end welfare as we know it." Nobody knew exactly what that meant or what reform would look like. The Clinton administration's support of the Personal Responsibility and Work Opportunity Reconciliation Act of 1996 (PRWORA) showcases how race, class, and the DLC ideology came together in this major event of the 1990s. One of the consequences of the passage of this law was that it removed welfare from the national discourse. Yet it also helped to consign some of the most vulnerable members of American society further into the muck of the underclass. Although the popular conception of black politics at the end of the twentieth century suggests uniform support for welfare, the growing black middle class also held views similar to whites who abhorred welfare, revealing the importance of class within the African American community.

Chapter 7 explores the President's Initiative on Race, constructed by executive order in June 1997. One of the best examples of the DLC philosophy at work and the problems inherent with it, the initiative fell apart not only because of the president's personal failings, but due to his emphasis on reconciliation. For a man considered among the best, purest political minds of his generation, Clinton not only failed to seize the moment to foster greater racial inclusivity and tolerance, but also failed to accurately judge the national environment in which he was operating. From its inception, the race initiative failed to foster a constructive atmosphere in which reconciliation could take place. Instead, it stands as evidence of America's inability and refusal to seriously tackle the seminal issue of race. The tortured year and a half of the initiative's existence, however, was ultimately the failure of a president distracted by personal issues. As historian and President's Initiative on Race Advisory Board chair John Hope Franklin noted, the president was simply too distracted by other issues to devote his full energies to the One America initiative.[42] This story captures the hope, promise, and failure of President Clinton and his administration to fulfill the promise that was displayed in the weeks after his election in November 1992. That promise was to usher in a new era of equality and justice. After twelve years of Republican rule, African Americans were hungry for political change, and the president failed to live up to those high aspirations.

Finally, chapter 8 examines the legacy of the Clinton years for African Americans. By using data concerning economic inequality, readers will obtain a clear picture of the complex state of African American life in the new century. Moreover, the ascendancy of Barack Obama to the presidency in 2008, using much of the same rhetoric Bill Clinton used in 1992, demonstrates the continuing influence of the Clinton years.

This book is one of the first scholarly examinations of the Clinton years by a professional historian, especially as they pertain to race and African Americans. Most scholars of the new political history have focused on the ascendancy of Modern Conservatism. My work offers an examination of a man shrouded in misconceptions, half-truths, and popular sentiment. It examines whether Clinton's policies matched the perceptions of him as "the first black president." These perceptions had strongly suggested that Bill Clinton was an honorary black person who had somehow slipped past the white power structure. In addition, this work demonstrates the growing complexity and nuance of African American politics at the end of the twentieth century. It dispels outdated notions of a monolithic community and replaces those ideas with evidence of a sophisticated and rapidly changing group of Americans.

This work does not, however, delve into the personal behavior of the president, unless his conduct impacted policy. This work is not designed to be comprehensive or definitive in scope. It is intended to continue and open debates about the meaning of the Clinton years and to place those years in the context of the times without the polarization, rancor, and animosity of the 1990s, thereby making sense of this perplexing and exciting era as it relates to Clinton's most loyal constituency, African Americans.

CHAPTER 1

The Democratic Leadership Council and African Americans

IT WAS NOVEMBER 6, 1984. The polls on the West Coast had just closed. CBS news anchor Dan Rather announced to the nation that Ronald Reagan had won reelection by an overwhelming landslide, an affirmation of his conservative political ideology. Back on August 23, at the Republican National Convention in Dallas, Texas, Reagan had unveiled his new campaign ad, "Morning in America." Judith Stein has written that Reagan "managed to knot his lofty rhetoric of freedom with the mundane economics of the day. Freedom was a staple in U.S. campaign rhetoric, but Reagan's definition harked backed to the nineteenth century."[1] Reagan's ability to deliver eloquent speeches that conjured up a mythical past was one of the most potent political weapons in his arsenal. Historian Gil Troy argued that Reagan's "optimism and pro-Americanism forged a governing template useful to future presidents from both sides of the aisle."[2] Republicans and Reagan Democrats around the country rejoiced in the afterglow of a historic victory. President Ronald Reagan defeated former vice president Walter Mondale in 1984 with 525 electoral votes and a plurality of 58.8 percent of the popular vote. Mondale lost every state except his home state of Minnesota and the District of Columbia. On Capitol

Hill, the mood for Democrats resembled that of a funeral. Democratic operatives, moderates, members of Congress, and their respective staffs sighed at the thought of another four years of Ronald Reagan.

Democrats' jeers could be heard from coast to coast. Walter Mondale was the wrong candidate to take on the Gipper. The party had lost its appeal to mainstream Americans. It had grown too liberal, too soft on crime, too dovish on national defense, too enamored with minorities and special interests. They believed that the Democratic Party had swayed too far from its traditional base.

In 1932, Franklin Delano Roosevelt, using the Great Depression as a political opportunity, formed a new Democratic coalition of labor, the working class, intellectuals, progressives, and minorities into the most dominant electoral coalition in the nation. Historians have long credited his campaign as the origins of the modern Democratic Party coalition. For African Americans, as well as for millions of other Americans, FDR made the Democratic Party attractive for the first time. Steven Lawson cites that Roosevelt's "New Deal extended economic relief to the one-third of the nation that was ill housed, ill clothed, and ill fed, which included blacks as well as poor whites."[3] President Roosevelt's effort to stop the economic carnage of the Great Depression impressed many who were caught in its grip. African Americans benefited from much of the New Deal, but not, as Steven Lawson points out, "because of their race; in fact, many New Deal agencies, especially in the South, were administered to preserve prevailing racial practices that maintained blacks in a subordinate position."[4] FDR's ability to capitalize on the ineptitude of President Hoover in 1932 and bring new factions of the American electorate into the Democratic fold resulted in twenty years of Democratic rule in the White House. Then-contemporary historians, such as Arthur M. Schlesinger Jr., argued that the Roosevelt years were the beginning of a new political epoch similar to the years of President Andrew Jackson. Schlesinger explained in detail the transformative period of the 1930s in several works, including *The Crisis of the Old Order, 1919–1933*; *The Coming of the New Deal, 1922–1935*; and *The Politics of Upheaval, 1935–1936*.[5] The 1932 election was a realignment in the American electorate that generally held until Reagan created a new national alignment in American politics in 1980.

The 1960s, however, tore at the soul of the Democratic Party.

Vietnam, civil rights, gay rights, women's rights, and the Great Society produced division not only within the Democratic Party, but throughout the nation as a whole. The role of liberals in these events provoked a backlash. As Maurice Isserman and Michael Kazin note, "The coalition of wage earners and intellectuals of all races and most regions that Franklin D. Roosevelt forged in the 1930s cracked apart during the late '60s and has not been rebuilt."[6] For the Democratic Party, Isserman and Kazin explain, "Taking its place on the left of American politics was a mélange of social movements—feminist, gay and lesbian, black nationalist, Mexican American, environmentalist—that swelled in size and became skilled at defending the rights and cultural identities of people who, before the '60s, had been scorned or ignored."[7] This new Democratic Party, so different from that of Woodrow Wilson and Franklin Roosevelt, frustrated the moderate-to-conservative Democrats that made up the Democratic Leadership Council into looking for alternatives.

The 1970s provided the impetus for massive political and cultural change. A decade crudely thought of as a throwaway or unimportant period filled with disco balls, Afros, energy crises, and heavy metal was a period of incredible activity that led to the Reagan revolution. As historians Bruce Schulman and Julian Zelizer write, the 1970s was a period in which social and cultural transformations and political culture dramatically changed and, thus, shaped the rest of the century.[8] These changes included antibusing movements, pro-business advocacy, neighborhood associations, religious zealotry, and antifeminist groups. These often disparate and disagreeable groups rallied to one another in common cause against what they perceived as the menaces of the 1960s: sexual permissiveness, alternative lifestyles, secularism, and anti-American behavior. Further, concern over the state of the American family prompted average Americans across the United States to become more civically active. This was often combined with fierce patriotism, moral themes, and propagandizing theories advocating the free market, free enterprise, and the rugged individualism of the nineteenth century. As Matthew Lassiter notes, "The ideological contradiction at the core of the conservative 'pro-family movement' has always resolved around the inherent tension between the enthusiastic celebration of free-market capitalism and the simultaneous defense of traditional family values."[9] These activists and their followers responded to calls for unity against liberalism. Moreover, their reaction toward the excesses of liberalism resonated even with those determined to hold the line, such as union workers.

If the 1950s and 1960s could be generalized as decades of successful struggles for freedom for minorities, women, gays, and the poor, then the 1970s and 1980s were the decades of backlash and revolt against those successes. Central to much of the conservative position was civil rights. During the civil rights movement evangelical leaders such as Jerry Falwell and Pat Robertson rejected political activism generally and civil rights specifically. Civil rights to them translated into special favors for minorities at the expense of whites. Considering themselves in favor of equal rights, conservative clergy thought that assimilation, order, and adherence to strictly pro-American behavior was the best way for African Americans to be treated as equal. They turned a deaf ear to the pleas of Dr. Martin Luther King and liberal clergy to push for full equality for all Americans. In addition, many portrayed the civil rights movement as a conspiracy by communists to create upheaval in the United States. However, by the beginning of the 1970s, clergy from the Sunbelt and South, along with other areas around the country, alleged that the 1960s contributed to the declining morals of the country.

The most sensitive area of interest was the schools. After *Brown v. Board of Education of Topeka* in 1954, white southerners began creating private schools.[10] Some of those schools were funded with taxpayer money. Often they were called day schools or Christian academies. By the 1970s it was clear that whites were using these schools to evade integration. As a result, the federal government began targeting these schools for denial of tax-exempt status. While the Internal Revenue Service was right in denying privilege status to such schools, the IRS contributed to the conservative movement's feelings of being under siege. Historian Joseph Crespino argued, "Republican Party operatives would continue to invoke this populist framework to position themselves as the chief defenders of conservative religious principles against a modern secularist enemy that was hostile to the interests of Christian Americans."[11] This combination of cultural politics, religious activism, family concerns, and fears of racial amalgamation propelled a massive conservative movement called the New Right to victory in 1980, with Ronald Reagan as its standard bearer.

The modern conservative movement began in the wake of World War II. Conservatives such as Robert "Mr. Republican" Taft, William F. Buckley Jr., and Senator Barry Goldwater began to vigorously oppose the New Deal, fair deal, and big government as threats to American freedom. The 1944 publication of *The Road to Serfdom*, by F. A. Hayek, greatly influenced intellectuals and conservatives about the inherent dangers of federal intervention in the economy.[12] Hayek's work, with its discussions of the threat of central planning to individual freedom and liberty, helped to motivate other conservative writers to warn against the expansion of the government. By 1963, economist Milton Friedman and Anna Schwartz had published *A Monetary History of the United States, 1867–1960*.[13] Friedman argued that the Federal Reserve should keep tight control over inflation and promote free enterprise. Esoteric debates over monetary policy were a veneer for frustration over the growing involvement of the federal government in the lives and pocketbooks of millions of Americans. Focus on "the invisible hand" of the market to control itself, along with market-based solutions to America's domestic problems, was central to conservatives' political persona. By the 1980s, deficit spending to boost the American economy fell by the wayside as the works and ideas of Hayek, Friedman, and Arthur Laffer—the economic theorist who convinced Ronald Reagan of the wisdom of supply-side economics—grew acceptable among much of the American public.[14] In addition, the liberalization of America's racial politics rankled conservatives supportive of equal rights for African Americans but not when equal rights came from the federal government. By the 1960s, social transformation brought on by the rights revolution of the 1960s gave conservatives new arrows to put in their quivers.

Social agitation for civil rights by African Americans, women, homosexuals, criminal defendants, Native Americans, Hispanics, and welfare recipients provoked a serious backlash among conservatives. In 1945, as the United States forced Japan to surrender with the atomic bomb, conservatives grew worried about communist infiltration of the United States. As Donald Critchlow has noted, no other force galvanized conservatives in the immediate aftermath of World War II more than anti-Communism.[15] In fact, the civil rights movement was dogged by allegations of disloyalty and communist ties throughout its history. Conservatives' distaste for growing secularization and revision of the meaning of America meant that a backlash was brewing against the forces of progressive change. Furthermore, violence in the cities, disrespect toward authority and tradition, and sexual permissiveness disturbed millions of Americans who felt excluded by the upheaval of the 1960s. By the end of the 1970s, numerous conservative groups sprouted up to oppose busing, liberalism, the peace movement, and the alleged decay of American society.

As conservatives changed the political and cultural environment, Democrats rethought the party's core positions. Historian Robert M. Collins has written that "the effects of Reagan's powerful gravitational pull could also be seen in the emergence within the opposition party of the so-called New Democrats."[16] "Reagan's success in dominating the national agenda, his early steamroller legislative victories, and especially his overwhelming victory in the 1984 election," explains Collins, "lent increasing urgency to the task of formulating a credible response to his leadership."[17]

Al From and Bill Clinton were among those who believed that the party's growing alignment with special interests was disastrous for the electoral fortunes of the party. In the wake of the greatest electoral humiliation for a major party since Lyndon B. Johnson devoured Barry Goldwater with 486 electoral votes and 61.1 percent of the vote, From, Clinton, and like-minded politicos formed the Democratic Leadership Council (DLC). The purpose of the nascent DLC was simple: recapture the center in American politics. As From and Will Marshall, the intellectual arm of the DLC, argued, "They are inventing a new politics that transcends the exhausted Left-Right debate that has immobilized our nation for too long."[18] Compromise and conciliation were the hallmarks of these New Democrats. At the center of the DLC's platform were strength abroad, economic prosperity at home, and the ideals of community, responsibility, and accountability. In order to understand the 1990s, President Clinton, and his legacy regarding African Americans, one must discover why these New Democrats saw an overt commitment to minorities as troublesome. By examining the DLC, its platform, and its membership, we can better understand not only why it was so popular, but also how it impacted political and policy choices.

In the popular conception of the Democratic Leadership Council, Reagan whipped Mondale, and then Al From and Bill Clinton jumped in to resurrect the Democratic Party. This conception, though exaggerated, was partially true. In fact, as early as President Jimmy Carter's defeat at the hands of Reagan in 1980, young, relatively new Democrats were opining that the party needed to change. Many of these Democrats were Watergate babies. They were elected to office in the years between 1974 and 1980, in part, because of the real and alleged criminal activity of the Nixon White House and their own commitment to political reform. The Watergate generation included officials that figured prominently in the New Democratic movement over the course of the next three decades, such as Bill Clinton of Arkansas, Chuck Robb of Virginia, Sam Nunn of Georgia, Dick Gephardt of Missouri, Al Gore of Tennessee, Tim Wirth of Colorado, and Bill Gray of Pennsylvania. The leader of the young, centrist Democrats was part of one of the most colorful families in twentieth-century American politics: Gillis Long of the Long family of Louisiana. A cousin of Senator Huey Long, Senator Russell Long, and Congressman Speedy Long, Gillis Long was himself a member of the US House of Representatives. By 1980 Long had become chair of the House Democratic Caucus. Among his chief lieutenants was the future founder of the DLC, Al From. In the aftermath of Carter's loss, the Committee on Party Effectiveness (CPE) was born. The CPE, Kenneth Baer discovered, was "the first organization embodiment of the New Democrats."[19] It had thirty-seven members and met regularly to discuss the problems of the party, legislatively and politically. As Baer has also written, this group should not be considered New Democrats, as they did not see themselves in such a light and did not separate themselves from the mainstream party in any significant way.[20]

According to Bill Clinton, the Democratic Leadership Council held key values. In his 2004 autobiography, Clinton wrote:

> I had helped to write, and deeply believed in, the DLC's five core beliefs: Andrew Jackson's credo of opportunity for all and special privileges for none; the basic American values of work and

family, freedom and responsibility, faith, tolerance, and inclusion; John Kennedy's ethic of mutual responsibility, asking citizens to give something back to their country; the advancement of democratic and humanitarian values around the world, and prosperity and upward mobility at home; and Franklin Roosevelt's commitment to innovation, to modernizing government for the information age and encouraging people by giving them the tools to make the most of their own lives.[21]

While there would be much debate about what these five "core beliefs" meant, President Clinton used them to accomplish a variety of triumphs, such as crime legislation, welfare reform, education initiatives, and balancing the budget. Furthermore, the New Democratic rhetoric as spoken by Clinton drew a much larger cross-section into the Democratic Party, at least at voting time, than any Democratic Party agenda since the Great Society.

There were significant differences between these more pragmatic politicos and the older Democrats in office. These New Democrats criticized welfare programs, which they considered negative because they inspired dependency. Policies that neglected to promote economic growth were hallmarks of a bygone era that needed to be jettisoned. New Democrats distanced themselves from objects of taxpayer resentment. Thus, by embracing the New Left, with its cadre of minority racial extremists and militants, feminists, environmentalists, defendant and prisoner rights advocates, welfare rights activists, and proponents of sexual rights—including abortion and the right to engage in sex outside of marriage or with same-sex partners—Democrats had ceded cultural authority to the Republican Party. Reagan's victories symbolized that the Republican Party—with its enthusiastic support toward and from Evangelicals, traditionalists, gun rights advocates, anti-communists, classical liberal governance proponents, and working-class whites—had seized much of the old New Deal coalition. The Democrats had become associated with minorities, women, and coastal elites.

The New Democrats saw no path to electoral success in the party's current formation against a unified, disciplined, rhetorically resonant Republican Party. Northeastern liberals, such as House Speaker Tip O'Neill, represented a dying past. Franklin Roosevelt, Harry Truman,

John F. Kennedy, and Lyndon Johnson were long gone. Many within the old Democratic coalition—labor, conservatives, women, minorities, anti-communists, and populists—had joined Reagan's revolution. Yet the old Democrats did not change their party's perception.

The 1984 election was the breaking point. By February 1985, the Democratic Leadership Council was formed. Baer wrote, "This new institutional manifestation was interpreted as a break with, if not a direct threat, [to] the party."[22] While party elders pooh-poohed the creation of the DLC, it soon gained traction with important people in the party. These supporters included Tennessee senator Al Gore, Georgia senator Sam Nunn, and Louisiana senator John Breaux. Over the next twenty years, DLC would have a tremendous impact on both national policy and Democratic Party orthodoxy. It reconstructed how the party approached sensitive issues of race and opportunity.

The legislative successes of the civil rights movement, such as the Civil Rights Act of 1964, Voting Rights Act of 1965, fair housing laws, education reform, and federal intervention on behalf of African Americans in areas such as busing, the targeting of the Ku Klux Klan, and welfare, had sparked a backlash from the citizenry and a "frontlash" from elites that reduced the Democratic National Committee's power.[23] New Democrats wanted several major changes to the party's platform that had negative consequences for many poor and working-class African Americans, reflecting the growth of class as a consequential dividing line in African American politics. This class element meant that middle-class African Americans would distance themselves from their lower-class brethren.

Market-Based Solutions

One policy that New Democrats wanted to become central to the party's platform was embracing the free market as the best vehicle for economic progress and opportunity. In *Winning in the Global Economy*, one of the founding documents of the DLC, Chairman Dick Gephardt wrote, "The DLC believes that continued inaction in the face of ballooning budget and massive trade deficits ultimately will put America's standard of living at risk."[24] Recognizing the danger of deficits was only one part of the DLC plans for reform. The DLC also wanted government to be more active in a Wilsonian manner by working within the current system to lift America out of its current fiscal problems and empowering small and middle-size businesses, the real engines of economic growth. In fact, there were strong similarities between President Wilson's 1912 campaign and his promotion of "the new freedom" and the platform of the Democratic Leadership Council. Wilson noted in the preface to *The New Freedom: A Call for the Emancipation of the Generous Energies of a People* that his principle was "an attempt to express the new spirit of our politics and to set forth, in large terms, which may stick in the imagination, what it is that must be done if we are to restore our politics to their full spiritual vigor again, and our national life, whether in trade, in industry, or in what concerns us only as families and individuals, to its purity, its self-respect, and its pristine strength and freedom."[25] The DLC wanted the government to "make strategic investments in growth and productivity: in literacy and education, research and innovation, job training and the public facilities that undergird our commerce."[26] The organization believed that these efforts would help restore America's economic viability and vitality. The DLC rejected Keynesian theories of deficit spending, large domestic programs, and military spending out of proportion with revenue projections and international threats. To New Democrats, the 1960s and 1970s showed that the Democratic Party and the Progressive agenda had to be retooled in order to stay relevant in an increasingly complex economic age. New Democrats were channeling their Progressive Era political ancestors and rebalancing the politics of the Democratic Party.

The Progressives at the beginning of the twentieth century represented the moderation, tolerance, and pragmatism that New Democrats hoped the party would embody by the end of the twentieth century. Baer argued, "The New Democrats started to draw parallels between themselves and the Progressive movement active at the beginning of the twentieth century."[27] Reforming the system wherever possible was preferable to government intrusion into the private affairs of business and individuals. The DLC, therefore, was crafting solutions to new problems presented by current economic and social circumstances. As Baer writes, "The New Democrats believed that they faced an equally significant change: from a national and industrial to a global and postindustrial—or Information Age—economy, and from a bipolar, Cold War world to an uncertain, multipolar one."[28] In this way, New Democrats were ahead of the Democratic establishment in responding to both the changing political atmosphere and the socioeconomic environment. Liberal Democrats such as the Rev. Jesse Jackson criticized the DLC as opportunistic, poll driven, and primarily concerned with electoral victories, not principled positions. For many liberals, politics reflected moral authority and righteousness, not bare electoral concerns. The African American political class, especially, had a long history of distrust of electoral concerns that dated back to the Abolitionist movement: political pursuits cheapened and corrupted their cause. The DLC challenged this thinking. By the end of the 1980s, the Progressive Policy Institute had been formed to deliver proposals to the DLC and New Democrats around the country. As then governor Clinton said in an interview with NBC in 1991, "We have worked very, very hard to go beyond the sort of established political orthodoxies of both the Republican and Democratic parties."[29]

Equal Opportunities, Not Equal Outcomes

The perception, real or imagined, that the Democratic Party imposed litmus tests for its national figures troubled the DLC. This was especially true as it related to women and minorities and thorny issues such as affirmative action. One particular development of the 1980s made the DLC especially nervous. On November 3, 1983, the Rev. Jesse Jackson announced the first of his two candidacies for the Democratic nomination for president of the United States. A black civil rights leader running for the nation's highest office seemed like a pipe dream to most. However, Jackson presented the first semi-viable campaign by a racial minority in American history. He collaborated not only with civil rights organizations and his own organizations, but with organized labor and progressive organizations around the country. Sensing the mood of millions of Americans disillusioned by the Reagan era, Jackson tapped into a populist vein that exposed the unhappiness brought on by conservative social and economic policies, along with external factors such as globalization, deindustrialization, and economic insecurity. Those Americans felt that their concerns were not being addressed by the Reagan administration. Jackson, at least, represented major aspects of their concerns. His platform was a laundry list of liberal solutions to America's ills; it included government guaranteed employment, universal health care, increased taxation to pay for social programs, neutering the War on Drugs, support for Palestinians, ratification of the Equal Rights Amendment, and increasing the amount of support from the government for America's farmers. Many of these issues were key to the interests of African Americans and the remnants of the civil rights movement. Since the 1960s, national Democrats represented many of the solutions that appealed to African Americans. As a consequence, African American politics became increasingly fused with liberal policies. These policies supported equal opportunity and the use of federal power to stop segregation, alleviate poverty, improve education, and combat terrorist organizations such as the Ku Klux Klan, John Birch Society, and White Citizens' Councils. As Reagan came to office intent on reducing the size of government and social programs, federal power to alleviate social problems came under serious attack. As Robert M. Collins notes, "The overriding political consequences of this defining fact of governance was its shattering impact on the sort of federal activism strongly identified with Democratic liberalism."[30] African Americans, therefore, were increasingly on the outside looking in, trying to prevent further erosion of the government's commitment to social justice.

In his first campaign, competing against Democratic Party heavyweights Walter Mondale and Gary Hart, Jackson garnered more than three million total votes. As a result of his success in 1984, when Jackson ran again in 1988, he had a better organization and more credibility. Ronald W. Walters notes that the politics of leverage—demonstrated by his widespread credibility within the African American community, crossover appeal to the wider progressive community, and appeal to the liberal roots of the party—gave Jackson incredible political strength.[31] However, the strength shown by Jackson made New Democrats nervous and, as a consequence, Jackson was disinvited from the DLC's convention in 1990. When asked why Jackson was not invited to speak, as he had been in previous years, DLC leader Al

From responded that Jackson represented the "old politics." Jackson's direct appeal to minorities, women, and the working class made many New Democrats uncomfortable because they were trying to move the Democratic Party away from the liberalism, as espoused by Jesse Jackson, that they considered so damaging to their electoral interests. They even tried to use the 1988 primary calendar to dismiss Jackson; according to Marshall Frady, "The megaprimary of Super Tuesday in the South . . . had been contrived as a baffle to filter out any liberal candidacy like Jackson's should it still be in the field, and to ensure that the candidates coming out of it would be of conservative disposition reflecting the supposed political temperament of that region—and, not incidentally, the temperament of the inner fraternity of similarly cautious-spirited party figures making up the Democratic Leadership Council, who had largely invented the strategy."[32] That Jackson won five states—including the cradle of the Confederacy, South Carolina— angered New Democrats. Baer pointed out, "The results of the Super Tuesday effort were destined to weigh on DLC leaders, for they raised fundamental questions about the New Democratic strategy and the overall viability of the organization."[33] Jackson's campaigns demonstrated that the DLC and New Democrats were uncomfortable with traditional appeals to African Americans, dismissive of the concerns of "rights groups," and programmatically determined to regain the political offensive by condemning what they considered to be liberal excess. What New Democrats needed was a politician who could, in a manner of speaking, neutralize Jesse Jackson while still remaining able to secure the African American community's recent support for the Democratic Party. Bill Clinton was that man.

In 1984, Walter Mondale made a big show of bringing Dianne Feinstein of California and Geraldine Ferraro of New York to his Minnesota home, in front of the media, as he decided which woman he would select for the vice presidency. (Eventually, Mondale chose Congresswoman Ferraro.) As William Galston and Elaine Kamarck noted in an influential policy paper for the Progressive Policy Institute, "Liberalism has been transformed. The politics of innovation has been replaced by programmatic rigidity; the politics of inclusion has been superseded by ideological litmus tests."[34] These litmus tests included such things as diversity, including diversity on the presidential ticket.

One policy that most exemplified New Democrat distrust with government solutions to social problems was affirmative action. These concerns over women and minorities undergirded New Democrats' opposition to the mainstream Democratic Party's organization and platform.

On affirmative action, liberals and minorities, it seemed, were forcing business and government to provide assistance unavailable to whites. In addition, affirmative action and race-based programs had not been constructed in a thoughtful, coherent manner. As Manning Marable saw it, affirmative action "per se was never a law, or even a coherently developed set of governmental policies designed to attack institutional racism and societal discrimination."[35] This inchoate formation of social policy allowed conservatives to malign affirmative action. As Marable further argued, conservatives "cultivated the racist mythology that affirmative action was nothing less than a rigid system of inflexible quotas which rewarded the incompetent and the unqualified (who happened to be black) at the expense of hardworking, tax-paying Americans (who happened to be white)."[36] Using the rhetoric of the civil rights movement and the words of Dr. Martin Luther King Jr., affirmative action opponents were able to promote a new racial ideology: the colorblind society. Conservatives such as Abigail and Stephen Thernstrom, Ronald Reagan, George H. W. Bush, Ward Connerly, and Thomas Sowell used Dr. King's most memorable speech—at the March on Washington in August 1963—to promote their view that only individual measures, not collective measures, were the best way to promote equality. The colorblind philosophy was incredibly effective at galvanizing support, putting supporters of affirmative action on the defensive, and making a mockery out of King's dream of racial equality.

Opponents of "collective measures" such as affirmative action failed to put King's remarks in their proper context or take into account King's last years, when King became far more radical in his beliefs and political positions. King became convinced by 1967 that class, not racial prejudice, was the dividing line in America life. The interests of poor whites, blacks, and browns were the same, yet race was used to ensure that no interracial cooperation existed. Furthermore, King was advocating for an end to the war in Vietnam, redistributive measures at home, and greater responsibility and morality by America in the conduct of its domestic and foreign affairs. So serious were Dr. King's emerging political positions that, as Taylor Branch cited, "J. Edgar Hoover was alerted to sensitivities over Vietnam . . . [when he received] a solicitous call from Attorney General Katzenbach [who] informed him that President Johnson and Secretary Rusk wanted an FBI investigation of the emerging King position on Vietnam, including possible Communist influences."[37] In fact, on April 4, 1967, at Riverside Church in New York, King delivered a blistering critique on America in a twenty-two-minute speech. Dr. King remarked, "A true revolution of values will soon look uneasily on the glaring contrast of poverty and wealth. With righteous indignation, it will look across the seas and see individual capitalists of the West investing huge sums of money in Asia, Africa, and South America, only to take the profits out with no concern for the social betterment of the countries, and say, 'This is not just.'"[38] King's words were prophetic in foretelling many of the problems of America in the age of globalization.

For the DLC, affirmative action presented a difficult dilemma. The DLC could support the controversial policy, like the mainstream Democratic Party, and isolate the very people they needed to persuade to retake the party. Or it could promote a more nuanced and moderate approach to affirmative action and equal opportunity that would appeal to moderates, independents, and many liberals. They chose the latter. As Galston and Kamarck and tried to argue, New Democrats wanted "an end to dogmatism, litmus-testing, and finger-pointing that have dominated discussion" about affirmative action.[39] At the DLC's fourth annual meeting in New Orleans in 1990, members stated unequivocally: "We believe in the protection of civil rights and the broad movement of minorities into America's economic and cultural mainstream, not racial, gender, or ethnic separatism. We will not tolerate another decade in which the only civil rights movement is backward."[40] Assimilation was central to New Democrat ideas about racial progress. Even old liberals such as historian Arthur Schlesinger Jr. pushed back against multiculturalism. In a controversial book written at the height of political correctness in 1991, Schlesinger wrote, "The ethnic upsurge . . . began as a gesture of protest against the Anglocentric culture. It became a cult, and today it threatens to become a counter-revolution against the original theory of America as 'one people,' a common culture, a single nation."[41] Schlesinger, like many New Deal liberals, placed the impetus for social betterment on the backs of those least able to bear the load.

The idea of "equal opportunity, not equal outcomes" acknowledged the grievances of white Americans and their growing suspicion of race-based measures to foster equality, while delivering nominal support to the traditional Democratic base of African Americans and their demands for equal opportunity. It was a sophisticated message designed specifically to appease both sides in what has been referred to as a "big-tent strategy." By embracing much of the colorblind rhetoric, however, the DLC conferred legitimacy to conservative arguments that denounced race-conscious measures to remedy social injustice.

Through Work Comes Salvation

The New Democrat position on welfare deepened the suspicions of many liberals and African Americans toward New Democrats. The creation of Aid to Dependent Children (ADC) in 1935, as a part of the Social Security Act, provided cash assistance to recipients. By the 1960s, the program had been amended several times and expanded to include more people, especially minorities. As welfare recipients and advocates organized for more rights and benefits, the nation was experiencing the economic anxiety and misery of the 1970s. Welfare recipients became an easy target for conservatives, Republicans, moderates, and even Democrats. After all, welfare flew in the face of American ideals of rugged individualism and self-initiative.

By the Reagan revolution of the 1980s, welfare grew synonymous with race. Reagan had spoken often of "welfare queens" in Chicago and other inner cities sitting on their duffs collecting multiple welfare checks and driving Cadillacs. Thomas and Susan Edsall informed the reader that for taxpayers, "taxes had come for many voters to signify the forcible transfer of hard-earned money away from those who worked, to those who did not. Taxes had come to be seen as the resource financing a liberal federal judiciary, granting expanded rights to criminals' defendants, to convicted felons, and, in education and employment, to 'less qualified' minorities."[42] In addition, "the continuing vitality of this coded language—a language of 'groups,' 'taxes,' 'big government,' 'quotas,' 'reverse discrimination,' 'welfare,' and 'special interests,'—became critical to the maintenance of the conservative presidential majority in the latter half of the 1980s."[43] This was the atmosphere in which Democrats operated during the 1980s.

The Democratic Leadership Council opposed traditional welfare for a number of reasons. First, New Democrats believed that welfare created a cycle of dependency among recipients and encouraged laziness. Therefore, it was imperative, as Elaine Kamarck and Will Marshall wrote in 1993, that America replace "welfare with a work-based social policy that reinforces mainstream values, rewards individual initiative, and demands responsible behavior from recipients of public assistance even as it expands opportunities to achieve self-sufficiency."[44] The most popular solutions included stricter work requirements, a two-year maximum stay on the rolls and five-year lifetime benefit, and eliminating Aid to Families with Dependent Children (AFDC). Welfare created a two-tiered system that forced taxpayers to care for those less fortunate, thus breeding resentment and anger that exposed class and racial lines. As Clinton's secretary of Health and Human Services, Donna Shalala, later said, the separated and parallel societies created by welfare were not good for anyone.[45] As a result of the growing economic inequality and political neglect by the Reagan/Bush administrations, Kamarck and Marshall write, a "yawning racial chasm that threatens to divide America into separate, unequal societies" grew dangerous for the future of the American republic.[46] Thus, government investment in education, crime prevention, and market-based measures would create opportunity for all Americans. By using market-based measures, along with limited, targeted government investment in programs such as health care, job training, and childcare, the politically difficult issue could be diffused and the American underclass could be uplifted.

Growing irritation among taxpaying Americans, as a result of sheer size and number of Americans receiving benefits, helped make welfare more vulnerable than at any other time since its creation in 1935. New Democrat and Progressive Policy Institute founder Will Marshall argued, "People are less concerned about the costs of welfare than about its failure to encourage and reward the values most

Americans live by: work and saving, marriage and family, individual initiative, and a sense of responsibility to one's community."[47] Marshall, echoing New Democrats around the country, criticized President Clinton in 1994 for waiting eighteen months to reveal the plan for reform. Marshall argued that "six shifts" needed to take place in order to reform welfare: (1) work must pay; (2) job placement through the government, nonprofits, and private businesses would be necessary for recipients coming off welfare; (3) community service jobs would have to be available; (4) access to health care would be universal; (5) child-support enforcement would be vigorous; and (6) people would be prevented from becoming welfare recipients in the first place.[48] Unlike conservatives, who advocated either completely abolishing welfare or severely restricting it, New Democrats wanted government to help those on the dole, but only so far. The market-based economy could help those who could not help themselves. These are the principles upon which the Clinton administration tried to execute welfare reform in 1996.

Welfare caused electoral troubles for the Democratic Party in an era where the country was clearly disenchanted with liberal solutions to America's social problems. The solutions of Franklin Roosevelt and Lyndon Johnson would no longer suffice. Pulling away from government solutions to societal problems deeply disturbed African Americans, who, after hundreds of years of government-endorsed abuse and neglect, were worried about losing the government assistance that had been recently gained over the last few decades. As *Black Enterprise* reporter David C. Ruffin noted in 1987, "Because the DLC is moving away from the liberal traditions of the Democratic Party, the group is viewed warily by some blacks and progressives."[49]

Lock Them Up and Throw Away the Key

To appeal to mainstream voters, Al From and the DLC responded to beliefs that America's cities were crime infested and that the Democratic Party had grown more interested in protecting the rights of criminals than those of victims. This perception began in the 1960s when, as a part of the rights revolution, the US Supreme Court ruled that those arrested had to be read their Miranda rights. Further, the Supreme Court ruled in *Gideon v. Wainwright* that defendants had the right to an attorney regardless of whether they were charged with a misdemeanor or felony.[50] Pell Grants and financial aid were given to inmates who wanted to improve themselves.

The Democratic Leadership Council promoted and embraced toughness against criminals. Central to the New Democrat approach were mandatory sentencing laws, victims' rights laws, community policing programs, more cops on the streets, gun restrictions, and drug education. As Ed Kilgore of the Progressive Policy Institute persuasively argued, "Crime is a cause, as well an effect, of poverty and social discrimination; and the victims of social injustice tend also to become the preeminent victims of crime."[51] Since conservatives had made the crime issue symbolic in nature, New Democrats proposed "real" toughness through "looking to the streets—where police officers can deter crime through creating increased risk of apprehension; where the most immediate causes of crime can be isolated and reduced; and where the community support critical to any anticrime initiative can be mustered and mobilized."[52] The hard-line approach to crime resonated with many middle-class voters, white and black. However, it also concerned African Americans, who were far more likely to encounter the criminal justice system than whites. President Reagan's War on Drugs and new statutory enhancements, such as the Drug Kingpin law, made many blacks Americans feel as though they were under attack.[53] The toughness on crime led to a number of laws, including the 1994 crime bill that Clinton signed into law, that dramatically increased the size and scope of the so-called prison industrial complex.

Blacks in the Democratic Leadership Council

In the general perception of the Democratic Leadership Council, it is an organization for southern Democrats mediating the political costs of the 1960s rights revolution. Black Democrats, however, have played a role in the organization. In the beginning, the DLC had "exactly two black members and a mere handful of Hispanics and women."[54] The initial lack of diversity created uneasy feelings among many liberal

African Americans who were fearful that the DLC members were the descendants of the southern Democrats of the Jim Crow era. Yet, as Jon F. Hale has written, "Many DLC members in the first group were themselves liberals. In 1987, forty-eight of one hundred DLC House members had Americans for Democratic Action (ADA) ratings of more than 75."[55] In addition, "as liberals, most did not want to see the party's substantive positions change; but as elected officials, most saw the wisdom in discussing ways to make the party positions more palatable to mainstream voters and in making themselves look more moderate in the eyes of their constituents."[56] The presence of these rather opportunistic Democrats made it easier for some African Americans to trust the DLC and its policy agenda, because it appeared to be more a strategy for gaining seats in the US Congress, state houses, and the White House, rather than an overarching attempt to recreate the Democratic Party.

Furthermore, the white southern politicians that made up the DLC were a product of the "New South."[57] They represented blacks, embraced blacks, and had none of the racial animus of the old southern Democrats. Several black Democrats became affiliated with the DLC. They included Philadelphia congressman William Gray, Virginia governor Douglas Wilder, former head of the National Urban League Vernon Jordan, Mississippi congressman Mike Espy, DNC chair Ron Brown, Georgia congressman John Lewis, Louisiana congressman William Jefferson, Baltimore mayor Kurt Schmoke, Atlanta mayor Maynard Jackson, and New York congressman Floyd Flake. Many of these Democrats came from the South and saw the problems facing the national party. Ideas and policy agenda items promoting responsibility, opportunity, and community were not opposite to the interests of African Americans, they were central to their personal and political positions. The messages of prosperity, opposition to redistributive measures, support of meaningful welfare reform, and updating of the government to be more responsive and efficient appealed to many middle-class African Americans. Baer notes, "Democrats were able to construct this coalition of the New Rich and the base of blacks and labor unions because many of them copied the New Democratic approach proved successful by Clinton."[58] African Americans, proving that they were not monolithic in their political orientation, reflected the wide range of views concerning economics, politics, and governance that white Americans did, especially as the black middle class grew significantly. The DLC's pronouncements embracing social justice did, however, assuage some Africans Americans troubled by the vagueness of the DLC's intent.

It helped that starting with a DLC annual meeting in Williamsburg, Virginia, in 1986, former Virginia governor Charles Robb made overt efforts to include more African Americans. As former Atlanta mayor Maynard Jackson remarked in 1987, "'There was an original perception, an initial perception that this was sort of a good old boys group.' But he added, there is certainly 'no validity' to such a notion today. 'I don't think the DLC is any more of a risk than the DNC.'"[59] In addition, as Jack Germond and Jules Witcover wrote in their column, "It is also a product of a growing and pragmatic recognition among more conservative white Democrats and liberal black Democrats that they need one another."[60] In other words, there was a real element of political pragmatism among New Democrats and liberal blacks, such as Andrew Young, John Lewis, and William Gray, that belied the idea that (1) blacks were politically monolithic and (2) that New Democrats were simply reactionaries or what Vermont governor Howard Dean would call nearly twenty years later "Republican-lite."

In 1989, Douglas Wilder, the Democratic nominee for governor in Virginia, made open efforts to distance himself from Jesse Jackson. While Jackson and Wilder had been friends for nearly thirty years, they were far apart on political issues. For instance, Jackson represented the populist, liberal wing of the Democratic Party. Jackson's 1984 and 1988 campaigns for the presidency were reflective of class conflict, conflict between the haves and have-nots. Jackson wanted to redistribute wealth to lift up America's poor and working classes regardless of what race they happened to be. Wilder had made his name as a moderate-conservative Democratic politician from the heart of the Old Confederacy. In the late 1980s, Jackson was not popular within the commonwealth. R. H. Melton of the *Washington Post* reported, "Wilder believes there are compelling political reasons to put as much distance as possible between himself and Jackson as he stumps for votes in generally conservative Virginia."[61] Further, Melton noted, "Wilder criticized Jackson's Rainbow Coalition for hurting the image and electoral chances of the national Democratic Party."[62] This episode demonstrated that Wilder and, by extension, other moderate African American candidates were leery of the liberal Democrats. In addition, it reinforced the reality that the African American community was diverse politically and ready to move forward from the intense, often vitriolic debates of the 1960s about social issues.

Ronald Brown, chairman of the Democratic National Committee and Clinton's future commerce secretary, also reflected the unease of moderate African Americans with the liberal politics of Jesse Jackson and the coastal elites. Brown was a product of a middle-class family and white preparatory schools and colleges. A prominent member of the National Urban League, Brown worked his way up in Democratic circles. In 1989, Brown was installed as chairman of the DNC. Brown promised liberals that he would help soften the appeal of the DLC during his tenure. But Brown also reflected the need for a moderate-conservative wing. As Jackson's forces and the DLC battled over convention rules regarding delegate allocation, Brown was forced to act as a bridge between both parties. E. J. Dionne pointed out, "Another problem, in Mr. [Stan] Greenberg's view, is the Republicans' success in using racial politics—President Reagan's opposition to affirmative action, for instance—to divide the Democratic coalition. That is one reason why the rules battle so rankles Ronald H. Brown, the new Democratic National Chairman. If the rules battles becomes a fight over Jesse Jackson, Mr. Brown said, the result could be 'bloody.'"[63] Dionne also noted that Ron Brown "sees himself as a bridge between the party's racial and ideological factions and he does not like confrontations."[64] Process aside, many African Americans, privately or publicly, agreed with the refocusing of policy and rhetoric that the DLC represented.

A perfect example of the need to refocus the Democratic Party was Harvey Gantt of North Carolina. A successful mayor of Charlotte, Gantt was the Democrats' best hope of defeating incumbent Jesse Helms in 1990. A series of racist advertisements—the "white hands" ad was particularly noxious as it characterized Gantt as a liberal black intent on equal outcomes. Gantt believed, as Thomas B. Edsall noted, "The party must directly address the issues of affirmative action and quotas. Asked how he [Gantt] would do this, he said Democrats must demonstrate there is not an 'epidemic' of reverse discrimination and that all efforts must be made to bring minorities into the work force to be internationally competitive."[65] That many African Americans, concerns about various personalities or rhetoric aside, were attracted to the DLC message and refocusing the Democratic Party demonstrated that these politicos understood they had to change in order to be elected and reelected. Further, the intense debates of the 1960s and 1970s had changed as the nation became more conservative. Lastly, the explosion of the African American middle class following the civil rights movement left deep divisions between the working and middle classes that manifested themselves in politics.

As Bill Clinton became the standard bearer of the DLC in 1990, many of these members knew Clinton or knew of him. They knew his record on racial issues as governor of Arkansas. Arguably, no other white politician did as much to confer legitimacy to the DLC among African Americans as Bill Clinton. As early as January 1992, many of these black DLC members and supporters endorsed the candidacy of Clinton. Thomas Edsall wrote in a *Washington Post* article in January 1992 that "Arkansas Gov. Bill Clinton, who had done considerable groundwork in the past, emerged yesterday as the immediate beneficiary of the freedom black leaders. . . . Mike Espy (D-Miss.) said he will endorse Clinton, and two other key black leaders in the South, Reps. John Lewis (D-Ga.) and William J. Jefferson (D-La.) are expected to quickly follow suit."[66] In addition, "H. Hartford Brookins, a prominent bishop of the African Methodist Episcopal Church who has been a major backer of Jesse L. Jackson in the past, is expected to endorse Clinton early next week."[67] These African American supporters would eventually include Jesse Jackson himself, Artur Davis of Alabama, Harold Ford of Tennessee, Michael Nutter of Philadelphia, and many others attracted to both a winning political agenda and the substantive agenda items that helped to refocus the Democratic Party. These politicos helped provide crucial support to Clinton among African American voters in 1992, especially after difficult issues arose involving a mentally defective death row inmate, controversial comments by a black rapper, and a very public tiff with the Rev. Jesse Jackson.

Black Suspicion of the DLC

The DLC embrace of market-based solutions made many African Americans uneasy, as they had historically been less likely to benefit from moderate-to-conservative approaches to economic policy. In an era where African Americans still lagged far behind whites in terms of wealth, educational achievement, occupational achievement, and health, any talk of limiting the government's role in American society conjured up fears of the devolution of the government's responsibility to the poor and working classes. Ideas such as deficit reduction, tax breaks, and free trade compounded the fears of a community that has been disproportionately impacted by racial backlash, globalization, and deindustrialization. Those ideas translated into budget cuts for domestic programs and agencies. In *Black Enterprise* National Urban League president John E. Jacob noted that President Clinton should have focused on job training and creation for disadvantaged and that "the President [should] press as hard for jobs as he did for NAFTA."[68] As William Julius Wilson has noted, many of the problems of the inner cities resulted from deindustrialization and job losses as much as racism.[69] This, in part, is what prompted the Rev. Jesse Jackson in 1991 to derisively refer to the DLC as "Democrats for the Leisure Class."

As early as 1985 Jesse Jackson was complaining about the insurgent Democratic organization. In a 1985 *Washington Post* article by Paul Taylor, Jackson was quoted as saying, "'The Democratic Leadership Council . . . is sending a clear signal' by 'traveling around the country as a group of all whites.'"[70] Jackson clearly had his finger on the pulse of the African American political class when he said that "'the shadow of Ronald Reagan hovers over the Democratic Party'" and that Reagan "'has intimidated the Democrats.'"[71] There may have been hyperbole in Jackson's remarks; however, his words did convey the feelings of those who felt that the DLC was trying to push the Democratic Party to the right of the political spectrum. Virginia lieutenant governor Douglas Wilder remarked in 1986 that his fellow Virginian, Charles Robb, and the DLC were a "'divisive' force in the national party whose members include 'me-too-ists who put on Reagan masks.'"[72] As time passed, however, critics, including Wilder, joined or supported the DLC. Public policy issues aside, this was a major reason why many blacks viewed the DLC with serious suspicion. They saw a faction of the Democratic Party that was growing stronger with each passing year and sounded more and more like the Republican Party with its message of moderation and responsibility. Many blacks saw these remarks as code for negating the public policy advancements of the previous twenty-five years.

It can be argued that the very presence of the DLC brought on hypersensitivity with the African American political class. Wilder noted at a Richmond hotel toward the end of 1986, "'It's demeaning to say you've got to appeal to those . . . to white southern males . . . and say to blacks, 'Hold still, we'll do something for you.'"[73] Concern over the white electorate, especially the southern white male voter, angered not just Wilder but others who saw such appeals as sympathetic to racists and a slap in the face to African Americans. Even Atlanta mayor Maynard Jackson, who viewed the DLC, generally, as positive, still "cautioned that blacks could not be praised for 'playing a key role in the success of the Democratic Party and then be asked to sit over in the corner and be quiet.'"[74] The perception that the DLC simply wanted all of the various "interest groups," especially blacks, to shut up, sit down, and be quiet, was central to African Americans' distrust of the DLC. These criticisms helped to force the DLC to take more of a big-tent approach to the politics they were trying to represent. His feuding with Wilder led Robb to state, "'We need to make room for those citizens who are now left out. . . . We have an obligation—both to the needy and to society as a whole—to help the poor move into the social and economic mainstream of our national life.'"[75] Robb's public statements at the annual meeting of the DLC in Williamsburg reflected the need of the DLC to shore up its sagging reputation within the African American political class. It also demonstrated the need of the DLC to grapple with the presence of Jesse Jackson and his millions of followers. At this same Williamsburg meeting, reporter John W. Mashek penned, "In their public discussions, some 70 elected officials will stick to the issues, but in their private discussions in the corridors of the Williamsburg Inn, a hot topic will be Jackson and how to deal with him without alienating large numbers of the black voters who have become so crucial to the success of the party."[76] Further, it demonstrated the sensitivity of New Democrats to direct and subtle claims of racism from African Americans. It was this balancing act, along with specific policy positions, such as those on welfare, crime, and affirmative action, with which the DLC most struggled.

The DLC's treatment of Jesse Jackson angered African Americans most. Jackson's 1984 and 1988 presidential campaigns emphasized the vast disparities between the rich and poor. They highlighted the growing economic inequality in American society. Jackson also said, often loudly and vociferously, that lack of commitment to the interest of America's most vulnerable had to be confronted with distinctions between the two major parties. In political parlance this sounded like the "class warfare" arguments that Republicans used so well to dismiss concerns for the poor and the downtrodden. Dating back to the Gilded Age, pronouncements about economic disparities often were responded to with cries of "class warfare." Therefore, any talk of redistribution of wealth and progressive taxation that would increase the tax liability for high earners resulted in criticism that progressives and liberals were attempting to destroy domestic harmony by highlighting these inequities. This issue greatly concerned the DLC, which saw such rhetoric and politicking as problematic. As Robb said in the spring of 1989, "'[Jackson] encouraged the public perception that the Democrats want to divide the country between the haves and have-nots.'"[77] This divisiveness threatened future electoral gains and, with it, the potential to change American domestic and foreign policies. Further, Robb said, "'The real challenge for our party and our country is to find and elect leaders who offer a practical, appealing, commonsense vision of the future of our government.'"[78] New Democrats, therefore, wanted to focus on another line of argument that ignored these inequities and promoted "pro-growth" policies that appealed to the masses without highlighting such issues. This was a part of the reason the DLC viewed Jesse Jackson with resentment, and why liberal African Americans viewed the DLC with suspicion.

When Jackson decided not to run for president in 1992, the DLC reacted with sheer joy. New Hampshire state chairman J. Joseph Grandmaison had already said to the *Washington Post*, "If he were to make that decision, there'd be many Democratic leaders who would breathe a sigh of relief."[79] His withdrawal helped the DLC in its effort to present itself as the home of centrist moderates who could appeal to the so-called middle class. Al From drove home the point in 1989 when he said to the *Washington Post,* "'When Jackson runs, he gets all the black votes so other candidates don't think it's necessary to campaign [for black votes] in the primaries. We have a challenge . . . to put together an appeal that unites the interests of middle-income whites and blacks because we need that kind of biracial coalition to win.'"[80] But millions of African Americans remained working class, so such rhetoric about the great middle class did little to address many black concerns about jobs, health care, education, and numerous other issues. Yet blacks moving into the middle class and many more that were close and aspired to be middle class found the rhetoric politically resonant.

The DLC's opposition to traditional welfare also angered many blacks. Republicans had long been enemies of welfare; the Democratic Party's embrace of welfare since 1935 had dramatically increased the number of recipients on the dole. Many of these people were black and had health problems, addiction issues, and little to no skills. In fact, between 1981 and 1992, as the Clinton administration pointed out, "the number of welfare recipients increased by 2.5 million (a 22 percent increase) to 13.6 million people."[81] African American politicians generally thought that reforming welfare was fine as long as recipients were not thrown off the rolls all together. The embrace of Republican notions of the alleged dependency and even laziness of recipients angered blacks who believed that the real aim of reform was not to uplift the poor but to demonize them. The Democratic Leadership Council believed that all able-bodied Americans should work. African American politicians and much of the black community felt the same; however, they quickly diverged once any details were presented. It appeared to many blacks that the DLC and later the Democratic Party were abdicating their responsibility to the poor by embracing ideas that promoted reforming and constricting America's safety net. The combination of Clinton's rhetorical appeals for responsibility and community along with his propensity toward deal making sent off alarm bells. After Clinton delivered his landmark speech to the DLC in Cleveland, where he outlined much of the DLC platform, he was cornered by many African American DLC members who demanded answers. A delegate to the convention, Henry Reddy of Pennsylvania, remarked to Dan Balz of the *Washington Post* that his "concern is that the DLC is pushing a wedge between the most loyal faction of the Democratic Party and themselves. . . . What he said to me is we've got to outdo the Republicans. We don't. We've got to be Democrats."[82] Core Democratic policies and issues, such as welfare, civil rights, and affirmative action, were central to this skepticism.

In October 1995, after Clinton defended affirmative action, he traveled to Austin, Texas, where he addressed a mostly white student body about the need to excise racism from American society. Moreover, the appeal of Louis Farrakhan and the Nation of Islam and its Million Man March in Washington prompted Clinton to address the thorny racial issue again. The *Washington Post* said, "[In] preparing for his speech over the past weekend, aides said, Clinton spoke with such African Americans as Jesse L. Jackson, Washington lawyer Vernon E. Jordan Jr. and Rep. John Lewis (D-Ga.). Among the white leaders he spoke with was Sen. Joseph I. Lieberman (D-Conn.), the chairman of the moderate Democratic Leadership Council."[83] While that John Harris article reported the president's intentions for his speech and the coming of the Million Man March, it also showed that the president himself, as demonstrated by his own aides' comments to Harris, recognized that interests of the Democratic Leadership Council and the African American political community were rarely the same. Beyond the DLC's "no quota" position, Clinton himself had argued at the 1991 DLC convention in Cleveland that affirmative action could lead to a quota system, thus affirming conservative arguments about the veracity of race-based programs. The DLC and Clinton made the point, forcefully, that "the role of government is to guarantee equal opportunity, not mandate equal outcomes. . . . We oppose discrimination of any kind—including quotas."[84] This ignored all relevant data that contradicted the notion of "reverse discrimination," bought into conservative ideas about a "colorblind society," and appeared to attack one of the most important policies that expanded the African American middle class.

African Americans had long complained that the Democratic Party had long taken them for granted. The Democratic Leadership Council had been founded, in part, to counter the perception that Democrats were too closely associated with minorities and purposely constructed its platform to appeal to whites, especially Reagan

Democrats. Ultimately, this was successful in winning the White House in 1992 and 1996 and expanding the influence of moderate Democrats around the country. Yet, when Democrats got into trouble politically, they often turned against one of their most loyal constituencies, African Americans. Such was the case in 1998 when President Clinton found himself in the most serious investigation of his presidency: Monica Lewinsky and allegations of abuse of power and perjury.

As noted scholar and journalist William Schnieder explained in December 1998, "Why are liberals so sympathetic to a President who has sold them out again and again? Because (in their view) he's being persecuted? Maybe. But more than that, Clinton is a hero to liberals because of his values—1960s values. A lot of [Democratic Leadership] council Democrats share with conservatives a resentment of the 1960s, when the McGovernite Left started to take over their party."[85] This persecution sentiment is well known to African Americans. More important, however, Clinton's embrace of much of the 1960s ethos resonated with African Americans. In fact, this was a major source of disagreement between Clinton and his colleagues at the DLC. As Schneider also noted, "In the council's view, the liberals' cardinal sin was to show disdain for traditional values. Exactly what Clinton did by his behavior in the White House, Lieberman argued."[86] Ironically, Clinton's peccadilloes and fondness for the social transformation obscured, for African Americans, many of his actual policies.

The idea of the loyal black constituency lost much of its veracity during Clinton's later years in office. Frustration with Clinton's personal flaws and his centrist, DLC agenda can be gleaned by examining a few pertinent facts. The Joint Center for Political and Economic Studies found that "there is comparatively little change in black partisan identification. . . . The level of Democratic partisanship has remained remarkably stable since the Joint Center's first National Opinion Poll in 1984."[87] These findings masked growing divisions within the African American community as to the national party agenda. Moreover, the recalcitrance of the GOP provided cover to Democrats and Bill Clinton, especially. The fluidity within the African American community demonstrated both frustration and irritation with the New Democratic philosophy and its focus on "values" issues that often assumed or insinuated that problems within the African American community were the result of group pathology.

Conclusion

The Democratic Leadership Council was the most important ideological and intellectual component of the Democratic Party during the Clinton years. It was also a strategy designed to relieve the Democratic Party of the albatross hung around its neck by the previous thirty years. As scholar Margaret Weir notes:

> This transformative strategy had three components: (1) To counter distrust of the federal government, policy would work through market mechanisms or the states and it would 'reinvent' government; (2) To counter racially-charged 'wedge' issues, such as crime and welfare, policy would set clear expectations for individual responsibility and impose sanctions on bad behavior . . .; (3) To counter arguments that social spending was too expensive, policy would highlight the long-term benefits of 'investing' in people so that they could be productive workers and citizens.[88]

So important were the New Democrats that the liberal wing of the party that had dominated the Democratic Party's agenda from the 1960s onward became a marginal factor in political and policy decisions. Ronald Walters explained, "The position of the DLC was a controlling factor in the selection of campaign issues in the era of Bill Clinton, as witnessed by Clinton's positions as expressed in the crime bill of 1994 and the welfare reform bill of 1996."[89] The DLC became legitimate as Clinton won the White House in 1992 and 1996. In addition, hundreds of Democrats nationwide credited the DLC as pivotal in their congressional, senatorial, and gubernatorial races for elective office. The anger of liberals, minorities, and progressives at the sometimes real and sometimes perceived retreat from the progress of the 1960s remained at a low boil. Success begat success. Acceptance from interparty opponents was reluctant but significant nonetheless.

At any rate, for Democrats nationwide, the centrism of the Democratic Party and the Clinton White House was better than having a Republican in office. This is especially true as Newt Gingrich,

Bob Dole, Tom Delay, and their allies around the country became increasingly antagonistic toward Clinton, with investigations of every part of the Clintons' lives. The 1990s explosion of cable news and extreme partisanship provided a crucial fig leaf for Clinton and his New Democrat agenda by diverting focus on the real and possible effects of his policies and allaying many of the fears of African Americans and liberals about the Clinton agenda.

Essentially, the DLC split black politicians into two groups: the old group defined more by its activism and reliance on government largesse and a new group that represented the growing class divisions within American society. The older, more established black politicians tended to view market-based solutions to societal problems as a cop-out designed to negate the legitimate concerns of African Americans. Moreover, their reliance on racial politics—a critical and necessary strategy in the Jim Crow and 1960s eras—put them at odds with an America that had moved on to new challenges. These challenges included class. An unspoken factor in the post–civil rights era, class arguably was most clearly seen within the African American community as a significant number climbed and clawed their way into the middle class. In addition, as those people became college graduates, businesspersons, professors, and professionals, they felt the backlash most acutely from the civil rights era. By succeeding, those blacks changed their views on numerous political issues, such as crime, affirmative action, welfare, and government spending and taxation policies. The DLC's embrace of a middle approach appealed to blacks for many of the same reasons that it appealed to whites: compromise, core principles, progress, and economic self-interest. Finally, the DLC demonstrated the salience of both class and the rise of a new, more centrist political style not only embraced by Bill Clinton in the 1990s, but also embodied by black politicians such as Artur Davis, Cory Booker, Kendrick Meek, and, most famously, President Barack Obama.

On June 16, 2009, the Democratic Leadership Council gathered to honor Al From. Bruce Reed, Clinton's former 1992 campaign aide and chair of the Domestic Policy Council, had taken over the centrist organization. Clinton then stepped up to the podium. More than eight years after he left office, in a completely changed political atmosphere, Clinton defended the DLC. Looking at Al From from the platform,

Clinton told everyone, "I would have never become president if it wasn't for you."[90] The Democratic Leadership Council's platform of devolution, "racial reductionism," welfare reform, values issues, and crime policy would be clearly on display during the eight years Clinton was in office. The first six months of Clinton's presidency, however, cast doubt on Clinton's commitment to the New Democratic philosophy. The next five chapters examine the salience of New Democratic ideas as espoused by President Clinton. First, the nomination of a black, female lawyer to a prominent Justice Department position tested Clinton's mettle, invoked the ire of African Americans, and drew Clinton back to the New Democratic foundation that he had seemingly abandoned.

CHAPTER 2

Race and Class
in the 1990s

THE AFRICAN AMERICAN struggle for freedom and equality remained unfulfilled as the 1990s began in earnest. In nearly every statistical category, white Americans surpassed and, at times, lapped African Americans. Moreover, the Reagan revolution and the ascendancy of conservatism brought a backlash toward the gains of the civil rights movement. President Reagan had criticized many of the civil rights measures that had been passed during the Great Society era, most notably, the Voting Rights Act of 1965. He even was resistant to reauthorizing key provisions of the Voting Rights Act on the grounds that it was insulting to the South.[1] Apparently, what was insulting was the act itself, especially section 5, which states that states could not change voting laws, regulations, or procedures unless they received prior approval from a federal judge or the US attorney general that the change did not discriminate against African Americans. In addition, federal observers could monitor activities within both the state and specific counties.[2] It was the Civil Rights Act of 1964 and Voting Rights Act of 1965 that finally broke down the de jure barriers of Jim Crow. African Americans, as a result, made tremendous political and economic gains.

Affirmative action policies and programs afforded certain blacks opportunities—admission into exclusive prep schools and universities and entry-level positions in companies, firms, and corporations—that previously were closed to them. Consequently, for the first time, a significant number of African Americans were able to move into the middle class. Middle-class African Americans were able to buy homes, purchase cars, invest, build up retirement nest eggs, start businesses, enroll their children in good public or private schools, and partake in the accoutrements typical of middle-class Americans. Yet those gains were unevenly distributed within the African American community. Further, those emblems of class status remained out of reach for millions of poor and working-class African Americans for whom educational, family, institutional, and structural barriers remained too high to successfully traverse.

While some blacks enjoyed their new status in the professional class, others continued to suffer. Those blacks who were beneficiaries of 1960s liberalism were often in positions which allowed them to easily step into opportunities. For instance, African Americans whose parents or family had political connections, some family money, or access to education were able to seize opportunities that were unavailable to others. As a result, a fissure developed within black America as certain blacks were, however reluctantly or grudgingly, accepted into mainstream society. The examples abound with tales of Clarence Thomas, Vernon Jordan, Barack Obama, J. C. Watts, Colin Powell: men who were, with their hard work, intelligence, and connections, able to benefit from the opening of America. As more blacks assumed seats in universities and positions within mainstream America, the fissures within the black community widened, leading to disappointment, anger, and class conflict.

These tensions mirrored the growing disillusionment within the United States as a whole. Just as many blacks were left with hopelessness after seemingly being left behind by political, economic, and technological advancements, so too were white Americans. The drawdown of the Industrial Age and the rise of the finance and service-related sectors left many working- and lower-middle-class whites with the same feelings of abandonment and resentment. Some of those sentiments, however, were directed toward those they felt had received the opportunities that once belonged to whites. These transformations in

American life were compounded by population shifts that devastated urban areas in the Midwest and Northeast. As Thomas Sugrue expertly notes, "The flight of capital was rooted in interstate competition, as rural states, especially in the Sun Belt, lowered taxes and discouraged unionization to create a 'favorable business climate' to attract companies from high-tax, high-wage cities like Chicago."[3] While this hurt many families, regardless of race, it had a disproportionate impact on African Americans. As jobs were transferred from the city to southern and suburban areas, many African Americans were trapped and left with decaying neighborhoods and public schools. In addition to the loss of jobs and economic activity, those cities often lost revenue they previously received from the federal government. This was devastating to the residents of those locales. The contrast between the suburbs and inner cities became even starker as state and federally supported projects, such as home construction, highway construction, and tax incentives to developers, encouraged those capable of migrating to the suburbs to do so.[4]

Dissolution, Disintegration, and Uneven Progress of the African American Community

Arguably the best way to describe the progression of the African American community is disintegration. *Washington Post* columnist Eugene Robinson discussed at length this concept in his 2010 book, *Disintegration: The Splintering of Black America.*[5] Most historians and commentators have focused on the positive aspects of the transformational changes wrought by the civil rights movement. People praise the integration of schools. People laud the breakdown of Jim Crow. People celebrate the end of overt racial discrimination. It is the assimilation of African Americans in mainstream (white) culture that is seen as positive. Moreover, we exalt the success stories, such as people graduating from college, finding work in white-collar jobs, and making important strides. This ignores the profound impact of integration on the African American community.

Blacks were a relatively tight community within the United States from slavery through Jim Crow. They did not have a choice.

Racial solidarity had a special importance and meaning for African Americans. It meant protection. It meant security. It meant millions of African Americans, regardless of ideology, philosophy, or difference of opinion, had the same basic interests: security of their person, home, job, and family. The civil rights movement was basic in its objectives. Those people simply wanted to the right to vote, receive an education, have some economic security, and equal protection of the law. While what they wanted, and largely achieved, was rather simplistic, it was revolutionary when one considers the obstacles they faced in fulfilling their mission. And it was received with little in return from white America. In fact, economically and racially, white America may have benefitted the most from the end of Jim Crow.

The institutions that were at the center of black life often fell into disrepair. Historically black colleges and universities across the South struggled to maintain their relevancy in an era of integration. Black high school seniors increasingly turned to white institutions of higher education. Alumni support began to wither as younger generations of black college graduates gave their money to the white institutions that awarded them degrees. Many of those schools had remained private, never becoming part of the state higher education system in their respective states, thus becoming increasingly vulnerable to neglect and decline.

Integration often closed the mom-and-pop stores that served the community. The rise of K-Mart and Walmart, along with other retailers, served to further destroy not just small businesses across the nation, but the very black institutions that had served local communities for decades. The need for cheap goods and services often trumped racial solidarity. Integration was never meant to be a cross-cultural exchange of institutions, cultural values, or ideas. It meant assimilation. As a result, the black cultural and business institutions took on an exotic aesthetic feel. A perfect example is the continuing fascination with soul food, barbeque, and other so-called black foods. The famed soul food joint Sylvia's, in Harlem, often draws white diners. It was somewhat reminiscent of the huge fascination with Asian and Native American culture that whites enjoyed during the 1970s and early 1980s. Finally, the growing popularity of hip-hop and rap music during the late 1970s, 1980s, and 1990s within white America was both impressive, because many whites simply enjoyed the new genre, and troubling, as it also signaled the growing acceptance and enjoyment of high-tech, late-twentieth-century minstrel shows.

Free from the politically damaging image of repression, whites could move forward as if nothing happened. With the doors finally opened, in a very narrow, legalistic sense, African Americans could be largely forgotten. No longer would whites need to maintain dual educational systems. No longer would whites need to actively police society to make sure blacks did not cross some line separating blacks from whites. No longer would whites need to do anything other than follow the basic tenets of the law. Still the institutional and systemic racism that was so much a part of the cultural DNA of American life could persist with ne'er a peep.

The onus was now on blacks to make the most out of the new "opportunities." Any failure to achieve could easily be assigned to the individual, no matter how high the barriers or how limited their life opportunities. Colorblindness was the order of the day. While race was overtly used to maintain control, the vanilla language used to advocate for such measures prevented others from alleging racism or bias. For instance, President Reagan's War on Drugs served to further alienate and control urban black youth. Poor kids and young men were sent to prison in droves during the middle 1980s and the 2000s. Welfare policies continued to vary depending on state and region. Educational opportunity narrowed as urban schools and minority-majority school districts received less funding, less attention, and poorer staffing. Economic transformation made the situation worse as lower-middle- and working-class blacks found it nearly impossible to transcend their station in life. In the second half of the nineteenth century, the concept of social Darwinism became a dominant theory of American society. Those at the bottom of the economic and social ladders deserved to be there. There was something wrong with those people. If they were any better, they would not be in the position that they were in. Survival of the fittest was the common belief. Furthermore, the arrival of a newly ascendant black middle class seemed to justify the continued belief in this flawed theory. To the extent that society could help the downtrodden, those people needed to redouble their efforts and focus on themselves. After all, the common perception, nurtured by a new and aggressive conservative movement, was that the Great Society programs that combated poverty, disease, and ignorance largely failed. As blacks who could get out of their circumstances left—as soon as the doors to greater opportunity opened—others were trapped and, consequently, left to die with the old liberalism, the old factories, and the old way of life. The end result was the fragmentation of the African American community. As Robinson has expertly noted, "In the end, one black America became four—Mainstream, Abandoned, Transcendent, and Emergent."[6]

Elite African Americans

There has always been an elite group of African Americans: doctors, professors, teachers, lawyers, businessmen, and clergy. These elite people held extraordinary influence and power within the African American community. They were the power brokers, the groups and individuals who could make things happen for other blacks and at least lessen negative things in the lives of others. The African American elite influenced what happened in the community. As fortunate blacks rose to these positions after the Civil War, they created schools, businesses, funeral homes, and churches. Through these institutions, they helped to erect economic, educational, and social institutions central to black life in the United States. Throughout Reconstruction and Jim Crow, prominent civic leaders often brought a group focus in terms of uplifting the race. The binary nature of black life made life uncomplicated. Life was hard, early death was a daily threat, and there was a strict line of demarcation between whites and blacks that was never to be crossed. The constrictive nature of life forced blacks to focus on what they could achieve and what could be controlled. Helping with these hard facts of life were elite blacks. Uplift would come through hard work, commitment to education, and a middle-class orientation.

Elite blacks, however, often acted as go-betweens with blacks and the larger white world. This was clearly seen as a succession of local and prominent blacks, such as Booker T. Washington, W.E.B. DuBois, and Martin Luther King Jr., pushed, prodded, and agitated for better freedom, opportunity, and equality. In doing so, many elite blacks were rewarded with power, money, and prominence. Sometimes some elites acted in ways contrary to the interests of the African American community. Some, such as the aforementioned, tried to do what they believed was in the best interest of their people. Despite black activism, little seemed to change. This was especially true for the elite blacks. As smart, accomplished, or talented as they were, they could never break the color line. That began to change with the second Reconstruction in the 1960s.

The civil rights movement accomplished what previous efforts, including Reconstruction, could not. Elite blacks, with the hundreds of thousands of unsung heroes, broke down the de jure walls of oppression and inequality. From 1945 to 1968, de jure segregation in public facilities, education, housing, and the workplace fell like a set of dominoes. The transformational change came in unexpected ways in the African American community, none more so than for elite blacks. Elites were, finally, routinely admitted to Harvard, Yale, and other world-class institutions. When they graduated, thanks to affirmative action policies that helped to even the playing field, and growing public disapproval of overt displays of racism and discrimination, they entered prestigious firms, companies, and corporations. Along with their valuable degrees and upper-class careers, elite blacks began to build wealth, connections, and networks, which allowed them to partake in opportunities unavailable to most Americans, black or white. Nowhere was this as clearly seen as in the world of politics. Minority-majority congressional districts were one way to move into powerful political positions. As members of US Congress, these African Americans were able to direct resources toward their home districts, promote legislation important to their constituents, and, when necessary, fight Republican attempts to roll back funding for important programs and projects, weaken key civil rights measures, and otherwise present regressive legislation. In fact, by the time Bill Clinton was sworn in as president, the Congressional Black Caucus was arguably the most powerful faction in the US Congress. Furthermore, blacks became members of the political establishment by working in political campaigns, becoming activists, and working through groups affiliated with the Democratic Party. The late former chairman of the Democratic National Committee and secretary of commerce, Ron

Brown, was perfect example of this upward trajectory for elite African Americans. Others chose a different route. Vernon Jordan parlayed his lifelong career in law and civil rights, including leading the venerable Urban League civil rights organization, into a lucrative second career as a high-priced attorney at a prestigious Washington, D.C., law firm and a highly influential insider of power politics in the nation's capital. While these two figures are just a couple of many, they are reflective of the growth of the elite African American community. It did, however, come at a price: separation.

As these elites began to climb the ladder of success, they often became more assimilated and distant from lower-class blacks. New opportunities compounded these success stories: new homes in elite communities, country club memberships, prestigious private schools, and such. The so-called end of manufacturing and the rise of service- and finance-related jobs helped to increase the stratification between elites and lower-class African Americans. The rise of black Republicans, a by-product of the Reagan era, is demonstrative of this fact. Cities such as Chicago, New York, metropolitan Washington, D.C., and Atlanta all had elite communities.

By 1990, African Americans were 12 percent of the population, constituting thirty million people. In fact, the African American community grew by 13 percent, which was higher than the national average. Most, 57 percent, exactly, lived in cities. Another 27 percent found homes in the suburbs. In fact, the African American suburban presence grew by 29 percent over figures for 1980. Contrary to popular belief, most blacks did not live in poverty; that was only a third of the community. Many others, though, teetered on the brink of poverty. But for the top 10 percent of the black community, progress was tangible, palpable, and, increasingly, enjoyable. These were important changes that reflected the growing divide between elites and lower-class blacks.[7]

Middle-Class African Americans

The black middle class has also boomed since the civil rights movement. While class can be difficult to determine—sociologists and others define it differently—there are some markers and indicators that are common enough that we can ascribe them to middle class. For instance, education is an important part of middle-class life. If education is the great equalizer, then it helps to explain the historic preoccupation within the African American community with schools and higher education. Further, as the twentieth century wore on, increasingly complex skill-sets were needed for upward mobility. This has been especially true since the end of the Industrial Age in 1969, as the economy moved toward the finance and service sectors. Therefore, education is central to middle-class status. As Mary Pattillo-McCoy has expertly noted, "The most strict definition of middle (for blacks and whites) includes only those with a college degree."[8] According to the National Center for Education Statistics, between 1976 and 1993 blacks went from earning more than 58,000 bachelor's degrees to more 83,000.[9] In the same time frame, blacks earning master's degrees went from 21,037 to 21, 986 per year in 1993.[10] In addition, blacks earned 1,253 doctoral degrees in 1976, compared to 1,385 in 1993.[11] Blacks also earned 2,537 professional degrees in 1976, compared to 4,444 by 1993.[12] As the doors to education were thrown open to African Americans, millions grasped at the opportunity to further education themselves and move into the middle class. It was the college experience that both hardened and opened up black graduates. They not only learned history, economics, and literature, but also developed relationships with other students, learned more about the world around themselves, and questioned long-held assumptions. While that is the mission of higher education, it had a profound impact on African Americans reaching for the coveted middle-class life. This had serious consequences for American economic and political life.

As middle-class African Americans left the ivory tower for the real world of work, family, and life, they encountered the hardships of often being the first in their profession or among the very few in an overwhelmingly white professional world. There were also great differences in the jobs assumed by whites and those assumed by blacks. Few African Americans were able to ascend to the heights of Wall Street or the executive ranks of corporations. Often blacks took jobs in the public sector, where they could, despite lower wages than in the private sector, earn good benefits, have better opportunities for promotion, and build a retirement through savings and a local, state, or federal pension plan. Thomas Holt argues:

> The job categories in which white-collar employment among blacks were distributed shifted dramatically: whereas teachers and the clergy had together made up almost half (46 percent) of such employees in 1940, they constituted just 28 percent in 1980, their former dominance shrunken by a rapidly expanding black managerial class. The sectoral sources of black income continued, nonetheless, to evolve in the same direction through the final decade of the century: by 1995 more than half of all black professionals were working in the public sector.[13]

These realities made it more likely that middle-class blacks would embrace the Democratic Party and progressive legislation. In fact, the number of black conservatives and Republicans remained relatively small, less than 10 percent of all adult African Americans. Black professionals, however, also grew more conscious and concerned about such issues as federal taxes, property taxes, and safety and more leery of federal programs that targeted the poor, seemingly at the expense of the middle class.

While most African Americans remained committed to the old concept of racial uplift and supportive of friends, relatives, and others that they knew that were further down on the socioeconomic scale, many adopted the concerns, fears, and even prejudices of white America toward the poor. This was compounded by white social and media infatuation with tales of black criminal pathology. The perception of blacks as a dangerous criminal element was nothing new. What was new was the War on Drugs and the mass incarceration of African Americans during the 1980s and 1990s. In addition to the gang violence and crack-cocaine epidemic, the urban landscape became something to avoid. In part a result of these factors, calls for responsibility were common among middle-class blacks. Demands for reform of America's welfare system were strong. Furthermore, pleas from middle-class blacks to politicians for help with urban and, sometimes, suburban violence were heard from Boston to New York to Chicago to Los Angeles and everywhere else where blacks lived in significant numbers. Author and journalist Ellis Cose discovered, while researching his 1993 bestseller, *The Rage of a Privileged Class*, that "the resentment many black professionals feel at being expected to accept responsibility for the underclass is palpable."[14] These problems made it extremely difficult for the black middle class to progress in an atmosphere in which the so-called underclass formed white perceptions of the entire African American community. The pressure placed on poor African Americans by middle-class blacks was not simply the result of middle-class paternalism. Instead, it was often the result of the pressure they felt from white America to uplift the poor.

The Reagan revolution and the backlash toward civil rights led to calls for the middle class to help the poor instead of using the power of the state to ameliorate those problems. Personal responsibility, in its proper political context, was more than political rhetoric. It was the vitriolic response to the end of Jim Crow, the rise of affirmative action, and the persistence of black demands for equal opportunity. As such, white politicians used political language that sought to place the blame and the burden for high crime rates, low graduation rates, decreasing rates of marriage within the black community, and dysfunction on blacks themselves. This included many Democratic politicians that saw old liberal rhetoric about uplifting the poor as political suicide. Most notably, the Democratic Leadership Council was formed, in part, to embody and articulate new values that emphasized responsibility and market-based solutions to complex social problems. Black politicians increasingly adopted this rhetoric in order to broaden their appeal to middle-class and white constituents. Nowhere in America's mainstream political discourse was there serious consideration—universities perhaps being the one exception—of the structural and institutional barriers to racial uplift. Despite the success of the black middle class since the end of the civil rights movement, they were seemingly always to blame for the problems of others. Moreover, rarely have Americans been responsible for the travails of their poor communities. The predictable result was twofold: on the one hand, increased pressure on poor blacks from the middle class and, on the other, the rising waves of discontent and anger among the black middle class, which had played by the rules, worked hard, and tried to advance their communities.[15]

Poor African Americans

By the beginning of the 1990s, the black poor found themselves more isolated and further behind not only whites, but also middle- and upper-class blacks. Out of thirty million people, 29.5 percent of all African Americans were living in poverty. This was less than half a percent better than the same statistics for the previous decade.[16] Moreover, black families earned 26 percent less than the federal poverty level.[17] Whites had a poverty rate of only 10 percent; thus, blacks were nearly three times as likely to be impoverished.[18] These disparities reflect the increasingly distant relationship between the middle class and the poor. Troubling economic data, in part, demonstrated why such a gap existed.

In order for one to understand these numbers, the numbers have to read in the context of the 1980s and early 1990s. Deindustrialization played a large role in decimating well-paying jobs in the private sectors in major urban areas, such as Chicago, Detroit, and New York. As those jobs moved to the suburbs or overseas, what were often left were hopelessness, despair, and severe need. The rise of the service industry, as a replacement for the closing factories, mills, and plants, created low-paying jobs—sometimes there were no jobs—that did not cover the monthly expenses of the worker. As William Julius Wilson famously noted, "The declining growth of the manufacturing, wholesale, and retail industries in the central city create[d] problems for many lower-income white and black middle class, whose members have access to the higher-paying white collar jobs in the expanding service-producing industries in the central city."[19] Along with the economic shift from manufacturing to service, economic downturns, and decreased federal money for municipalities, many cities across the nation reduced services, scaled back capital projects, eliminated "unnecessary" school programs, pumped money into law enforcement, and hired what were often the lowest-paid and least impressive teachers in kindergarten through twelfth-grade education. Thus, economics did for poor blacks what race did for many middle- and upper-class blacks: hold them to their position with, especially for the poor, little hope of escaping to better environs or enjoying upward mobility.

The 1990s served to only deepen the misery of the black poor. As the controversial and highly influential late legal scholar Derrick Bell noted:

> The race problem had worsened greatly in the 1990s. A relatively small number of blacks had survived the retrogression of civil rights protection, perhaps 20 percent having managed to make good in the increasingly technologically oriented society. But, without anyone acknowledging it and with hardly a peep from the press, more than half of the group had become outcasts. They were confined to former inner-city areas that had been divorced from their political boundaries. High walls surrounded these areas, and armed guards controlled entrance and exit around the clock. Still, despite all precautions, young blacks escaped from time to time to terrorize whites. Long dead was the dream that this black underclass would ever "overcome."[20]

Those people truly became the forgotten. Ignored, despised, and feared, poor urban blacks became the face of black America. No amount of elite blacks, ones like Colin Powell, Ron Brown, or Clarence Thomas, could dislodge the overwhelmingly popular image of the young brother on the street corner looking to commit a felony.

Conclusion: Political Impact of Division

The divisions between the various classes of African Americans presented major issues for their community. Integration and assimilation made it more difficult to cope with the conservative onslaught of the 1980s and 1990s. As middle-class African Americans moved to become a part of the mainstream, they often took positions that were at odds with the interests of the poor. Class became intertwined with race in ways that were new to the American experience. President Clinton's appeal to the black community was not so much directed at the poor as it was the middle and upper classes. Clinton's class-based politics fostered an environment in which market-based solutions, largely for the middle class, trumped older commitments to the poor and dispossessed. This was how Clinton was able to sell welfare reform, the crime bill of 1994, and regulatory reform to a community disproportionately impacted by such efforts. It is also fair to say that such concerns and political tendencies also reflected the growing dis-union, largely along class and cultural lines, which infected American society during the 1990s.

The new economy of the 1990s was a microcosm of the trans-formative changes of the decade. High technology and the Internet demonstrated clearly how much class had become a dividing line between the poor and everyone else. Computers, high finance, and service-related work effectively split the nation into the past and the future. This meant that half the nation was slowing dying as the other progressed. As the older, whiter America declined, the newer, younger, and more educated America quickly surpassed them, creating an untenable situation in which the politics of race and class influenced every political decision made by political elites, such as President Clinton. Moreover, as whites saw their fortunes decline, they vented their anger on society's most vulnerable: African Americans. Middle-class blacks, feeling the pressure to conform and wanting to protect their hard-gotten gains of the past thirty years, were complicit in the fleecing of the poor. Finally, moving forward, middle-class blacks were able, through their example, to set the stage for greater racial progress during the 2000s. Barack Obama's election to the US Senate in 2004 and the White House in 2008 would have been impossible without the class-based nature of American domestic policymaking and President Clinton's embracing of centrist values.

CHAPTER 3

The Politics of
Racial Appointments
The Nomination of Lani Guinier

AT THE WHITE HOUSE on June 4, 1993, after several weeks of controversy, President Clinton notified the leader of the Congressional Black Caucus, Kweisi Mfume, that he was withdrawing Lani Guinier's name from consideration for the post of assistant attorney general for the Civil Rights Division of the Department of Justice. The ham-handed way in which the president handled the nomination was evident in both its rollout and how it was terminated. As Steven F. Lawson explained, "Clinton tried to assuage the bitter disappointment of the Congressional Black Caucus, which steadfastly backed Guinier, by personally telephoning Representative Mfume with his decision even before he told the nominee."[1] Clinton had not bothered to tell Guinier at their Oval Office meeting that he had already decided to withdraw her name from Senate consideration, preferring instead to tell her on the phone less than an hour later. A brutal Senate confirmation was averted, preventing a vicious confirmation battle that would have imperiled Clinton's legislative agenda.

A little over a month later, at the eighty-fourth NAACP annual meeting in Indianapolis, those in attendance gathered to hear the typical speeches about the state of the race, progress made, achievements left to realize, and awards to be given. However, this conference was different. An air of excitement was present due to the changed political atmosphere in Washington. The most sought after speaker that day was not Ron Brown or Hazel O'Leary or Benjamin Hooks, but Lani Guinier. Guinier had been unceremoniously dismissed by a president that the NAACP had strongly supported in the 1992 presidential election. Guinier had become, as the NAACP magazine *Crisis* referred to her, a "Cause Celeb."[2] But questions concerning whether Guinier was a victim or another unfortunate dupe of Bill Clinton miss the meaning of the incident. Her outspokenness, passionate defense of the Voting Rights Act, and controversial legal theories presented a conundrum for Clinton. It conjured up images of radical black activists so despised and distrusted by mainstream white America and conservative activists. Despite her legal credentials, civil rights legal work, and elite education, Guinier simply did not conform to class-based expectations for acceptable political nominees and, in the process, played into the media narrative of a radical black female circa 1968.

A former attorney for the NAACP Legal Defense Fund, Guinier was a top-notch attorney and law professor who had served in the Carter administration, tried numerous cases involving civil rights and voting rights, and pursued equality in education, the workplace, and the political arena. The fervor started after her nomination in April 1993 to become the assistant attorney general for the Civil Rights Division of the Department of Justice. She was to become the nation's chief civil rights officer, charged with the responsibility of monitoring disability issues, criminal issues as they related to civil rights, housing and civil law enforcement, special litigation, voting rights, employment fairness, immigration issues related to unfair employment, and educational opportunities. The Civil Rights Division had been created as a part of the 1957 Civil Rights Act. This was the first time that a woman had been nominated to lead the division.[3] Yet that nomination resulted in a media firestorm. Due to her legal opinions, writings, and previous work as a civil rights attorney, Guinier was labeled a "quota queen," a quota queen allegedly determined to take from white Americans for the benefit of black Americans.

A Brief History of Racial Nominations

Prior to President Clinton's first inauguration in January 1993, appointments and nominations of African Americans had become routine. Racial appointments had become events in which the incumbent could gain kudos from supporters for their appearance of inclusion. In addition, it presented the opposition party with a golden opportunity to score political points with its own supporters by attacking the legitimacy and credibility of the men and women selected for various positions. Appointing members of the various factions of his party enabled the president to broaden his influence, keep a lid on criticism, reward loyal supporters, and score political points with the American people. This is especially true as it relates to the selection of minorities, such as Jews, blacks, Catholics, Hispanics, and women. These appointments, as Clinton entered office, took on added meaning because Clinton had campaigned, in part, on creating a government that resembled America. The new president and his spokesmen noted to news outlets that the Clinton cabinet and White House "'will look like America'" in terms of race and gender.[4] The appointments were widely watched since it was the first time in twelve years that a Democratic president had been in office, thus creating excitement for many African Americans that had been shut out of government service during the Reagan years. There was hope that the new administration would bring in new people who not only represented the various factions and wings of the Democratic Party but also represented the United States' diverse population.

Dating back to the administration of Abraham Lincoln, presidents had used elite blacks to, as historian John Hope Franklin noted, "gauge the pulse of the African American population through one or more community leaders."[5] This pattern continued unabated through the Hoover administration. By 1933, this pattern was dramatically expanded as President Franklin D. Roosevelt brought in his so-called black cabinet. While FDR's black advisers were numerous in comparison to previous administrations, he, as Harvard Sitkoff noted, often ignored their advice.[6] Their presence was, nonetheless, a watershed moment for African Americans in politics. By the time John F. Kennedy was elected president in 1960, African Americans were pushing harder than ever, not only for civil rights, but for representation at the federal level. President Kennedy and his brother, US attorney general Robert F. Kennedy, brought numerous blacks into both the administration and the federal judiciary. Kennedy's promises and agenda, as well as that of his successor, Lyndon B. Johnson, demanded greater outreach to African Americans. This pattern of appointing African Americans often served raw political purposes. It also, however, gave a select few an entrance into the heady world of presidential power and politics. It usually meant that African Americans in those privileged positions could advocate for the race. As the Carter years came to a close with the election of Ronald Reagan in 1980, racial appointments would be subject to broader political concerns, such as ideology, philosophy, and greater policy aims. The incoming administration would have limited diversity and that diversity would usher in new policies.

The change began in the 1970s, influenced by the politics of backlash and rage in the wake of the urban rioting, Black Power, forced busing, and a fight over precious resources. The modern Right profited off of the resentments boiling within white America. Furthermore, conservatives used the ethnic, working-class, and suburban anger to fuel contempt and even hatred toward the state. As scholar Eric Porter has noted, "The Nixon, Ford, and Carter administrations were unable to solve these problems, which helped fuel attacks on the liberal state in ways that were explicitly or implicitly racially coded."[7] The growing polarization between the two major political parties, and much of the electorate, meant that race remained a battlefield in the 1980s. President Carter's support for African Americans, combined with the hostage and energy crises, stagflation, and disillusionment after years of war and scandal, helped propel Ronald Reagan to the presidency in 1980. Reagan immediately moved to scale back the liberal state, but he needed able hands to help him do it. John Ehrman wrote, "Socially conservative and working-class voters disturbed by urban unrest and unhappy with liberal support for affirmative action, abortion rights, and other cultural shifts, began to move away from the Democrats."[8] As a result, a new schism developed. The old pattern of racial appointments evolved to accommodate new political concerns such as race and class.

Most African American politicos held the Reagan administration in contempt. To them it was clear that Reagan was trying to roll back the gains of the previous two decades. In a July 1981 article in *Black Enterprise* magazine, the venerable black news source noted, "The 'substantive roles' blacks have been given in the Administration have not been in sufficient quantity to satisfy even black Republican supporters of the President."[9] In addition, the Reagan administration had difficulties trying to find blacks who would carry out the administration's agenda. *Black Enterprise* also noted, "Another problem is the Administration's controversial approach to issues affecting blacks. Blacks have turned down jobs for fear that they will be asked to carry out policies that are not in the best interest of the black community."[10] The blacks that did join the administration often brought with them a commitment to the new conservatism of the Reagan revolution.

Several dozen African Americans served in the Reagan administration, including Clarence Thomas, Colin Powell, Anita Hill, Samuel Pierce, Arthur Teele, Melvin Bradley, and Alan Keyes. These figures, with some exceptions, held several views in common: lower taxes, opposition to affirmative action, desire for limited government, criticism of the welfare state, and distrust of liberal, big government solutions to complex and vexing social problems. Further, they were clean cut, deeply patriotic, devout, and closely aligned with the unthreatening "Huxtable" image promoted by the famous 1980s situational comedy, *The Cosby Show*. In an era of increasing distrust of liberal solutions to societal problems, black conservatives promoted the socially and fiscally conservative brand of Reaganism.

The African American community was becoming more diverse politically. As Joseph Lowndes argued in *From the New Deal to the New Right: Race and the Southern Origins of Modern Conservatism*, the new white conservative movement began before the ink dried on the New Deal.[11] The Great Society was, in certain respects, as controversial within the black community as it was in the white community. Traditionally conservative in their personal affairs, many African Americans resented the increased presence of the government in their lives. By Reagan's election in 1980, many African Americans were emerging from colleges and universities and moving into professional positions and higher tax brackets. Some middle- and upper-class blacks were attracted by Reagan's condemnation of taxes, federal intrusion, and regulation. These blacks disagreed with liberals who believed that government had to play a role in society. In addition, conservative blacks felt that economic conditions had to be improved in order to uplift the black community. *Black Enterprise* reporter Isaiah J. Poole noted in February 1981, "These blacks do not disagree with their liberal counterparts on the severity of problems in the black community. . . . Low-skilled black youth, for example, are not held down so much by racism as by a minimum wage law which makes it unprofitable for companies to hire them."[12] Some, such as Clarence Thomas, were appalled by such well-intentioned programs as affirmative action. The nascent black conservative movement emerged at a time when the country had realigned with a new center-right political prospective. The Republican Party embraced these black conservatives, in part, because they provided crucial political cover. It was hard to label mainstream conservatives as racist when they often deployed black conservatives to carry the message.

The new divisions within the black political community also portended contentious confirmation battles. For instance, Reagan's nomination of Robert Bork and Bush's appointment of Clarence Thomas for the Supreme Court in 1987 and 1991, respectively, meant the nomination of Lani Guinier in 1993 would face stringent scrutiny from both the media and senators on Capitol Hill. In the so-called colorblind era, with its emphasis on coded language, nonracial rhetoric, and individual rights, conservatives, both black and white, appeared to favor a more classically liberal form of government. Someone, such as Guinier, proposing greater enforcement of civil rights law challenged desires for more limited government.

Past Associations between Clinton and Guinier

In the immediate aftermath of the civil rights victories of the early 1960s, universities began making concerted efforts to integrate not only their student bodies, but also their faculties, graduate schools, and professional schools. For the first time America's most prestigious schools sought African American students with demonstrated potential. Lani Guinier, a 1971 graduate of Radcliffe College, was granted admittance to Yale Law School. Yale during the 1970s was very liberal, both in grading and temperament. Bill Clinton would later note, "At Yale, the only grades were Honors, Pass, or Fail."[13] Guinier found herself in classes with several figures who would later play a prominent role in American life. Clarence Thomas, the future US Supreme Court justice, was a member of her class. Robert Reich, Samuel Alito, Sonia Sotomayor, John Bolton, and Stephen Carter all graduated during the 1970s. Bill Clinton and Hillary Rodham were students there, albeit a year and two years ahead of Guinier, respectively. When the couple headed the Yale Barristers' Union, they agreed, at the insistence of a mutual friend, to give Guinier assistance with a school problem. Guinier reflected, "They were admired. We looked up to them, respected them because they were known to be fair. They were among the half dozen or so friends from law school who had attended my wedding."[14] For Guinier and others, Clinton represented a new generation of southern white males opposed to the racial animus of the past.

After the Clintons departed New Haven in 1973 following graduation, they began their respective careers. Rodham took a position as a lawyer of the Watergate committee investigating President Nixon. Clinton became a law professor at the University of Arkansas and began planning his entrance into electoral politics. Guinier graduated in 1974, and after some early work as a law clerk and juvenile court referee, she took a position as special assistant to the assistant attorney general for the Civil Rights Division, Drew Days, in the late 1970s.[15] Before the age of thirty, Guinier had become a known figure inside civil rights circles, in the fight to preserve hard-won civil rights advancements, and in the Carter administration.

A Cabinet That Looks like America

As the newly elected president, Clinton had hoped that he could put together a government more representative of the American people than his predecessors had done. Presidents Reagan and Bush, while they did appoint minorities, tended to reflect an America more representative of the 1950s than America near the end of the twentieth century. This process was ongoing throughout the Clinton presidency.

First, Clinton nominated Zoe Baird, then Kimba Wood, both white women, to the position of attorney general. Both were unsuccessful, as tax issues and the revelations that undocumented workers were in their employ surfaced. Clinton was finally able to get Janet Reno confirmed to the position.

Clinton appointed a record number of African Americans to other positions in his cabinet. In fact, Clinton's pronouncements about the need for diversity within the cabinet and subcabinet and White House actually served as an albatross around his political neck. Liberals, eager at the thought of greater inclusion, wanted new faces that represented their particular race, gender, or ethnicity. Conservatives were watchful for any sign of quota hiring. In addition, the media closely followed the announcements coming from the administration about Clinton's selections. *Washington Post* political journalist David S. Broder remarked in a Christmas 1992 article, "The scramble to meet that goal produced a remarkable last-minute shuffle of people and jobs, demonstrating that for the first Democrat to win the White House in 12 years, the need to showcase the ethnic, racial, and gender variety of his party overrode any ideological litmus tests, any concerns about internal policy cohesion and, with few exceptions, any claims based on political loyalty, interest group or geographical representation."[16] The very issue that New Democrats abhorred—quotas—seemed to be a priority within the Clinton administration.

The media coverage highlighted the concerns of diversity. One article, by M. Rucci of the *Courier Mail* (Brisbane), explained, "By opening Cabinet posts to more women and minorities such as blacks and Hispanics, Mr. Clinton has now answered calls from special interest groups who demanded his government be more representative."[17] This "call" for greater representation was intense. Joel Kotkin reported in a *Washington Post* article, "After a dozen years of smug middle-American cultural domination, the White House is now besieged by representatives of groups that felt cheated during the Reagan-Bush years. For some prominent advocates, the issue is no longer simply access but the 'political correctness' of those appointed to office."[18] Kotkin was arguing against the very multiculturalism that many in liberal politics were pushing. Some media commentary even went so far as to enumerate the alleged failings of white men and their decline in status in recent years, generally, and during the early months of the Clinton era, specifically. David Gates of *Newsweek* revealed, exactly a month before the Guinier nomination, "Suddenly white American males are surrounded by feminists, multiculturalists, P.C. policepersons, affirmative-action employers, rap artists, Native Americans, Japanese tycoons, Islamic fundamentalists and Third World dictators, all of them saying the same thing: You've been a bad boy."[19] In this climate of majority (white) and minority (black, Jew, female, Hispanic) hypersensitivity, Clinton's rhetoric and actions to bring previously ignored groups into high-level government positions served to heighten the collective sensitivities of the American populace. Further, it meant that Clinton had to pay close attention to the records and reputations of the men and women he was nominating and appointing to office, lest he find himself trapped in the identity politics of the early 1990s.

As the list of nominations and appointments was rolled out in the weeks before and after the inauguration, each one was given extra scrutiny to determine both Clinton's governing philosophy and his commitment to centrist politics. These nominations and appointments included three African American members: Ron Brown as secretary of commerce, Mike Espy as secretary of agriculture, and Hazel O'Leary as energy secretary. All of these people were close friends and political allies of the president and had supported his campaign in 1992. They were also supportive of and a part of the Democratic Leadership Council. Clinton would also appoint other minorities to important cabinet and subcabinet posts, such as Joycelyn Elders (surgeon general), Jesse Brown (Department of Veterans Affairs), Alexis Herman (Labor), Norman Mineta (Commerce), Henry Cisneros (Housing and Urban Development), Federico Pena and Rodney Slater (Transportation), Bill Richardson (Energy), Togo West (Veteran Affairs), and David Satcher (surgeon general). So in these early months of the Clinton administration, there was an emphasis on securing minority candidates and fulfilling the campaign pledge regarding diversity. Unfortunately, that played into the hands of Clinton's political enemies.[20] Above all others, Lani Guinier exhibited the very personal and ideological traits that so infuriated conservatives.

The Nomination of Guinier

One of the great questions surrounding the nomination of Lani Guinier is, Why? Why did Clinton nominate her in the first place if she and her writings were so troublesome? The answers are complex. First, the president desired to put people in office that, generally, shared his center-left positions. Second, Clinton honestly believed that she was suited to fill the post. Third, the president was convinced by First Lady Hillary Rodham Clinton to place her in the Justice Department. It was widely assumed at the time and confirmed by eyewitness accounts of the early Clinton years that the president and the first lady tried, in some respects, to have a co-presidency. Hillary Clinton took an office in the West Wing, a first for a presidential spouse. Furthermore, as Nigel Hamilton has noted, "Hillary and her cabal of female staffers and associates—Patsy Thomasson, Susan Thomases, Melanne Verveer, Eleanor Dean Acheson—added yet another obstacle . . . [by] proudly picking Lani Guinier."[21]

According to Taylor Branch, Clinton never read her writings or personally vetted her for the post.[22] On one hand, Clinton was nominating a "friend," somebody whom he respected. On the other hand, her educational credentials and middle-class orientation might have relaxed any suspicions that would have normally accompanied a high-level nomination. In addition, while assistant attorney general is a high-level post, Guinier was nominated to the subcabinet, not a cabinet post. The failed nominations of Zoe Baird and Kimba Wood for attorney general and the near failure of Webster Hubbell for associate attorney general consumed tremendous political energy and time. Finally, the president had promised a "cabinet that looks like America," and Guinier fit the bill as an African American woman.

The Furor Ensues

The morning after the announcement, April 30, storm clouds appeared over the nomination of Lani Guinier. The *Wall Street Journal* published an op-ed by former Reagan administration official Clint Bolick entitled "Clinton's Quota Queen."[23] Immediately questioning

Clinton's judgment, Bolick noted, "'New Democrat' Bill Clinton has taken a sharp left turn by appointing two civil rights ideologues to major posts."[24] Lani Guinier was appointed to head the Civil Rights Division of the Justice Department, and Norma Cantu, counsel for the Mexican American Legal Defense and Educational Fund (MALDEF), had been nominated for assistant secretary for civil rights in the Department of Education. Bolick acknowledged the intellectual "firepower" of Guinier and Cantu as well as the depth of their experiences in law and advocacy. However, Bolick attacked numerous academic articles that Guinier had written as a law professor at the University of Pennsylvania.

Bolick argued that Guinier's writings called for "racial quotas in judicial appointments." Further, Bolick argued that Guinier wanted to make health care, employment, job training, and other social needs as permanent entitlements for all Americans. If Guinier was confirmed, she would "graft onto the existing system a complex racial spoils system that would further polarize an already divided nation."[25] Bolick also claimed that Guinier wanted to expand, revise, and augment the Voting Rights Act of 1965. Using her own words against her, he suggested that if confirmed, she would eliminate the principle of one-man, one vote. "Whether or not these proposals have merit as public policy, Ms. Guinier clearly believes they are compelled by the Voting Rights Act, which she would be charged with enforcing as assistant attorney general." Finally, Bolick closed the piece by not so subtly saying that Clinton's appointment of Guinier and Cantu would "blur the lines between advocacy groups and government agencies, as they were in the pre-Reagan years." They would bring back the "in your face civil rights agenda" of the 1960s.[26]

Rarely does one media piece, in the nation's premier economic daily no less, attract as much attention or have as much impact as did Clint Bolick's op-ed piece in the *Wall Street Journal*. Within hours the media in Washington and New York had picked up the piece and began reporting on it. An obscure, former bureaucrat and current think tank fellow was driving the media cycle. Other conservatives sensed an opportunity to shake the new president on the third rail of American politics: race. A fusillade of media coverage and written pieces followed about the president, Guinier, and quotas that completely caught the Clinton White House by surprise. The *New York Times* reported that groups such as the Judicial Selection Monitoring Project saw Guinier as a "radical whose impatience with 'one-person, one-vote' can be used to make her unacceptable to most Americans."[27] The *Washington Times* pointed out, "She called for racial quotas, and committee sources said the White House is concerned over challenges to the Guinier nomination."[28] *USA Today* said, "She says the system thwarts the goal of the Voting Rights Act to deliver more political power to minorities. The 1965 federal law was meant to guarantee legislative success for minority interests, she says, not just the election of more minority candidates."[29] Now the nomination was in peril and the media was complicit in driving the story.

The story sparked old debates about affirmative action and important questions about the role of government and the law in extending equal opportunity and full citizenship rights. The use of the term "quota queen" took off on Ronald Reagan's rhetoric of "welfare queens," lighting a fuse of racial resentment and anger. The *New York Times* published an article with the title "Lani Guinier's Agenda Provokes Old Enemies." Guinier did not help her cause when she responded to a question about who was responsible for the lack of activism during the Reagan/Bush years by saying "William Bradford Reynolds."[30] Reynolds had been the assistant attorney general during the Reagan years. He was also the mentor of Clint Bolick, the author of the op-ed that ignited this great brouhaha. The *Times* article conveyed the sense that the "counter-counter-revolution'" that Guinier was allegedly planning would somehow wreck the country and exacerbate the deep fault-line of race in America. It helped to implant the notion that there was something untoward about Guinier's views. Further, the *Times* article revealed that there was more to the story than simply a controversial nomination. There were harsh feelings between Guinier and her conservative tormentors. Her fierce criticism of the Reagan and his civil rights legacy reflected the personal animus between the two camps. In addition, Guinier represented the liberal-leaning circle of civil rights activists that conservatives blamed, in part, for the growth of the federal government and, in part, for the redistribution of resources by the federal government that discriminated against white Americans. It is noteworthy that most of the news stories did little to explore the tangled relationships between Clinton's nominee and the conservative activists until after the nomination was over. In fact, the confrontation was more interesting than focusing on the back story that clearly showed more personal and philosophical differences between the two camps.

Michael Isikoff of the *Washington Post* became a prominent reporter on the nomination. On May 21, 1993, Isikoff published an article entitled "Confirmation Battle Looms over Guinier; Critics Target 'Extreme' Views in Law Review Articles by Justice Dept. Civil Rights Nominee."[31] This article, among others, helped to plant seeds of doubt in the minds of members of the Senate. As Isikoff wrote, "in recent weeks, conservative activists, mirroring the tactics of liberal groups during confirmation fights over Supreme Court nominees Robert H. Bork and Clarence Thomas, have combed Guinier's writings, extracting passages they say reveal her as an 'extreme' left-wing activist with a far-reaching social agenda."[32] Isikoff hit on an important point—the desire to seek revenge after the defeat of Bork and near-defeat of Thomas, all within the previous six years. Isikoff then left his perch as journalist and attempted to become a constitutional and legal scholar. He wrote:

> In one controversial 1992 *Virginia Law Review* article, Guinier argued that the mere election of more black lawmakers is an insufficient measure of voting rights success if those lawmakers have little influence in the state legislatures.[33]

This analysis resulted from Isikoff's scant review of Guinier's writings. As Laurel Leff noted, "[Isikoff] defended his use of the quotations, saying he spent 'about an hour' with the two law review articles, totaling 119 pages, to get 'enough of a flavor' to make sure the 'quotes in there were not twisted out of context.'"[34] Isikoff's reporting lent credence to the political attacks coming from Clint Bolick and the *Wall Street Journal*. *Los Angeles Times* reporter David Savage, quoted in the *Columbia Journalism Review*, remarked, "The Wall Street Journal and Clint Bolick really went after her and managed to kill off this nomination."[35] If it was only Bolick, then this argument would have fallen apart, but others piled on. In an op-ed on May 7, 1993, Paul Gigot of the *Wall Street Journal* quoted, often out of context, Guinier's writings in ways that made her appear extreme.[36]

All of the news networks—ABC, CBS, NBC, and CNN—picked up the story, adding to a media circus that put the nomination in jeopardy before confirmation hearings could even be scheduled. Journalists fed off the two-dimensional battles between the president and his political opponents. It made for great copy. As Leff notes:

> Too many reporters uncritically accepted Bolick's and other con-
> servatives' depictions of her views, the same quotes appearing
> over and over again in such publications as *Newsweek*, the *Los
> Angeles Times*, and *U.S. News & World Report*. . . . And too many
> reporters substituted code words, such as "quotas," "affirmative
> action," and "reverse discrimination," for a genuine dialogue on
> the sensitive subject upon which her writings focus—the con-
> tinuing effort to thwart blacks' effective participation in the polit-
> ical process.[37]

Numerous stories about the controversial nomination focused mainly on her alleged radicalism. Only afterward did the media focus any attention on the organized opposition to the nomination. For example, while Isikoff had been part of what Leff called "that drum-beat" of opposition, he subsequently revealed, after the fact, that there were powerful enemies behind the campaign against her.[38] On June 6, 1993, in a *Washington Post* article entitled "Power behind the Thrown Nominee: Activist with Score to Settle," Isikoff wrote, "They produced a drumbeat of press releases, reports, and op-ed articles that portrayed the University of Pennsylvania law professor as a pro-quota, left-wing 'extremist' bent on undermining democratic principles—labels that stuck and helped frame the debate over the Guinier nomination in terms that made it difficult for her allies."[39] In addition, Isikoff revealed that Abigail Thernstrom, a conservative activist, had tipped Bolick off to the nomination two months before it was announced, thereby giving Bolick and his conservative allies ample time to prepare the campaign against Guinier. (Speculation swirled since the election about who would be nominated for important posts in the new adminis-tration.) Thernstrom was quoted by Isikoff as telling Bolick at a D.C.

hotel near the White House, "Clint, you're going to love her."[40] The opponents of the president certainly were pleased. With the cooperation of the press, unexpected assistance from the president, and little time to sort the issue out, opponents had accomplished in fewer than thirty-five days what it took other opponents of other nominations months to accomplish.

As the media drove the story, President Clinton felt increasing pressure from both liberals and centrists to make a decision. Consequently, some of the most influential people within the Democratic caucus, also spooked by the media coverage and more concerned with the economy and pressing international events, encouraged the president to drop the nominee.

The Actual Writings and Ideas

Lani Guinier's work under US assistant attorney general Drew Days III in the Carter administration and her sterling reputation as an attorney for the NAACP's Legal Defense Fund made her a target for conservatives. Her vociferous attacks on President Reagan's civil rights record as well as on his chief civil rights officer, William Bradford Reynolds, quickly drew the attention of conservatives once she was nominated. Her academic musings, combined with her strong advocacy for the Voting Rights Act of 1965 and fierce challenges through legal advocacy, provided opponents of her nomination with ammunition to exploit fears of racial radicalism.

As an untenured law professor at the University of Pennsylvania, Guinier had engaged in extensive research and writing. This was not the first time that nominees' intellectual opinions had gotten them in trouble. In 1987, Judge Robert H. Bork, a former Nixon solicitor general and acting attorney general, had carried out Nixon's orders to fire Archibald Cox during the "Saturday Night Massacre." It was his legal opinions and writings that provided liberals with the ammunition to defeat his nomination to the Supreme Court. Led by Senator Edward M. Kennedy, liberals tore the nominee apart by arguing that Bork opposed the rights of women and minorities. Further, Bork's ideas about original intent and privacy rights, once disseminated to the nation, destroyed any chance Bork had of being seated on the Supreme Court. After the Bork hearings, "Borking," as it came to be known, became an expected part of the confirmation process. Clarence Thomas upon his nomination in 1991 for the Supreme Court, found himself and some of his ideas subject to "Borking" by liberals in the Senate and women's groups outside of Congress. The Guinier nomination followed the model created by the Bork hearings in 1987. Abigail Thernstrom, the *Wall Street Journal* editorial board, and congressional Republicans picked out the most easily manipulated passages from her writings to warn the American public that Guinier was a dangerous radical who would subvert American democracy and the principle of "one man, one vote."

Central to conservatives' opposition to Guinier was her fervent support for the Voting Rights Act of 1965.[41] The landmark civil rights law provided protections and mechanisms that ensured African Americans would have the right to vote. The law provided federal supervision of elections in the South and targeted especially notorious places in the South that historically denied African Americans the right to vote. With the passage of this act, combined with passage of the Twenty-Fourth Amendment, which prohibited the use of poll taxes, conservatives and southerners felt that the federal government had overstepped its proper boundaries, thus fueling the anti-statist fervor percolating throughout conservative intellectual circles. By the 1990s, however, the Voting Rights Act was settled law. Conservatives were no longer challenging the legitimacy of the landmark law. They were challenging new interpretations that would extend the reach of the law. When Reagan was running for president, the heart of the arguments was that the Voting Rights Act was an extralegal step. As Earl Ofari Hutchinson noted, "[In] 1980 Ronald Reagan told biography Laurence Barrett that the 1965 Voting Rights Act was 'humiliating to the South.'"[42] This humiliation resulted from the supervision of the federal government over the electoral process that was traditionally that domain of the states. In 1993, the argument against Guinier was that she would dramatically expand the power of the Voting Rights Act, thus extending its enforcement power. For conservatives, traditionally, the Voting Rights Act was both an affront and an unnecessary intrusion of the federal government into the internal workings of southern states. However, by the 1990s, the fight was no longer about the legitimacy of the law, but the use of the law. Guinier's support for the measure and her fight in 1982, along with many others in the civil rights community, to preserve its most important provisions and possibly re-conceptualize how to fulfill its intent had contributed to some of the harshest criticism of her.

On August 6, 1965, President Lyndon B. Johnson signed the Voting Rights Act of 1965 into law. The VRA finally addressed the shortcomings of the Fifteenth Amendment by enforcing its provisions with the assistance of the Justice Department and his Civil Rights Division. Federal examiners were authorized to oversee elections in the South, especially in areas that had a history of intimidating voters, denying citizens the right to vote, and using mechanisms such as poll taxes, literacy exams, property-holding rules, or other forms of obstruction. Moreover, penalties, such as fines of up five thousand dollars and five years in prison, were all authorized by the act. In the eyes of white southerners opposed to equal rights, US district courts were given jurisdiction to enforce both the act, generally, and key provisions such as section five, prohibition on voting qualifications, and twelve, financial penalties for denial of voting rights, specifically. The centrality of voting rights to effective and meaningful citizenship was enshrined in the Voting Rights Act of 1965 and informed the work of activists such as Guinier. Political and legislative schemes created by white lawmakers to dilute minority voting strength signaled, for Guinier, the need to re-conceptualize voting rights, legislative effectiveness, and equal political representation. Her writings as a University of Pennsylvania professor of law tried to tackle these continued political inequalities.

Guinier outlined three distinct generations of political and legal activism. The first generation agitated and bled for the passage of the Voting Rights Act of 1965 in places such as Selma. The second generation fought against what Guinier called "qualitative vote dilution." This meant that white officials shifted political power from district or precincts to at-large districts, thus accepting the presence of black politicians and groups yet denying them any influence over the political and legislative process. In essence, black votes were diluted by a process that prevented minorities from receiving effective political representation. The third generation fought against the logical next step in stifling the legislative interests of African Americans. As African Americans gained more seats in representative bodies, white incumbents shifted and changed the legislative rules by which legislators could be effective. By changing legislative rules, the majority, which tended to be white, could prevent minority legislators from effectively representing their constituents by preventing votes and legislation, denying chairmanships, and carrying out a variety of other things. Guinier noted that the effects of these subtle actions taken by the majority undermined the intentions and spirit of the Voting Rights Act of 1965. Krista Helfferich remarked that Guinier's work and proposals to correct these problems resulted from her belief in the "Madisonian Majority," a reference to James Madison's belief that when the majority is constant and unmovable, it will crush the interests of the minority. Therefore, the majority should be continuously shifting, based on the issue at hand. Helfferich continues, "This 'rule of shifting majorities' means that sometimes individuals will win and sometimes they will lose. But the participants' ability to take turns deepens faith in the fairness of the system."[43] As Guinier herself explained in a 1991 article in the *Michigan Law Review*, "My purpose has been to attempt to conceive of a deliberative process in which racism does not control all outcomes."[44]

Guinier promoted the idea of cumulative voting. Cumulative voting strengthens the political position of the minority by helping them to elect representatives. Voters would be allowed to cast several votes, depending on the size of the district, in order to demonstrate their respective preferences. For instance, if a district has ten seats, then each voter would be given ten votes. With ten votes to cast the voter could concentrate all his or her votes on one candidate or divide them between several candidates, thereby intensifying and empowering the voter who otherwise would be at a disadvantage in seeking effective representation. This would empower the minority voters in any district regardless of their race. Further, the process would require candidates for public office to pay close attention to the needs and political desires of the constituents they seek to represent. Doing away with specific districts or precincts, at-large seats would become the norm, thereby creating more realistic political communities instead of heavily weighted conservative or liberal communities wherein the representative has little to no need to concern himself with the needs and interests of the other part of the district. Guinier wrote, "It is even more consistent with some notions of one person/one vote than geographically based districting because it equalizes the number of votes each representative represents without gerrymandering or artificially creating communities of interest."[45] Moreover, Guinier noted that this strategy "fulfills the dual vision of the Voting Rights Act that minority groups should enjoy equal voting weight and equal voting power."[46] If implemented, such a strategy would displace serious, vested interests not only by allowing voters to register the intensity of the political preferences, but also by allowing the minority community to have some meaningful influence in the electoral and legislative process. She also argued that "the remedy at the electoral stage would be a modified at-large voting scheme, and its counterpart at the legislative phase would be rules that allow cumulative voting and encourage consensus decisions."[47] To change the procedures and mechanisms of American political behavior, Guinier argued for a more utopian, fairer system in which communities—African American, Jewish, Hispanic, white, or other—would have an equal opportunity to not only participate but effect change in the manner in which a governing body at the local, state, or federal level represents its constituents.

A central tenet of the US political system is the concept of "one man, one vote." Another central element is the concept of winner take all. In a winner-take-all system, the winner of the election need not represent all 100 percent of the electorate; he or she only needs to represent a plurality or 50.1 percent. Under this system, a minimum of 49.9 percent of the electorate could be ignored and their political and legislative interests submerged. Since upwards of half the electorate at any given time has no meaningful political and legislative representation, democracy itself is negated, as well as the promise of equal protection stated in the Fourteenth Amendment to the Constitution. While many disagreed with this interpretation, Guinier argued that was precisely what occurred when almost half the population, or various racial and ethnic groups, had no effective political voice. In fact, this tension between the majority and the minority dates back at least to Alexis de Tocqueville.[48] African Americans and other minorities are the most vulnerable to this type of voting system. As African Americans represent less than 15 percent of the population, they are far less likely to receive adequate and equal representation and influence in the decision-making process. This is the principal concern of Guinier and the target of her written ideas.

In order to address these concerns Guinier proposed "proportionate interest representation." For instance, if a state has ten congressional districts and African Americans constitute 10 percent of the state, then African Americans would get one seat, which would be equal to 10 percent. Moreover, this translates into proportional power within the legislative branch of the federal and state governments. As Guinier noted, "Proportional interest representation contains strategies for reform at both the electoral and legislative level to address some of the process defects in black electoral success theory that have failed to yield substantive justice."[49] Proportional interest representation, if implemented, would threaten vested interests in political power.

These ideas of cumulative voting and proportional interest representation were not new ideas. They were used, Guinier noted, in both foreign countries and Wall Street.[50] However, to use these strategies in politics and voting would not only upset traditional norms, but play into the arguments of conservatives that Guinier represented black radicalism. The esoteric and dense nature of her writings did not lend itself to simple interpretations. In fact, the writings seemed only to confirm what her opponents had already said about her: she was a radical who would use the power of her office to eliminate one-man, one-vote and institute a system in which equal outcomes would be the goal.

Guinier believed that her ideas followed the democratic tradition of the Voting Rights Act. She believed that the Voting Rights Act's purpose was to extend and protect representative democracy for America's most vulnerable communities. Using new methods to ensure access to power and a voice in American politics were justified by the enforcement provisions of the Voting Right Act, according to Guinier. However, the complex nature of her proposals, along with the concept of each voter holding multiple votes, disturbed many Americans. The concepts of one-man, one-vote and winner take all were hallmarks of American democracy. To change that seemed un-American to most people. But the controversy placed the articles in another, more negative light. Georgetown law professor Mari Matsuda reflected that "the deeply racist and misogynist underpinnings of the pejorative label 'quota queen' with its linguistic predecessor, 'welfare queen,'" was a major component of the conservative attack on her nomination.[51] Regardless of whether Guinier's ideas had merit, they provided ammunition for Clinton's political enemies. She had become the Sister Souljah of the early Clinton administration.

The Nervous New Democrats

Republicans lined up to oppose Guinier's nomination. Senate minority leader Robert Dole had warned that Guinier was "hostile to the principle of one person-one vote, consistently hostile to majority rule and a consistent supporter not only of quotas but vote-rigging schemes that make quotas look mild."[52] Democrats were also nervous about the nomination. The media version of her writings made Guinier appear to be a dangerous legal scholar intent on radically changing America's political institutions and systems. After months of contentious confirmation battles over Janet Reno, Zoe Baird, and Webster Hubbell, Democrats had little appetite for another long, damaging confirmation over a woman who appeared to be so outside the mainstream.

Guinier also seemed to conflict with New Democratic attempts to downplay the importance of race in American life. Placing conciliatory approaches above confrontational ones, New Democrats saw Guinier's full-throated support for innovative approaches to problems of racial equality at the end of the twentieth century as destructive to the policy and electoral interests of the Democratic Party. Strongly supportive of equality rights, New Democrats saw her overt, controversial approaches as not only problematic, but representative of the old racial politics that preferred confrontation rather than cooperative approaches to equality. Like conservatives, New Democrats were not disturbed by the Voting Rights Act; however, they were concerned about an enforcement of the Voting Rights Act that challenged mainstream views of American democracy. The Delaware senator and chairman of the Judiciary Committee, Joe Biden, remarked to reporters that she had "to come prepared to defend her writings" and that those writings gave him "great concern."[53] In a *U.S. News & World Report* article published just after the nomination was withdrawn, Donald Baer noted, "The White House had no reason to be caught off guard. . . . Senate Democrats warned Clinton aides before the nomination about Guinier's articles. Aware that she was a friend of both the president and Hillary Rodham Clinton, the White House counsel's office cautioned them about the articles. The Clintons insisted on the nomination anyway."[54] These Senate Democrats included moderates such as Dennis DeConcini, Howell Heflin, and Herb Kohl, liberals such as Carol Moseley-Braun, and strong conservative Republicans such as Strom Thurmond, Orrin Hatch, Alan Simpson, and Chuck Grassley. All expressed serious doubts about the nomination. Even liberal titans such as Edward M. Kennedy, Paul Simon, and Howard M. Metzenbaum were skeptical of Guinier and her writings. Clinton himself reported to Taylor Branch that Kennedy, Biden, and others in the Senate were advising him that the nomination could not survive.[55]

The leaders of the New Democrats, such as Al From and Will Marshall, advocated replacing Guinier with a more moderate and acceptable nominee. The politics of race and class—enveloped as it was in the colorblind rhetoric of the last two decades of the twentieth century—suggested that open displays of racial recognition were out of step with both cultural and political realities. From acknowledged such realities in an op-ed in the *New York Times*, saying that the civil rights groups had "rightly pressed their interest in her nomination. But the president has a different and greater responsibility—to represent the interests of not just the civil rights community but everyone in the American community."[56] Five years later From summarized the views of New Democrats by writing, "The tension created by the nomination reflects a fundamental difference between new and old Democrats on the issue of equality. Whether the issue is education or employment, New Democrats believe equality should be defined in terms of opportunity, not outcomes."[57] Will Marshall told the *New York Times* that if Guinier had succeeded in her quest to become assistant attorney general for civil rights, it "would have had a devastating effect on race relations."[58] Vermont senator Patrick J. Leahy said, "If the writings I've seen so far reflect the way she feels about how the Civil Rights Division should be run, then it would be a complete aberration and in no way would be acceptable to me."[59] Oklahoma representative Dave McCurdy, a prominent member of the DLC, told the *Washington Post,* "I don't think she'll get through. She'll become such an incredible lightning rod that either she or the administration will be discredited. Majority rule is what this country was built on. This is not South Africa."[60]

Views as strong as these, from the president's friends no less, could not and would not lend themselves to compromise. In a rare display of bipartisan unity, Republicans and Democrats alike lined up to oppose this nomination, leaving the president with little room to maneuver if he wanted central aspects of his agenda to pass.

Death by a Thousand Cuts: The Withdrawal

By the end of May, the unraveling nomination had become a serious embarrassment and distraction to the Clinton White House. President Clinton's few attempts to save his own nominee did little to change the perceptions implanted in the public's mind. Guinier herself did not do herself any favors once she was finally given the opportunity to express and defend her positions in the media. Previously denied the opportunity to speak directly to reporters, she went on Ted Koppel's *Nightline.* The venerable newsman peppered her with questions about the meanings of her numerous writings. Guinier believed that the White House staff "felt that I should have used the *Nightline* forum to talk about my views in instead of my feelings, but that I shouldn't have asked for a hearing. I kept talking about the need for a hearing in order to express my views fully and that was inappropriate. That made them angry. They had concluded that I was not a team player. As a result, the next morning, I was forbidden to do more interviews."[61] Guinier's performance, while lauded by her friends and colleagues, came across as sanctimonious to those in the White House. Her decision to stand her ground and defend herself rankled those within the administration who believed she should have fallen on her sword. Taylor Branch explained, "She emphasized her opinions rather than her willingness to represent the administration, arguing that she could convince the senators. . . . Regardless of the outcome, her hearings would guarantee several weeks of bad publicity when the administration already was 'bleeding in the water.'"[62] While Guinier may have been right on the merits of defending her position, she was, in the White House's opinion, wrong on the politics. There were larger issues to contend with, such as the economy, other nominations, and the stimulus, that demanded more attention. It appeared as though Guinier had forgotten the cardinal rule of politics: thou shall not injure the boss.

Guinier's seeming lack of political awareness continued as she prepared to meet President Clinton in the oval office. The president's aide Ricki Seidman informed Guinier on the morning of June 3 that she had lost any hope of being confirmed. She asked Guinier to withdraw. It was clear that the president and his staff were trying to cut their losses. It was also apparent that Seidman was given the uncomfortable task of getting Guinier to voluntarily withdraw herself for the administration and the president. Guinier refused to consider withdrawing. In a tense conversation, Seidman told Guinier, "'I think maybe some of these people are right that you are not a team player and you weren't the right person for this job.'"[63] Guinier snapped and informed her that no one at the White House had lifted a finger to help her and that she didn't trust "any of you to be acting in my best interest or in the interest of the administration or frankly in the interest of effective civil rights enforcement."[64] But as Guinier arrived at the White House later that afternoon for a meeting with the president, the mood became surreal. Photographers camped outside the White House, waiting for word of the president's decision and to get reactions, if possible, from Guinier.

Finally, in the Oval Office, the two began to discuss the controversy. The president was troubled by some of her writings. He informed her that the issue of proportional interest representation, one of the articles that provoked the ire of conservatives, was "balkanizing."[65] The president did not like that appearance of an us-versus-them approach to civil rights policy. Guinier tried to inform the president that while she understood his perspective, he had misunderstood the main thrusts of her writings, particularly in the context of her nomination. In addition, as Guinier notes, the remedies of super majorities and minority rights had already been applied in the US Senate, public corporations, and certain counties in the South to achieve fairer electoral and legislative results.[66] The president was unmoved by her arguments. He told her that key senators, including Edward Kennedy, Joe Biden, Herb Kohl, and majority leader George Mitchell, had also pleaded with him to drop the nomination, especially if he wanted to get an economic program passed.[67] President Clinton confided as much to Branch, who wrote, "He would have defended the nomination and Guinier had it not been for the bruising Senate politics."[68] The president informed her that if the process was to continue then it would be death by a thousand cuts.[69] In less than an hour the meeting was over. Guinier did not know what was going to happen next. However, she felt confident that she had made her case and given the president some important things to think about. Surely, President Clinton would not abandon her and would allow her time and space to defend herself.

Within a half hour of returning to the Justice Department, Guinier received a call from the president. The nomination would be withdrawn. At a press conference at the White House, Clinton said, "At the time of the nomination I had not read her writings. In retrospect, I wish I had. Today, as a matter of fairness to her, I read some of them again in good detail. They clearly lend themselves to interpretations that do not represent the views that I expressed on civil rights during my campaign and views that I hold very dearly, even though there is much in them with which I agree."[70] Echoing the DLC philosophy, Clinton argued, "My campaign for the Presidency was based on trying to unite Americans on the basis of race, opportunity, and responsibility, the idea that we could all work together to reach common solutions. And I regret very much the bitterness and the divisiveness which has occurred already."[71] What was not said, and what was at the heart of the DLC vision on racial issues, was that equal opportunity was the primary goal: but if that goal created strenuous political difficulties, then it would be dispensed with.

Aftermath/Conclusion

In the weeks, months, and years following the Lani Guinier episode, much has been made of President Clinton's decision to "abandon" her. The NAACP awarded Guinier the Torch of Courage award in July

1993, in part because of her distinguished career and in part because of her ordeal with the Clinton White House. By 1998, Guinier had been hired as the first black, female, tenured faculty member at Harvard Law School. She continued to write articles, op-eds, and books. In 1994, Guinier published *The Tyranny of the Majority: Fundamental Fairness in Representative Democracy*, a compilation of her previous works. She also published *Lift Every Voice: Turning a Civil Rights Setback into a New Vision of Social Justice,* which examined the nomination and her vision of social justice. Guinier also became more involved in the push for equality and democracy. In 2002, she published *The Miner's Canary: Enlisting Race, Resisting Power, Transforming Democracy* and, in 2011, published *Tyranny of the Meritocracy: How Wealth Became Merit, Class Became Race, and Higher Education Became a Gift from the Poor to the Rich.*[72] She has maintained her public presence in the nearly twenty years since the nomination failed. She has never expressed any doubts about the righteous nature of her position.

Yes, the president was right to withdraw her name. The politics of the process in the Senate would have drained precious political capital and possibly endangered the president's legislative agenda. But the withdrawal nevertheless demonstrated that Clinton lacked a certain gravitas, a demonstrative political toughness. That perceived lack of conviction was seized upon by many African Americans, his most loyal supporters. They felt betrayed by his actions. For some, it was a signal that he could not be trusted. An editorial in *Crisis*, an organ of the NAACP, summed up the sentiments of many African Americans. After allegedly ignoring the plight of poor Haitians trying to escape a brutal regime and implementing the reviled "Don't Ask, Don't Tell" policy, "Clinton suffered a triple dose of amnesia after backing-off on his appointment of the outstanding Black lawyer Lani Guinier. . . . How many more 'snow jobs' will the disenfranchised, the working class folks of color, and others who are oppressed, have to see and hear before they come to the conclusion that many Americans truly cast their votes for a Slick Willie."[73] For the African American political class it was a signal that its interests would be submerged in the interests of political reality.

African American support for President Clinton remained high throughout the 1990s. His belief in equality and justice resonated with African Americans. Yet, like the Sister Souljah moment of 1992, the Lani Guinier nomination and subsequent withdrawal led to the perception that, under pressure, the president could be steamrolled. As Eleanor Clift noted after the debacle, "abandoning Guinier looks less like a shrewd move than a Clintonesque cave in to conservative pressure."[74] This is perhaps what so angered the Congressional Black Caucus (CBC) and liberals around the country: if the president cannot stand for a friend on a routine nomination, then how can he stand up against stiff opposition to other elements of the Democratic and Progressive agenda? Kweisi Mfume, head of the Congressional Black Caucus, noted, "The incident would create problems for Clinton's future relations with the 38-member Caucus."[75] That is precisely what happened. From the crime bill of 1994 to welfare reform of 1996 to the race initiative of 1997–98, the CBC and its allies in the media attacked Clinton and many of his proposals. In the end, however, Clinton knew that the CBC would stick with him. As Clift noted, when Clinton called Mfume and other CBC members, he was engaging in "a ritual laying on of hands with the knowledge that they have nowhere else to go."[76]

CHAPTER 4

Responsibility and Accountability

The Politics of Crime

IN 1981, RICKEY RAY RECTOR, a poor black man from Conway, Arkansas, murdered a man at a dance. Following days of searching for the widely acknowledged dim-witted man, Rector's sister called the Conway Police Department to report that her brother wanted to turn himself in. Officer Robert Martin entered the home of Rector's mother, where he was staying, and talked casually with Mrs. Rector. Suddenly Rector walked into the room. Martin noticed him and asked him how he was doing. When Rector said, "Hi, Mr. Bob," Martin returned to his conversation. Without warning or provocation, Rector shot the officer.

Officer Martin was mortally wounded. Rector ran out of the back of the house into the yard. Perhaps realizing for the first time what he had done, or resigned that he might be murdered himself, or perhaps fearful of returning to prison, Rector took the loaded firearm, pointed it to his head, and fired. The resulting wound was nearly fatal. Emergency room physicians and nurses in Little Rock worked to save the cop killer. They were successful. But in order to save his life the doctors had to remove three inches of brain tissue, from the forehead to nearly the middle of his head. Effectively, Rector had given himself a crude frontal lobotomy. What Rector did not take care of, the doctors did. He was left with the capacity of a five- to seven-year-old. Subsequently, Rector was declared competent to stand trial by a white Arkansas judge and convicted by an all-white jury. The sentence: death.

For years, Rector went through the long, winding road of appeals with no results. But in 1992, Governor Bill Clinton needed to demonstrate his toughness on crime. Despite the pleas from doctors, civil rights groups, and Rector's attorneys, Clinton refused to budge. Clinton even flew back to Little Rock from New Hampshire to oversee the last few days of Rector's life. It is also noteworthy that this occurred at the same time that Clinton's longtime paramour, Gennifer Flowers, was revealing their affair and the Clinton campaign was reeling. On January 24, 1992, Rector was put to death by lethal injection in Cummins, Arkansas. Many argued, then and later, that it was clear, given the circumstances, that Rector should have been given a stay of execution and his punishment reduced to life imprisonment. Even those who had examined Rector admitted to one degree or another that Rector was childlike and of questionable competence. Years later Clinton continued to maintain that the execution was legitimate. In an interview on National Public Radio with Amy Goodman on Election Day 2000, Clinton argued that Rector "was not mentally impaired when he committed the crime. He became mentally impaired because he was wounded after he murdered somebody. . . . Had he been mentally impaired when he committed, I would never have carried out the death penalty, because he was not in a position to know what he was doing. That is not what the facts were."[1] For Clinton this was a "value" issue: Rector murdered someone, a cop no less. The fact that Rector gravely injured himself after the fact did not absolve him from the crime of murdering a police office.

Clinton's actions followed the New Democrat philosophy on crime: compassion for victims, tough on criminals. Rector's alleged incompetence was not a factor in Clinton's decision, since he was fully competent when the crime took place. That Clinton was willing to allow this execution to proceed, despite the widespread pleas coming in from across the nation, was a notice about the direction in which he would take the Democratic Party and the nation in the years to come. The Rector case is a window through which Clinton can be understood. Older notions that argued environmental concerns helped dictate behavior—somewhat an article of faith among liberals—divided America between criminals and victims, thus tearing at the fabric of society and destroying the vision of community, opportunity, and responsibility that Clinton was advocating.

In 1994, Congress passed and President Clinton signed the Violent Crime Control and Law Enforcement Act. The law implemented federal restrictions on assault weapons, increased penalties for domestic violence, and provided funding for crime prevention. The legislation also put more than a hundred thousand police officers on the streets, provided billions for new prisons, and expanded the federal death penalty. The tougher approach to the issue of crime resonated with white, middle-class Americans who were central to Clinton's electoral coalition and his fight against stiff Republican opposition to his legislative agenda.

Many in the African American community, especially clergy and the middle and upper classes, were receptive to the new law and supported its passage. Blacks, statistically, were far more likely to be victims of crime, especially violent crime. Their support was illustrative of the class divisions within the African American community. The effects of the law continue to be felt a decade and a half after it was signed into law. President Clinton's political skill in manipulating black class divisions through values-oriented rhetoric helped lead to the passage of this controversial piece of crime legislation. It had a disproportionate impact on the poor African Americans who were further stigmatized, harassed, and imprisoned by the new law and those chosen to enforce it.

William Julius Wilson has written in *When Work Disappears: The World of the New Urban Poor* about how the loss of jobs due to outsourcing, the information age, and deindustrialization have contributed to crime and poverty.[2] In *Streetwise: Race, Class, and Change in an Urban Community*, Elijah Anderson examines the travails of blacks and whites in the inner city.[3] Andrew Hacker writes in *Two Nations: Black and White, Separate, Hostile, Unequal* about racial and class divisions, inequality, inequity, politics, and crime.[4] Another important contribution to the literature has been David B. Holian's "He's Stealing My Issues! Clinton's Crime Rhetoric and the Dynamics of Issue Ownership." This important article in *Political Behavior* demonstrates how "Clinton not only changed the dimension over which the parties discussed crime, from a focus on punishment to stressing prevention, but also served as an agenda setter for media coverage of crime using this new emphasis."[5]

Both Republicans and Democrats historically used the volatile issue of crime to persuade voters to pull the lever next to their name at the ballot box. After the civil rights movement ended with the burning of American cities, Black Power, and the assassination of the Rev. Dr. Martin Luther King Jr., crime became synonymous with supposed black pathology. As Ishmael Reed has noted, "network news shows have become 'profit centers,' news producers have found a lucrative market in exhibiting black pathology, while coverage of pathologies such as drug addiction, child abuse, spousal battering, and crime among whites and their 'model minorities' is negligible."[6] Richard Nixon, Ronald Reagan, and George H. W. Bush exploited Americans' fear of crime to win a combined five of the six previous presidential elections leading up to 1992. It was within this atmosphere that Bill Clinton emerged from the political shadows in 1992. He promised to be a New Democrat. He vowed to center his administration on the principles of "opportunity, responsibility, and community." Unlike New Deal liberals who focused on the quantitative reasons for social breakdown and Great Society liberals who sought answers to our national problems through qualitative and empirical research, Clinton took a middle-of-the-road approach to social policy. He attempted to balance the competing interests and tensions between traditional Democratic orthodoxy and the centrism of the New Democrats after concluding that many parts of the national Democratic orthodoxy had failed to achieve the desired results in American society. As he proclaimed repeatedly, "the old debate between prevention and punishment is a false choice; we need both."[7]

Reasons to Refocus the Democratic Party on Crime Issues

In 1980, then governor Clinton lost his reelection bid in large part because of his perceived left-of-center politics and policies regarding crime, education, taxes, and the death penalty. He had raised taxes, moved to modernize the education system of Arkansas, been reluctant to use the death penalty, and failed to prevent President Jimmy Carter from putting Cuban immigrants in the state. This unfortunate episode in his life was a seminal moment in his political career. Losing that race forced Clinton to rediscover the middle ground in American politics. When he ran for governor again in 1982, Clinton demonstrated a new willingness to adhere to the popular winds as reflected in polls, focus groups, and media opinions. Moderation on political issues such as race, crime, and social policy reflected the growing consensus among many Democrats that the coastal elites and special interest groups had for far too long controlled the Democratic Party, with disastrous results for the nation and for the party. Following the thumping of Governor Michael Dukakis in 1988, Clinton began to position himself for a presidential run of his own in 1992. He started making speeches around the country on critical domestic policy issues such as crime. Ostensibly, this was to promote the Democratic Leadership Council. For Clinton, it was something more: it was the beginning of his taking over of the levers of power and thought within the Democratic Party. In addition, Clinton advocated for victim's rights and the use of the death penalty. Reluctant to use punishment with as much finality as execution in his first term as governor, 1979–1981, Clinton demonstrated little reluctance in his subsequent terms. From 1983 to 1993, he repeatedly ordered the Arkansas Department of Corrections to schedule execution dates for Arkansas Death Row inmates. As David Maraniss noted, Clinton had stated as early as 1976 that "he supported the death penalty" and that the real question was not "is this the right thing to do, but it is always the wrong thing to do."[8] Clinton was struggling with both the moral and political implications of using the death penalty.

Crime on a National Level

Among the central policy positions of then governor Bill Clinton in 1991 and 1992 was crime. Public safety and social order are necessary elements of any successful presidential campaign, as the previous Democratic presidential nominee, Dukakis, learned the hard way. In

1988, after the spectacular collapse of Colorado senator Gary Hart amid revelations of marital infidelity, Massachusetts governor Dukakis secured the nomination. Dukakis had long supported a little-known benefit program in Massachusetts law that allowed prisoners to be furloughed for days at a time. According to a *New York Times* report, most states had a furlough program, and for the most part, they were considered successful.[9] Some inmates had to be arrested again for not returning on time. Other inmates committed crimes—these including both misdemeanors and felonies—while on furlough. The most notorious of these felons was a man by the name of William R. Horton. Horton, black and menacing-looking in mug shots, became one of the central domestic issues of the 1988 presidential campaign. In 1974, William Horton and a friend robbed and murdered a cashier at a gas station in Massachusetts. Horton was given a furlough in 1986 and he fled to Maryland, where he assaulted a man and raped his wife. Opposition research by the Bush campaign staff revealed Dukakis's support for the soon-to-be controversial program. Previously, the Horton case had been of little interest outside of Massachusetts and Maryland; it was just another local crime.

Vice President George H. W. Bush's campaign strategist Lee Atwater, considered by many in both the political and media worlds as a brilliant and dirty operative, ran a campaign ad featuring William Horton and Governor Dukakis's support for the controversial program. Dukakis had supported the program throughout his tenure in office. However, in 1987 he finally gave up supporting it as he was running for president, but it was too late. The damage had been done. The ad was condemned by many as racist but was very effective in labeling Dukakis as weak on crime. After the ad ran, his poll numbers dropped precipitously, while Bush's rose. During a fall presidential debate, CNN's Bernard Shaw asked Dukakis whether he would support the death penalty if his wife, Kitty, was raped and murdered. Dukakis responded by saying, "I have opposed the death penalty during all of my life. I don't see any evidence that it is a deterrent."[10] The response, while in line with his views on the volatile issue, helped to implant serious misgivings about his judgment and manhood. As historian Michael Schaller has noted, "Without making overt racial statements, the Bush campaign linked Dukakis to white fear of black crime and sexual assaults."[11] In November Bush overwhelmed Dukakis at the polls to win the nation's highest office. It was this legacy with which Clinton most urgently had to reckon.

Anticrime Efforts Take Center Stage in the Clinton Administration's Domestic Agenda

Among the many things the newly minted President Clinton wanted to do upon taking office in 1993 was crime prevention. He had talked about it throughout the campaign. That Clinton put crime at the top of his domestic agenda—along with health care reform, welfare reform, and economic stimulus—signaled a dramatic shift in Democratic priorities. Unlike in the Estes Kefauver and Robert Kennedy organized crime hearings of the 1950s, Clinton actually sat at the head of the Democratic Party, thereby forcing Democrats to place crime prevention at the top of their domestic agenda. At the heart of Clinton's efforts was controlling assault weapons by supporting the pending Brady Bill and the community policing of neighborhoods, cutting the size of federal law enforcement, and adding more than a hundred thousand police officers on the streets.[12]

Major metropolitan areas such as Los Angeles, Chicago, New York, and Boston had seen their violent crime rates skyrocket by the beginning of the 1990s. Many whites who had not already abandoned the cities by the late 1980s were leaving in droves by the time Clinton took office. The reason for the exodus was threefold: the allure of life in the suburbs, dwindling property values, and fear of crime. Black crime and lingering opposition to integration, combined with the prospect of high-quality, overwhelmingly white public schools, contributed greatly to the phenomenon known as "white flight." Beginning in the late 1960s white middle-class families left the cities for the suburbs not only to enjoy single-family homes but also to avoid integration at all costs. Historian Kevin Kruse, in *White Flight: Atlanta and the Making of Modern Conservatism*, uses Atlanta as a window through which one can view the response to the end of segregation, examining how regular, everyday whites developed a social movement to escape the coming of integration.[13] Kruse's work demonstrates the continuing relevance of race at the center of conservatism. Scholar Matthew Lassiter, in *The Silent Majority: Suburban Politics in the Sunbelt South*, convincingly demonstrates how race-neutral strategies of white resistance led to densely populated urban centers that were overwhelming black and how the growth of the suburbs became nearly completely white.[14] The suburbs were at the center, as Lassiter argues, and the suburbs transcended the South. Gang violence spurred on by the crack-cocaine epidemic, along with growing class divisions within the black community, served to entrap the inhabitants of these forsaken communities. As Wilson has written, the plight of the inner city is directly linked to the lack of affordable health care, quality education, decent housing, and well-paying jobs.[15] Further, the seismic forces of globalization and outsourcing ate away at blacks' hard-fought economic gains since World War II and the civil rights movement. "Crime" became a code word for "black." Travis L. Dixon has explained, "An accumulating body of research has provided evidence that television news commonly depicts African Americans as criminals while portraying Whites as officers and victims. . . . Conversely, Whites were underrepresented as perpetrators on television news compared to crime reports while being overrepresented as officers compared to employment records."[16] Mentioning drugs, gangs, murder, and rape triggered images of black thugs to the average media consumer, including many middle-class and upper-class blacks. In order to maintain his hold on the middle class, Clinton had to dedicate significant energies to putting a stop to criminal behavior.

Clinton argued that more money, energy, and focus had to be put on community policing, passing the Brady Bill to prevent gun violence, starting Boot Camps for young offenders, reforming drug addicts, passing Safe School legislation, implementing anti-gang initiatives within the Department of Justice and state law enforcement, initiating national service, and creating economic incentives for distressed communities. Finally, Clinton wanted to use the "Bully Pulpit to call attention to crime, violence, and the collapse of social institutions essential to civilized life: family, community, and work."[17] By couching his rhetoric and plans in the language of family, community, work, and responsibility, Clinton was able to appeal to a broad cross section of the electorate. A January 1994 strategy memo from the president's aide Rahm Emanuel says, "The crime bill is a means to a further end. The crime bill is also a vehicle to communicate to the public a set of strongly-held values that the President embraces, as well as the President's tough stance on crime and criminals."[18] The president toured the nation to talk about crime and prevention, hitting all of the regular hot spots: schools, public housing projects, and churches. At a meeting of senior officials, such as Bruce Reed, Jose Cerda, and Domestic Policy Council staffers, in the Roosevelt Room of the White House on November 15, 1993, participants discussed ideas and made plans. The purpose was to build up a head of steam going into 1994 and the new legislative session. Included in the discussions were plans to have the president travel around the country promoting the crime package. Some of the major suggestions issued at this important meeting included grants in the amount of $150 million from a spring supplemental funding bill for community policing, restrictions on the importation of firearms of a military nature, consolidation of drug grants, movement of former soldiers to law enforcement, and the formation of the Midnight Basketball League.[19] The bill itself, with the exception of the ban on assault weapons, was relatively uncontroversial as most Americans recognized the need for greater control of the crime plaguing America's streets. However, one part of the bill, the Racial Justice Act, provoked tremendous controversy.

Congressman Don Edwards of California introduced the Racial Justice Act on March 11, 1994. H.R. 4017 was designed to prevent racially discriminatory capital sentencing, to prohibit the execution of a defendant because of race, and to provide access to death-penalty case data. The most controversial aspect was Section 2921, "Prohibition against the execution of a sentence of death imposed on the basis of race." Further, the bill allowed individual defendants to present evidence that "race was a statistically significant factor in decisions to seek or to impose the sentence of death in the jurisdiction." If the defendant could present such evidence, then "the death sentence may not be carried out unless the government rebuts the inference by a preponderance of the evidence."[20] Since there was ample evidence of racial discrimination in applying the death penalty, as demonstrated by the Baldus study, African American politicians wanted to bring parity to the judicial process.[21] Most conservatives, however, saw the issue in a polar opposite way. They saw any type of racial justice act as an attempt to defy the will of the people. It would be a giveaway to criminals who had harmed others. Conservatives saw it as fundamentally unfair to law-abiding citizens who followed the rules and simply wanted to protect themselves, their families, and their property. Like affirmative action, conservatives saw the Racial Justice Act as discriminatory against the majority of Americans by giving special consideration to defendants over victims. In fact, throughout the 1990s, conservatives and President Clinton debated the appropriateness of a Victims Rights Amendment that would ensure that inmates served their time and that victims could pursue monetary damages against the offenders. Implicit in this argument was race. Since African Americans were far more likely to be standing in front of a judge, trumpeting victims' rights was a way in which politicians could not only play to their base supporters, but play on the fear of white Americans of black-on-white crime.

Although the Racial Justice Act ultimately failed to pass, the debates it generated are a window through which one can understand the complexity of race in the age of Clinton. The origins of the proposed Racial Justice Act dated back to a 1987 decision by the US Supreme Court in *McCleskey v. Kemp*. In 1978, Warren McCleskey, an African American, murdered a white police officer in Georgia during a furniture store robbery. He was convicted and sentenced to death. In court McCleskey argued that racial bias predetermined his sentence, and therefore it was unconstitutional under the Fourteenth Amendment's equal protection clause. The Supreme Court's ruling, in a decision written by Justice Lewis Powell, affirmed the decision of the district court and the Eleventh Circuit Court of Appeals. Justice Powell wrote, "It is not the responsibility—or indeed even the right—of this Court to determine the appropriate punishment for particular crimes."[22] As Illinois senator Carol Moseley-Braun noted on the Senate floor, "the Racial Justice Act was developed after the U.S. Supreme Court explicitly stated in the case of McCleskey versus Kemp that the evidence of racial discrimination in that case was, and I quote, 'best presented to the legislative bodies,' who could develop the appropriate solutions."[23] During the proceedings a report—the Baldus study—proved that blacks were more likely to be sentenced to death than whites, especially when the victim was white.[24] In the aftermath of the court's decision, a progressive coalition that included African American politicians sought to remedy the situation through the legislative process. This meant that the court's ruling had to be challenged. Moreover, it had to become easier for defendants to introduce evidence of bias and abuse by prosecutors.

The second case leading to the push for the Racial Justice Act was the Anti-Drug Abuse Act of 1988.[25] One part of the act, called the "Drug Kingpin Death Penalty," created the death penalty for those guilty of committing murder in the act of drug trafficking.[26] According to a staff report by the Subcommittee on Civil and Constitutional Rights of the Judiciary Committee, with assistance from the Death Penalty Information Center, "analysis of prosecutions under the federal death penalty provisions of the Anti-Drug Abuse Act of 1988 reveals that 89% of the defendants selected for capital prosecution have been either African American or Mexican-American."[27] These were staggering numbers that did not even have a veneer of parity. Death penalty opponents tried to get the Racial Justice Act passed following the Supreme Court's decision in *McCleskey*. But it was always rebuffed by the Senate and Republican presidents Reagan and Bush. When the 1994 crime bill came to the forefront of the legislative calendar, there was a Democratic president in the White House, a strong Congressional Black Caucus, and the support of many white Democrats. The Racial Justice Act seemed to be a major part of the final bill.

In the 103rd Congress, Democrats controlled an overwhelming majority in the House and a very robust majority in the Senate.[28] House Democrats were easily able to pass the Racial Justice Act in April 1994 to the pleasure of African American leaders and death penalty opponents around the country. While Republicans could do little in the House, they waited for the bill to move to the Senate to produce the final bill. There they seized on the measure as a giveaway for violent, dangerous criminals. In a rebuttal to the provision, "Sense of the Senate," New York senator Alfonse D'Amato, speaking for himself and Senators Slade Gorton and Pete Domenici, urged that the Racial Justice Act be removed from the final crime bill.[29] That suggestion was mild compared to those of others in the Senate and in the media. Congressman Steven Horn of California argued that the Racial Justice

Act "would result in the effective abolition of capital punishment."[30] One of the most vociferous opponents was Florida congressman Bill McCollum, who said that the Racial Justice Act "would abolish the death penalty in America."[31] At a time when crime was considered one of the nation's most important problems, such visceral language served as red meat for a public terrified of crime, violence, and the prospect of black thugs coming to visit violence and destruction upon them. Inflaming the issue further was the language that framed it.

In a report published just four years before the signing of the crime bill, the General Accounting Office released a report detailing widespread disparities in death penalty sentencing.[32] Testimony from the director of Administration of Justice Issues, Lowell Dodge, before the Subcommittee on Civil and Constitutional Rights of the House Judiciary Committee revealed that "in 82 percent, or 23 of the 28 studies, race of victim was found to correlate with being charged with capital murder or receiving the death penalty."[33] The purpose of the Racial Justice Act was to allow defendants to present credible evidence of racial disparity at sentencing and on death row.[34] Liberals in the House, with the strong and enthusiastic endorsement of the Congressional Black Caucus, pushed the measure through over the objections of more conservative Democrats.

But President Clinton, along with Senate Democrats and moderate House Democrats, managed to drop the measure during the formulation of the conference report. Arguably, it could have passed the Senate; however, such a legislative fight would have damaged the president and vulnerable Democrats even further as the midterm elections neared. Many liberals were quite angry over the removal of the Racial Justice Act from the final bill. A *New York Times* editorial summed up the frustration with the president and Senate Democrats by saying, "The last straw was President Clinton's surrender to the Senate conservatives who oppose a provision to allow minority defendants to introduce statistical evidence of racial bias in the application of the death penalty. Compromising is always a part of lawmaking, but the abandonment of the racial justice provision tips the scale."[35] There is no federal statutory language addressing the disparity in death-penalty cases today.

The Congressional Black Caucus represented the black middle and upper classes, while also trying to represent the interests of the poor and vulnerable. As demographics of the black community changed after the passage of the Civil Rights Act of 1964 and the Voting Rights Act of 1965 and the various programs of the Great Society, the black leadership shifted from its activist roots. They chose inclusion and access instead of exclusion and agitation. At the same time, however, they tried to pay due respect to traditional concerns about equality and justice; hence both their fervent support for the Racial Justice Act and eventual capitulation to the Clinton White House.

The civil rights movement hierarchy became more pragmatic and concerned with the issues of the new middle- and upper-class blacks, such as higher educational access, higher property values, occupational achievement, and social mobility. Black members of Congress in large part represented this new "civil rights leadership." It is why, in the end, they ended up supporting the crime bill. In addition, these new concerns and priorities were well received by many blacks who considered themselves apolitical. This is not to say that these politicians and leaders abandoned their political responsibilities, but that as the black community became more diverse and invested in mainstream America, its aims, concerns, and values changed to reflect such diversity.

When the Racial Justice Act of 1994 was discovered in the massive crime bill, the public fervor was immense. The Democratic Leadership Council along with the Clinton White House did not want to see the crime bill fail and thus give the Republicans more ammunition for the fall elections. In July, after the bill cleared the House and Senate in the late spring and early summer, respectively, and as conferees were trying to reconcile the bill, the Racial Justice Act of 1994 was dropped. This was due to fierce Republican opposition as well as concerns from moderate and conservative Democrats that the provision would create an unfair privilege for minorities. The Congressional Black Caucus was bitterly disappointed and proved a roadblock, albeit a temporary one, to passage of the crime bill. In the end the majority of the Congressional Black Caucus supported the bill. The CBC also supported the bill because it contained preventative spending and the assault weapons ban. As CBC chair Kweisi Mfume noted, "People accused us of being obstructionists and said it would be detrimental to the party and we would never get the assault-weapons ban—but we got it. . . . We threatened again to tie up the entire process if we didn't get a narrowing of the 'three strikes and you're out' provision, because it was too broadly applied. . . . We forced it, because it was a matter of principle, and we won."[36] By narrowing their losses and securing some small victories, the Congressional Black Caucus could secure a moral victory on the Racial Justice Act and a substantive victory on the other hand. The CBC victory derived from the ability to take on a president of their own party, hold his feet to the fire, and secure some compromise on other issues. Lastly, helping to pass the crime bill would insulate its members from political attacks and build goodwill with the Clinton White House.

The Racial Justice Act was defeated after it became associated in the public's mind with African American criminality. As Darren Wheelock and Douglas Hartmann have argued, "deeply entrenched images and ideas associating crime with young African American men had the rhetorical effect of heightening the threat of crime and raising serious questions about preventative programs. This ultimately shifted the balance between punitive and preventative appropriations in the bill."[37] After Republican exploitation of this issue and the willingness of the Democratic leadership in Congress to drop the measure, the president himself decided to abandon the program, thus politically slapping African Americans in the face. As Democratic Party strategist Donna Brazile has noted generally, "Prior to the 1996 election, there was a lot of dissatisfaction with him [Clinton] over some of his policies . . . about his backing of some conservative initiatives."[38] The crime bill was a perfect example of their dissatisfaction. At the very least, he demonstrated political caution when it came to matters of race.

Conservatives and pro–death penalty advocates, such as Congressman McCollum, argued that the Racial Justice Act amounted to a quota system for justice. Despite efforts to correct the perception of the bill, members of the Congressional Black Caucus and liberal Democrats found that they had little support from the Clinton White House. President Clinton refused to signal his support for the controversial measure despite the pleadings of members of Congress and the media. As the *New York Times* urged in an editorial when the bill stalled in July, "It is time for President Clinton to take a stand for racial justice in administering the death penalty . . . [and] the president is silent about it."[39] Politically, it was understandable that the Clinton White House would support the removal of the controversial provision. As senior advisor George Stephanopoulos remarked, "We didn't have a choice; in a rabidly pro–death penalty Congress, the 'Racial Justice Act' was a poison bill."[40] Yet Clinton also wanted a bill that could be signed into law and addressed the troubling issue of crime. He would not allow himself to be dragged into the thorny issue of racial equality. In addition, securing half a loaf was better than getting nothing. Here was the New Democrat philosophy on social policy: focused on popular, values-oriented solutions to complex problems. As Clinton discussed with his in-house historian Taylor Branch in late August 1994, "By concentrating on the more popular elements—100,000 new community police officers, plus more prisons, prevention and treatment programs, and tougher penalties for terrorist crimes—they sought to recapture members from those rural districts most vulnerable to the gun lobby."[41] The Racial Justice Act was dropped from the final bill.

On July 21, 1994, the administration tried to work out a deal with members of the Congressional Black Caucus on the Racial Justice Act provision. According to the *New York Times*, "The Administration offered two alternatives to the Racial Justice Act. One would have President Clinton issue an executive order to prosecutors to use extra caution in seeking the death penalty and demand that various checks and balances be used before it is applied. The other would set up a commission to study the death penalty."[42] As the *Times* article noted, there was already a study proving the disparity in sentencing, thus nullifying the need for a second one. According to the report to Senate and House Committees on the Judiciary, "more than three-fourths of the studies that identified a race of defendant effect found that black defendants were more likely to receive the death penalty."[43] Leon Panetta, White House chief of staff, approached members of the CBC to try to work out a deal on studying the issue further. It was a weak and unserious gesture on Panetta's part, as reflected by Congressman Charlie Rangel's remark after the meeting that the "death penalty section was 'dead as a doornail.'"[44]

Ultimately, on August 11, 1994, the conference bill, without the Racial Justice Act, was brought before the House for a procedural vote on the rule.[45] In a stunning defeat for the White House, members of the Congressional Black Caucus, led by John Lewis and Kweisi Mfume, joined with Republicans to defeat the rule, 225 to 210. This was a protest vote on the part of African Americans. There was little else the Congressional Black Caucus could do to demonstrate its displeasure with the final bill other than to vote against allowing the bill to come to a final vote.

One week later, the Clinton White House was able to pick up the tepid support of Representatives Lewis and Rangel, as well as others who had voted against the rule. Heavy political pressure from the president and the congressional leadership coerced members of the Congressional Black Caucus to vote for the rule, allowing the bill to come for a final vote. Members of the Congressional Black Caucus had many reasons to switch their vote on the second round of voting. A defeat of one of the president's signature legislative items would have delivered a devastating blow to Clinton less than three months before the midterm elections. In addition, the CBC recognized that the bill did contain significant monies for preventative measures. Therefore, the political survival of the president and the billions of dollars in aid for cities to fight crime with preventative efforts forced many black members of the House, reluctantly, to change their votes to let the bill pass. African American bitterness remained, however, as the Clinton administration was willing to deal with conservative Democrats and Republicans to get the deal passed.

The Congressional Black Caucus, as Clinton himself had done, did what it had to do to protect its interests against the deal making of Clinton and his New Democratic agenda. The political exigencies of race in an overly racialized era compelled Clinton to move in a more pragmatic manner. As Harry Chernoff, Christopher Kelly, and John Kroger pointed out, "The administration seemed to go back and forth on whether such a provision was in any way acceptable, but [Senator Joe] Biden was quite clear, eventually saying: 'We don't have the votes for anything that has 'racial justice' in it, even the word 'racial.'"[46] "An eventual compromise on a racial justice executive order was worked out," according to Chernoff, Kelly, and Kroger, who had knowledge of the inner workings of the Clinton White House.[47] In an interview with the *Los Angeles Times*, congressman and CBC chair Kweisi Mfume explained such a compromise by stating, "What we were going to get was an executive order by the President and a commission."[48] The purpose of this gesture was to placate the CBC by drawing attention to racial disparities in sentencing and trying to persuade law enforcement and the courts to not discriminate against African Americans. The president's promise to look further into this critical issue and to direct his administration to monitor such disparities in the future led to the vast majority of the Congressional Black Caucus members changing their votes from no to yes on the final bill.

The crime bill also included the expansion of the death penalty, dramatic increases in construction and funding of prisons, truth-in-sentencing requirements, and financial support for prosecutors. These had a mostly negative impact on the lives of poor and working-class African Americans. The new programs and the money allotted to them gave police even more of an impetus for incarcerating African Americans.[49] African Americans went to prison at a rate that was disproportionate to whites. For the year 1999, Legal Services for Prisoners with Children, based in San Francisco, showed that African Americans represented 12.7 percent of the population but 48.2 percent "of American adults in state and federal prisons and local jails and 42.5% of prisoners under sentence of death."[50] In 1993, the year before the passage of the crime bill, there were more than 500,000 African Americans behind bars, according to the Department of Justice's Bureau of Statistics. Ten years after the passage of the crime bill that number rose to more than 800,000.

The president's stance on this issue demonstrated the potency of the New Democrat message and policy positions as embodied by Clinton. It was yet again a disappointing event for racial progressives, as the president supported a crime bill that was more draconian than constructive. After the Racial Justice Act was dropped and some Democrats joined with the Republicans to prevent the conference bill from coming to the floor, the bill finally passed the House on August 21 and the Senate on August 25. President Clinton signed the Violent Crime Control and Law Enforcement Act of 1994 into law.[51]

The Rest of the Crime Bill

The Violent Crime Control and Enforcement Act of 1994 was designed to alleviate the problems of crime in the inner cities. Spurred on by the crack-cocaine epidemic of the late 1970s and 1980s, as well as gang violence, the use of automatic weapons, assaults, shootings, rapes, murders, and other assorted crimes, the fabric of urban life was ripped apart. To complicate matters further, as whites fled to the suburbs in the wake of the civil rights movement and integration, the major cities saw their tax revenue dwindle. As white, middle-class residents sought the comfort of the suburbs, blacks, who historically had been enticed to migrate to metropolitan areas, found themselves stuck in the muck and mire of an urban landscape stripped of high-quality educational opportunities, good-paying jobs, and political attention. Poverty-bred crime and the loss of local, state, and federal funding during the Reagan/Bush era left many areas in disrepair. Funding that once went to combat poverty now went to law enforcement. Shortly after the Reagan administration was sworn into office, Michelle Alexander argued, "The Justice Department announced its intentions to cut in half the number of specialists assigned to identify and prosecute white-collar criminals and to shift its attention to street crime, especially drug-law enforcement."[52]

President Clinton argued that the common-sense approach to crime should be more community policing, more officers on the streets, and more money for drug courts and prisons. In remarks at a town hall meeting in Detroit on February 10, 1993, Clinton argued that three things needed to be done: (1) pass the crime bill that failed in Congress in 1992, (2) pass the Brady Bill, and (3) enact Governor Douglas Wilder's plan to limit the purchasing of handguns to one a month.[53] In a major speech delivered to the Convocation of the Church of God in Christ in Memphis in November 1993, Clinton chastised African Americans who accepted violence and bad behavior, to the shock and applause of those in attendance, by saying, "The freedom to die before you're a teenager is not what Martin Luther King lived and died for."[54] The ability to combine a preacher cadence with the tough-love message of an older brother was a powerful and authentic voice of hope for those in the audience that day and for others around the country, as Clinton pleaded for the passage of the crime bill.

Such messages of tough love resonated with African Americans precisely because Clinton had tapped into a vein of popular discontent. The drugs, HIV-AIDS, gangs, youth pregnancies, and family breakdowns of the previous quarter of a century had devastated the inner cities. As some African Americans moved from poverty to working class to middle class, their realization of the self-destructive behavior became acute. Clinton understood just how powerful these concerns were for African Americans and used them to promote crime legislation. The president tapped into a pulse of the African American community and its concerns, desires, fears, and obstacles; however, he genuinely wanted to rectify the situation and help provide the security and opportunity that he knew the African American community had never enjoyed. This is where the New Democratic rhetoric paid dividends with those African Americans who were largely non-ideological, partisan only in reaction to Republican policies, and worried about the future of the race.

The crime bill also called for community policing, grants for correctional facilities, truth-in-sentencing grants, punishment for young offenders, the incarceration of illegal aliens, prohibition of Pell Grants for prisoners, the utilization of the private sector, grants for prosecutors, federal penalties for sex crimes, penalties for violence against women, the National Domestic Violence Hotline, drug courts, mandatory life imprisonment (Three Strikes) for certain felonies, enhancement of penalties for drug trafficking and dealing drugs in drug free zones, increased penalties for drunk driving and gun crimes and terrorism, the prosecution of youth offenders as adults for crimes of violence, funding for law enforcement training, and increased penalties for assault, manslaughter, civil rights violations, trafficking in counterfeit goods and services, conspiracy to commit murder for hire, arson, and drug trafficking near public housing.[55] Most of those elements were solid policy for crime control. Others, however, demonstrated a punitive focus. As this legislation concerned African Americans, several of these rules and laws had an adverse impact.

Under Sec. 1701, the attorney general was given the power to make grants to the states for the purposes of increasing police presence and addressing crime problems. In addition, grants were to include funding for former servicemen to be hired as police officers in their local communities. This had a positive effect in that many former servicemen and women were hired, greater police presence reduced criminal offenses, and violent crime statistics collected by the Department of Justice revealed that crime reached all-time lows during the Clinton presidency. Its downside, however, was the repeated arrests of criminals and suspected criminals. It led to a dramatic increase in the prison population and the scourge of police brutality. That policy sent clear signals to law enforcement that criminals or suspected criminals were to be pursued vigorously. As more officers were put on the beat, the higher was the likelihood of violations of peoples' civil and constitutional rights.

Under section 20411, the bill prohibited Pell Grants to prisoners. This stripped the right of prisoners to receive educational assistance from the federal government. In this section, the Higher Education Act of 1965 was amended.[56] Congress and the Johnson administration saw rehabilitation as crucial in order to create the Great Society. Pell Grants were created in 1972 to address the disparity in educational funding by creating the Basic Opportunity Grant Program; in 1980 it was changed to the Pell Grant Program in honor of its chief sponsor, Rhode Island senator Claiborne Pell.[57] A major argument for including prisoners in this program was the belief that education helped inmates rehabilitate and prevented subsequent returns to prison. While Pell Grants were not the only way for inmates to finance an education, the overwhelming majority of inmates had little access to other sources of funding. Taking student loans, with little opportunity to repay them, was not practical. For African Americans, this new law meant that those who were inclined to take classes to better themselves could no longer find the means to do so. As a result, these inmates were left with little else to do in prison but sink deeper into the morass of the criminal lifestyle, often with repeated trips to prison. Michelle Alexander explained that "30 percent of released prisoners in its sample were rearrested within six months of release. Within three years, nearly 68 percent were rearrested at least once for a new offense."[58]

The Three Strikes law meant that criminals were now subject to mandatory life sentences for three or more criminal offenses that result in conviction. While this law was reserved for federal offenders, many states also took up the rule in the rush to demonstrate their toughness against criminals. African Americans disproportionately faced the brunt of this law as they were statistically more likely to be arrested, convicted, and sentenced to prison. William L. Sabol wrote in his analysis that black males were six times "more likely to be held in custody than white males."[59] As Bill Moffitt of the National Association of Criminal Defense Lawyers remarked in testimony before the US Commission on Civil Rights, "Our 'war on drugs' virtually guarantees that three strikes sentencing will fall primarily on African Americans, because drug sales count as prior felonies. . . . The federal "three strikes" law enacted in the 1994 Crime Act seeks to politically 'fix' a system that is not broken."[60]

The federal death penalty was expanded to include about sixty offenses, including crimes resulting in the death of a police officer, drug trafficking, and drive-by shootings and carjackings resulting in death; in other words, crimes typically associated with African Americans. It also impacted minority communities more than others. As the Justice Department's own records have shown, between 1995 and 2000 there were thirteen African Americans sentenced to death, compared to four whites. At the state level the statistics were grim. The American Civil Liberties Union noted in 2003, "People of color have accounted for a disproportionate 43% of total executions since 1976 and 55% of those currently awaiting execution." In Pennsylvania, Louisiana, and Colorado, that number was to 70 percent, 72 percent, and 80 percent, respectively.[61] The federal impetus on the use of the death penalty encouraged state prosecutors to seek the death penalty and governors to sign the death warrants. While such organizations as the Innocence Project were proving hundreds of defendants innocent through the use of DNA evidence, there was no pause from the Clinton White House or other New Democrats. What did concern them was inequity within the system, not the death penalty or incarceration itself. Discussing the horrific dragging death of James Byrd in 1998, Taylor Branch uncomfortably noted that Clinton "perceived a side benefit for the death penalty in the fair and impartial conviction of white supremacists for capital crimes against black victims. Such progress would reduce the empirical bias in executions—a victimization by race, controlling for all other factors—which could answer a principal line of argument against capital punishment."[62] This is not to say that the president was untroubled by innocent people going to prison or being put to death. In fact, he was concerned about it; however, the need to foster safe communities where parents could work and raise their children was more important. Like affirmative action, welfare reform, and other social issues, the system would get better over time.

The bill also demanded more prison time for offenders, block grants to the states for local and state governments to construct prisons, and Truth in Sentencing Incentive Grants. The use of block grants dated back to the New Federalism of President Richard Nixon, who followed the conservative doctrine that the states were better equipped to spend taxpayers' dollars than the denizens of Washington. The aim of this measure was to encourage states to sentence defendants and force them to serve at least 85 percent of the time handed down. While comforting to the victims and their families, it did little to ameliorate the prison-overcrowding issue. The block grants program was a response to the growing distrust of some Americans with the federal government. Instead of the Department of Justice and Federal Bureau of Investigation acting on their own authority, the Justice Department would simply act as an administrator in dispersing federal dollars to states that met certain criteria. These arrangements gave greater control to the states but also allowed for states to make optimal use of private corporations to build and run these prisons. At the same time, using convict labor to make a profit helped serve the financial interests of the prisons, states, and private citizens alike. The International Committee of the Fourth International (ICFI) reported in May 2000 that there were more than "80,000 inmates in the US employed in commercial activity, some earning as little as 21 cents an hour. The US government program Federal Prison Industries (FPI) currently employs 21,000 inmates, an increase of 14 percent in the last two years alone."[63] In fact, Clinton did not so much as pivot from the Reagan era as he simply reconfigured it to serve the Democratic Party's needs. This was the DLC's New Democrat philosophy at work.

How It Passed

Passing the crime bill was not easy. Many interests vied for the opportunity to influence the bill: Democrats and Republicans, law-enforcement and defendant rights organizations. During his late first term, Clinton had entered a tenuous position as his political capital was waning. The original bill dated back to the previous Congress, where it had failed to secure enough votes. The combination of bans on assault weapons, increased spending for preventive programs, and the perception that the bill would force the government to take an increasingly active role in the American life made it difficult to pass. On January 25, 1994, President Clinton stood before the House of Representatives to deliver the annual State of the Union address. Acting from a position of moral strength, Clinton asked that Congress shed political and ideological differences and pass a crime bill that would reduce violence, save children, and restore the American community. Expounding upon old Reagan themes against the government, the president informed the Congress and American people, "Our problems go way beyond the reach of Government. They're rooted in the loss of values, in the disappearance of work, and the breakdown of our families and our communities."[64] The values message was designed to resonate with an American public concerned with the disintegration of societal norms and institutions.

Afterward, the president's staff considered scheduling events that underscored the "values" discussed by the president during the State of the Union in such venues as town hall meetings, interviews with the media, and national town hall meetings.[65] Already, groups and politicians were lining up against the bill. Most prominent was the National Rifle Association. Zealous opponents of any type of gun control, the NRA mounted an expensive campaign to undermine the bill's assault-weapons ban section. This campaign helped to weaken the bill, distract voters, and scare conservative and vulnerable Democrats in both houses of Congress who knew that they would face harsh attack ads in their fall reelection campaigns.[66] Like many advocacy groups, the NRA published voting records and ratings of members of Congress that influenced elections. Christopher Kenny, Michael

McBurnett, and David Bordua note that the NRA was particularly successful in influencing the midterm elections of 1994 as a result of the "electoral prowess" and favorable political conditions, in part, created by the passage of the crime bill.[67] While the crime bill would pass, along with the assault weapons ban, the NRA and gun advocates were able to gain revenge in the fall elections. Finally, the White House staff wanted to present the president as "tough on crime by highlighting specific components of his crime bill proposal [and] identify the president as a person of deeply-held values, a moral leader for this country."[68] By May the House and Senate had passed their respective versions of the bill and the Congress went into conference committee to reconcile the final bill for a vote in late July or early August.

The issue that served as a racial lightning rod was the addition of the Midnight Basketball League program. In July and early August 1994, as conferees were trying to finish the bill, conservatives heavily criticized this program. Pilot programs in California, Maryland, and other areas in the late 1980s and early 1990s demonstrated promising results in helping young, predominately black males stay out of trouble and out of gangs by providing operating funds for basketball courts. The prevailing notion was that if high-risk children and young adults had a place to go where they could blow off steam, engage friends, and participate in a healthy and popular activity such as basketball, they would be less likely to engage in drug use, crime, or gang activity. As Darren Wheelock and Douglas Hartmann have noted, "Midnight basketball accounted for $50 million of the original $33 billion bill, barely a tenth of a percentage point of the funding, a mere fraction of a fraction."[69] As Wheelock and Hartmann also note, "midnight basketball represented . . . a symbol for something else."[70] The symbol was taxpayer dollars spent on undeserving and dangerous youth. Implicit in that symbolism were the ghosts of government programs past. Harkening back to the 1960s, specifically the Great Society, programs that sought to address inequality and poverty were seen as a failure. Buttressing such arguments were facts, such as the increase in crime, violence, and disorder and the failure to eradicate poverty in the 1960s, that suggested government spending on social programs did little to dispense with the problems. Actually, conservatives contributed to the problem, making a bad situation worse at taxpayer expense. Race and partisan politics were very much at work here. Democrats scarcely put up a fight. Mainly, Democratic arguments said that the bill was simply preventative in nature and not solely designed for poor, young, urban people.

Funding for such preventive programs as Midnight Basketball was dramatically reduced. The Congressional Black Caucus, angry over the changes in the bill and the reluctance of prominent Democrats to fight against the distortions by opponents of the bill, joined Republicans in voting against its passage on August 11, 1994, in a key procedural vote. This was a setback for President Clinton. By August 21, 1994, however, the House of Representatives passed the conference report by a recorded vote of 235 to 195. Four days later, on the twenty-fifth, the Senate passed the conference report, 61 to 38. The bill, now passed by both Houses of Congress, was presented to President Clinton on September 12 and he signed it into law on the next day.[71]

African American Support

Why did African American members of Congress and the African American community at large support this legislation? The answer reveals the complexity of African American life at the end of the twentieth century. Most Americans, black and white, believed crime was a major problem at the beginning of the 1990s. The impact of suburbanization, deindustrialization, crack cocaine, gangs, and dwindling tax revenues created a crisis for American cities. Furthermore, the impact of integration dislodged some of the black support for preventative cures to urban problems. As more and more African Americans removed themselves from black communities to attend better secondary schools, integrated universities, and integrated residential communities, they became attracted to the anticrime rhetoric emanating out of Washington. Historian Steven F. Lawson notes, "The economic recovery that had accompanied Clinton's program of increasing taxes and reducing the deficit benefitted middle-class African Americans, for whom the results of the civil rights movement and affirmative action were finally paying off."[72] Polls showed African American support for anticrime measures to be at least equal to that of whites. As

Gwen Ifill noted in a prescient article in late 1993, "Representative Charles B. Rangel, the New York Democrat who has been pressing the Administration to spend more time addressing narcotics and crime, said the speech touched a chord in the black community. We have not spoken out about the cancers we have in our own bodies. . . . But the violence has reached a point where we need help."[73] In 1990, in a speech at city hall, New York City mayor David N. Dinkins said:

> Fear is the ugliest of emotions. It is the child of ignorance and the father of hatred. It can spawn intolerance, greed, and disorder. Unchecked it may become the greatest criminal of all, robbing us of every freedom, crushing our birthright and burning our future before us. And fear has seized American cities this summer. In Los Angeles and Atlanta, in Chicago and Milwaukee and Dallas, in Washington, Baltimore, Philadelphia, and here in New York as we know all too well, we have shattered all previous records for carnage in our streets.[74]

Along with concerned community groups and clergy, African Americans were in many ways just as concerned as whites with the issue of crime. It is here that President Clinton, who possessed credibility within the African American community, could find support for a crime bill that had a disproportionate impact on the very community that supported him most. A perfect example was Clinton's actions following the bill's first defeat in early August 1994. The president made two crucial speeches in the wake of that setback, one in Minneapolis and one in Maryland. On August 12, 1994, the president flew to Minneapolis to speak at the National Association of Police Organizations convention. There the president tried to pressure law enforcement and, by proxy, members of Congress to support the crime bill by driving home the message of toughness on criminals. "We never had a bill before that was endorsed by every major law enforcement group in the entire United States."[75] Two days later Clinton traveled to a black church, Full Gospel A.M.E. Zion Church in Temple Hills, Maryland, to work on his most loyal constituency. Instead of simply discussing law enforcement, like he did in Minneapolis, Clinton focused on values, community, and the urgency created by the nation's moral decay. Clinton praised the church for "filling that void from the ground up and from the inside out."[76] Then he drove the message home:

There are children in this church who have been gunned down: I know it. The least we can do is to help you to be protected. The least we can do is to put people on the streets who cannot only catch criminals but prevent crime as good law enforcement officers. The least we can do if people are totally hopeless is to get them out of your hair so they won't be bothering you. And the least we can do is to, yes, give your children more things they can say yes to, not just things they can say no to.[77]

Clinton was able to drive the point home with aplomb. He candidly discussed the problems facing America, especially Black America. Few white politicians could walk into a black church and, with the rhetorical cadence of a black minister, speak on such sensitive issues. Thirty religious leaders, including the minister at Full Gospel A.M.E. Zion Church in Temple Hills, gave a strong statement in support of the bill released by the White House on August 16. In part, they said, "While we do not agree with every provision in the crime bill, we do believe and emphatically support the bill's goal to save our communities, and most importantly, our children."[78] African Americans religious leaders strongly voiced their support.[79]

Despite the absence of the Racial Justice Act, the president persuaded African American politicians and regular citizens on the moral dimensions of the legislation. The irony is that New Democrat rhetoric, with its mixed impact upon the African American community, was so persuasive. It is also indicative of the progress of African Americans, in terms of class achievement, that a bill heavy on punishment was so receptive to many African Americans. Sadly, the impact of the legislation paled in comparison to the rhetoric and promises Clinton delivered. The US Commission on Civil Rights reported at the end of the Clinton presidency, "An agonizing reality exists alongside statistics showing a decrease in the use of deadly force by police officers and a reduction of crime in many communities: the persistence of police misconduct."[80] The pressure to address the troubling rise in racial profiling and misconduct led Clinton to meet with thirty members of the civil rights and legal communities to discuss the problem. In a February 1999 letter, Mary Frances Berry, chair of the US Commission on Civil Rights, urged and hoped that the president would get "the Attorney General . . . involved in the investigations of the latest incidents."[81] In addition, many members of Congress continued to press for new crime control measures, often with the support of the administration, throughout the remainder of the Clinton years.

African American members of Congress finally supported the bill because it authorized $7.9 billion dollars for such preventive efforts as drug treatment, the Midnight Basketball League, anti-gang initiatives, and programs for children in the summer. This provided political cover for them in that the crime bill was not just a punitive action directed toward criminals, minorities, and the poor. As Steven A. Holmes of the *New York Times* noted, "that money—and the prospect that an even more draconian crime bill could be enacted, with less money for social programs and without a ban on 19 different types of assault weapons—was enough to induce 28 of the 38 black Democrats to vote . . . to allow the bill to be considered by the full House."[82] Some of the most powerful CBC members, such as Cleo Fields of Louisiana, John Lewis of Georgia, and Charlie Rangel of New York, switched their support because of the so-called sweeteners in the bill. It was better to get half a loaf than to get nothing.

The Crime Bill's Impact on African Americans

The Violent Crime Control and Law Enforcement Act of 1994 has had myriad and long powerful repercussions on African Americans. This law helped to dramatically increase the prison population; it also increased police harassment and brutality, causing devastating destabilization of the African American family and community and a measurable reduction in educational and occupational achievement. These developments occurred during a time in history when global forces, market pressures, and growing international interdependence made capturing the so-called American dream more and more difficult. While some of the effects of the bill were invisible, others, such as racial profiling, were apparent and so widespread that the Clinton administration was forced to address the issue within a few years.

The prison population rose dramatically as a result of this major piece of social legislation. The Executive Office of the President, Office of National Drug Control Policy reported, "From 1990 to 1998, the

Federal prison population almost doubled, reaching 123,041 offenders. The State prison population also increased significantly between 1990 and 1998, from 708,393 to 1,178,978 inmates.[83] While these statistics examined drug-related offenses and offenders, they are indicative of a larger trend pervading the criminal justice system: dramatic increases in the number of persons who have encountered it, especially African Americans. Ten years after enactment of the law, the incarceration rate for blacks was 2,531 per 100,000 residents, among the highest of any racial group.[84] The incarceration rate for whites was only 393 per 100,000 residents.[85] Ronald Kramer and Raymond Michalowski argued that Clinton's rhetoric and actions, which included billions for punishment, led to what Elliott Currie called a "'stunning imbalance between punishment and prevention.'"[86] The build-up of prisons ignored fundamental and underlying problems affecting African Americans: joblessness, poverty, and lack of opportunity. While being disadvantaged is not an excuse for bad behavior, failing to address the mitigating circumstances that lead to crime in the first place is a recipe for social disaster. As Kramer and Michalowski have noted, "the flaw in conceptualization is that violence is a problem rooted in personal or group traits that can be corrected independent of the social structure."[87] One obvious effect was the disruption it caused in the lives of young black men.

Sociologists Becky Petit and Bruce Western, using patterns of social integration, argued that imprisonment "further delay[s] entry into the conventional adult roles of worker, spouse and parents. They [ex-cons] are also less likely to get married or cohabit with the mothers of their children. By eroding employment and marriage opportunities, incarceration may also provide a pathway back into crime."[88] This had a disproportionate impact on African Americans as they were sent to prison at a higher rate than whites. As legal scholar Dorothy E. Roberts notes, "Because poor black men and women tend to live in racially and economically segregated neighborhoods, these neighborhoods feel the brunt of the staggering prison figures. Research in several cities reveals that the exit and reentry of inmates is geographically concentrated in the poorest minority neighborhoods. As many as 1 in 8 of the adult male residents of these urban areas is sent to prison each year and 1 in 4 is behind bars on any given day."[89] No other group of Americans had such experience with the criminal justice system. Lacking social integration and located in heavily populated urban areas, the African American community felt the impact of these incarcerations more than other racial/ethnic groups.

To complicate matters, such predicaments caused a particular problem for black women: the lack of available, unencumbered mates. Black women outnumbered black men as a part of the population by 1,727,820 in 2000. Numerically, there were fewer mates for black women compared to white women. There were 96.4 white males for every 100 whites females. The ratio for black men was 90.5 for every 100 black women.[90] According to a special report by Lisa Thomas-Laury of WPVI-TV of Philadelphia, by the beginning of March 2010, "there [were] 1.8 million more African American women than black men."[91] The dearth of eligible black men has forced some black women to remain single or date outside the race. While there is nothing wrong with interracial relationships, it is troubling that black women who want to date and marry black men are compelled to look elsewhere. As Thomas-Laury notes, "Statistics now show that the number of black women married to white men or someone other than a black man has doubled in the last decade."[92] Black women, in general, also have higher educational levels and, often, higher occupational earnings than many black men. According to a recent report from the Census Bureau, out of 8,463,809 black households, more than 3,872,192 were headed by women. Furthermore, only 3,787,030 of their total households had a married couple, making up about 46 percent of all black households. For whites, nearly 80 percent of their households had a married couple.[93] So many black men are either in prison, on probation, or on parole that legislation such as the 1994 crime bill has poured gasoline on a growing fire within the black community. As black men fall farther behind other men and often live with the belief that they will have a criminal record, rates of domestic violence toward their mates has increased. According to the National Organization of Women, "when we consider race, African American women face higher rates of domestic violence than white women."[94] These types of issues were supposed to be curtailed by the Violence Against Women Act, which was a part of the omnibus crime package of 1994. That it has accelerated in the decade after passage suggests that a one-stop crime policy that is overly focused on punishment rather than prevention can help lead to violence within the homes of America's most vulnerable communities.

By December 31, 1998, more than four years after the enactment of the law, African Americans accounted for 616,106 of the 1,299,096 prisoners in both state and federal prisons.[95] Of that number, 577,289 were black males. By 2007 the prison population had increased from 992,000 in 1994 to 2.3 million in 2007; at the same time, African Americans' presence in state and federal prisons increased from 501,672 to 814,700 inmates. By 2007, African American men represented the largest percentage (35.4 percent) of inmates held in custody, followed by white males (32.9 percent) and Hispanic males (17.9 percent).[96] The spike in immigration, especially from poor Latin American countries, prevented the percentage of black males in prison from increasing because law enforcement has redirected its resources to address the growing diversity. Clinton's and Congress's failure to address the disparities in drug crimes, convictions, and sentencing made a bad situation worse.

The 1994 Crime Bill failed to reduce the growing gap in the sentencing of defendants for possession, use, and sale of powder and crack cocaine. The United States Sentencing Commission recommended in April 1995 that disparities between prison terms for crack cocaine and powder cocaine be reduced to a more equal level. Timothy Messer-Kruse has noted, "In 1994, 90 percent of people convicted of possession of crack were jailed, whereas fewer than one-third of those convicted of possession of powder cocaine were jailed. . . . African Americans composed only 13 percent of regular drug users in the nation, but represented nearly three-quarters of those given prison sentences."[97] Those statistics represented data collected through 1995. All too often the targets of criminal investigations and prosecutions were black dealers and users, not those responsible for the major trafficking operations that brought the drugs to foot soldiers in the illicit trade. Roberts has noted, "The explosion of both the prison population and its racial disparity are largely attributable to aggressive street-level enforcement of the drugs laws and harsh sentencing for drug offenders. . . . The War on Drugs became its own prisoner-generating machine, producing incarcerations rates that 'defy gravity and continue to grow even as crime rates are dropping."[98] The 1994 crime legislation did nothing to alleviate this problem. In fact, it compounded the issue by focusing on putting one hundred thousand police officers on the street and moving in favor of state control. In a report prepared for the US Commission on Civil Rights, Marc Mauer, assistant director of the Sentencing Project, argued, "Much of this legislation has been not just mean-spirited but counterproductive as well, by limiting prisoners' access to the acquisition of skills that might be used constructively upon their return to the community."[99] The War on Drugs failed to stop the growing drug trade in the United States and, in fact, helped to accelerate it. The so-called revolving door of prison contributed to undermining the African American community since they were the ones who were usually caught in law enforcement's dragnet.

African Americans continued to suffer police brutality, an issue unaddressed by the 1994 crime bill. One of the most infamous instances of police brutality occurred shortly before the passage of the crime bill, the beating of Rodney King by Los Angeles Police officers during a traffic stop. Other incidents, however, occurred on Clinton's watch that shocked the nation's conscience. On August 9, 1997, Haitian immigrant Abner Louima was arrested by New York City police officers and then transported to a police station in Brooklyn. There the thirty-one-year-old was sodomized with a toilet plunger and beaten savagely. Tyisha Miller, a nineteen-year-old woman, sitting in her car in Riverside, California, was shot to death by four Riverside police officers in December 1998. Amadou Diallo was murdered when New York police officers shot him nineteen times in the foyer of his apartment in the Bronx on February 4, 1999. He was unarmed. So voluminous were the problems associated with racial profiling and police brutality that the Clinton administration had to publicly condemn those and other actions and encourage stricter enforcement of standards and procedures. Polling in 1996 found that 42.7 percent of the black population believed that police brutality was a serious problem where they lived. Only 12.9 percent of the white population believed the same.[100] Those opinions correlate with a 2002 Justice Department report that stated, "During a traffic stop in 2002, police were more likely to use force against a black (2.7%) or Hispanic (2.4%) driver than a white (0.8%) driver."[101] In 1997, there were 10,516,707 arrests in the United States, according to the FBI's Crime in the United States records. However, blacks accounted for 3,201,014 of those arrests while whites made up 7, 061,083 arrests.[102] At first glance this numbers suggest that whites were more likely to encounter law enforcement. Taking in population percentages, however, blacks made up 30.4 percent of the arrests that year while only being 12 percent of the entire population.[103] African Americans, in general, were more likely to not only confront law enforcement, but also be searched, confined, arrested, and convicted. Since African Americans were more likely to have contact with law enforcement, for them this meant a higher likelihood of police brutality or other misconduct.

The 1994 crime bill also failed to address these issues of racial profiling and the often resulting violence toward suspects. In later years, the Clinton administration was forced to notice the concerns of civil rights leaders Jesse Jackson and Al Sharpton. Further, Mary Frances Berry, chairperson of the US Commission on Civil Rights, sent a letter to President Clinton in February 1999 urging him "once again to clear the atmosphere of the underlying bigoted assumptions that appear to have taken on new strength in our land."[104] Although the 1994 crime bill required the attorney general to collect accurate data on excessive force by law enforcement officers (apparently with the hope of curtailing such abuses of power), a culture of police misconduct was allowed to persist at all levels of American society. In fact, a 1999 report by the Bureau of Justice Statistics noted, "Police were more likely to search a vehicle driven by a black (8.5%) or Hispanic (9.7%) than a white (4.3%)."[105] Clinton's enthusiastic support for such a punitive piece of social legislation compounded a bad situation for those subject or potentially subject to the criminal justice system.

The impact of incarcerations, prosecutions, and violence perpetrated upon African Americans at the hands of the police has also had a catastrophic effect upon working- and lower-class African American families. As Demico Boothe, a former inmate from Memphis, Tennessee, has noted, the lack of available men and jobs has led to black women on welfare. In addition, once those inmates were released, paroled, or given probation, they had extremely difficult experiences trying to rebuild their lives. Often those inmates found themselves, since their first conviction, repeat guests of the prison system. Bureau of Justice statistics found that black men who reached the age of twenty had a 28.5 percent chance of going to prison during their life. Further, at age twenty-five and at age thirty black men had a 25.3 percent and 17.3 percent chance of going to prison, respectively.[106] Lastly, incarceration itself often did little to redeem the person, often setting the inmate up for prison violence, rape, contraction of HIV-AIDS and other sexually transmitted diseases, and improvement on whatever criminal skills they already possessed. Sexual violence in prison, long a joke to those never incarcerated, was prevalent within the walls of America's prisons. According to the Bureau of Justice Statistics National Inmate Survey for 2008–09, at least 49.4 percent of male inmates who spent more than thirty days in prison experienced some form of sexual victimization. Women experienced some form of sexual victimization, according to the same criteria, at 65.7 percent.[107] At a time of globalization, removal of trade and regulatory barriers, and stagnant or declining wages, African Americans caught in the grip of the criminal justice system were, generally speaking, consigned to America's permanent underclass.

African American imprisonment takes a major toll on the inmates' parents, children, and spouses or cohabitants. Professor Rose M. Brewer has found that "over half of incarcerated Black men with children lived with those children before incarceration. Any emotional and economic support provided by the fathers has been removed."[108] Without the presence of both parents, many children fall between the cracks. Scholars of the criminal justice system refer to this phenomenon as "collateral consequences." In testimony before the House Judiciary Subcommittee on Crime, Terrorism, and Homeland Security in June 2010, Marc Mauer reported the tragedies that befall these communities. Mauer testified, "The conglomeration of collateral consequences can now touch every aspect of an individual's life, affecting employment, housing, education, military service, public benefits, driver's licenses, child custody, voting, and jury service, among others."[109] Far-ranging consequences of imprisonment on the individual, the family, and the community meant that society's most vulnerable children often fell into poverty and dangerous personal behavior. African American men were far likelier to go to prison, especially between the ages of fourteen and thirty-four, which obviously is during the peak childbearing and childrearing years. Because of the fact that those men were not there to help raise those children, those youngsters were more likely to fall into crime, poverty, and prison.

Making the situation worse were spatial considerations. Roberts notes, "Because poor black men and women tend to live in racially and economically segregated neighborhoods, these neighborhoods feel the brunt of the staggering prison figures. . . . As many as 1 in 8 of the adult male residents of these urban areas is sent to prison each year and 1 in 4 is behind bars on any given day."[110] Therefore, mass incarceration contributed to the breakdown of African American communities. As might be expected, the vast majority of these convicts come from poor backgrounds. Race and class often condemned these inmates by raising obstacles that they could not possibly overcome.

Once those inmates were released from prison, they found themselves in the often impossible position of trying to find a job. Recent studies demonstrate that minorities, especially black men, have extreme difficulties finding full-time jobs after their release from prison. Many cannot even get a call back from prospective employers for an interview. Even when they do, they find that white applicants, sometimes with similar records and credentials, get the jobs. The buildup of the so-called prison industrial complex, strengthened by Clinton's 1994 crime bill, made a bad situation even worse. The effects of imprisonment on lower-class black men are staggering. Pettit and Western have discovered that "among black men born between 1965 and 1969, 30 percent of those without college education and nearly 60 percent of high school dropouts went to prison by 1999. The novel pervasiveness of imprisonment indicates the emergence of incarceration as a new stage in the life course of young low-skill black men."[111] Further, Devah Pager wrote, "A criminal record presents a major barrier to employment, with important implications for racial disparities."[112] Beyond employment difficulties, if drugs were at least part of the reason for their incarceration, then they could lose their access to public housing. As Alexander explained, "Clinton also made it easier for federally-assisted public housing projects to exclude anyone with a criminal history—an extraordinary harsh step in the midst of a drug war aimed at racial and ethnic minorities."[113] Ex-convicts found themselves without jobs or a home in many instances, which, according to Pettit and Western and Pager, prevented them from moving into adulthood, with all the responsibilities that apply.

Occupational hurdles, such as the attachment of felony records to defendants, have long-lasting repercussions for the entire society. Jeff Manza and Christopher Uggen point out that "the case of felon disenfranchisement is a powerful reminder that even the most basic elements of democratic governance, such as a universal right to vote, can still be threatened in a polity otherwise asserting its democratic credentials."[114] The crime bill, ironically, helped shape the 2000 presidential election because hundreds of thousands were denied the right to vote because of prior criminal acts. As Lawson argued, "the first presidential election of the twenty-first century underlined both the importance and the vulnerability of black ballots . . . [and] the ensuing struggle [in Florida] revealed new forms of black disenfranchisement, though revelations of injustices failed to reverse the results of the election."[115]

With spiking incarceration rates and the resulting, troubling impact on families and former convicts, and with growing domestic and international economic competition, African Americans found themselves even further from the so-called American dream. Other minority groups, such as Asians and, in some cases, Latinos, were surpassing African Americans politically, economically, educationally, and socially for prominence as the twenty-first century dawned. Finally, to add insult to injury, the dramatic increase of African Americans in prison, on probation, or parole means their political participation is diminished. Mauer testified, "As a result of laws that disenfranchise felons and ex-felons in various states, an estimated 1.4 million African American males, or 13% of the black male adult population, is either currently or permanently disenfranchised as a result of a felony conviction. . . . Thus, not only are criminal justice policies contributing to the disproportionate incarceration of African Americans, but imprisonment itself then reduces the collective political ability to influence these policies."[116] Without greater participation in the political process, African Americans collectively were placed at a significant disadvantage to improve their position through the political process. In the presidential elections of 2000 and 2004, thousands of potential African Americans voters could not vote because of felony convictions. In states such as Florida and Ohio, Republican George W. Bush was able to declare victory and take the presidency, in part, because of the lack of higher voting participation among African Americans. It was a cruel irony for Al Gore and John Kerry that their strong support for get-tough crime legislation helped to deny them the White House. Lastly, the decision to support such legislation and not to reform already existing drug laws contributed to Republicans reaching the zenith of political power between 2001 and 2007 in all three branches of government, two decades after the Reagan revolution.

Conclusion

Presidential authority is a vague concept. Scholars in the fields of history and political science and government spend entire careers examining the trends, various events, and empirical data, searching for the source of a particular president's power and authority. While it is true that a president does not pass legislation, it is equally true that a president can and often does hold great sway. The 1994 crime bill did include such measures as the Violence Against Women Act and an increased focus on terrorists. But the New Democratic philosophy of the Clinton White House helped contribute to the mass imprisonment of millions of African Americans. As Alexander notes, "This move, like his 'get tough' rhetoric and policies, was part of a grand strategy articulated by the 'new democrats' to appeal to the elusive white swing voters. In so doing, Clinton—more than any other president—created the current racial undercaste."[117] It destroyed too many lives by putting forth the solution of building more prisons over rehabilitative measures that might actually increase security, save lives, and improve American society. President Clinton's endorsement of the withdrawal of the Racial Justice Act and his cynical manipulation of the American public's fears led to the passage of a bill that was punitive in scope and intent, as well as demonstrative of the pernicious effects of a "values" agenda. Clinton, as well versed as anyone in the various theories on crime, knew or should have known that simple solutions, such as locking them up and throwing away the key, were not only inadequate but often compounded the problem. Violent crime had actually been dropping since the beginning of the decade, without serious investigation into why violent crime was decreasing during the 1990s to all-time lows. It was simply believed that the 1994 bill, combined with a booming economy and lower deficits, was the reason for the decline. In fact, the Clinton White House's rationale for the decline was simply that there was more funding and more enforcement since prioritizing crime as a major issue. Bruce Reed, senior advisor and head of President Clinton's Domestic Policy Council, wrote in *Blueprint*, a New Democrat magazine, in the early months after Clinton left office, "The Justice budget doubled under Clinton because the nation chose to confront crime as a national problem."[118]

Some pundits have compared the often-unruly American electorate to an irrational mob; even some of the founding fathers sought to diminish the influence of those so-called commoners. America's often-hysterical reaction to crime, as spurred on by politicians and the media, provided President Clinton with the wiggle room to push the Congress to pass this legislation. As Vesla M. Weaver has argued in a prescient article on the development of crime policy after the Civil Rights Act of 1964 and Voting Rights Act of 1965, "punitive policy intervention was not merely an exercise in crime fighting; it both responded to and moved the agenda on racial equality."[119] This concept of *frontlash*, as presented by Weaver, is a policy whereby "formerly defeated groups may become dominant issue entrepreneurs in light of the development of a new issue campaign."[120] Clinton played, willingly, into the hands of those groups that sought to criminalize, demonize, or otherwise ostracize African Americans. In his determination to keep his coalition together, he pushed crime policies that rarely took into consideration other avenues to crime prevention.

President Clinton held strong majorities in both the House of Representatives and the Senate, the trust of the African American and white communities, and the personal ability to craft legislation in a more progressive fashion. While he had those majorities in Congress, as Randall Kennedy wrote, "he had made it plain that his sympathies lay predominately with 'the middle class.' For those below it, he offered chastising lectures that legitimated the essentially conservative notion that the predicament of the poor results primarily from their own conduct and not from the deformative deprivations imposed on them by a grievously unfair social order that is in large part a class hierarchy and in smaller part a pigmentocracy."[121] In *The New Jim Crow: Mass Incarceration in the Age of Colorblindness*, Alexander argues that the "law and order perspective, first introduced during the peak of the Civil Rights Movement by rabid segregationists, had become nearly hegemonic two decades later." Further, she writes, "Ninety percent of those admitted to prison for drug offenses in many states were black or Latino, yet the mass incarceration of communities of color was explained in race-neutral terms, an adaptation to the needs and demands of the current political climate."[122] This adaptation, as Alexander calls it, was found in the political rhetoric, political behavior, and, ultimately, the Violent Crime Control and Law Enforcement Act of 1994. Clinton did not cave in to Republican demands for punishment so much as he fulfilled the New Democratic vision of crime policy. In the process, he helped to create what Alexander called a "new racial caste system." Clinton's good intentions were at odds with the often-horrific consequences. Since crime policy overwhelmingly impacted poor African Americans, it was more acceptable to the American public. Besides, as many politicians remarked at the time, those people only had themselves to blame for their lot in life and they to be held accountable. However, on another controversial issue, affirmative action, Clinton's actions would win back support from the African American political class that he had sacrificed to get Congress to pass the Violent Crime Control and Law Enforcement of 1994.

CHAPTER 5

"Mend It, Don't End It"

The Politics of Affirmative Action

AFFIRMATIVE ACTION! Rarely in American politics does a two-word phrase conjure up so many different meanings, so much resentment, and so much passion. Opponents of affirmative action argued that it promotes division, acts as reverse racism, and is antithetical to American ideals of individualism, fairness, and merit-based opportunity. Supporters of affirmative action consider the program a necessary step to ensure equal opportunity in the workplace and education because of persistent racism and discrimination. It has been a favorite target of campaigning politicians since President Richard Nixon began implementing the Philadelphia Plan in the late 1960s and early 1970s. By the beginning of the Clinton administration in 1993, the politics of affirmative action had reached a boiling point.

Since 1978, when the US Supreme Court decided *Regents of the University of California v. Bakke* and forced the admission of Allan Bakke to its medical school, opponents of affirmative action had looked to the courts, as well as to the political process, to eliminate these programs.[1] President Bill Clinton's support of affirmative action, however, had been a critical link to his African American supporters. He campaigned on supporting the program in spite of a New Democratic philosophy that viewed affirmative action suspiciously. As New Democrats noted in the New Orleans Declaration of 1990,

"We believe the promise of America is equal opportunity, not equal outcome."[2] In the wake of the president's withdrawal of Lani Guinier from consideration for assistant attorney general for civil rights and the passage of the crime bill without a racial justice provision, Clinton had a fresh opportunity to demonstrate his civil rights bona fides by supporting the controversial program after the Supreme Court delivered its decision in *Adarand Constructors, Inc. v. Pena*.[3] The Supreme Court's ruling that race-based programs must be able to survive "strict scrutiny" compelled Clinton to defend the program while also adhering to the law. His response galvanized his supporters and angered his opponents. The president's strong defense of affirmative action unveiled critical answers as to the politics of race and class during the 1990s.

Brief History of Affirmative Action

The principle of affirmative action dates back to the Kennedy administration in the early 1960s. President John F. Kennedy signed Executive Order 10925 on March 6, 1961, establishing the Presidential Committee on Equal Employment Opportunity. In section 201, Kennedy ordered the committee to "scrutinize and study employment practices of the Government of the United States, and to consider and recommend additional affirmative steps which should be taken by executive departments and agencies to realize more fully the national policy of nondiscrimination within the executive branch of the Government."[4] In other words, the origins of affirmative action would start at the federal level, with emphasis placed on dislodging discrimination and opening opportunity to African Americans in employment. Further, federal contractors were targeted by the Kennedy administration for biased practices. In section 301 of Kennedy's executive order, he ordered that contractors "will take affirmative action to ensure that applicants are employed, and that employees are treated during employment, without regard to their race, creed, color, or national origin."[5] These major steps toward equal opportunity took on a new meaning after Kennedy's assassination in November 1963.

Lyndon B. Johnson promised to carry on Kennedy's efforts in the civil rights arena. Beyond pushing for the passage of the Civil Rights Act of 1964 and Voting Rights Act of 1965, Johnson assessed race relations in the 1960s and concluded that laws were not enough. In one of his most important speeches on race at the commencement exercises at Howard University, President Johnson outlined the rationale that would be used by supporters ever since:

> Freedom is the right to share, share fully and equally, in American society—to vote, to hold a job, to enter a public place, to go to school. It is the right to be treated in every part of our national life as a person equal in dignity and promise to all others. But freedom is not enough. You do not wipe away the scars of centuries by saying: Now you are free to go where you want, and do as you desire, and choose the leaders you please. You do not take a person who, for years, has been hobbled by chains and liberate him, bring him up to the starting line of a race and then say, "you are free to compete with all the others," and still justly believe that you have been completely fair.[6]

Historian David C. Carter has noted that "the increased attention that the Howard address paid to glaring and persistent economic inequalities faced by the majority of African Americans served as the harbinger of passionate and often angry debates over what historian Hugh Davis Graham has labeled 'compensatory justice.'"[7] What Graham called "compensatory justice," or affirmative action, and what Carter called the Johnson administration's increased concern over "persistent economic inequalities" was the real concern that laws were not enough to rectify the situation. Essentially, race and racism were coded into the American DNA. Laws could deter or prevent lynchings, beatings, and intimidation, but laws, by themselves, could not compel white Americans to treat African Americans fairly in education or the workplace. Therefore, at the heart of Johnson's message was the recognition that America's racial past and present presented significant barriers to equal opportunity and economic, social, educational, and political mobility. In order to address this conundrum, "affirmative" steps must be taken to give those without privilege an opportunity to realize their potential. The government would coerce employers doing business with the government to open opportunity to minorities. Educational institutions, spurred on by the Rights Revolution and the governments' example, by the end of the 1960s were admitting African Americans to their student ranks.[8] These changes, part and parcel of the civil rights movement, led to dramatic changes in American society.

President Johnson's desires to eradicate poverty, educate the uneducated, and bring equality to blacks eventually were at odds with his foreign policy. The morass of Vietnam, however, put increasing pressure on Johnson to choose priorities. On one side, Martin Luther King Jr., A. Phillip Randolph, most of organized labor and Chicanos, and Johnson aide Walter Heller argued that the war was a threat to the Great Society. The other side, pushing Johnson for escalation in Vietnam, included Mississippi senator John Stennis, Arizona senator Barry Goldwater, and conservative foreign policy hawks in his own administration determined to prevent communist advances in Southeast Asia. Further, as Carter noted, "more conservative forces were pressuring the administration to go slow on antipoverty programs. Some like Mississippi's John Stennis, had even threatened to hold Vietnam appropriations hostage."[9] In the wake of the recent assassination of John F. Kennedy, Johnson felt compelled, as historians Maurice Isserman and Michael Kazin argue, "to prove to the Republicans that he was tough on communism, he also had to prove to his own party that he was as strong a leader as the slain president."[10] So Johnson was confronted with a combination of pressures from conservatives, liberals, rights' activists, and his own conscience. As far as affirmative action and the Great Society were concerned, Johnson "felt a challenge in gaining support from black America for the Vietnam War, and the conflict cast a long shadow over the relationships between the Johnson Administration and black protest movements in this period."[11] The growth of peace activism within the civil rights community increasingly put activists at odds with Johnson, thereby creating an almost unbearable situation of tension, resentment, and mistrust. LBJ's decision to escalate the Vietnam War spelled the end of the Great Society and contributed to growing animosity between him and the supporters of progressive domestic policies. The heavy lifting regarding affirmative action, therefore, was left to his successor, Richard Milhous Nixon.

President Nixon rode a wave of resentment and anger into the White House in 1968. While he appealed to racists with his law-and-order rhetoric, he also viewed America as an upward-running escalator where there was room for more middle-class people. Nixon, like many of his contemporaries, believed in the idea of a full employment economy. Besides a growing black middle class, the Republican Party could garner support from a voting bloc that by 1964 had become solidly Democratic, thereby further splintering the old New Deal coalition. Christopher Edley wrote, "The Nixon Administration introduced affirmative action goals and timetables . . . precisely because the nondiscrimination command alone had not changed job patterns at firms with federal contracts."[12] In essence, Nixon envisioned room for blacks and whites to move beyond their present condition. Arthur Fletcher, who was black and assistant secretary of labor, developed the Philadelphia Plan. Building upon the Kennedy and Johnson initiatives, Fletcher and his superiors decided that those engaged in work on behalf of the federal government had to develop hiring goals for blacks. If they failed to meet those goals, then they would be penalized. It became the model for affirmative action in business programs. Compelling businesses to comply with all applicable laws and to foster an atmosphere of inclusion and equal opportunity, Fletcher's design brought more African Americans into the mainstream. Yet, it was also a cynical tool to split the Democratic coalition of black and white labor, taking from one to give to the other. The carrot-and-stick approach used for the rest of the century to create equal opportunity and full employment practices by the business community often fostered division. By accepting and promoting diversity in the workplace, corporations could boost that they were open-minded and inoculate themselves from potential lawsuits alleging racial or sexual bias. However, conservative complaints about Nixon's affirmative action plans and his liberal social policies forced Nixon to roll back his public support for programs that helped minorities as he ramped up his campaign for reelection in 1972.

By the 1990s, affirmative action was responsible, in part, for the growth of the black middle class. Sharon Collins noted in a 1983 study that as a result of government efforts to "improve the economic and social position of blacks . . . blacks have moved into a wider range of professions and higher income brackets, creating a black middle class."[13] Yet this growth remained inferior to the white middle class, deepening the support from African American politicians, middle class professionals, and activists for a policy that had provided significant gains toward economic stability. Mary Pattillo-McCoy notes, "Unlike most whites, middle-class black families must contend with the crime, dilapidated housing, and social disorder in the deteriorating poor neighborhoods that continue to grow in their direction."[14] Ironically, as a result of the Civil Rights Act of 1964, women of all colors benefited—white women most of all—from affirmative action. The result of this social experiment was not only greater opportunities for those previously excluded, but also debates as to its fairness and constitutionality. Those opposed looked to the courts when a young, white, prospective medical student challenged a state university's decision to reject his application.

Legal Challenges to Affirmative Action

By the 1970s most institutions of higher education were eagerly seeking minority students for undergraduate, graduate, and professional programs. While businesses were compelled to provide equal opportunity to minority applicants, higher education officials, prompted by pressure for cultural diversity, created intricate admissions systems that set aside seats for minority students. The main argument for creating what amounted to a two-tiered system was that the presence of minorities, especially African Americans, enriched the intellectual atmosphere on campus. In addition, the education provided to the student body would increase from different life experiences of minorities and women. While these systems made significant improvements in integrating African Americans into white institutions, they also provoked resentment from white applicants who believed that they were denied admission based on race.

In 1973, and again in 1974, Allan Bakke was denied admission into the School of Medicine at the University of California at Davis. Bakke sued the university and its governing body, the Regents of the University of California, seeking relief from the courts in the form of admission into the medical school. Central to his case was the argument that the point system and special preferences of the medical school violated his constitutional rights, specifically, the Fourteenth Amendment and the Equal Protection Clause. Sixteen out of one hundred seats at UC Davis were set aside for minorities; the courts ruled that the policy therefore constituted a quota system. UC Davis was ordered to admit Bakke forthwith. Justice Lewis Powell, who wrote the majority opinion for the Supreme Court, argued:

> Racial and ethnic classifications of any sort are inherently suspect and call for the most exacting judicial scrutiny. While the goal of achieving a diverse student body is sufficiently compelling to justify consideration of race in admissions decisions under some circumstances, petitioner's special admissions programs, which forecloses consideration to persons like respondent, is unnecessary to the achievement of this compelling goal, and therefore invalid under the Equal Protection Clause.[15]

In laymen's terms, the court ruled that quotas were illegal and a violation of the Fourteenth Amendment. The decision, however, was a partial win for proponents of affirmative action as it upheld the underlying motivation—to increase diversity in higher education and professional schools because it served a compelling societal interest.

In *Fullilove v. Klutznick*, the court heard "several associations of construction contractors and subcontractors and a firm engaged in heating, ventilation, and air conditioning work, [who] filed suit for declaratory and injunctive relief in Federal District Court, alleging that they had sustained economic injury due to enforcement of the MBE [Minority Business Enterprise] . . . violated, inter alia, the Equal Protection Clause of the 14th Amendment and the equal protection component of the Due Process Clause of the 5th Amendment."[16] It was argued by the government that the set-asides were legitimate and constitutional because they did not discriminate against non-minorities and narrowly focused on a small percentage of the business community. Chief Justice Warren Burger, writing the majority opinion for the court, opined, "The MBE provision of the 1977 Act, on its face, does not violate the Constitution."[17] In a victory for affirmative-action supporters, the court declared the quotas were permissible in business and that the 1977 Public Works Employment Act's MBE was constitutional.

In what came to be called *Wygant v. Jackson Board of Education* in

1986, the plaintiffs appealed the decision of the Sixth Court of Appeals to the Supreme Court for certiorari.[18] As the Supreme Court notes, the district court upheld the constitutionality of the provision "as an attempt to remedy societal discrimination by providing 'role models' for minority schoolchildren," and an appellate court affirmed the decision.[19] Once again Justice Powell wrote the opinion for the court, saying, "Societal discrimination is too amorphous a basis for finding race-conscious state action and for imposing a racially classified remedy."[20]

In 1988, a case in which the plaintiff had been denied a contract based on Richmond, Virginia's Minority Business Utilization Plan reached the high court. This case came to be known as *City of Richmond v. Croson*.[21] The Minority Business Utilization Plan was designed to include businesses that were at least 51 percent owned by minorities. While African Americans were the principal target, Latinos, Asians, and Indians were also included in the plan. Richmond, being the former capital of the Confederacy, certainly had a racial history steeped in discrimination against African Americans. However, none of this history, or any empirical data, was presented to justify the city's plan to set aside 30 percent of each contract. Instead, the city declared the plan to simply be a "remedial effort" to correct past wrongs. The J. A. Croson Company sued for relief after being denied a contract despite being the only bidder. The lower federal courts upheld the plan as constitutional, following the city's reasoning that *Fullilove v. Klutznick* allowed such plans. The Supreme Court, however, saw the case differently and ruled the plan was unconstitutional and in violation of the Fourteenth Amendment's Equal Protection Clause. Justice O'Connor wrote, "The city has failed to demonstrate a compelling governmental interest justifying the Plan, since the factual predicate supporting the Plan does not establish the type of identified past discrimination in the city's construction industry that would authorize race-based relief under the 14th Amendment's Equal Protection Clause."[22]

While the public remains skeptical of race-based programs such as affirmative action, they have been supportive of programs that do not exclude whites altogether. As a result of the right of Modern Conservatism, hundreds of magistrates, district court judges, appellate judges, and Supreme Court justices have been appointed and confirmed, thereby guaranteeing more conservative interpretations the law.

The Ronald Reagan and George H. W. Bush administrations, with their power to nominate judges and justices, were presenting a major challenge to traditional Democratic orthodoxy about the legitimacy of race-based solutions to complex societal problems. The colorblind philosophy, however, was not only appealing to conservatives and Republicans but to moderate Democrats and Democratic advocacy groups, such as the Democratic Leadership Council, suspicious of such programs and eager to retake the American center.

The Colorblind Philosophy

Affirmative action has come to mean different things to different people. For some it is a well-intended effort to help those historically disadvantaged by racism and discrimination, often with positive results for the beneficiaries as well as society. Others have viewed it as a form of reverse discrimination against whites, taking away from whites for the benefit of unqualified blacks. Since there is no general consensus on what affirmative action actually is, even by experts, the policy has been vulnerable to mischaracterization and vilification. Despite the confusion over this controversial policy, there are some ways to describe it. Affirmative action is a policy which allows educators, bureaucrats, and businessmen to take race into consideration when a minority person applies for a job, seeks admittance into school, or attempts to build his or her company by obtaining government contracts for goods and services. Furthermore, it was clear by the passage of the 1964 Civil Rights Act and the Supreme Court's decision in *Brown v. Board of Education of Topeka* that mainstream, white America would not integrate willingly.[23] This is evidenced by the thousands of "private academies" and "Christian schools" that were created in the fifteen years after *Brown*. Yet, beyond attempts to maintain separation, whites—especially southern whites—tended not to hire African Americans for anything except manual labor or low-level work. So affirmative action was seen as the remedy to such entrenched racism. Thus, the government would compel mainstream society to accord equal opportunities to blacks. This, however, was not the first time the government had acted in such a provocative and deliberate manner. Ira Katznelson notes that the federal government, after the Civil War, has passed the Thirteenth, Fourteenth, and Fifteenth Amendments to the Constitution, enacted civil rights laws to protect those rights guaranteed by the civil rights amendments, and even created new institutions, such as the Freedmen's Bureau, to encourage and offer "remedial support to African Americans."[24] The end of Reconstruction and the implementation of Jim Crow laws, along with eventual government approval, prevented those initial steps toward equality from taking place. A hundred years later those questions of equality were still taking place in what historian C. Vann Woodward called the "Second Reconstruction." As such, race-conscious measures developed in the 1960s would be questioned by many—whites and blacks, Republicans and Democrats—as to their veracity and legitimacy in the 1980s and 1990s.

Conservatives and moderate Democrats responded to the social transformation of the 1960s by adopting the language of various movements, especially the civil rights movement. Legal scholar and Clinton aide Christopher Edley explained, "Critics of race-conscious measures often invoke Martin Luther King, Jr.'s 'content of their character' passage in urging that we hasten the realization of a color-blind society by insisting on color-blind practices now."[25] It is too much to say that opposition to affirmative action is solely based on tribal concerns. Edley also wrote, "A more sensible notion is that color should not be a consideration in public or private decisions about important economic and social opportunities."[26] Thomas Sowell, a black economist, argued that affirmative action takes away from those who benefit from it.[27] Supreme Court justice Clarence Thomas, a beneficiary of affirmative action during his undergraduate and law school years, came to view affirmative action as detrimental to the very people it was supposed to help. In his autobiography, Justice Thomas explained, "I'd long believed that the best thing to do was to stop government-sanctioned segregation, then concentrate on education and equal employment opportunities."[28] Government efforts, such as affirmative action, were misguided to Thomas. Colorblindness was the most desirable goal.

Thomas and Sowell were not alone in viewing race-conscious

measures as suspect. The growth of the black middle class in the 1970s and 1980s led to division within Black America as to what policies should be pursued. Hoover Institution scholar Shelby Steele refers to the affirmative action arrangement as one where blacks gain power through such "entitlement programs," while whites who support affirmative action can assuage themselves of guilt and gain innocence.[29] In *The Content of Our Character*, Steele argues that "what was wrong was that both races focused more on the goals of these mandates than on the means to the goals. Blacks can have no real power without taking responsibility for their own educational and economic development."[30] This is at the heart of much of the colorblind philosophy: equality of opportunity, fairness, merit-based selection, and personal and communal responsibility.

Yale law professor Stephen L. Carter, in *Reflections of an Affirmative Action Baby*, writes at length about his experiences in school and the workplace. Criticism of black professionals who benefited from affirmative action and suspicion of their credentials pervades the American landscape. Carter argues that affirmative action is the reason for such suspicion. Further, Carter argues that such programs not only complicate the lives of those who benefit from it, but also instill hostility from mainstream white America. In addition, Carter notes that affirmative action programs are redistributive, which interferes with American notions of self-reliance and equal opportunity.[31] Yet Carter touches on one of the important, but unspoken, gripes that conservatives often have against affirmative action: affirmative action has the ability to build a more inclusive society through the largesse of others, thereby eliminating individual initiative and increasing the role of government in the lives of the American people.

Former University of California–Berkeley professor and Manhattan Institute fellow John McWhorter has also been a vocal critic of affirmative action. Equally important, he has been an articulate critic of black culture and its impact on young blacks' chances for success. Neatly summarizing his and other affirmative action opponents' views in 2003, McWhorter noted, "People who recognize the folly of racial preferences are no more opposed to diversity in this sense than critics of 'gangsta' rap are opposed to music. What they do reject is the condescending notion that a diverse campus demands lower admissions standards for brown students, and that, in 2003 America, brown students need crutches to make it."[32] The difference between black critics such as Thomas, McWhorter, Sowell, and Steele and their white peers is that they can criticize affirmative action without being tarred as racist.

Liberals and many African Americans, especially in the political class, have used any opposition to affirmative action as grounds to denounce someone as racist. Particularly noteworthy is the fierce response from the Congressional Black Caucus, NAACP, National Urban League, and many black academics. Whites opposed to affirmative action promote like-minded black public intellectuals and politicians, demonstrating that colorblindness is not some nefarious plot to deny equal opportunity. Noted political scientist Andrew Hacker points out, "To support their position, they cite black conservatives— Thomas Sowell, Clarence Thomas, Shelby Steele—who assure them that blacks have played the victim too long and must be judged by the same standards as other Americans."[33] This does not deny the veracity of their position; in fact, it is demonstrative of the passionate debate raging within American society during the 1990s. That debate cannot be easily characterized as pro-minority or anti-minority; it is a dialectic over the progress of the civil rights movement and its implications for the present and future. The promotion of colorblindness has been embraced by both those opposed to racial progress and regular, average Americans of all colors and political leanings. The rise of black conservatives is demonstrative of the fact that perceptions of race-conscious remedies are no longer held in near universal acceptance within the African American community. Lastly, neo-conservatives and neo-liberals, both groups dissatisfied with the 1960s, found that much of their earlier support for liberal racial policies was misguided. Georgetown University sociologist and popular progressive writer E. J. Dionne has noted that these neoconservatives blamed the liberalism of the 1950s and 1960s—with its focus on rights, minorities, women, and diversity—for the problems of America in the 1970s and 1980s.[34] By promoting diversity, along with programs and initiatives that do not benefit all Americans, a schism is created within American society. Those who benefit from such programs are, therefore, forever tainted as suspect.

In fact, it is this conundrum that confronted President Clinton and the Democratic Leadership Council during the late 1980s through the 1990s. As the "Third Way" faction of the Democratic Party, it had to straddle the line: embracing the ascendant colorblind philosophy while recognizing the benefits that affirmative action had provided to both African Americans and women. This understanding was grounded in acceptance of different popular views of affirmative action. Ward Connerly, an African American member of the Regents of the University of California and opponent of affirmative action, argued that "state and federal policies should not be dictated by the assumption that college enrollments must reflect the population patterns of a state."[35] Civil rights icon and George Mason University history professor Roger Wilkins countered, "The fact is that the successful public relations assault on affirmative action flows on a river of racism that is as broad, powerful and American as the Mississippi."[36] Polling data from 1997 demonstrated that 82 percent of African Americans thought affirmative action should be increased or kept the same, while 51 percent of whites believed the same.[37] But the presence of a growing cabal of black conservative/anti-affirmative-action advocates presented a new dynamic in the debate of the controversial issue. The Democratic Leadership Council was ahead of the national Democrats in this regard.

The DLC's moderate position attracted middle-class African Americans who were also skeptical of such measures. The DLC adopted a resolution at their meeting in Cleveland, Ohio, in May 1991, that stated, "We believe the role of government is to guarantee equal opportunity, not mandate equal outcomes. We reaffirm the Democratic Party's historic commitment to secure civil, equal, and human rights. We oppose discrimination of any kind—including quotas. . . . Where others seek to exploit racial differences for political advantage, we support a broad opportunity agenda to give all Americans the tools to get ahead."[38] Clinton argued five days later that the colorblind versus race-conscious solution was a "bogus debate" because "the Republicans have set it up so that, if you are for the civil rights bill [of 1991], you have got to be for quotas, so that if you are not for quotas we have to say you are for discrimination."[39] Clinton argued instead for a middle approach that recognized the grievances of whites while endorsing the need to help those discriminated against because of race. The colorblind philosophy, appealing to many, was politically dicey as numerous academics, intellectuals, and politicos used the affirmative action issue to support their own causes. This contentious debate confronted President Clinton head-on when the Supreme Court of the United States handed down a rigid ruling that forced his hand.

The Critical Case:
Adarand Constuctors, Inc. v. Pena (1995)

In early 1995 the Supreme Court heard a case brought by a construction company, Adarand Constructors. Adarand Constructors sought relief through summary judgment because the Small Business Administration (SBA) maintained a special clause in its contracts, as did most of the federal government, to give incentives to companies to hire minority subcontractors who were determined to be disadvantaged by the SBA. According to the syllabus attached to the court's decision, "The District Court granted respondents summary judgment. In affirming, the Court of Appeals assessed the constitutionality of the federal race-based action under a lenient standard, resembling intermediate scrutiny, which it determined was required by *Fullilove v. Klutznick*, 448 U.S. 448, and *Metro Broadcasting, Inc. v. FCC*, 497 U.S. 547."[40] The plaintiffs claimed that the SBA's plans, specifically, sections 8(a) and 8(d), violated the Fifth Amendment's Due Process clause.[41] Justice Sandra Day O'Connor wrote the majority opinion for the court. The lower courts' verdicts were vacated and the case was remanded. O'Connor stated that Adarand "has met the requirements necessary to maintain its claim by alleging an invasion of a legally protected interest in a particularized manner, and by showing that it is very likely to bid, in the relatively near future, on another Government contract offering financial incentives to a prime contractor for hiring disadvantaged subcontractors."[42] The court rejected the "intermediate scrutiny" argument of the lower courts, saying, "All racial classifications, imposed by whatever federal, state, or local governmental actor, must be analyzed by a reviewing court under strict scrutiny."[43] Therefore, the less stringent standard of intermediate scrutiny used up to that point was no longer valid; the courts had to ascertain whether or not the program in question was not only constitutional, in a broad sense, but whether or not it served a "compelling governmental interest."

The reality of this decision was that the Clinton administration would have to reevaluate all 130 affirmative action programs at the federal level to make sure that they complied with the Supreme Court's latest decision. In addition, the use of the "strict scrutiny" standard delivered a harsh blow to affirmative action proponents and made it more difficult to sustain affirmative action programs. Using the intermediate standard to judge whether an affirmative action program was constitutionally viable allowed government, business, and education officials more latitude in implementing their own programs. The court's determination that programs must be able to survive strict scrutiny marked a turning point in jurisprudence. It narrowed the ability of these actors to install such programs and pushed them to find more race -neutral measures to secure equal opportunity. As a result, openly race-conscious programs fell off as various actors tried to conform to the court's new position. African Americans, therefore, faced fewer opportunities to gain a foothold into mainstream society. Affirmative action was imperiled and African American members of Congress, advocacy groups, and liberals demanded a strong response from President Clinton. Anticipating the court's ruling, Clinton ordered, on March 7, 1995, a comprehensive review of affirmative action programs in the federal government.

White House Affirmative Action Review (1995)

As the Supreme Court pondered the arguments presented in *Adarand v. Pena*, the Clinton administration began to consider the implications of the court's decision on the future of affirmative action. Clinton asked three specific questions to his administration in evaluating federal affirmative action programs: (1) What are these programs? (2) Are they working? (3) Is there some other way we can reach any objective without giving a preference by race or gender in some of these programs?[44] The president was looking for the review to be "a valuable starting point for a national conversation on the challenges of creating truly equal opportunity."[45] The White House staff saw the issue as one where the president could fulfill his commitment to diversity, to equal opportunity, and to the African American political community. Also, the affirmative action review would give the administration a chance to reform preference programs ahead of possible challenges to their legitimacy.

In order to accomplish these tasks, the report produced by George Stephanopoulos and Christopher Edley "summarizes that evidence and, where appropriate, offers preliminary conclusions of fact based on that evidence."[46] The specific policy objectives and challenges presented by the president included these: to "restore the American Dream of opportunity," to find "common ground," and to "bring the American people together into a stronger community."[47] Whereas the president and the DLC crowd were being criticized from both the left and right for practicing a politics based on consensus, the affirmative action issue for Clinton became a matter of opportunity. If the president could engage the public in a civil discussion on the benefits of affirmative action in ensuring equal opportunity, then a program considered by most African Americans and independents as more helpful, or at least more benign than destructive, could be defused of its politically divisive nature. If it could be defused, then a major fault line in late twentieth-century race relations could be neutralized.

A memo written more than a year earlier illustrates that the administration was concerned about substance as well as appearances. On January 28, 1994, Alexis Herman, advisor to the president, sent a memo to Clinton regarding civil rights policy. Trying to make the best of the president's upcoming nominee for assistant attorney general for the Civil Rights Division of the Department of Justice in the wake of the Guinier episode, Herman pointed out that the lack of a head for the Civil Rights Division had "heightened the discussion that the Administration lacks a coordinated civil rights policy. We have an opportunity to articulate a framework/philosophy when you announce the intent to nominate the Assistant Attorney General for Civil Rights next week."[48] While the rumination about the nomination of a subcabinet official, at first glance, bears little in common with the review of affirmative action, this memo is revealing for its emphasis on moving past just enforcing the law to actually promoting the very type of opportunity that affirmative action could provide. As Herman explained, "even after we eliminate barriers to justice and create opportunities, we must still empower people to help themselves."[49] Affirmative action, conducted properly, was a policy Clinton embraced because it could be based on themes central to his political persona: responsibility, opportunity, and community. In essence, people doing what they should be doing should be helped by the federal government, especially when evidence demonstrated that African Americans often were discriminated against in education and the workplace. For most African Americans, as well as the Clinton administration, affirmative action was a civil rights issue.

As the administration began its review, academics, journalists, pundits, and governmental agencies trained their lenses on whether or not affirmative action actually worked as advertised by its supporters. An internal report by the Department of Labor concluded that "there is 'no widespread abuse' of affirmative action programs in employment and that there are only a small number of reported reverse discrimination cases by white males—a high proportion of which have been dismissed by federal courts."[50] The report also concluded that based on an analysis of four years of federal court cases involving job and employment discrimination, between only "1 and 3% of some 3,000 reported employment discrimination cases between 1990 and 1994" involved reverse discrimination.[51] This type of empirical data was important for an administration trying to debunk allegations that affirmative action led to "reverse discrimination" and that race-based programs were inherently biased, which was one of the central tenets of a conservative, colorblind orthodoxy. Opponents further argued that race-based preferences seek to correct a historical wrong at the expense of white Americans who had no role in the oppression of African Americans and women, and they contend that affirmative action unnecessarily penalizes those it is designed to help the most: minorities and women. The affirmative action review, however, revealed that "before the Civil Rights Act of 1964, the median black male worker earned only about 60 percent as much as the median white male worker; by 1993, the median black male earned 74 percent as much as the median white male. The male-female wage gap has also narrowed since the 1960s: median female earnings relative to median male earnings rose from about 60 percent during the 1960s to 72 percent in 1993."[52] The Glass Ceiling Commission, created by President Bush in 1991, concluded that "the fears and prejudices of lower-rung white male executives were listed as a principal barrier to the advancement of women and minorities."[53] The Glass Ceiling Commission only confirmed what empirical data had already proven: whites had an almost insurmountable advantage in access to education, employment opportunities, and upward mobility.[54] In general, the review found that affirmative measures, along with statutory enhancements such as the Civil Rights Act of 1964, had contributed substantially to the growth of the black middle class. These improvements led to the perception that whatever the drawbacks of such programs, their existence had to be protected from judicial revision and political acts by affirmative actions' opponents.

While charges of abuse and inefficiency plagued affirmative action and hurt non-minorities, the Clinton administration review revealed this:

> There is no systemic qualitative evidence that productivity is lower in contracting firms as a result of OFCCP. The one systematic study found that contractors do not appear to have lower productivity, suggesting that OFCCP has not caused firms to hire or promote less qualified workers.[55]

The Office of Federal Contract Compliance Programs, which ensures that companies doing business with the government do not discriminate against minorities and administers federal affirmative action programs, disabused the notion that affirmative action resulted in lower-quality work and lower productivity from companies engaged in race-based measures.[56] Further, "OFFCP administers and enforces three legal authorities that require equal employment opportunity: Executive Order 11246 as amended; Section 503 of the Rehabilitation Act of 1973, as amended; and the Vietnam Veterans' Readjustment Assistance Act of 1974, as amended, 38 U.S.C. 4212 . . . [and] require Federal contractors and subcontractors to take affirmative action."[57] What the affirmative action review revealed was that it did not lead to blatant discrimination. In fact, it was as good for business as it was for minorities. Business often needed those minority faces in order to attract customers, shoppers, and consideration from local, state, and federal agencies to secure contracts.

The affirmative action review urged that government agencies "establish a process to review the effective and fairness of affirmative action programs on a continuing basis, using the principles described in this report."[58] The report demanded the elimination of any program that "creates a quota; creates preferences for unqualified individuals; creates reverse discrimination; or continues even after its equal opportunity purposes have been achieved."[59] Clinton himself went much further in a memorandum to the administration dated the same day as he delivered an address at the National Archives. He wrote that "in every instance, we will seek reasonable ways to achieve the objectives of inclusion and antidiscrimination without specific reliance on group membership. But where our legitimate objectives cannot be achieved through such means, the Federal Government will continue to support lawful consideration of race, ethnicity, and gender under programs that are flexible, realistic, subject to reevaluation, and fair."[60] To protect against a knee-jerk reaction on the part of government agencies, the assistant attorney general, Walter Dellinger, in a memorandum to general counsels throughout the government, warned that "no affirmative action program should be suspended prior to such an evaluation" to determine if they "comport with the strict scrutiny standard" set by the Supreme Court in *Adarand v. Pena*.[61] With the review concluded and the orders sent government-wide, now it was the president's turn to publicly state his and the government's position. This position would deepen America's commitment to affirmation action while acknowledging that there were some flaws.

President Clinton's Support for Affirmative Action

The fight to preserve affirmative action reveals the importance President Clinton placed on merit-based opportunity for all Americans. As the child of a lower-middle-class family, Clinton was acutely aware of the importance of affirmative action programs for historically disadvantaged groups. There is arguably no group of Americans—aside from Native Americans—more historically disadvantaged than African

Americans. When the review of affirmative action concluded with the final report presented to the president in July 1995, Clinton delivered a major speech on affirmative action at the National Archives and Records Administration in Washington, D.C. On July 19, 1995, Clinton spoke unequivocally in favor of the controversial program.

Justifying his support for affirmative action, the president told the audience that:

> The purpose of affirmative action is to give our Nation a way to finally address the systemic exclusion of individuals of talent on the basis of their gender or race, from opportunities to develop, perform, achieve, and contribute. Affirmative action is an effort to develop a systematic approach to open the doors of education, employment, and business development opportunities to qualified individuals who happen to be members of groups that have experienced longstanding and persistent discrimination.[62]

Beyond stating what many already knew and giving the obligatory tip-of-the-hat to slaves, women, and civil rights heroes, Clinton defended race-based programs by trying to dispel the notion that quotas and unqualified people were being given unfair advantages. He said that the employers "may cut corners and treat a flexible goal as a quota. They may give opportunities to people who are unqualified instead of those who deserve it. . . . But it isn't affirmative action, and it is not legal."[63] In acknowledging that some whites may have legitimate claims that such programs hurt them, Clinton was able to straddle the proverbial fence by relieving the doubts of many whites that his administration would fight against such illegal actions, while defending a program considered sacrosanct by members of the Congressional Black Caucus and the broader African American community.

Clinton said, "Most economists who study it agree that affirmative action has also been an important part of closing gaps in economic opportunity in our society, thereby strengthening the entire economy."[64] Tying in economic benefits with social benefits conferred more legitimacy to the now vulnerable program. To drive his point home, Clinton remarked, "A group of distinguished business leaders told me just a couple of days ago that their companies are stronger and their profits are larger because of the diversity and the excellence of their work forces achieved through intelligent and fair affirmative action programs."[65] After delivering a firm defense, in general, of affirmative action, Clinton unveiled the results of his administration's review.

The review, as noted earlier, did not reveal critical problems that would warrant ending affirmative action programs. Clinton's administration would "mend" programs that could be or were being abused. Clinton took the Supreme Court's ruling in *Adarand v. Pena* as a challenge to be embraced in the name of uplifting Americans.[66] Clinton told those in the audience that summer day:

> If properly done, affirmative action can help us come together, go forward, and grow together. It is in our moral, legal, and practical interest to see that every person can make the most of his own life. In the fight for the future, we need all hands on deck, and some of those hands still need a helping hand.[67]

Clinton's speech was arguably the most sophisticated, erudite defense of affirmative action since Lyndon Johnson's famous address at Howard University. Clinton's ability to boil down affirmative action to a specific set of goals and to convey the importance of such programs to America's economic and moral health would remain just that without following through on the policy and political ends. But his support of the policy also demonstrated his belief in opportunity: affirmative action gave opportunity to deserving people who otherwise would have been shut out of a school, university, and job. Clinton's defense of affirmative action at the National Archives in July 1995 was the beginning of his administration's efforts to defend the controversial policy against a wave of popular opposition.

The Defense of Affirmative Action after the Review

In the wake of the president's strong defense of affirmative action, the Clinton administration simultaneously tried to balance its constitutional obligation to enforce the law as declared by Congress and the Supreme Court and maintain its commitment to race-based programs. The first impulse of the administration was to build upon the recommendations as listed in the review. In evaluating the effectiveness of

Department of Labor's Office of Federal Contract Compliance, the administration found that the use of affirmative action to promote equal opportunity in the workplace of business engaged in work with the government "has been and continues to be valuable, effective, and fair."[68] However, the likelihood of such programs in federal contracts being exploited by left and right and black and white remained high. In response, Edley and Stephanopoulos argued that the secretary of labor should be directed to "underscore and reinforce current law and policy regarding nondiscrimination, the illegality of quotas, the enforcement focus on 'good faith efforts,' and the relationship of equal opportunity to legitimate qualifications, by instituting appropriate changes in the administrative guidelines."[69] Expressing clear guidelines on race-based programs and allowing for race-neutral policies that were serious in their mission to provide "good faith efforts" toward diversity helped in removing misguided notions of such programs while also maintaining them.

The military, which had been arguably the most successful example of integration and affirmative action, was looked at to see how and why it was so successful. Edley and Stephanopoulos discovered that the armed forces had successfully integrated the enlisted ranks and set firm policies—called the pipeline—to do the same with the officer corps. These efforts included "setting explicit goals to increase minority representation," outreach and recruiting activities through the Reserve Officer Training Corps (ROTC), and increasingly diversity at the service academics, such as West Point and Annapolis. Especially important to this effort were the selection procedures that encouraged upward mobility without quotas, the rigorous training programs, and management skills that increased the likelihood of diversity within the officer corps. The Clinton staff saw room for duplicating the military's success by "instructing DoD [Department of Defense] officials to share with other agencies the materials that DoD has developed for its equal opportunity training for senior military and civilian officials." The review strongly encouraged President Clinton to meet with the military to "underscore" the importance of diversity and correct the last bastions of white, male leadership: "the flag and general officer ranks," as well as the "technical specialties, where underrepresentation remains substantial."[70] These were commitments that the president held dear as they advanced his agenda of diversity and merit-based advancement.

Next, the review examined the thorny issue of federal procurement policies as they relate to increasing minority entrepreneurial opportunities. Beyond race-based programs that benefit minorities in education, race-based programs for business were an especially juicy target for affirmative action opponents. The review found that Small Business Administration records showed that affirmative action in procurements and federal contracting had helped increase minority participation. Since the programs in existence adhered to existing law and regulations and did not engage numerical straitjackets, they were flexible and in compliance with Supreme Court jurisprudence. Interestingly, the review also argued that, since there was little data available on race-neutral options, "moving from social and economic disadvantage to focus on economic disadvantage only would seriously undermine efforts to create entrepreneurship opportunities for minorities and women, given continuing patterns of exclusion and discrimination."[71] Instead, the review team argued that several steps should be taken to address waste and fraud and enhance the efficiency of the programs. These steps included (1) tightening the economic disadvantage test so business owners could not hide assets to gain contracts, (2) tightening requirements for graduation from sheltered competition, (3) enforcing stringent safeguards against "fronts" by authenticating the credentials of these Small and Disadvantaged Businesses by certified accountants, and (4) establishing measures to reduce regional/industry concentrations by identifying sheltered programs that could be eliminated after successful inclusion of disadvantaged minorities and women.[72] The purpose was to make affirmative action programs leaner and more efficient. In addition, by buttressing these programs to conform to the *Adarand* decision and other laws, regulations, and judicial decisions, the Clinton administration was trying to ensure the long-term solvency of affirmative action programs, at least until there was a general consensus that they were no longer needed—something no reasonable person thought possible during his or her lifetime. It would take generations more, according to some, to eradicate the racism and discrimination within American society.

The administration's review of affirmative action, however, took a much harder line on educational opportunity. Educational opportunities were possibly the most contentious issue facing affirmative action. These race-based programs have the perception in the public as social engineering projects that used innocent children, usually white children, to effect social transformation. The growing economic inequality resulting from deregulation, globalization, and deindustrialization fostered resentment among many whites that their children were being disadvantaged to remedy historical wrongs in which they played no part. Despite all evidence to the contrary, this perception was the inverse of what was actually happening. The review found that targeted programs in the Departments of Education and Human and Health Services were needed because there "is the continuing underrepresentation of historically discriminated against groups in key professions and in institutions of higher education." Equally important was that "a great many institutions and professions have never made an effective break with their history of discrimination and exclusion." Since the administration considered educational institutions as the "engines of opportunity," it was vital to ensure inclusion in order to make "the promise of equal opportunity a reality." These programs have "few adverse effects on nonbeneficiaries, and . . . in general the criticisms raised can be answered. Concerning minority-targeted scholarships, for example, DoEd estimates that only 40 cents of every $1000 in Federal educational assistance funding was devoted to such targeted programs." This directly contradicts the notion of wasteful spending on minorities. To continue forward with such programs, Edley and Stephanopoulos wrote that the Office of Management and Budget should work with all agencies to make sure that all programs remained effective and fair and that equal opportunities and measures were included to adhere to the Government Performance and Results Act.[73]

Defending affirmative action, however, became more difficult as the legal and political environment shifted to limit its scope. Eddie Correia, special counsel to the president, noted in a memorandum to Deputy Chief of Staff Sylvia Mathews, "Affirmative action efforts have been a major part of administration policy in several areas, including public and private employment, procurement, education, and voting. In all these areas, the courts have narrowed the range of situations when government can take race or gender into account in developing and implementing public policy."[74] As a result, the administration pursued a two-pronged strategy that involved "defending traditional affirmative action programs and revising them where possible to meet constitutional requirements. The second track involve[d] strengthening our effects to achieve the goal of equality through race and gender neutral programs."[75] It emphasized voluntary affirmative action arrangements by business and education. Those race-neutral remedies proffered by businesses, however, had to demonstrate "good faith" efforts.

In a court decision in Texas in 1996, the Fifth Circuit Court of Appeals ruled in the case of *Hopwood v. Texas* that four prospective white students, denied entry in the University of Texas Law School, were denied their constitutional rights under the Fourteenth Amendment.[76] The University of Texas had been using affirmative action to diversify its student ranks. Cheryl J. Hopwood alleged that she had been denied admission in favor of lower-qualified minority students. The US District Court for the Western District of Texas ruled that the law school did have a compelling interest in diversity; however, the Fifth Circuit Court ruled in March 1996 that race could not be used as a factor to make decisions regarding admission. The Clinton administration was put into a difficult position. In essence what the Fifth Circuit Court had done was invalidate the Supreme Court ruling in *Bakke v. California* (1978).[77] This decision did not apply to the rest of the nation, only to the states within the jurisdiction of the Fifth Circuit Court.

The Clinton administration was sufficiently disturbed by the ruling that it filed a brief in support of Texas. As Richard Hayes, from the Office of Public Liaison, noted, "[Clinton] instructed the Justice Department to file a brief in support of the State of Texas's petition to the Supreme Court to overturn this decision and uphold the University of Texas Law School's interest in promoting the racial diversity of its student body through legally permissible means."[78] Despite the pleas of Texas and the Clinton Justice Department, the Supreme Court declined to hear the case in July 1996. The Clinton administration, however, took solace in the fact that "Justices Ginsberg and Souter recognized the issues were important and needed to be addressed. But they said that this was not the appropriate case to resolve them—

because the program in question had already been abandoned by the University."[79] Despite the court's decision not to hear the case, Clinton and his Justice Department not only had challenged the *Hopwood* decision, but also went to court to try and reverse it. Eventually, the *Hopwood* decision was reversed by the Supreme Court in *Grutter v. Bollinger* (2003), in which the court determined that using race, narrowly, in admissions was permissible because the University of Michigan Law School had a "compelling interest" in producing a diverse student body.[80]

In another sensationalized case the Clinton administration took a strong stand in favor of affirmative action: *Piscataway Township Board of Education v. Taxman*.[81] Piscataway, New Jersey, came under severe scrutiny in 1996 as a result of its board of education's 1989 decision to lay off a white teacher, Sharon Taxman, instead of a black one, Debra Williams. Under New Jersey state law employees were to be laid off in the order of least seniority. However, if that resulted in creating or compounding a lack of diversity, then white employees would be laid off first to preserve diversity. When the school board needed to lay off employees, both Sharon Taxman and Debra Williams had equal qualifications, credentials, seniority, and performance evaluations. Piscataway decided to lay off Taxman in order to keep some level of diversity in the Business Education Department. As Clinton's acting solicitor general, Walter Dellinger, wrote, "That was the first time petitioner had used its affirmative action plan in making an employment decision since the plan's adoption in 1975."[82] Further, Dellinger argued that Ms. Taxman's request "for a writ of certiorari should be denied."[83] This case was one of the most controversial of the 1990s and demonstrated the difficulties of pursuing diversity and equal opportunity at the end of the twentieth century.

It certainly provoked anxiety within the Clinton Justice Department and White House. In a June 1997 memorandum for the president, written by White House counsels Charles F. C. Ruff, Dawn Chirwa, and Bill Marshall, they informed the president of actions of the Justice Department and argued, "We believe that this brief achieves two necessary goals: (1) answering the Court's request; and (2) forestalling potential criticism that Justice has distanced itself from its position before the circuit court. It also represents a sound legal position. Because of its unique and troublesome facts, Piscataway does not invite a favorable decision on affirmative action."[84] In addition, the White House attorneys argued, "It is notable that no civil rights organizations are filing briefs in support of the school board in the case."[85] In the absence of a viable fight on the affirmative action front, the administration, instead, sought to persuade the court not to hear the case based on its fears of losing, but also because the case easily played into opponents' arguments that race-conscious measures were unfair.

When Taxman was reinstated, the school board was in the process of eliminating its "non-remedial" policy. However, the district court had awarded Taxman back pay and other monetary damages, which Taxman continued to demand. The Third Circuit Court "affirmed" the decision of the lower court in regard to the damages awarded. Strategizing on how to diffuse the volatile case, Walter Dellinger wrote Attorney General Janet Reno a month before briefs were due to argue that, "after weighing several options and consulting with representatives of major civil rights litigation groups, I have concluded that we should file a brief arguing that the money judgment awarded to Taxman in this should be affirmed on the narrow ground that the Board failed to offer or defend an adequate justification for this particular race-based layoff decision."[86] Moreover, Dellinger argued that by endorsing the "narrow" justification for the award, the "Court would then not have to reach the broad question whether Title VII always precludes non-remedial affirmative action."[87] In terms of Clinton's decision to fix the flaws in affirmative action instead of ending it, this strategy would demonstrate "that we are serious in our commitment to mend (without ending) affirmative action. . . . If we nonetheless attempt to support the Board, the Court is apt to conclude that we will support any use of race that is labeled affirmative action."[88] Dellinger's memo reinforced the notion that there are practical grounds on which affirmative action is not only necessary but profitable, but that affirmative action can also lead to abuses. As a result, the "mend it, don't end it" policy was successful in acknowledging the need for such programs while also understanding its weaknesses. Furthermore, it helped to protect the vulnerable program from attack by an increasingly antagonistic federal judiciary.

The President's Initiative on Race—the subject of chapter 6—was another opportunity seized by the Clinton administration to defend affirmative action and educate the public about its importance. The Initiative on Race hoped to foster dialogue about race in America and encourage reconciliation. In concrete terms, there was no other issue that more symbolized the divide between the races than affirmative action. The Race Initiative Advisory Board was selected because of each member's ability to contribute substantively to a debate on race. In addition, the president used the opportunity to engage personally on the issue of race-based programs. In announcing the creation of the race initiative at the University of California, San Diego, Clinton challenged those in the audience and elsewhere, who were opposed to affirmative action, to "come up with an alternative. I would embrace it if I could find a better way."[89] In addition, Clinton said, "I believe a student body that reflects the excellence and the diversity of the people we will live and work with has independent educational value."[90] Citing the Kerner Commission from the 1960s, Clinton also noted that it was no longer a situation of "two Americas," but multiple Americas; the growing diversity of the United States made not only affirmative action but reconciliation imperative.

In December 1997, Clinton and Vice President Al Gore, as a part of the Race Initiative Outreach Meeting with Conservatives, took on some of the most fervent opponents of affirmative action. Among those in attendance were University of California regent Ward Connerly, conservative intellectuals Abigail and Stephan Thernstrom, the wife of Republican senator Mitch Mitchell, Elaine Chao, and Florida congressman Charles Canady. In a back-and-forth debate Clinton stuck to his defense of affirmative action as fair and just. In responding to a question and comment about whites' legitimate fears and grievances from Stephen Thernstrom, Clinton denounced the idea of a colorblind America. Further, Clinton shredded Professor Thernstrom's contention that "it is a reality that certain neighborhoods, predominately black neighborhoods in inner cities are very dangerous places at night. And they are very dangerous places largely because there are black criminals who are committing criminal acts. . . . [W]hites express those fears and they can be dealt with, they can be discussed, but they shouldn't be dismissed." Clinton turned the tables by arguing, "The other day we had a group of African American journalists in here. . . .

[E]very man in that office, every single, solitary one, had been stopped by the police when he was doing nothing, for no other reason than he was black. And you say that's because there's a rational fear because of the fact that what occurs in some neighborhoods. . . . That is a race-based public policy." Abigail Thernstrom quickly backed off, saying, "We agree with that. We agree with that. It's unacceptable to me."[91]

This exchange encapsulated a significant portion of the debate over affirmative action. Although white conservative opponents pointed to real and perceived white grievances over race-based programs, they often ignored other race-based programs that impacted African Americans in negative ways. Police profiling, drug interdiction, sentencing disparities, and other, more pernicious preferences, such as the denying of loans, mortgages, financial assistance, and employment, had been in place much longer than any affirmative action program. That was Clinton's point and why, in part, he supported affirmative action: the vestiges of not only slavery but institutional and systemic racism continued to impact the lives of African Americans in unhealthy and unfair ways.

At the heart of the colorblind philosophy was the notion that race itself was taboo. An acknowledgement of race was passé in the post–civil rights era, because it seemingly dismissed not only ideals of individuality and fairness but Dr. King's dream of an America where people would be judged "not by the color of their skin but the content of their character." The debate between those for and against affirmative action all too often relied on worn dogmas that either race did not matter or that the policy should be defended no matter what. Clinton disputed these dogmas in an effort to seek comity between blacks and whites on one of the most contentious and important domestic issues of the late twentieth century.

What Clinton's Approach Says about Race during the 1990s

At first glance President Clinton's defense of affirmative action appears standard for a Democratic leader in the post–civil rights era. In fact, most leaders of the Democratic Party since Lyndon Johnson's famous speech at Howard University outlining affirmative action have supported, if not explicitly, then implicitly, race-based programs to address historical inequities and discrimination. By the time Clinton came into office in 1993, African Americans had become an important faction of the Democratic Party. African Americans had demonstrated their loyalty through voting, financial support, and often fierce opposition to Republican policies. Media narratives of the affirmative action review and the subsequent defense of affirmative action programs have generally revolved around these traditional perceptions of Democratic loyalty. Closer examination reveals that Clinton did not simply defend the program; he challenged the program's existence in a way that gave it much-needed viability. Challenging the efficacy of affirmative action had been called for by New Democrats for years. As future Clinton aides Elaine Kamarck and William Galston noted in an influential 1989 paper for the Progressive Policy Institute, "It is hard to escape the conclusion that Democrats are afraid even to probe questions such as affirmative action, crime, and policies to alleviate poverty."[92] Instead of a repudiation of liberal policies, New Democrats sought a reevaluation of these programs. Clinton used New Democratic principles to access affirmative action's strengths and weaknesses, plotting a path forward for the controversial programs, revealing the often unspoken need to reform programs to changing social and political circumstances.

In addition, while the initial impetus for reviewing the programs resulted from growing political and legal challenges, it also came from the need to address the growth of class, a major element in recent decades, as an impediment to full equality and opportunity. Since de jure segregation and discrimination had long ended, class, especially in light of globalization, had at least gained parity with race in American life. The main recipients or beneficiaries of affirmative action, white women and middle-class African Americans, clearly demonstrated the salience of class. An article in the *New Democrat*, a DLC-affiliated publication, discussed the need for Clinton and other Democrats to recognize the black middle class.[93] Alan Wolfe bluntly warned, "If the Democratic Party does not change to accommodate new racial realities in America, new racial realities will change the Democratic Party."[94] Furthermore, "as more African Americans move to the suburbs [and take on middle-class sensibilities], some will, in all likelihood become Republican."[95] It is, in part, this new reality that Clinton responded to with his support for affirmative action.

The president's actions on affirmative action represented the fullest ideals of New Democratic philosophy: equal opportunity, not equal outcomes. Seymour Martin Lipset of the Progressive Policy Institute, the intellectual arm of the Democratic Leadership Council, argued in a 1995 article that "to rebuild both the Democratic base and the national consensus on civil rights and racial justice, affirmative action should be refocused, not discarded."[96] This is precisely what Clinton did in his July 1995 speech at the National Archives.

The fiercest support for affirmative action policies has come from those who have benefited the most: middle-class African Americans and white women. Due to this reality, they were the least likely to support reform of race-based programs. What Clinton had realized was that the program had created significant division between those it helped and those who felt discriminated by it. This so-called angry white male syndrome arguably had more to do with globalization and deindustrialization than blacks specifically. But the public perception was that blacks were given special preferences to the detriment of whites who had not discriminated against them. Clinton realized this and carefully framed his defense of affirmative action in the language of opportunity, reconciliation, and equality. However, despite Clinton's sensitive defense of these programs, he also realized that, as Joel Kotkin noted, "for poorer blacks, affirmative action has been utterly useless; since 1970, the proportion of black families living in poverty has grown from one-fifth to one-quarter."[97] Clinton thus committed to increased access to higher education, national programs such as AmeriCorps, and community empowerment zones. Affirmative action had proved effective for those African Americans with at least rudimentary skills necessary for social and economic mobility. While many saw affirmative action as a singular issue, Clinton saw it as one part of his overall civil rights program that combined political, rhetorical, social, economic, and policy initiatives. This nuanced strategy helped not only defend the controversial policy but also earn and reaffirm the continuing support of African Americans. As Joe Klein revealed, Clinton's support was personal and political, practical and principled, revealing the complexity of race and class through personal experiences and principled beliefs about America.[98] It represented the growing importance of class at the end of the century. While other policies, such as welfare reform and crime, clearly had a deleterious effect on the black poor, affirmative action benefited the middle class. The black middle class was in a position to take advantage of the opportunities afforded by the policy in a way that the black poor could not. Clinton's defense of the policy further split the African American community along class lines. These class dynamics contributed to the growing division between the haves and have-nots, thus mirroring the increase in economic inequality that had risen since 1980. Those in the middle class that could take advantage of the policy of affirmative action were, in Clinton's mind, members of a community that was responsible, productive, and accountable.

Conclusion

Affirmative action during the 1990s was a hot-button issue. Conservatives used the controversial issue to drum up support from their base. Liberals and African Americans used the issue to mobilize their forces. Even entities such as corporations and the military rose to defend the vulnerable program. Randall Kennedy explained, "The amorphous and malleable idea of 'diversity' provided much needed buoyancy to affirmative action, especially in the 2003 University of Michigan affirmative action cases when 65 major companies, including American Express, Coca Cola, and Microsoft, asserted that maintaining racial diversity in institutions of higher education is vital to their efforts to hire and maintain a diverse workforce."[99] Further, members of Congress rose to defend affirmative action when Republicans presented legislative challenges to it. For instance, on July 10, 1995, Republicans senators Mitch McConnell, Bob Dole, Richard Shelby, Don Nickles, and Hank Brown filed S. 1085 to effectively abolish affirmative action inside the federal government.[100] In response to this proposed legislation, Democrats rallied to affirmative action's defense. On the floor of the Senate, Illinois senator Paul Simon argued, "It has made America a better place and is making America a better place."[101] California congressman Esteban Edward Torres passionately said, "I have benefited from it all my life. That is because I am white, I am male, I am Anglo and I am Protestant. . . . The real affirmative action is also indirect and at work twenty-four hours a day, seven days a week, year in and year out. Because it is informal and indirect, we tend to forget or deny just how all-important and all-pervasive it really is."[102] Georgia congressman John Lewis, after the decision in *Adarand v. Pena*, noted, in language similar to that used by President Clinton, "Affirmative action is an important tool to address the persistent of racial and gender inequality and discrimination. Now more than ever before, we need affirmative action because the scars and stains of racism and bigotry are still deeply embedded in the American society."[103] These are just some of the thousands of floor statements enunciated by supporters of affirmative action in and around the time of Clinton's historic speech in July 1995. Organizations such as La Raza, the NAACP, NOW, the Leadership Conference, and much of corporate America defended affirmative action on grounds that it increased opportunity, diverse, and profits. As a result of the increased efforts to defend affirmative action, no piece of legislation passed during the Clinton years that restricted or abolished affirmative action. It was, in part, because of Clinton's support for it and Congress's inability to restrict it that opponents directed their attention to ballot initiatives, in places such as California and Michigan, and executive state action, such as in Florida under Governor Jeb Bush.

The usual supporters of affirmative action were not the only people and groups to rally to the defense of the controversial program. Businesses and corporations around the nation also stepped up their efforts. According to the Federal Glass Ceiling Commission, that group included, but was not limited to, Fannie Mae, Hewlett-Packard, JC Penney, Procter & Gamble, Exxon, SC Johnson Wax, AT&T, Dow Jones & Company, CIGNA, Avon Products, Inc., American Airlines, McDonald's, US West, Pacific Gas and Electric, Pacific Bell, Apple Computer, Eastman Kodak Company, and Johnson & Johnson.[104] What these corporations realized is that affirmative action and related programs of uplift regularly increased their profits, broadened the clientele, insulated themselves from legal attacks, and fostered better community relations. Dozens of these corporations rallied to the defense of affirmative action in the Michigan cases in 2003.[105] Further, they continue to support race-conscious and class-conscious measures today. It greatly helped that President Clinton provided crucial support to the controversial policy at a time when affirmative action could have been abolished altogether. The president stood tall in the face of stiff cultural and conservative opposition.

The New Democrats used the issue to promote a new direction in affirmative action. Clinton used the issue to reflect the growing dynamics of race and class in the 1990s. Clinton's actions in this regard reflect three main themes about the New Democratic philosophy: (1) reform was needed to correct abuses and outdated ideas, (2) affirmative action was needed, albeit in a more restricted form, and (3) affirmative action was not contrary to ideas about merit and equal opportunity as long as those policies were put in the context of opportunity, responsibility, and community. Arguably, from a policy standpoint, this was the boldest move of Clinton's tenure in regard to race. The president's actions turned the old two-sided debates over affirmative action into a more nuanced, sophisticated, and broader civil rights strategy that included the earned income tax credit, more student loans and Pell grants, an increase in the minimum wage, increased enforcement against discrimination, use of market-based solutions to assist distressed communities in the form of grants, business activity, and federal support, and dialogue with the American public about the necessity of inclusive policies and politics.

CHAPTER 6

Welfare Reform

The New Democratic Ethos and African Americans

DO THE GOVERNMENT and the taxpayers have a political, moral, or legal responsibility to materially protect the most vulnerable citizens? At the beginning of the twentieth century, progressives and conservatives fought ferociously over this issue. By the start of the Great Depression, after the failure of the government, under Presidents Warren Harding, Calvin Coolidge, and Herbert Hoover, to respond effectively to the growing economic inequality of 1920s and the stock market crash, progressives were able to convince large numbers of Americans of the need for greater governmental involvement in the social and economic life of the country. The passage of the Social Security Act of 1935 created the predecessor for welfare legislation, including the Public Welfare Amendments of 1962, which created Aid to Families with Dependent Children (AFDC).[1] Including married men for the first time, this act changed the dynamics of the system. It disregarded the strong public sentiment against able-bodied men receiving public assistance and deepened the resentment toward those on the dole. Further, as southern politicians, working-class ethnics, and the leaders of the Republican Party began to adapt their political rhetoric to the changing times, welfare became a pernicious code word for black. As sociologists Kenneth J. Neubeck and Noel A. Cazenave noted in 2001, "The racialization of welfare has reached the point where politicians can now exploit racial animus to promote their political ambitions and goals simply by speaking the word welfare."[2] Using the term "welfare" had serious repercussions for race relations and the plight of those trapped in America's underclass. It deepened both the fear and animosity toward those least able to defend themselves and bred resentment among the minority toward the majority.

In August 1996 President Bill Clinton signed the Personal Responsibility and Work Opportunity Reconciliation Act into law.[3] After sixty years of federal commitment to the poor through cash assistance, housing, and food stamps, the disadvantaged were now required to get jobs and were subject to a maximum lifetime benefit of five years of assistance. African Americans were disproportionately impacted by the law. Clinton's decision to sign this legislation revealed the propensity of the New Democrat philosophy to jettison the interests of the poor and minorities in the pursuit of a middle road that rejected liberal orthodoxy and embraced the key themes of modern conservatism: family, responsibility, and limited government. Moreover, this philosophy relayed serious doubts among many Americans as to the effectiveness of government programs in uplifting the downtrodden.

When Clinton first ran for president in 1992, among the litany of policy changes he proposed was ending welfare as an entitlement and moving those on welfare to work. Clinton was speaking of what most consider to be traditional welfare, Aid to Families with Dependent Children (AFDC). This program gave assistance to lift people out of poverty; benefits included cash assistance, health care, food stamps, and other necessities such as housing. In the three decades between the Public Welfare Amendments and Clinton's inauguration as president, welfare had become a major wedge issue. Conservatives stigmatized those on welfare, particularly women and minorities, as freeloaders, ne'er-do-wells, burdens on the taxpayer, and symbols of what was wrong with America. To be sure, the American welfare state bore little resemblance to its European counterparts as Americans worked more hours, received fewer benefits, and condemned any meaningful assistance for the poor as socialism. The lack of a realistic appreciation about its effects, its recipients, and its impact on the national economy resulted in welfare becoming a punching bag for not just conservatives but liberals too. Clinton had to react to this shift in priorities and political commitment.

Clinton's years as a governor of a small state had taught him that the system was "broken." In fact, Clinton had been a proponent of welfare reform as governor of Arkansas. Clinton spoke of a new "contract" with welfare recipients: "Recipients would commit to strive for independence in return for the benefits, and the government would commit to help them."[4] In addition, since Clinton's first term as governor, 1979–1981, he had eagerly implemented a "workfare" program that Arkansas had been selected for by the Carter administration. He was also a proponent of the 1988 welfare reform law that mandated that teen mothers stay in school and live at home in order to receive benefits. States had the responsibility of carrying out the federal mandates regarding welfare, but governors often believed that mandates were ineffective and even dangerous. Following the New Federalism model established by President Richard Nixon, Clinton thought that the states needed more control over the system, while welfare recipients needed to move from welfare to work.

Brief History of American Welfare

At the height of the New Deal, reformers within Franklin D. Roosevelt's administration were concerned with the needs of the average American and the provision of a social safety net for those trapped at the bottom of the socioeconomic ladder. Applying an already conceived program of aid for women and children, the Congress passed the Social Security Act of 1935. This piece of legislation redistributed income. As welfare scholar and former key congressional staffer Ron Harkins put it, "thus nestled among the seedling Social Security and unemployment programs in the Social Security Act of 1935 was the little welfare acorn called Aid to Dependent Children (later called Aid to Families with Dependent Children)."[5] ADC, and later AFDC, became the primary focus of conservatives opposed to the redistribution of tax revenue for the benefit of the poor. Unlike other government programs such as oil depletion allowances, social security for the aged, tax breaks through the use of exemptions or itemizations, or publicly funded education, there were few arguments to justify such governmental action when welfare recipients could simply work. Welfare ran counter to American notions of self-reliance, individual initiative, and responsibility.

The use of public measures to assist the indigent also greatly concerned southern politicians worried over the potential for taxpayer dollars being spent on African Americans. Throughout the sixty-year history of welfare, vitriolic and incendiary language was often used to vilify African Americans who were thought to be unworthy. Julian E. Zelizer notes, "The historical scholarship on Social Security has focused on benefits, particularly on the racial and gender dynamics behind who received different amounts of benefits. This research argues that the two-track structure of Social Security tended to benefit white male retirees, who had been industrial wage-earners, and their dependent wives (social insurance), while Social Security provided meager assistance to single women, African Americans, and the unemployed (public assistance)."[6] Robert C. Lieberman has noted that that the Roosevelt administration compromised on the creation of the Social Security Act to exclude African Americans. Equally important, Lieberman argues, "Each of these programs [Old-Age Insurance, Unemployment Insurance, and Aid to Dependent Children] challenged the racial structure of American society in a distinctive way, creating new benefits or encouraging states to create or expand benefits that might have undermined the tight racial control that white Southerners maintained over their society and economy."[7] Creating such a program was threatening to the vested interests of the southern landowners, thus creating and maintaining an uneven, racially stilted system of benefits and beneficiaries.

Jason Deparle notes, "The last thing Congress intended in the thirties was to move black women out of the fields and onto the welfare rolls. . . . Southern members of Congress controlled the presiding committees and made sure the law did nothing to interfere with the South's supply of cheap field labor."[8] While these programs were intertwined with race and racism, the proponents of welfare programs in the United States took special notice of the economic concerns of property owners and other employers. In no meaningful way did they want to disturb the traditional balance in the South and other places by giving African Americans a way to lift themselves out of the poverty and misery of the Jim Crow lifestyle. The economic needs of planters superseded the needs of their poor African American workers.

Welfare was also racialized in such a manner as to confer pathology on the African American community; welfare was already seen a handout to lazy people who would not work. The prospect of blacks receiving cash benefits arose; it played into long-held notions of black inferiority, shiftlessness, and inability to be accountable and responsibility. What made it palatable to enough members of Congress for passage was that it did not threaten, initially, to undo the carefully constructed and strictly maintained system of white privilege and black subjugation that the nation had so enthusiastically embraced.

"The ease with which political elites abolished the Aid to Families with Dependent Children program—the primary safety net protecting poverty-stricken mothers and children—would have been impossible," Neubeck and Cazenave note, "had not many politicians, along with policy analysts and the mass media, spent decades framing and morphing welfare into a supposed 'black problem.'"[9] Further, because of this supposed "black problem," the welfare state's political and rhetorical promise of equal rights and opportunity was betrayed. As Jill Quadagno has noted, "the equal opportunity welfare state was replaced by a welfare state that encouraged racial isolation and the concentration of the black poor in inner cities."[10] This created a two-tiered system in which whites, even those in need of assistance, remained ahead of blacks, thus securing their position of supremacy.

The use of welfare, however, was limited prior to the Great Society, when President Lyndon Johnson's War on Poverty created "new social programs and spending on social programs grew dramatically."[11] Even the liberals in the Johnson White House and in Congress were not seeking to continue or expand government handouts. They were promoting a version soon to be called "workfare." As Maurice Isserman and Michael Kazin wrote, "Under the war on poverty, poor Americans would be encouraged to take advantage of job-training programs and other forms of educational assistance that would allow [them] to benefit from the opportunities provided by an expanding national economy—hence the title given [Sargent] Shriver's package of legislative proposals, the Economic Opportunity Act of 1964."[12] This included a jobs program along with other incentives, such as federal funding of training programs to assist the poor in uplifting themselves. As more African Americans became recipients of government benefits during the 1960s, the more controversial welfare became. The application of character and value-laden characterizations on those receiving welfare, specifically African Americans, gained credibility from one of the most prominent political intellectuals of the last forty years of the twentieth century: Daniel Patrick Moynihan.

In March 1965, Moynihan, assistant secretary of labor in both the Kennedy and Johnson administrations, issued a report entitled *The Negro Family: The Case for National Action*.[13] Moynihan described the numerous problems and afflictions of African Americans. Moreover, he pointed out that race relations were suffering as a result of the continued subjugation of African Americans. Central to his theories about major issues confronting the African American community was the family. More specifically, the lack of proper family role models contributed to joblessness, crime, and dysfunction. The domineering presence of the women as heads of household, Moynihan argued, led to group pathology that took on cyclical dimensions, thus passing on bad character traits and habits from one generation to the next. Equally important, the "breakdown of the family" led to dramatic increases in "welfare dependency." While sympathetic to the enormous challenges confronting African Americans in the mid-1960s, Moynihan blamed the victims for their conditions. And in blaming the victims, Moynihan conferred upon them the mantle of "pathological." Without white, middle-class value systems and assistance from the federal government to stop the disintegration of the black family, African Americans would continue to slide further downward, thus perpetuating the misery, dysfunction, and social suicide of a major group in America.[14] Yet there were no analyses of white issues regarding poverty and dependency. As David C. Carter has noted, "the lack of comparative data on white families from similar socioeconomic backgrounds fueled the suspicions of those who thought that Moynihan— like earlier writers—sought to demonstrate that the great majority of African Americans were 'beyond the melting pot.'"[15] Conservatives and other opponents of government aid programs would soon use

Moynihan's words and theories about dysfunction, dependency, and values to promote the argument that welfare stigmatized, harmed, and otherwise condemned the very people it was designed to help. As the report circulated among politicians, academics, and average Americans, it became easier for most Americans to see welfare as a black problem, not a white one, especially with the growing violence and tension of urban America.

As early as the Nixon administration, politicians were looking for ways in which to scale back the various public assistance programs. President Richard M. Nixon attempted in 1971 to create the Family Assistance Plan to provide every American with a minimum level of income. Part of the rational of FAP was that by providing a basic level of income, overall costs of entitlement programs could be reduced. FAP would stop penalizing poor Americans who chose to work. As Rick Perlstein has noted, "the Nixon-Moynihan 'Family Assistance Program' was cleverly devised to ameliorate its [AFDC] structural flaw: AFDC penalized work. Get a job, and you couldn't get welfare."[16] The measure failed to secure enough support in large part because it was considered too radical by conservatives and too little by liberals (on Capitol Hill). Dean Kotlowski noted, "Nixon wished to prune the costs, excesses, and failures of the New Deal and Great Society without scrapping them outright."[17] Finally, Democrats probably suspected that Nixon's plan was a Trojan horse designed to begin the process of eliminating public assistance and to break public support for the New Deal coalition, which, while badly strained, was still popular with the electorate. In fact, Joseph E. Lowndes notes that Nixon never really wanted to pass FAP, but really wanted to "blame liberals for the death of FAP."[18] Nixon, having run a racially tinged campaign in 1968, could appeal to moderates by showing that he was interested in helping the poor, even African Americans. The failure of the civil rights movement to successfully address economic disparities in opportunity, education, and income contributed to the growing crisis over welfare. The failure of government, vis-à-vis the War on Poverty and entanglement in Vietnam, to deliver on President Johnson's desire to eradicate poverty and the violence in places such as Watts, Newark, Detroit, Harlem, and Washington contributed to the belief that liberal solutions to vexing social problems were actually making them worse. Inherent in this belief was that welfare programs and government assistance of assorted kinds were actually promoting a "culture of dependency" that was threatening the domestic tranquility of the nation. As energy crises, Middle East disturbances, and the twin evils of inflation and high employment—stagflation—swept through the 1970s, conservatives' arguments about welfare, including those that implied racism, gained greater salience in mainstream America. Ronald Reagan would be able to make the same pitch, although with a smile on his face, that would change the nature of the debate on welfare and begin the first real policy challenges to welfare since the Social Security Act passed in 1935.

In 1980, voters shifted their political support to the Republican Party on the national level. At the apex of his political powers, Reagan used his rhetorical flourishes to denigrate welfare recipients, particularly African American women. Reagan's speeches about so-called welfare queens struck a chord with millions of Americans who, regardless of their political affiliation or region of the country in which they lived, felt that government was, in the words of Reagan, the problem. Barack Obama noted in *The Audacity of Hope*, "[That] Reagan's message found such a receptive audience spoke not only to his skills as a communicator; it also spoke to the failures of liberal government, during a period of economic stagnation, to give middle-class voters any sense that it was fighting for them."[19] Once in office, Reagan turned his anti-welfare speeches into reality. As Thomas Edsall and Mary Edsall have noted, "in federal social spending, the largest percentage cuts during the Reagan years were made in means-tested programs serving heavily black populations, programs staffed, in many cases, by black personnel. The basic welfare programs, AFDC and food stamps, were cut by 17.4 percent and 14.3 percent, with the result that at least 400,000 families lost their eligibility for welfare, and nearly one million individuals lost eligibility for food stamps."[20] As the 1980s wore on, interest groups, think tanks, and Democrat-affiliated organizations such as the Democratic Leadership Council also began to target welfare for reform. As R. Kent Weaver has noted, "several factors helped to put work-oriented welfare reform on the national agenda in the 1980s. The increase in the number of middle-class mothers with young children who are in the paid labor force increased political support for requiring AFDC mothers to work."[21] As more women entered the workforce, to support their families as well as to pursue their respective careers, it put pressure on welfare recipients to work. Conservatives exploited a dynamic which they previously had criticized, the changing social and economic norms that used to dictate that women stayed at home with the children while men brought home the bacon. If those women could work and raise children, then women receiving welfare could work as well.

The debate surrounding welfare had changed to focus more on illegitimacy and long-term dependency, with race an underlying subtext.[22] As a result of the changing political environment, Congress pushed for greater responsibility, accountability, and work requirements with the passage of the Family Support Act of 1988. After the greater work requirements of the 1988 reform, attention from Democrats and Republicans alike was put on eradicating the welfare system. New Democrats like Clinton bought into socially conservative ideas that linked illegitimacy and dependency with welfare, though they also wanted to provide additional assistance for recipients to get an education, job training, and family care assistance.

Intellectual Opposition to Welfare in the 1980s and 1990s

Publications such as the *National Review*, the *Wall Street Journal*, and the *Washington Times*, along with conservative members of the academic elite, eviscerated welfare as cruel, corrupt, and unnecessary. Charles Murray warned in *Losing Ground* that America's welfare system was a disincentive for recipients to work and often trapped them in an unending cycle of poverty and misery, at taxpayer expense.[23] Since the beginning of the Reagan era, the Republican Party had focused more on the social dynamics of welfare, such as dependency, illegitimacy, and undeserving recipients, as opposed to older arguments such as the appropriate role of the federal government, rugged individualism, and economics. Race was a key factor in this regard. A predominate belief that welfare disproportionately favored minorities fostered resentment among whites toward African Americans. Neubeck and Cazenave showed that "like 'the drug problem' and 'the crime problem,' welfare had become an effective resource in the lexicon that politicians could mobilize to exploit whites' racial fears and animosities."[24] Demonizing African Americans on welfare, then, became politically salient. Using the rhetoric of colorblindness, political and media elites attacked those on welfare with little concern about blowback from critics alleging racism.

When Ronald Reagan attributed America's decline to "welfare queens" too lazy to work, he laid the rhetorical groundwork for the assault on welfare and poor people in 1996. Further, as Kevin Phillips explained in *The Politics of Rich and Poor: Wealth and the American Electorate in the Reagan Aftermath*, resentment toward the state and welfare programs grew as a result of Reagan's emphasis on tax cuts, defense spending, deregulation, and overseas borrowing.[25] By the 1990s growing public acceptance of controversial social science data provided the credibility needed to push forward welfare reform. More than anything else, however, the growing furor over welfare reflected not just frustration with a system that was out of balance, but the lingering divisions over race in the United States during the 1990s.

Conservatives did not corner the market on opposing welfare. Peter Edelman, a noted liberal who had worked for Senator Robert F. Kennedy, has noted, "I hate welfare."[26] The differences, however, boiled down to three things: (1) the appropriateness of the government redistributing taxpayer money to the poor, (2) the belief that able-bodied adults should provide for themselves, and, if they cannot, then private charity should help, and (3) the politics of race. Liberal supporters of welfare argued that American society was unequal and minorities were incapable of surviving on their own—a patronizing, often insulting argument. Neubeck and Cazenave note, "In the 1980s, liberal and moderate politicians quickly came to join conservatives in making the need for new control-focused welfare policies a key national political issue," though combined with liberals' benevolent notions of social justice and social uplift.[27] The actual needs of poor African Americans and others were often ignored.[28]

As Weaver notes, "the overrepresentation of racial minorities among AFDC recipients has reinforced racial stereotypes about family structure and weak work ethics among African Americans."[29] Republican messages of opposition to welfare and promotion of welfare cuts, tax cuts, and across-the-board cuts in social entitlement spending found an accepting and receptive public. By making government the enemy of the people and casting doubts upon the legitimacy of entitlement programs, the Reagan revolution opened the door for a serious assault on welfare. In fact, by 1988, for the first time, a welfare reform bill was passed and signed into law that mandated some level of work for recipients.

One of the major critics of welfare was the controversial scholar Charles Murray. In his influential 1984 tome, *Losing Ground: American Social Policy, 1950–1980*, Murray describes an utter failure of a system.[30] Murray claimed that welfare not only created greater dependency but also increased the number of illegitimate births. For many conservatives, Murray's argument that "the guarantee of welfare benefits—not only cash but also food stamps, Medicaid, housing, and many other programs—helped lead young men and women to a reduced state of vigilance in avoiding pregnancy before marriage" rang true.[31] Illegitimacy had by the beginning of the 1990s become a major concern of anti-welfare activists. However, as Ron Haskins notes, the empirical studies "are weak and somewhat inconsistent, the results provide only moderate evidence that welfare is linked with illegitimacy."[32] Both liberals and conservatives used existing social science data to justify their policy positions. In doing so, both made the issue increasingly difficult politically.

As early as 1986 policy groups were being formed to examine welfare and decide whether it should be completely overhauled. Policy experts at the Olin Foundation, Bradley Foundation, and American Enterprise Institute in Washington organized a group of policy experts for the purpose of determining how to reform welfare. The working seminar, as it was called, linked welfare with behavioral dysfunction and dependency. It claimed that work and responsibility must be part of any welfare reform effort.[33] This group included Democrats such as Alice Rivlin, Barbara Blum, Franklin Raines, and Robert Reischauer, adding greater credibility to this seemingly impossible issue.

Lawrence Mead's book *Beyond Entitlement: The Social Obligations of Citizenship* is considered one of the leading works on welfare in the years leading up to 1996.[34] Mead, a Republican, believed that America's social policy was deeply flawed. In essence, without a reciprocal arrangement whereby recipients are expected to do something in return for benefits, it is a system that promotes selfishness and dysfunction. As sociologist Margaret Weir wrote in a critical review of Mead's work, "by not requiring the recipients of public assistance to do anything in return for aid, the state effectively prevents the poor from attaining the social competence necessary to be integrated into the larger society."[35] Legitimate and serious issues such as these added to the persistent belief that welfare was harmful to its recipients and a drain on society. Taxpayer money was making the situation worse.

A new class of black Republicans and conservatives eagerly took to the airwaves and print media, including Thomas Sowell, Juan Williams, Walter Williams, Shelby Steele, John McWhorter, and Larry Elder. John McWhorter notes, "Rejecting mainstream norms became vibrantly fashionable in young America, and in black America this often translated into a bone-deep wariness of 'white' norms. Secondly, welfare became an open-ended opportunity, led by people actively seeking people to bring onto the rolls."[36] For most black conservatives, welfare and blacks participation in welfare was a values issue. Their participation in the debate over welfare conferred legitimacy to conservative arguments that welfare actually hurt people. In addition, black critics of welfare, by their very presence, were able to undermine the Congressional Black Caucus's position that welfare reform was simply a nod to racists or other conservatives hell bent on ending the program. To accept welfare was to tempt long-term dependency, illegitimacy, and dysfunction. Moreover, why would African Americans, considering their tortured history with the US government, want more involvement from government officials? Welfare was cruel, they argued, and academic elites needed to stop coddling recipients and encourage responsibility, work, and accountability. This sentiment was echoed, as revealed by Clinton advisor Elaine Kamarck, by the most powerful element within black America: the church.[37] Conservative rhetoric about work, combined with the New Democrat message of President Clinton about responsibility, community, and accountability, resonated with a growing black middle class that had matured and splintered since the end of the civil rights era.

The State of American Welfare
at the Beginning of 1992

In 1992, President Clinton began talking opening and forcefully about ending welfare as we know it. He was able to confer legitimacy upon the controversial proposal to end welfare by delivering values-laden rhetoric that emphasized the importance of work and a normal life. Clinton's own rhetoric, combined with the Republican victories in 1994, meant that the president had to take welfare reform even more seriously, as the Republicans controlled both houses of Congress. Clinton speechwriter David Kusnet notes that for Clinton a "normal life" had profound meaning; "he realized, as most presidents and most successful professionals in this country do not realize, that to have a normal life is a great accomplishment. . . . What Clinton was thinking was that having a job gives structure to your life."[38] Ending Aid to Families with Dependent Children—traditional welfare based in part upon cash payments to recipients—was seen by the DLC and Clinton as a necessary step in order to rectify a supposedly dangerous system that trapped poor Americans in a vicious cycle of dependency and misery. As part of his plan to end AFDC, Clinton proposed doubling the Earned Income Tax Credit.[39]

No other piece of legislation, regulation, or tax manipulation was more important in terms of abolishing AFDC than this part of the tax code. The Earned Income Tax Credit was created in 1976 to offset the Social Security taxes of low-income workers with children and to provide those taxpayers with an increased incentive to work.[40] Senator Russell Long, for decades one of the foremost tax experts in Washington, offered the credit in Congress in hopes of making sure that only those who deserved it actually received it. Long, a Democrat from Louisiana, opposed not only President Nixon's Family Assistance Plan but also taxpayers' money going into the pockets of the "undeserving." Unlike AFDC, which was politically controversial, EITC was politically popular and acceptable because of its focus on work. EITC, New Democrat ideology, an electoral disaster (for President Clinton and the Democratic Party), and a growing polarization of the American polity would lead to a monumental change in America's safety net in less than four years. As Joe Klein noted, "He expanded the

Earned Income Tax Credit from $15.9 to $21.2 billion in the first year, which, in effect, cut taxes for fifteen million families."[41]

The cornerstone for this development was the "Republican Contract with America," published in the fall of 1994.[42] The Personal Responsibility Act was designed to abolish the old program with a very narrow—somewhat punitive, some argued—replacement program that forced recipients to work and promoted responsibility. Its mission was simple: to "discourage illegitimacy and teen pregnancy by prohibiting welfare to minor mothers and denying increased AFDC for additional children while on welfare, cut spending for welfare programs, and enact a tough two-years-and-out provision with work requirements to promote individual responsibility."[43] In 1991, some forty House Republicans formed a meeting group called the Wednesday Group. Its cochairmen were Vin Weber and Bill Gradison. As economist Mary Reinstma noted, "as early as October 1991 this group had published a paper entitled 'Moving Ahead: Initiatives for Expanding Opportunity in America' which recommended, inter alia, mandatory work and time limits."[44] The ideas of the Wednesday Group, combined with the "Contract with America" focus on eliminating welfare and Republicans' newfound power after the 1994 elections, meant that welfare reform was going to be among the first issues taken up by the new Congress in 1995.

Disconnect: African Americans and African American Political Leaders

African Americans were not monolithic in their views of welfare. Nearly sixty years of experience, direct or indirect, with the welfare system had provided many African Americans with strong opinions of the benefits and drawbacks of this most controversial social entitlement. Thirty years after the passage of the Civil Rights and Voting Rights Acts, racial integration had fundamentally changed the dynamics of the African American community, creating class divisions that brought many middle- and upper-class blacks into general agreement with whites on this issue. One notable difference, however, was that whites often saw welfare as a sign of group pathology while blacks saw it as intrusive and damaging to racial uplift.

President Clinton both understood and relied upon this growing dichotomy to achieve his legislative and political goals. Elaine Kamarck noted that President Clinton "went into black churches and sold welfare reform. . . . [W]e focus-grouped welfare reform with black audiences. . . . They were mad as hell about the welfare system."[45] Stan Greenberg, another Clinton aide, noted, "The fact that he came out of the South and had the support he did with black clergy meant that he could raise these issues in ways that others couldn't."[46] The president's values-oriented rhetoric resonated, as in his memorable 1993 speech in Memphis to a large black church. Clinton's power with African Americans, in large part, reflected a yearning within the African American community for an earlier time, before integration, crack cocaine, gangs, prisons, and globalization upended the traditionally tight familial and communal bonds of the African American community. No place was this more apparent than in the vitriolic debate over welfare reform. It was the African American political class that appeared behind their constituents in relation to the African American masses. Since the vast majority of Congressional Black Caucus members represented traditional, liberal-leaning districts, their political interests differed from those who represented more middle-of-the-road districts that wanted welfare reform. Furthermore, the CBC, a powerful voting bloc in Congress, had overlooked the demographic, political, financial, and social changes that had been occurring since the 1970s. As more African Americans climbed the ladder to the middle class, they viewed social entitlement spending as counterproductive to the interests of their community. It foreshadowed a powerful schism within African American politics that came to symbolize the nuance of black politics at the end of the twentieth century.

Once the welfare debate began to heat up after the Republican takeover of Congress in 1995, African American members of Congress took to the floor to denounce measures to reform America's social safety net. Georgia congressman John Lewis rose to attack the bill on March 21, 1995. Quoting Hubert Humphrey, Lewis said, "The moral test of government is how that government treats those who are in the dawn of life—the children; those who are in twilight of life—the elderly; and those who are in the shadow of life—the sick, the needy, and the handicapped. Mr. Chairman, this welfare proposal attacks each and every one of these groups."[47] The next day California congresswoman Maxine Waters, a former social worker, spoke from the well of the House and said, "No one has the corner on wanting reform. We would all like to see reform in the system. . . . We need to deal with the root causes of this problem, and we need to build into welfare reform the real opportunity for people to become independent by offering real jobs, job training and child care."[48] They, along with other liberals and members of the Congressional Black Caucus, were reacting to such Republican proposals as a family cap to cut off aid to young mothers who continued to have children, two years of maximum aid for welfare recipients, and deep cuts in food stamps and medical care. For African American members of Congress, the reforms signaled something much more alarming: an attempt by conservatives to end not only the federal government's responsibility to assist those who could not help themselves, but also the government's commitment to help African Americans. Since the Great Society programs of the 1960s, the government was perceived to have taken up the responsibility of helping to uplift African Americans. To Waters, Lewis, and others in the CBC, it appeared that that commitment was coming to an end.

Since the Clinton administration welfare reform plan died in 1994, after the president made clear that his top legislative priorities were health care reform and the crime bill, welfare reform increasingly became a Republican issue in 1995 and 1996. In the mindset of the CBC and its liberal allies, reform was a Republican issue more than a Clinton issue, freeing congressional Democrats to attack the bill with few concerns as to the political consequences. CBC members seemed to view Clinton's welfare reform as more of a political overture to independent-leaning Americans than a serious attempt to reform America's safety net. Jacob Weisberg of the *New Yorker* noted, "The broad challenge for Clinton on welfare has been to seize the center without losing the left."[49] Evelyn Z. Brodkin of *Dissent* noted that the decision to sign welfare reform in 1996 into law brought a "rebuke from the Congressional Black Caucus. But Clinton's decision effectively took the welfare issue away from the Republicans and highlighted Clinton's 'new Democratic' appeal to critical swing suburban and blue-collar, crossover voters."[50] Besides, Clinton's original proposals included billions in aid to help people get a fair opportunity to leave the welfare system. Believing that Clinton was more liberal on the issue, the CBC cast welfare reform as a Republican attempt to eliminate a critical entitlement to appease white racists and economic conservatives.

With the support of liberal interest groups such as the Children's Defense Fund, Liberal members took to the floor of Congress and the airwaves to attack the conservative measures as dangerous, mean spirited, and morally repugnant. Further, Republican welfare reform was believed to be a tax maneuver to reduce costs at the risk of the poor. On March 23, 1995, Pennsylvania congressman Bob Walker attacked Charles Rangel's defense of welfare as "actually corrupt and it is immoral."[51] In response, Rangel took to the floor the next day, saying, "Is this to reduce the deficit, is this for our national interests? No, it is for special interests. Let us see who is immoral and who is corrupt."[52] Liberal members, especially those in the CBC, represented districts that were traditionally liberal and opposed to centrism. While African American members were sincere in their criticisms of the bill, any change to the entitlement system was seen as a threat to their power, their influence, and the interests of the poor. What was not fully considered were the interests and opinions of the African American community. These vociferous political attacks were frequently stinging. They came not just from African American members of Congress but from the NAACP, the Children's Defense Fund, Jesse Jackson and the Rainbow Coalition, Al Sharpton of the National Action Network, and the National Organization for Women.

Ron Brownstein of the *Los Angeles Times* reported that 73 percent of blacks polled supported welfare reform that would require recipients to work to keep their benefits and the two year maximum time allowable to remain on the dole.[53] This data is obviously at odds with the lockstep support for the welfare system within the Congressional Black Caucus. It demonstrated that Clinton's New Democrat message on changing welfare as we know it resonated with more than just middle-class whites resentful of social entitlements that allegedly had run amok. This was lost on many black members of Congress.

Sharon D. Wright notes, "Only two of the thirty-nine black members of Congress voted for the welfare reform legislation, despite poll showings that 58 percent of black voters and 66 percent of white voters supported it."[54] The two that did vote for the bill were Republican House members J. C. Watts of Oklahoma and Gary Franks of Connecticut.

The issue of reforming welfare became more about politics and opposition than the policy itself. When the Republican Party took over control of Congress in 1995, they brought with them all the zeal and anger fit for a party that had been out of control in Congress for four decades. African American politicos therefore were skeptical of any changes to the ADFC program, because they originated from the Republican Party. The Congressional Black Caucus saw welfare reform in political and racial terms as opposed to policy terms. The leaders had been forged in the crucible of the 1960s and its aftermath. Where there could be some general consensus on issues such as crime after decades of increasingly racialized debate and characterization of public programs for the poor, there would be little compromise on welfare. Everyone dug into their respective positions, convinced of the sinister motives of the other.

Welfare Reform, 1993–1995

As the Clinton administration took office in January 1993, few issues were as important as the economy. The massive tax cuts, combined with skyrocketing defense budgets, not only had put the nation in a huge fiscal hole but had contributed to the deep recession that had propelled Bill Clinton the Oval Office in the first place. While economic stimulus was the top priority in 1993, conservatives thought that the opportunity to reform America's safety net had finally arrived.

President Clinton took office promising to usher in a new era of opportunity, responsibility, and community. Instead, he became consumed with the national deficit, his economic plan, and the one piece of old Democratic legislation dating back to the New Deal that was still unfulfilled: health care reform. Concern over the so-called crisis in health care made sense when one considered the relevant facts. According to the Bureau of the Census, more than 15.3 percent of the population in 1993 was not covered by any health insurance.[55] The crisis in health care was growing as millions of Americans lost jobs due to layoffs, outsourcing, and reductions in benefits made available to American workers. Furthermore, as Jason DeParle noted, "Clinton had reasons to proceed as he did. There were 14 million people on welfare, but three times as many without health insurance. Medical inflation was out of control, and if recipients were going to live decently as workers, they would need health care."[56] The overriding concern for health care allowed Republican and conservative critics to label Clinton as a typical Democratic big spender. As DeParle and others noted, this was a decision he came to regret for years to come. In fact, New Democrats were upset that Clinton appeared to have fallen into the old liberal trap of identity politics that did not enjoy a broad consensus of support. At the same time, liberals accused Clinton of opportunism in pushing welfare reform, anti-crime efforts, and NAFTA. Kenneth Baer noted, "These observers argued that Clinton had inherent tendencies to compromise and had 'vacillating desires.'"[57] Baer also pointed out that such political behavior was also a part of his personality and that he was "a total tactician."[58]

In an attempt to alleviate concerns about the administration's progress on welfare reform, Clinton took direct aim at the issue during a speech before the National Governors' Association. Besides noting that he would soon appoint a welfare reform task force, Clinton also said, "[I] wanted to tell you the principles . . . that will guide my administration as we work with you to reform welfare. First, welfare should be a second chance, not a way of life. I want to give people on welfare the education and training and opportunities they need to become self-sufficient. To make sure they can do it after they do go to work, they must still have access to health care and to child care."[59] The governors became increasingly important participants in the welfare debate because of a sense that power for themselves and their respective states could be grabbed, while the states' fiscal commitment potentially could be lessened. Also, there was no shortage of governors looking for political stardom. These governors were looking to use the issue to further their own political careers.

Clinton had been centering his arguments about welfare around work since he was governor of Arkansas. While he himself believed in the importance of work, he also understood the unique dynamics of welfare and how easily the welfare issue would and could be used to attack minorities, women, immigrants, and others. By the 1990s, African Americans constituted the highest percentage of recipients on the welfare. According to the *Green Book*, published annually by the US House of Representatives' Ways and Means Committee, in 1994 more African Americans were living in poverty than any other racial group: 30.6 percent or 33,353,000.[60] As Elizabeth Lower-Basch of the Office of the Assistant Secretary for Planning and Evaluation at Health and Human Services noted, there were some 1,700,000 AFDC/TANF black families between 1992 and 1995.[61] There were a multitude of reasons for such disparity in American society. Problems unique in sheer scale to the African American community included malnutrition, violence, lack of high-quality education, persistent job discrimination, structural and institutional barriers, globalization, and lack of access to capital and wealth. As the nonpartisan Urban Institute pointed out, "more than thirty years after the passage of civil rights legislation, significant economic and social inequalities persist amongst racial and ethnic groups in the United States."[62] The ideas of equality and fairness rang hollow for those left outside the so-called American dream. Globalization and deindustrialization continued and exacerbated inequality.

Welfare Reform, 1995–1996

Following the devastating midterm elections of 1994, Democrats on Capitol Hill and in the White House were in disarray. When the Republican Party captured control of both the House and the Senate, it gained the power that naturally comes along with majorities in Congress: subpoena power, committee chairmanships, budgetary control of the government, control of the amendment process, control of the influential rules committees, and control of the legislative calendar. President Clinton found himself in troubled waters with his domestic agenda in tatters. On welfare reform, Clinton found himself vulnerable as conservative Republicans sought more conservative solutions to reform welfare than they previously thought possible.

Clinton had initiated the conversation on welfare in 1992, but with the election of 1994, he had lost control over the important specifics of the welfare reform effort. Ron Haskins, one of the leading staffers on the House Ways and Means Committee, recounted in his tome about the historic bill, "The welfare system the nation had constructed over a half century was vulnerable as it never had been before."[63] Moreover, Clinton needed to win reelection in 1996. Peter Edelman explained, "Clinton made a brilliant political deal for himself: The deal was, implicitly, the Republicans get to keep the House because they can point to this achievement, and Clinton gets reelected president. As far as the Republicans were concerned, he was going to be reelected anyway. He took out election insurance."[64] As Clinton tried to balance his agenda with the political realities of Congress, more and more aspects of the Republican plans for welfare reform appeared to be tolerable, such as grants to the states, abolishing aid for immigrants, and time limits for aid. As Edelman understood it, "the message coming from Washington to the states was get people off welfare."[65] On March 24, 1995, the Republican-led House of Representatives tried to do just that by passing the Personal Responsibility Act of 1995. On the floor of the House, Hawaii congresswoman Patsy Mink and Pennsylvania congressman Chaka Fattah chastised the bill as "cruel." In addition, Fattah attacked the GOP for the "85 billion dollars worth of welfare subsidies for corporate America."[66] Other noteworthy Democrats also criticized the bill, such as New York senator Daniel Patrick Moynihan, who told the *New York Times* that the House bill was a "draconian measure."[67] In his weekly radio address, Clinton said, "The House bill would actually make it harder for many people to get off and stay off welfare. . . . It removes any real responsibility for states to help people gain the training and skills they need to get and keep jobs. It even cuts child care for working people struggling to hold down jobs and stay off welfare."[68] Clinton wanted market-based solutions to complex problems such as poverty, lack of education, and lack of opportunity. It was not so much a left or right shift as it was seeking the political middle ground and putting people to work. African Americans were treated as an afterthought. Pushing millions of people off the welfare rolls without education, training, or specialized help with child-care needs would have a disproportionate effect on African Americans.

While the Clinton administration was obviously concerned with the GOP proposals in the House and Senate, it was also growing more concerned with the punitive measures inserted into the new legislation. Despite her later support for the Welfare Reform Act of 1996, the secretary of health and human services, Donna Shalala, expressed grave reservations about the impending bill. In a memorandum written to the president in January 1995, Shalala wrote, "We believe this may be a defining issue for your presidency. . . . By contrast block grants largely abandon the hope of bold national change toward a welfare system more in keeping with the nations." In addition, she warned that block grants implied that they had no real national goals or vision for their social welfare policy. But Shalala also noted that the block grants were appealing to the administration in comparison to the "draconian cuts the Republicans have on the table now. And they seem consistent with your strong commitment to state flexibility."[69]

In 1995, as the budget and government shutdowns dominated the news cycle, the political attention on welfare reform waned. What little momentum Clinton had, which helped his standing among African Americans, came from his two vetoes of welfare reform. Among the key reasons for Clinton's vetoes of the first two welfare reform bills was what he considered unacceptable and mean-spirited cuts to vital social problems such as Medicare/Medicaid and early childhood education programs. The negotiations between Clinton and the Republican leadership were tense. In addition, Clinton was growing weary of the posturing of the GOP on domestic issues. As Taylor Branch said, "They all wanted to balance the budget, but they would throw 380,000 kids out of Head Start. Or slash college loans and Medicaid. If he must close the government to uphold countervailing value, so be it."[70] After the second veto on January 9, 1996, Clinton emerged victorious from the budget battle, and he had successfully framed the welfare debate in terms that made the Republicans look like they were going to end Medicaid. By the end of the spring, however, the GOP had regained political momentum with its push for a balanced budget agreement. The idea of a balanced budget, a central tenet of Republican philosophy, resonated with Middle America. In addition, as Haskins noted, the spring of 1996 brought new political forces into the fray that helped to "Revive the Revolution," as nearly every governor from both political parties supported reform.[71] This, combined with an election coming in November, meant that Republicans were resurgent going into the late spring and summer of 1996.

In Congress, Democrats appeared resigned to the fact that welfare reform would pass by the fall of 1996. As Haskins noted, "[The] subcommittee markup on June 5, about two weeks after the bill [had] been introduced, did nothing to dissuade us from the view that not only had Republicans become more focused, but Democrats had too. . . . Whereas the 1995 subcommittee markup had lasted three days, the 1996 markup lasted a little more than seven hours and was completed in one day."[72] As the House passed its version on July 18, and the Senate its version on July 23, the stage was set for a new showdown with the president.

President Clinton tried to preempt some of the coming changes by "requiring all 50 states to follow these states' lead and ensure that JOBS participants move into work after two years."[73] Moreover, Republicans wanted to end AFDC, impose its replacement Temporary Aid to Needy Families (TANF), end all assistance to immigrants, create block grants for the states, virtually eliminate federal control over the system, provide abstinence education, and impose a two-year limit of aid, a work requirement, and a five-year lifetime limit to aid. Unable to reach a decision internally, the Clinton White House stalled for time, and in the process left Democrats on the Hill with little or no direction. ·

As the White House debated the pros and cons of supporting and signing welfare reform into law, members of the Congressional Black Caucus took to the floor of the House and Senate to denounce the bill. In the upper chamber, Senator Carol Moseley-Braun delivered a blistering attack on the legislation, saying, "This bill is still an abomination, which is what I called the previous bill, and I intend to vote against it for precisely that reason—and I keep coming back to the question, and no one has answered the question: What about the children? What happens to them when all is said and done, with all the cuts and the changes that we are making with this legislation?"[74] Other members also expressed concern with its impact of minorities, women, and children. Florida congresswoman Carolyn Meeks argued, "Children are in that minority of legal immigrants you are talking about. You want to ban food stamps from these people and these children, you want to ban SSI from them, and you want to keep them from becoming what they could, and, that is, true American citizens as you have become."[75] Asian American congressman Robert Matsui of California remarked, "This debate is all about—to jeopardize 9 million children who will be affected by this bill just to put the President of the United States in a box."[76] Congressman Charles Rangel acknowledged the importance of work and recipients finding work but also expressed frustration that "the Republicans will throw 2 million people, children, into poverty, and my President will only throw 1 million into poverty."[77] Jim Clyburn of South Carolina told the House, "Rather than being a constructive debate, the welfare reform debate has become, for the most part silly talk of budgetary savings and time limits. . . . With the talk of personal responsibility being tossed around, I find it ironic that at the same time our Nation's most vulnerable families are being required to do more for themselves, our States are being asked to do even less."[78] These were but some of the numerous pleas coming from members of the Congressional Black Caucus. CBC members, sensing the anger brewing among conservatives, prevented by decades of Democratic control of Congress, to end a social entitlement they believed to be un-American, had nothing left but moral indignation and scorn. However, with the president vacillating on the controversial legislation, there was nothing that could be done to stop it.

The final bill was filed after midnight on the night of July 31. Clinton met with his top advisors to decide what to do. According to Haskins, no advisor, except for Mickey Kantor, advised the president to sign the pending legislation. After the meeting with his top advisers and a post meeting wrap up with Al Gore, Leon Panetta, and John Hilley, Clinton decided to sign the bill into law. It was not the perfect bill by any stretch; however, it accomplished goals dear to the president, such as moving recipients from welfare to work, time limits, more control for the states, and market-based measures for the employment of recipients. In addition, many of the worst Republican additions to the bill, such as the severe cuts to Medicaid, were either eliminated or scaled back. The only problems Clinton had with the bill, the cutting of funds to immigrants and for nutritional supplements, could be reinstated at a later date. By a vote of 328 to 101 in the House of Representatives and

78 to 21 in the Senate, the conference report passed. This was after 98 Democrats in the House and 25 in the Senate voted in favor of the new law.[79] After decades of division, the welfare reform was a new reality. The Personal Responsibility and Work Opportunity Act of 1996 was signed into law by President Clinton at the White House on August 22, 1996.[80] This new reality would come, often, at a high cost to those unfortunate enough to be associated with it.

Impact of Welfare Reform on Blacks

The impact of welfare reform on African Americans was myriad. The United States Commission on Civil Rights, citing the Citizens' Commission on Civil Rights, "concluded that 'due to the disproportionately large numbers of women and minorities who rely on Medicaid for health care coverage, these changes will have a disparate impact on their ability to obtain medical services.'"[81] The argument that welfare recipients simply needed to work ignored that many of those people faced staggering problems in the workplace and home. As the Citizens' Commission on Civil Rights noted, the cyclical patterns of people coming off welfare and then returning at a later date "revealed a more fundamental problem: many participants were encountering difficulties finding or keeping a job because of specific barriers that hindered their ability to stay employed."[82] African Americans found the transition from welfare to work the toughest. As Lydia L. Blalock, Vicky R. Tiller, and Pamel A. Monroe note, "race plays a role in persistent poverty in the United States, with the U.S. Census Bureau reporting the poverty level for Blacks at around 26%. For Blacks, race may be a more significant predictor of poverty than other factors like education."[83] These barriers included educational deficiencies, lack of job skills, language barriers, child-care issues, transportation, substance and abuse troubles, and mental health problems. Working often did not cover the recipient's monthly expenses. Since so many of those recipients were women, once they entered the workforce they were often earning less than their male counterparts, which compounded the problem.[84] These problems were reflected in statistics that demonstrated "welfare caseloads now have larger proportions of minority clients than ever before and increasingly are concentrated in large urban areas that typically have higher concentrations of minorities."[85] Complicating the issue was that the current status of many former recipients was unknown.

Another issue resulting from the passage of welfare reform was the privatization of services. Using block grants appropriated by the federal law as well as the lenient guidelines regarding the operation of AFDC's replacement, Temporary Aid to Needy Families (TANF), many states hired private companies to administer the program. In states such as Wisconsin, New York, and Arizona, Maximus, Inc., ran the new welfare program. In Florida, Workforce Florida controlled the distribution of benefits. Other states also tried to figure out ways to outsource their welfare caseloads. The major impact of such arrangements was that millions of people, a disproportionate number of whom were African Americans, were thrown off welfare so that these companies could maximize their profits by meeting goals for caseload reductions given by the state. As Jason DeParle noted, the only way private companies could turn a profit was by pushing people off welfare and into work assignments. In addition, DeParle noted that in Milwaukee, from 2000 to 2003, despite its work programs, "the unemployment rate surged to 9.7%."[86] Many African Americans who needed assistance were denied by the very people that were supposed to help them. The National Association of Black Social Workers grimly noted, "Despite the significant decrease in all state caseloads in numbers, overall the percent of Blacks (and Latinos) on TANF caseloads are increasing."[87] The persistence of high unemployment, lack of affordable health care, job dislocation, and low-wage labor had a disproportionate effect on the African American community.[88]

Using the private sector as a main instrument in distributing welfare benefits and pushing recipients into the world of work was typical of the centrist philosophy of President Clinton. As Will Marshall wrote in the *New Democrat*, "a redesigned welfare policy should decentralize decisions and resources, force the bureaucracy to compete with private and civic actors in helping move people to self-sufficiency, and [be] financed through cuts in government programs and subsidies rather than through new taxes or borrowing."[89] The federal government reduced its responsibility to the nation's poor.

Due to the problems associated with TANF, it is clear that welfare reform better assuaged the resentment of the American public than used government resources to assist recipients' transition to work and independence. Clinton's support for the bill, in a case of unintended consequences, justified and legitimized the character attacks against African Americans and others on the welfare.

Labor problems for African Americans also resulted from the new law. Labor unions, generally among the strongest supporters for the working poor, resented the placement of welfare recipients in entry-level jobs. Many employers cooperating with the various states were given incentives to hire welfare recipients. As CNN noted two years after the new law took effort, "Labor Unions object to hiring welfare recipients for entry level jobs. . . . [They are] fearful of a new crop of very cheap labor replacing union workers."[90] Not only did this law pose issues for organized labor but arguably led to exploitation of new workers. Since African Americans were being pushed off the welfare rolls in larger numbers than members of other races, they were more likely to feel the resentment of those who were unionized. While the AFL-CIO encouraged the proposed transition from welfare to work, it wanted those new employees to have rights. Under the new law, welfare recipients had to work twenty to thirty hours a week to continue benefits. As Jeffrey B. Fannell noted, "in 1997, the AFL-CIO Executive Council passed a resolution declaring its support of efforts to organize welfare workers by integrating them into existing bargaining units and creating new bargaining units."[91] Many of these workers were placed in entry-level, low-paying minimum wage jobs that did little to uplift them out of their present circumstances. Growing economic inequality and class stratification only accelerated in the years after the bill became law. In a prophetic speech before the National Baptist Convention a little over a year before welfare reform passed, Secretary of Labor Robert B. Reich warned that the United States was "surging toward still greater inequality at an alarming pace and called the development "the country's most virulent threat to family values."[92] Clinton's own Labor chief was presenting a key argument that those opposed to this welfare reform bill used before and after the passage of 1996 welfare reform law: it would be useless unless the growing social inequity in American society was addressed. The monumental changes brought on by deindustrialization and globalization presented special problems for the uneducated and low skilled. Welfare reform would present unique barriers and seemingly intractable problems for those moving from welfare to work.

The law also hurt the prospects for the African American family. Despite President Clinton's assertion that the Personal Responsibility and Work Opportunity Reconciliation Act "demands personal responsibility, and puts in place tough child support enforcement measures . . . [and] promotes family and children," the bill itself never addressed the hidden realities of the postindustrial world of work.[93] African Americans transitioning from welfare to work found an often-unforgiving economic environment. As Arloc Sherman and others have noted, "even among parents who leave the welfare rolls for work, few earn enough to support a family, either because their wages are very low or their jobs are unstable."[94] This unpleasant fact affected African American families more than others. Even the National Governors' Association expressed concern over the low pay and the prospects of recipients lifting themselves out of poverty.[95]

Once the new law went in effect, children were often without parental supervision. States often lacked the financial resources to provide child-care services or subsidies to those who needed it. Making the matter worse, states often did poorly in educating their citizens about the child-care assistance that was available. As revealed in the Children's Defense Fund/National Coalition for the Homeless report, "in South Carolina, for example, over half of former recipients surveyed by the state were unaware of child care assistance."[96] In states with a sizable population of African Americans—California, New York, Michigan, South Carolina, Georgia, Pennsylvania, Illinois— such a lack of resources presented significant barriers to those seeking employment. Without adequate care, children were often left to their own devices. Mothers had to leave small children, from infants to kindergarteners, with others; sometimes these babysitters were relatively unknown to the mother. This was how it was for most urban welfare recipients. Jason DeParle quoted a recipient in Milwaukee, Wisconsin: "'We're surviving! . . . 'Cause that's what we have to do.'"[97] For people like the ones DeParle studied for his book, welfare reform removed what little support many of these people had. It also put women in a precarious position by not providing the material and financial support they needed to actually transition into a position of security where they could pay their bills, raise their children, and live a decent, modest life away from government assistance programs. Obviously, this presented a major dilemma for African American mothers struggling to adhere to the new law and take care of their children at the same time.

The effect of the Personal Responsibility and Work Opportunity Act of 1996 was to compound the problems of America's underclass. In raw numerical terms, welfare reform was a success, because millions of Americans left the rolls. That fact, however, masked deeper structural and economic problems faced by those no longer able to receive welfare benefits. By forcing recipients into work, the new law compelled people to take a job, any job, and it did not have to be a good one. Millions took low-paying jobs with no benefits and no future prospects. Often these jobs were in fast-food restaurants, janitorial services, call centers, landscaping, and other menial jobs. The work provided them with no escape from the depravities of living in poverty. To the extent that welfare reform was passed and implemented in an allegedly colorblind manner, it had a disproportionate impact on African Americans. James Jennings demonstrated that "welfare reform ha[d] differential racial and ethnic impact in those predominantly black and Latino neighborhoods with high number of recipients compared to other neighborhoods."[98] Further, Jennings pointed out that various studies showed that African Americans had more negative experiences trying to get jobs or getting referred to educational programs before being required to get a job, and they often received less welfare benefits than white recipients.[99] This was the hazard of implementing a policy which sought to address welfare by attacking the individuals on it instead of the larger macroeconomic issues such as education, health care, child care, domestic malfunction, and structural and institutional barriers. In a study of ten families that were once on the welfare rolls, Blalock, Tiller, and Monroe wrote, "Although some of the women were employed, the lives of these families cannot be classified as economically self-sufficient, and many of the families were in as deep a state of poverty as they had ever been."[100] Such results confirmed the concerns of the Congressional

Black Caucus, the Children's Defense Fund, and liberal scholars of the American welfare state. Moreover, the deep strain felt by former recipients was indicative of the punitive and narrow-minded approach to fixing welfare.

In a 2002 report prepared by Z. Fareen Parvez for the Sociologists for Women in Society, it was shown that African Americans actually increased as a percentage of the welfare rolls. In 1996, the year that welfare reform was signed into law, African Americans made up 37 percent of the welfare rolls. By 2000 that number had increased to 39 percent. Furthermore, Hispanics increased from 21 percent of the rolls in 1996 to 25 percent in 2000. In comparison, whites decreased from 36 percent in 1996 to 31 percent in 2000.[101] Since women made up 90 percent of TANF recipients, and black women were far more likely to be single with children, the new law impacted minorities more than it did whites. These trends continued throughout the 2000s as African Americans remained disproportionately the recipients of welfare. At the height of the economic bubble of the 2000s, in 2006, according to the Department of Health and Human Services, African Americans were 36 percent of the TANF recipients, whites accounted for 33 percent, and Hispanics made up 26 percent.[102] Parvez notes, "Blacks are also the only racial group that experienced an increase in the percentage of low-income, non-welfare recipients. Studies show that white TANF recipients are referred to educational programs in much higher percentages than Black recipients."[103] In addition, a pattern developed after welfare reform became law where blacks were far more likely to be threatened with sanctions than whites, who were more likely to receive benefits because of increased income as opposed to punishment by welfare authorities.[104] These reports evidenced that the welfare reform law compounded the problems of the black poor, which accounted for fully one-third of the black population in the United States.

According to the Urban Institute there are five criteria that make up the black underclass: (1) single female-head households, (2) welfare dependency, (3) chronic unemployment, (4) criminal recidivism, and (5) marginal education. While welfare rolls dropped by more than 50 percent since the enactment of the 1996 reform law, the black underclass remains stubbornly entrenched. Marriage rates in the black community remain far behind those for whites. Poor blacks continue to face staggering obstacles to employment, especially employment that would be sufficient to raise a family. Black men face the high likelihood of going to prison and then, after release, being sent back to prison on new charges. Finally, blacks remain behind their white counterparts in terms of educational achievement, leaving them further behind their peers, less likely to climb into the middle class, and more vulnerable to the vagaries of the marketplace. Welfare reform ultimately served the purpose of Washington elites and middle-class America. That purpose was, as Edelman remarked, "to get people off welfare": it does not matter how you do it, as long as you do it.[105] Forcing people into low-level employment and stripping them of assistance often placed recipients in a position worse than the position they were in before. Moreover, the larger economic forces at work since the 1970s compounded the problems of poor, especially the black poor. In fact, as John Schmitt reported in 2009, the last thirty years "mark a significant departure from a five-decade trend toward greater economic and social equality."[106] The African American poor were the easiest to blame for America's troubles. Clinton's decision to sign what essentially was a Republican bill into law reflected the growing class and political divisions of the 1990s. It served the purpose of reducing the commitment of the American taxpayer, individual and business, to those who were living in poverty. The transition from manufacturing to finance, as noted by Judith Stein in *Pivotal Decade*, had major consequences for those at the bottom of the socioeconomic ladder.[107] No group of Americans benefited less than African Americans, who faced uneven, sometimes discriminatory treatment at the hands of caseworkers and employers, as well as personal, structural, and institutional barriers that limited their ability to reach self-sufficiency. With the very notable exception of the crime bill of 1994, no other law passed during the 1990s so clearly demonstrated the class and political divisions rifling through the American body politic during that crucial decade. Political scientist Marcus D. Pohlmann noted, "[Welfare reform] will enhance the position of the owning class by providing them with an easily exploitable group of workers in what essentially will amount to a condition of indentured servitude."[108]

Lastly, the Personal Responsibility and Work Opportunity Act of 1996 promoted and reinforced the pernicious notion that African

Americans were mooches, derelicts, and undeserving of taxpayer money. President Clinton failed to acknowledge the fact that most people on welfare, including African Americans, already worked. Nor did he recognize that the AFDC did not give those recipients enough to live on or a realistic chance at moving out of poverty. In a 2002 position paper, the National Association of Black Social Workers stated, "Five years of welfare reform has created little relief from poverty for poor African American families who continue to stagger under the strain of continued high levels of unemployment; job dislocation; and low wages."[109] This was confirmed in an article by *USA Today* ten years after the law was signed: "Today, 1.9 million families get cash benefits; in one-third of them, only the children qualify for aid. About 38% of those still on welfare are black, 33% white and 24% Hispanic."[110] If anything, African Americans were more of a presence on welfare than before. This is due, in part, to the ease with which whites on welfare found jobs compared to blacks and the ease with which political elites jettisoned the interests of the poor.

Conclusion

As Weaver astutely observed, "welfare reform succeeded in 1996 . . . because the racially stereotyped image of AFDC recipients made it especially vulnerable when the 1994 elections led to an upswing in support for Republicans."[111] For Clinton, welfare reform's racialized impact was, perhaps, unintentional; however, the damage was done. This was a risk Clinton was willing to take. His proposals and acceptance of the final bill "had strong political roots in a broader New Democratic political project of making the Democratic Party more attractive to Reagan Democrats and Perot voters, despite deep divisions between them and congressional Democrats on the issue."[112] The hands-off, unbridled faith in market-based solutions to complex social problems was a hallmark of the New Democrat approach. Compromise in the face of stiff political opposition, combined with Clinton's failure to address welfare reform successfully in his first two years when Democrats controlled both chambers of Congress, led to the a law which Edelman called "the worst thing Bill Clinton has done."[113] President Clinton later acknowledged the problems resulting from a lack of jobs in the cities in a speech before the Democratic Leadership Council in December 1996: "We must bring the freshest ideas to bear on how we can bring the power of private business to the inner city, where today there are simply not enough jobs for those who will no longer be eligible for permanent welfare."[114] Clinton said this less than four months after the bill became law. To his credit, the president did give serious thought and effort to bringing big and small businesses to the inner cities through his empowerment zones and enterprise community program.[115] The resources, however, were not in place to assist African Americans and others in their transition to work when welfare reform passed.

The disconnect between African American political leaders and ordinary African Americans was apparent in this controversial episode in the Clinton presidency. Blacks in Congress were clearly behind the growing national consensus regarding welfare. The growing national consensus was demonstrated as liberals and welfare advocacy groups became more marginalized during the debate over welfare in 1995–96. Ann Devroy, of the *Washington Post*, noted that the elections of 1994 and Clinton's own rhetoric in 1992 had changed the political atmosphere. Going further, Devroy noted that even one of the president's most senior aides, George Stephanopoulos, said "What has changed for Clinton is not his principles but his environment."[116] The environmental changes were clearly reflected in polling data that suggested most Americans were concerned about the austere measures proposed by the GOP. However, as David Hess of the *Philadelphia Inquirer* noted, "polling found strong support for reforming welfare."[117] Mainstream Americans, black and white, were supportive of limiting the reach of government, distrustful of government programs, and sensitive about any changes to middle-class programs such as Social Security and Medicare. Welfare reform was not one of their primary concerns. It demonstrated both the importance of class divisions in the 1990s and the continuity of Reaganism nearly a decade after he left office. These divisions were broad and far-reaching, yet indicative of the growth of political diversity, as well as division within the African American community. Such divisions within the broader middle-class African American community reflect a growing maturity based upon social and financial mobility. For African Americans this legislation not only had profound repercussions but led to a new era of race relations.

The unexpected consequence of welfare reform is that it removed welfare from the front burner of American politics.[118] More specifically, it removed the racialized debates surrounding welfare. No longer were there vitriolic, racially tinged debates about AFDC, welfare queens, and burdens on the system. Eliminated with it was the notion that there was a parallel system that penalized workers and taxpayers.[119] While many African Americans suffered from the punitive legislation, others benefited from the expansion in the economy, increased funds for Pell Grants, student loans, and educational/vocational support. Perhaps this was the effect Clinton was after all along: the elimination of a nasty debate that divided Americans along racial lines, income groups, and regional affiliations.

Clinton's endorsement of the legislation was the ultimate display of the New Democratic philosophy at work: conciliation, cooperation, and values-oriented solutions. On the tenth anniversary of the signing into law of welfare reform, President Clinton wrote an op-ed in the *New York Times* trumpeting its success. "While we compromised to reach an agreement, we never betrayed our principles and we passed a bill that worked and stood the test of time. This style of coopera- tive governing is anything but a sign of weakness. It is a measure of strength, deeply rooted in our Constitution and history, and essen- tial to the better future that all Americans deserve, Republicans and Democrats alike."[120] Ultimately, the fervor of welfare reform would pass and African Americans supportive of the overhaul were grateful for the president's actions. Yet the overhaul and Clinton's decision to make it law, in hindsight, were questioned extensively in the wake of the recession of 2001–02 and the Great Recession of 2007–09. What is the proper role of government in relation to the material need of the citizenry? Clinton's answer was that the primacy of work super- seded anything else. Through work came salvation, respect, and inde- pendence. Work, however, was not the soothing balm that healed the wounds of America's most vulnerable citizens; it was the solution that compounded the plight of the most vulnerable.

CHAPTER 7

A Missed Opportunity

President Clinton's Race Initiative, 1997–1998

RACE REMAINED A major impediment to progress in the 1990s. The social upheaval after the 1991 acquittal of the Los Angeles Police Department officers of beating Rodney King demonstrated the violent, contentious, and peculiar nature of race relations in the United States in the post–civil rights era. Politically, the nation mirrored the debates occurring in Washington, D.C. Those debates included the Congress, the Republican Party, the Democratic Party, think tanks, and activists. By the mid-1990s right-wing individuals and organizations, spurred on by the Republican Party, began to attack policies such as affirmative action that directly impacted the lives of African Americans. Attacks on affirmative action further fueled the resentment of whites toward African Americans and created a far more contentious atmosphere in the workplace. Those policies were being attacked in the courts as well as in popular culture. Scholars and others have written extensively about the unique racial dynamics at the end of the twentieth century. Those works include Shelby Steele's *A Dream Deferred* and *The Content of Our Character*, Cornel West's *Race Matters*, John McWhorter's *Winning the Race*, Christopher Edley Jr.'s *Not All Black and White: Affirmative Action and American Values*, and Lani Guinier's *Lift Every Voice*.[1]

One America was President Clinton's initiative to improve race relations, to open discussion, and to make recommendations for policy change. The combination of scandals, political rancor, and lack of public support for serious inquiry prevented the President's Initiative on Race from reaching its full potential. The PIR was a major failure of the Clinton White House. Clinton, his staff, and the Advisory Board failed to establish clearly defined goals for the initiative, address the critical attention in the media in a more forceful way, and control unethical behaviors that drew public attention away from the work of One America.

Beginning

On October 16, 1995, Louis Farrakhan and the Nation of Islam conducted the Million Man March in Washington, D.C. This event was supposed to be a clarion call to African American men to stand up and be counted, to take responsibility for themselves, and to stop the self-annihilation that Farrakhan saw blacks perpetuating on themselves. This was the backdrop for a major race-relations speech the next day at the University of Texas by President Clinton. Instead of the typical liberal speech that had come to be expected of Democratic politicians, Clinton spoke in the parlance of the New Democrat ethos he had embraced years before: it's about responsibility. "No good house was ever built on a bad foundation. Nothing good ever came of hate. So let us pray today that all who march and all who speak will stand for atonement, for reconciliation, for responsibility."[2] Clinton's words that day reflected the division within the African American community. Those divisions included disagreements over impartial mechanisms to achieve fair play in educational, economic, and professional opportunities. "To be sure, there is old, unfinished business between black and white Americans, but the classic American dilemma has now become many dilemmas of race and ethnicity."[3] The president's own words were also indicative of the sometimes fierce debates inside the White House. Since the 1992 presidential campaign, Clinton had been talking about race, affirmative action, and diversity, which he believed to be in the best interest of the nation and the African American community collectively. He appointed a number of high-profile black individuals to high-ranking positions within his administration.

In June 1997, the president took a dramatic step forward, trying to not only study but also work out some solutions to the nation's most perplexing problems: race relations and racial discontent. In a speech at the University of California at San Diego, Clinton announced that he had created "One America in the 21st Century: The President's Initiative on Race." By Executive Order 13050, he established a President's Advisory Board on Race that was charged with looking at ways to:

> (1) Promote a constructive national dialogue to confront and work through challenging issues that surround race;

> (2) Increase the Nation's understanding of our recent history of race relations and the course our Nation is charting on issues of race relations and racial diversity;

> (3) Bridge racial divides by encouraging leaders in communities throughout the Nation to develop and implement innovative approaches to calming racial tensions;

> (4) Identify, develop, and implement solutions to problems in areas in which race has a substantial impact, such as education, economic opportunity, housing, health care, and the adminis-tration of justice.[4]

Only three comprehensive, government-sponsored studies had ever been done on African Americans and race relations in history. The first one was *The American Dilemma* by Gunnar Myrdal in 1944.[5] Originally, the project began under the auspices of the Board of Carnegie Corporation. Myrdal was selected to write the report because he was Swedish and, therefore, believed to be able to impartially eval-uate America's racial problem. The book, critics wrote at the time, "is one of the best political commentaries on American life, because it places its discussion of politics in a well-rounded social science set-ting."[6] The second study was *To Secure These Rights: The Report of the President's Committee on Civil Rights*.[7] President Harry Truman commissioned a study to examine America's recent racial history and provide solutions for ensuring the civil rights of African Americans throughout the United States. The third study was the famous—or infamous—*The Negro Family: The Case for National Action*, which was published in 1965.[8] It was written by Daniel Patrick Moynihan during the height of agitation for civil rights and first-class citizenship for African Americans. The report discussed "pathologies" within the black community and outlined ways in which to assist uplifting blacks to educational, economic, and political parity with white Americans. It also discussed ways in which perceptions of African Americans have served as a major stumbling block to black advancement in the United States. At the time it was attacked for being paternalistic and even racist. While such studies can be helpful in promoting healthy race relations, they also can be fodder for distraction and partisanship.

Clinton's Initiative on Race was the latest attempt to reckon with the politically contentious matter of race in American society. Historians, as a result, have yet to examine in detail this important topic, and the scholarly literature on the President's Initiative on Race amounts to only a few articles. Political scientist Claire Jean Kim discussed the PIR in a *Polity* article from 2000, in which she placed the initiative in the context of Myrdal's work.[9] Renee M. Smith provided a critical examination of the problems of the initiative in a *Presidential Studies Quarterly* article in 1998.[10]

On June 12, 1997, five men and two women gathered in Washington, D.C., in the Oval Office to meet with President Clinton. At the meeting were famed historian Dr. John Hope Franklin, Los Angeles attorney Angela Oh, former New Jersey governor Thomas Kean, Bronx Christian Fellowship pastor Suzan D. Johnson, former counsel to the Assembly Special Committee on the Los Angeles Crises Robert Johnson, executive vice president of the AFL-CIO Linda Chavez-Thompson, and former Mississippi governor William Winter. This group was intentionally diverse in order to provide a broad range of opinions, perspectives, and possibilities for success. During the meeting the president informed the newly assembled Advisory Board that "he hoped that we would spark a serious dialogue on race and, on the basis of that dialogue and other findings, make recommendations to him for action."[11] The following day the board accompanied the president aboard Air Force One to San Diego for his speech at the University of California, San Diego.

One of the major reasons for this speech was the attack on

affirmative action by conservatives through court cases and voter referendums. The most notable and disconcerting case at the time of the address, in the opinion of President Clinton and civil rights organizations such as the NAACP, was California Proposition 209. In November 1996, a majority of California voters voted in favor of ending affirmative action practices in the state's higher educational system.[12] As a consequence of this controversial measure, enrollment of African Americans decreased significantly. Clinton was compelled to respond after this most recent attack on equality and opportunity for African Americans. In fact, conservatives had been challenging affirmative action through the courts since the 1970s.[13] Failing to make significant headway there, they turned their attention to the voters, often using much of the rhetoric of the civil rights movement and rhetorical flourishes about a colorblind society. Acknowledgment of race as a major factor in American life was likened to just bringing up the past or playing the race card. Once one argued that race was a factor, he or she was dismissed as either an opportunist or as someone engaged in grievance politics.

Clinton informed his listeners that they "faced a different choice: Will we become not two but many Americas, separate, unequal, and isolated? Or will we draw strength from all our people and our ancient faith in the quality of human dignity to become the world's first truly multicultural democracy? That is the unfinished work of our time, to lift the burden of race and redeem the promise of America."[14] Unlike the first two major studies on race, this effort was the result "not of a crisis, but of a unique opportunity."[15] The President's Initiative on Race had three major components: (1) the Advisory Board, (2) significant presidential events/actions throughout the year, and (3) outreach, consultation, and leadership recruitment.[16] Yet problems surfaced because the public lacked a clear understanding of the Advisory Board's authority and mission. Even the Advisory Board was somewhat flummoxed by these challenges. The Clinton White House did not adequately respond to rectify this public relations mistake. The PIR never was given the authority to investigate problems of a legal nature. One man, who had been allegedly unjustly fired from his job in New Jersey, traveled to the Durham home of Advisory Board chairman Dr. Franklin to plead his case. Franklin informed him that the PIR was not equipped to handle such issues and that the Equal Employment Opportunity Commission would have to take it up.[17] Despite that Franklin's visitor was a working-class man and not a media figure, the story indicates just how much confusion there was in the public over the actual mission of the PIR. However, beyond avoidable confusion over the role and responsibilities of the PIR, this incident illustrates the lack of direction, authority, and investigative powers imposed on the board by the Clinton White House.

The major media networks and publications relentlessly questioned the motives and legitimacy of the PIR. In a June 16, 1997, article in the *New York Times*, reporter Steven A. Holmes wrote, "Many said they believed that better relations between the races was a critical issue, though they were unsure how the President's speech or his appointment of a commission to study the problem would improve the country's racial climate."[18] This was an important critique of the PIR; however, that this article was written just after the announcement of PIR was demonstrative of the media's cynicism. *Time* tried to frame the issue as a Clinton/Democrat versus conservative/Republican fight. Eric Pooley wrote of Clinton and Proposition 209 advocate Ward Connerly: "While the initiative weathers a court challenge, Connerly has been traveling the country making speeches and accepting awards from conservatives who hail him as a hero fighting for his vision of a colorblind society, a black man whose rags-to-riches story suggests that preferences aren't necessary for black achievement."[19] This division and Connerly's campaign lent credence to the idea that preferences were no longer necessary and that America had reached a point where racism remained a vestige among the fringe elements within society.

Perhaps unknowingly, President Clinton also played into the vicious media whirlwind by participating in the now famous town hall meetings. Renee Smith writes, "By using a town-hall meeting approach, Clinton all but guaranteed that media coverage of his race initiative would be episodic, focusing on each meeting as a discrete event rather than focusing on the issue of race within its societal and historical contexts."[20] The public nature of the Advisory Board also reflected a major impediment to the successful execution of the president's stated goals. By law, the board was not allowed to meet in private; consequently, opponents with nefarious motives, as well as others simply curious about the boards' activities, were able to interject and frustrate the board's work. Those who sought to obstruct the work of the initiative were Republicans, radio talk show hosts such as Rush Limbaugh, Native American interest groups, and the media. They interfered by protesting the work of the initiative at every stage of its existence, casting doubt on the president's motives, and helping to further divide an American public that was already split along racial, sectional, regional, and class lines.

The Public

Public response to the president's initiative was mixed. During the 1980s and 1990s, public views on race sharpened to a degree not seen since the end of the civil rights movement. President Ronald Reagan had ushered in a new wave of conservatism that manifested itself along racial lines. By the 1990s, a new era of political correctness had begun to submerge the free expression of ideas, speech, and beliefs. It was no longer acceptable to voice vitriolic, homophobic, racist, or sexist opinions in public, and this contributed greatly to an under-lying reservoir of contempt and dissatisfaction among a great many Americans, especially whites. Many scholars have examined the polit-ical and rhetorical shift from the end of the World War II to the 1990s. In a dynamic work, Matthew Lassiter discussed the changing ethos in growing suburbia that resulted in the push for the "color-blind" soci-ety.[21] In another critical work, Joseph Lowndes noted the importance of language, political identity, and party-building efforts of conser-vatives, southerners, and Dixiecrats.[22] In *White Flight*, Kevin Kruse details how the city of Atlanta resisted the push for civil rights by maintaining their old systems under new paradigms.[23]

Considering the clumsy manner in which the Clinton adminis-tration often handled matters of race, it was no surprise when vocal opposition to the race initiative arose. On issues such as welfare and crime the president had raised the ire of many. That clumsy man-ner was apparent during entire span of the race initiative. Further, concerns and outrage over this were brought to the attention of the Advisory Board. One example of such sentiment was a letter from a senior pastor to Advisory Board member Dr. Susan Johnson-Cook. J. Alfred Smith Sr. wrote, "We are very unhappy with the disparity between President Bill Clinton's words against racism and his approval and support of unjust welfare reform. . . . The failure to enforce civil rights laws that are on the books is unforgivable."[24] Such opinions on the One America initiative reflect the prevailing view that the president had a somewhat mixed record on matters of race.

While some Americans viewed One America through a skeptical lens, others were incredulous at the very notion of drawing Americans together. One African American/Native American female wrote the president to say, "[I don't] think I'll live to see the harmony I've outlined in my letter, hopefully my children will."[25] She informed the president that she was "having a very hard time understanding why you and others feel an apology at this late stage would make a difference."[26] This woman's concerned letter to the White House demonstrates the underlying anger and incredulity present during the existence of the race initiative.

Another aspect of the public discontent with the president and his One America creation was the "angry white man."[27] When the Democratic Party lost the midterm congressional elections of 1994, many political observers noted the somewhat disturbing trend of angry white males who opposed any consideration given to minorities or women and, consequently, shifted their political allegiance to the Republican Party. Viewpoints such as these were reflected in letters to the editors of newspapers across the country, as well as in correspondence with One America's office in the New Executive Office Building in Washington, D.C. A veteran from California wrote to tell the board that he believed, "We've already given the Blacks zillions of dollars in welfare money . . . [and] enough is enough."[28] Not all letters were as negative as this one. For example, another Californian wrote to say, "Those who practiced slavery are now all gone, and the practice of long past and best forgotten."[29] Mr. Gibson's letter is just one of many that reflect the sense that America's racial debate had long passed. There was a desire among many that it was best to just let sleeping dogs lie and not open up old wounds. The evidence of large-scale discontent and racial animus to the contrary, many Americans thought that the effort and money being spent on One America was wasteful and nonproductive.

For other Americans, the open wound of racial strife and conflict remained too close to the surface for serious contemplation and discussion. The divisions within the United States during the 1990s were so acute that it was often difficult for people simply to discuss their feelings in a serious and open way. To many, the efforts of the president smacked of political opportunism. In a hasty and angry response to One America executive officer Randy D. Ayers, a woman from Connecticut said that the entire effort was nothing more than "b.s., political propaganda" and that "Barry Goldwater was right not to sign the Civil Rights Bill—government has intruded in everyone's rights to their own opinions, to free speech, to the right to not integrate, to the right to think as you please."[30] Classically conservative as well as emotional viewpoints such as these demonstrated the frustration with efforts to normalize and humanize race relations at the end of the twentieth century. The negative responses from American citizens came from all over the country and exemplified that most Americans were not ready to deal with race in a substantive manner.

The public's perceptions that the Advisory Board itself was lacking in diversity was just one more major hurdle facing the race initiative. The lack of a Native American on the Advisory Board infuriated many who initially had great hopes for One America. For instance, a twenty-nine-year-old Oglala Sioux Tribe female expressed her frustration and disappointment at the lack of racial diversity on the Advisory Board: "I felt disappointed because I did not see the Native American people represented."[31] This was among the contentious issues that faced the race initiative. In fact, despite that the members represented a broad cross section of America, many were still upset that their particular group was not prominently displayed on the Advisory Board. Such feelings testified to the strong desire of minorities—of all hues and background—to see faces in high places. It did not matter that the Advisory Board spent considerable time examining issues relating to Native Americans. These criticisms revealed a critical weakness of the initiative: its inability to address the growing diversity within American society. The Clinton administration's failure here was to view America's race problem through the narrow lens of the black-white conundrum. According to the 2000 US census, whites made up 75.1 percent of the population, blacks made up 12.3 percent of the population, and Hispanics made up 12.5 percent.[32] The repeal of the discriminatory Johnson-Reed Immigration Act of 1924 by the Hart-Cellar Immigration Act of 1965 allowed millions of people to enter the United States who previously had been denied.[33] The 1965 law led to unprecedented growth of the Latin American population in the United States. The Center for Immigration Studies noted in 1995, "The unexpected result has been one of the greatest waves of immigration in the nation's history—more than 18 million legal immigrants since the law's passage over triple the number admitted during the previous 30 years, as well as uncountable millions of illegal immigrants."[34] In addition, the new law "opened the doors to mass entry of people from Asia and Latin America (regions where people are far more likely to want to emigrate, and the law's emphasis on family reunification ensured that those through the door first would be able to bring in their relatives, freezing out potential immigrants from Europe and from other developing nations."[35] The explosion in diversity followed its predecessors by joining blacks, women, gays, the aged, and others in identity politics by pushing for attention to their respective issues, national influence, and more rights through recognition of past wrongs at the hands of the majority white population. Such an influx, essentially changing the demographical dynamic of the United States, created new and difficult challenges for the body politic. As the twentieth century neared its conclusion, America's increasingly diverse population provoked new problems that impacted social, political, and racial relations.

By the mid-1990s, the United States had grown exponentially due to massive waves of immigrants from Eastern Europe, Latin American, and Asia. With so many people trying to take part in the so-called American dream, the race initiative faced huge obstacles in maintaining order through all the clamoring voices. This served to only further hamper the efforts toward racial reconciliation. One notable incident that reflected the fear and loathing of many whites occurred in December 1998 during a meeting of the Advisory Board in Fairfax, Virginia. A man named Robert Hoy launched into a diatribe about how he was soon to be in the minority. "There's no one up there [referring to the Advisory Board] that's talking about the white people."[36] This outburst caused a considerable outrage among many. Outrage among whites more often reflected anger that someone espoused such views in open public rather than the fact that someone held such views. The politically correct movement of the 1980s and 1990s was reflective of this fact. It should be noted that Hoy had ties to the former head of the Ku Klux Klan, David Duke, but it does not in any way negate that many whites around the nation may have held similar views. It was not only the Clinton administration but the Advisory Board itself that failed to take adequate note of the diversity of the United States in the 1990s.

The changing racial dynamics of the United States by the 1990s created an increasingly complex atmosphere. With Latinos shaping politics in areas of the country such as Los Angeles, and with waves of Asian immigrants from Vietnam, China, Japan, Thailand, Laos, and Korea entering the country, politicians began to cater to an increasingly complex set of identity politics. The explosion in immigration often pitted the newer Americans—Latinos and Asians—against Americans of older stock, such as blacks, Native Americans, and white women. For the Democratic Party, these new circumstances created interparty warfare at times between the various groups. Racial animus or resentment could be found within the Advisory Board itself. The debates between its chairman, John Hope Franklin, and his fellow member, Angela Oh, reflected this division. Oh's concern that Franklin and others simply wanted to focus on the white-black issue demonstrated the new nature of minority politics at the end of the twentieth century. These facts, combined with growing white resentment at the changing mosaic of America, led to supremely vexing problems for such an ambitious undertaking.

The Clinton White House failed to anticipate the sheer diversity of opinion in the United States and the intractability of racial animosity. The multiethnic, exceedingly diverse nature of US society had served to further confuse and obstruct efforts toward reconciliation. There is no evidence that this problem was seriously considered by the president, the White House staff, or the Advisory Board and staff of the President's Initiative on Race. As board member Linda Chavez-Thompson noted, "The people weren't ready for a race conversation."[37]

The Media

One of the biggest impediments to the successful execution of the President's Initiative on Race was the print, radio, and television media. Since October 1991, when Clinton had announced his candidacy for president, the media had closely followed, and at many times pursued, Clinton and his administration. Journalism in the 1990s had changed considerably since the heyday of Bob Woodward and Carl Bernstein.[38] Journalists became more interested in steamy details of alleged trysts, criminal behavior, and scandalous activity that would increase circulation and viewership. No longer were the details of important legislation or actions on the part of the government worthy of serious coverage. Several authors/scholars have examined post-Watergate journalism and its effects on American politics and society.[39] Stories concerning the Whitewater scandal, Paula Jones, and Monica Lewinsky ate up more time and energy than issues like race, poverty, and activities of Congress, the courts, and the White House. The media dictated the way that Americans thought about such issues and topics but also reflected the views of the public at large.

From the beginning, major news organizations such as the *New York Times*, the *Washington Post*, the *Chicago Tribune*, *Time*, and the *Rocky Mountain News* cast doubt, in one way or another, on the viability of the initiative. At times the coverage of the race initiative took on a mean-spirited tone. Advisory Board members such as chairman Franklin spent considerable amounts of time responding, both in writing and by telephone conversations, to the negative coverage. In a May 20, 1998, letter by Franklin to Toby Harshaw of the *New York Times,* Franklin raked over the coals of the "grey old lady of journalism" for its lack of professionalism and bias.[40] *Times* reporter Steven Holmes had reported that Franklin had said that conservatives were not welcome at board activities, which prompted the chair to say, "I had never said that conservatives had not been invited to speak."[41] This was not the first time that Franklin tried to correct misinformation being spread by the media. The *New York Times* had also refused to print an op-ed piece Franklin wrote in January 1998. In fact, this was one of the disturbing aspects of the race initiative's time in existence.

The media often sensationalized the proceedings of the Advisory

Board through manufactured conflicts. One media-incited dispute that arose was between Franklin and California businessman and University of California regent Ward Connerly in late November 1997. Using Holmes's *Times* article, reporters had quickly informed Connerly of what Franklin supposedly said regarding representation on the board and its activities. Franklin wrote that Connerly was "understandably outraged because, on the basis of subsequent media reports, he had been grievously misinformed about what I said."[42] In fact, the *New York Times* "never did publish one of any dozen letters that I wrote to the editor of the *New York Times*. . . . [Y]ou can't distort a lie; these are lies that you are publishing."[43] Such biased reporting by the media only served to hamper the efforts of the Advisory Board to seek solutions to America's race relations problems. The media even reported that Franklin had little contact with the president, which was an egregious error. Franklin flatly disputed these accounts of little contact with the president. "Whatever I talked to the president by phone or in the Oval Office or on Air Force One, where I traveled with him a lot during this period, . . . we talked about policy issues, problems, and I never felt that he was leaving us in a lurch."[44] "From that time of the closing of the offices of the President's Advisory Board on Race in September 1998, from that time until the day he left office, he consulted with me and the groups of people, in my presence, about the very points that we made while we were in existence and what we thought he ought to do."[45] This directly contradicts the media assertion that the president was unavailable.

The Denver, Colorado, meeting on March 26, 1998, is further evidence of how the media hampered progress of the race initiative. The meeting was protested by many who were upset about the president's decision not to appoint a Native American to the Advisory Board. Franklin noted, "A rumor had circulated through the Native American community that I had prevented the president from appointing a Native American to the Advisory Board because it might interfere with my plans to keep the attention of the board and the president focused on the problems of African Americans."[46] Considering that Franklin is part Native American, such attacks on him and the board reflected a basic lack of knowledge of the initiative, its members, and its mission. An examination of some of the headlines showed the binary way in which the media covered the race initiative and its basic knowledge. For example, Guy Kelly of the *Rocky Mountain News* headlined the "Race 'Conversation' one sided" on March 25, 1998; the *Providence Journal-Bulletin* called it nothing more than "smoke and mirrors."[47] The list goes on and on. It was as if the media was incapable of discussing anything other than the protests in Denver. Such public events only played into the manipulative hands of the media. Criticism from the media and Native Americans on issues of fair representation was something that was not initially considered by the Advisory Board or the White House. The issue of representation was brought up early and often by Native American activists, and it was partially drummed up by the media to attack the legitimacy of the race initiative. In June 1997, the executive director of the National Association of Social Workers, Josephine Nieves, wrote to the president that she wanted to "extend a sincere gesture of support regarding your national effort on race and request that you expand the Advisory Board . . . to include Native American representation."[48] This prompted the White House director of presidential personnel and assistant to the president, Bob J. Nash, to respond by saying that the president "felt that appointing a large board covering all racial minorities in the country would not be as beneficial as a small number of people who would feel a sense of individual responsibility for their work and advice."[49]

The media's main interest in the President's Initiative on Race was to cover a main event and to fulfill its need for circulation/viewership. More specifically, the editorial boards and columnists wanted to advance their own political objectives. Arguably, the most serious and troublesome action by the media was its coverage of the Lewinsky scandal. In January 1998 the media, beginning with the Drudge Report, revealed that President Clinton had engaged in questionable conduct with a White House intern named Monica Lewinsky. The media seized upon the scandal with such intensity that it appeared that the president would be removed from office within a few weeks. The crux of the issue was the allegation that the president had lied under oath in a deposition forced upon him by the head of the Office of the Independent Counsel, Kenneth Starr. From this time forward the media refused to seriously focus on anything else. They hounded and badgered staff employees, members of Congress, and senior members of the White House staff. Despite that even the most impartial observers of America's ultimate political drama realized that the matter was not serious enough to rise to the level of an impeachable offense, the media presented the story as a grave case that imperiled the nation. Clinton later revealed that he did have an affair with the young intern and lied about it. However, ignoring the large public sentiment against impeachment, the Republican-led House of Representatives impeached the president in a partisan vote and sent the charges to the Senate for trial. In the end, the Office of the Independent Counsel spent more than forty million dollars and a year of the public's time and energy to prove that the president had engaged in an extramarital affair and lied about it. Further, the investigation did not lead to a conviction of the president and only served to embarrass and distract the White House from its normal duties. The media added fuel to the fire in its efforts to sensationalize private conduct. In the process, it drew much needed attention away from the work of the Advisory Board and the president's efforts toward racial reconciliation.

The White House

The Clinton White House contributed to the lack of success of the race initiative. Clinton knew from the beginning of his presidential campaign in 1991 that the media and his political opponents were gunning for him. Yet he proceeded to engage in behavior that only deepened the desire for revenge. Some of this behavior regarding Whitewater, Paula Jones, FBI files, and political disputes was in the role of his public responsibilities; some was not. Clinton had embraced a strategy of moving to the political center when circumstances became tough. The One America initiative was a perfect example of such tendencies.

Clinton's decision to address race through a presidential order and commission resulted from movement on both of Clinton's political flanks. The president was forced to address the Million Man March and pushed to examine the racial components surrounding Californians' decision to remove affirmative action from its higher-education system.[50] In his June 1997 speech announcing the One America initiative at the University of San Diego, he told the audience of dignitaries and graduates, "Remember too, in spite of the persistence of prejudice, we are more integrated than ever."[51] This statement, perhaps, reflected the president's ambivalence at the thought of special hiring and admittance practices as well as his understanding of the inherent abuses of power perpetuated on African Americans by white society. This somewhat hasty formation of the race initiative reflected the ambivalence of Clinton on the volatile issue of affirmative action.

When the race initiative was created in June 1997, it did not have a staff, offices, or the most basic rudimentary elements of an efficient, well-organized government commission. The only element it did possess was its Advisory Board. One America did not develop a plan until September, which only served to allow its enemies to attack it at will. As Franklin remarked, "By early September 1997, the Advisory Board had developed a work plan, including the schedule of monthly meetings of the full board to plan and discuss various issues, meetings of board committees, activities of individual board members, and the coordination of the board's work through its executive director and her staff."[52] Such organizational, logistical, and directional planning should have been done before the announcement of the race initiative was made public in June 1997.

Another factor that was not adequately addressed was the president's ongoing legal difficulties. Board member Chavez-Thompson explained, "I think we could have had more [support from the administration], but I think that about that time there were other things happening in the White House that had other people busy."[53] With ambitious plans for his second term, Clinton lumped too much together at once. With the legal attacks coming from the media and Republicans, the president had to cut corners on the details of his agenda. In addition, there was a lack of support from Congress due in no small measure to the fact that congressional Democrats were often busy fending off Republican attacks on the president.[54] Without a doubt this led to the somewhat haphazard manner in which the Advisory Board was created and its lack of defined purposes. The tasks assigned to the board were not clear enough, nor specific enough to prevent criticism of the race initiative. They were supposed to meet with the public, examine solutions to contemporary race problems, and make recommendations for the president to act upon. The PIR was little more than symbolic politics. It had neither the authority nor the apparatus to effect substantive change.

The President's Initiative on Race struggled with the multiethnic approach to addressing America's problems. The president could have made clear that the initiative was to focus solely on black-white relations. At the same time, Clinton could have created a second commission to address the concerns of Native Americans and other minorities that had been entering the country over the past thirty years, such as Latinos. However, the decision not to address the longest-lasting social problem, black-white relations, served to only confuse, hamper, and ultimately stifle racial reconciliation efforts in the United States.

Finally, the greatest impediments the White House brought to its own race initiative were the Lewinsky scandal and Vice President Al Gore's presidential ambitions. By January 1998, President Clinton and his White House staff were embroiled in the Monica Lewinsky/Whitewater/Paula Jones fiasco. The White House scheduling records for the president show no discernable evidence that the president spent any great amount of time working on the race initiative as opposed to other issues.[55] As Franklin points out, "the White House was distracted from doing its daily duty."[56] Franklin, Chavez-Thompson, Kean, and others have noted that the immense pressures on the president at the time kept Clinton from giving more attention to the President's Initiative on Race. The amount of stress on the president undoubtedly forced him to redirect his attention toward self-preservation. Disregarding any moral indictments of the president, it is imperative to understand just how much this was a failure of Clinton in his professional capacity. He needlessly helped to distract the nation from the work of the Advisory Board and prevented more substantive discussions about race to occur. Clinton knew that his political opponents were looking for a reason, no matter how trivial, to ruin his administration; to conduct himself in such an unflattering and undignified manner was disastrous. Further, the staff of the vice president and, to a certain extent, the president's staff were concerned with the 2000 election and did not want to get too close to such a sensitive issue. Governor Kean recalled:

> [I was] being told by friends of mine in the administration that
> the president was distracted and that the vice-president's people
> . . . really didn't want bold recommendations. Because I was told
> by people in the White House that politically race is not only a
> divisive issue in the Republican Party and the country but a divi-
> sive issue within the Democratic Party and that quite naturally
> the campaign people who were going to be running the Gore
> campaign did not want very bold recommendations on race as
> part of the campaign.[57]

The combination of scandal and pure political calculus worked against
the aims of this initially bold effort. Politically, as time went by and the
looming elections came closer, the importance of the PIR diminished.
Cabinet officials who in the beginning were very interested in helping
began to abandon the effort. According to Kean, they attended the first
couple of meetings and then dropped off the radar to focus on other
issues.[58] The lack of political weight bestowed on the PIR contributed
to its symbolic quality as opposed to a substantive, policy-oriented
effort. The staff also presented a problem because it was beholden to
the White House rather than the PIR. Judith Winston and other members of the staff were White House employees. Although no board
member has publicly criticized the staff, it underlines central problems
in the PIR: lack of independence and its ultimately fatal vulnerability
to political pressures.

The President's Initiative on Race

While the president and the White House contributed greatly to the
failure of the race initiative, the Advisory Board also did its part to
hamper progress. For example, as the board's chair, Franklin later said
that he "didn't know that we were in such bad shape, racially."[59] Franklin
had long been known as a thoughtful and serious critic of contemporary America. If he did not know the extent to which race remained
a vexing problem in American life, then how could any of the other
six members (or the wider population for that matter) know? A Joint
Center for Political and Economic Studies 1997 National Opinion Poll
revealed that "black and white Americans continue to view the race

question in fundamentally different ways." This was demonstrated by the differences within the advisory board itself. At the first meeting in the summer of 1997, Franklin had a noted disagreement with Angela Oh and the intentions and focus of the board. "Dr. Franklin believes that the focus and mission ought to be around the black/white conflict, which he sees as the nucleus for every other race problem this country has endured. . . . [C]ommissioner Oh suggests that the work of the commission really ought to be about multiracial and multiculturalism."[60] Even disputes between members of the board further disrupted the progress of the initiative. The lack of a unified front in the public view was a disturbing sign of things to come. But the PIR's failure was also symptomatic of the American public's inability to reconcile itself with its racial past. "These differences in perception present a special challenge for President Clinton's 'race initiative'"[61] Further, it should have been apparent to the members of the board that it was going to be tough and that procedures needed to be put into place in order to avoid, or at least minimize, "the hecklers" that were hounding its efforts.[62]

The Advisory Board did not shy away from the very public spectacle that the media created. The public nature of the meetings of the Advisory Board ensured that media coverage would be extensive. This was problematic as it gave the proceedings a disjointed feel, which opened the door to criticism of the president's agenda on these matters.[63] The Advisory Board was forced by law to hold its discussions in public, which allowed the meetings to turn into loud and, at times, obnoxious harangues. If the board and its plans had been more thoughtfully developed before the announcement of One America, maybe a more sensible arrangement could have been worked out. As it was, however, the board spent incredible amounts of time addressing the political battles surrounding the initiative.

The conceptual framework in which the race initiative was placed was also problematic. The three major previous explorations of America's race problem were studied and written about during a time of widespread racial strife and violence that was open and visible to the public. Both the race initiative and the president framed this mission as "not a crisis, but an opportunity."[64] The videotape of the brutal police beating of Rodney King in 1991, the spectacle of

O. J. Simpson's trial for two counts of murder, and the horrific dragging death of mentally disabled James Byrd Jr. in Jasper County, Texas, are testaments to continued racial violence, animus, and division. The race initiative failed to engage these divisions in serious terms because that train of logic ran contrary to the president's public positions. There was confusion within both the race initiative and the Clinton White House over the relevance of the project.

They were simply too many issues for the Advisory Board to face to efficiently do its job in such a short period of time. While the board took a broad look at race relations, it also confronted many other related aspects of American life such as school vouchers, affirmative action, multiculturalism, enforcement of civil rights laws, promotion of dialogue between the races, and media representations. In addition, the board examined issues such as health care, quality of life, and educational achievement and opportunity.[65] The organization of the race initiative was far too broad and all-encompassing to exhaustively investigate race in America. It did not take into account the large diversity of people living in the United States. Further, the top-down nature of the race initiative made it easy for others to pick away at it. The massive scale of this project led to errors of judgment and misunderstandings of its mission. The president had told the board that its mission was to "articulate the president's vision of racial reconciliation and a just, unified America." He also instructed it to find, develop, and implement solutions in critical areas such as "education, economic opportunity, housing, health care, crime, and the administration of justice for individuals, communities, corporations and governments at all levels."[66] The totality of this mission was simply too massive. Entire government agencies and departments, such as the Departments of Education, Labor, and Justice, are dedicated to helping American citizens in these areas. How could one initiative, with a budget of $2.9 million and a small staff, uncover everything there was to know?[67] The answer, of course, was that it could not. It only had a little over a year to do its work. Scholars have spent entire careers searching for answers to the highly complex and often perplexing problem of race. By the time that the President's Initiative on Race ended it was on life support. It produced a massive body of work that remained virtually unknown to the general public. As a result, race relations were not significantly affected by the panel's work, and as the current problems in America suggests, the effort toward One America still has a long way to go.

Conclusions

The President's Initiative on Race was blown asunder by a multitude of factors that, in hindsight, could have been partially averted. The combination of the media, public sentiment, and critical flaws within the initiative itself served to derail the PIR from its mission to promote racial reconciliation. It was for these reasons that Tom Kean, a board member, was very happy in the beginning of the initiative but ultimately disappointed with its outcome.[68] President Clinton can be commended, as well as the members of Advisory Board, the One America staff, and the White House staff who contributed, for efforts to resolve a difficult and perplexing problem. Yet the haphazard manner in which it was conducted should force historians and scholars to reconsider how the Clinton White House confronted African Americans and the race issue. Finally, this effort could have really helped to educate Americans to become more knowledgeable, tolerant, and thoughtful about our fellow citizens. Instead, it only contributed to the deepening of racial animus that continues to rip at the social fabric of the nation. By the end, "One America in the 21st Century: The President's Initiative on Race" was a missed opportunity to move the nation forward from a problem that was four hundred years in the making.

CHAPTER 8

The Clinton Legacy

Bush, Progress, and Obama

AS PRESIDENT BILL CLINTON left Washington on January 20, 2001, the country he left behind was in many ways changed from the one he inherited just eight years before. In 1993, Clinton had taken control of the federal government at a time when white backlash and resentment was on the rise. (At least until President Barack Obama was elected in 2008.) Affirmative action, racial diversity, and tightening economic prospects created an acute sense of victimization among many white Americans. It was Clinton's responsibility, in part, to bring the nation, as he said many times, into the twenty-first century. It was a balancing act for Clinton. He tried to do his best to appeal to both groups: resentful whites and minorities. The New Democratic ethos was designed to assuage the fears of the majority while preserving the gains of the minority. Welfare reform was indicative of this realization of changing atmospherics. The 1996 landmark act was passed in part to confirm and, then, alleviate the fears of the majority, even though whites disproportionately were beneficiaries of public assistance. Welfare was coded as black, and, therefore, had to be scaled back. At the same time, more and more African Americans were entering the middle class. In fact, two-thirds of all African Americans were not poor or working class, they were firmly entrenched in Middle America. The fact that many blacks also supported welfare reform was indicative of the changing racial and political dynamics of the 1990s and early 2000s. Such transformative undercurrents were harbingers of things to come.

The growth of African Americans, Asians, and, most importantly, Latinos as powerful voting blocs and economic forces in American life eviscerated any hope some may have had that the United States would return to the pre-Clinton years. This fact was not lost on many Republicans. The growth and progress were demonstrated in economic, political, and social ways that were hard to ignore. This chapter examines the Clinton legacy through the prism of the rapid changes of the 1990s and 2000s. Moreover, by examining the presidencies of George W. Bush and Barack Obama, we can gain a better understanding of the various cultural, financial, political, and racial undercurrents that swept the United States.

Economic Progress

Most Americans were in a much better economic position in 2001 than they were in 1993. The progressive economic and tax policies of the Clinton administration, along with the tremendous growth of the technology sector and the Internet boom, helped to stamp out the most severe poverty and despair in the country. The largest peacetime expansion of the economy did much to help lift most boats. As the Clinton administration prepared to leave office in the fall of 2000, the Treasury Department announced that the nation's debt was brought down to "under 35 percent of GDP from its peak of nearly 50 percent of GDP in 1993."[1] In addition, the nation had a surplus of $237.00 billion. As Lawrence Summers and Jacob Lew noted, "this year's surplus at 2.4 percent was the largest since 1948. This is the first time there have been three consecutive years of surpluses since 1947–49."[2] The nation generally felt good about itself. The heady years before 9/11 (September 11, 2001) boosted American confidence and optimism. Such optimism was reflected across class and racial lines. So good was the atmosphere that many Americans, black and white, turned their attention toward social issues, such as abortion, contraception, and morality, instead of bread-and-butter economic issues.

In 2000, the annual unemployment rate was 4.0 percent nationally.[3] For African Americans, the unemployment rate was 7.6 percent. The number was down from annual rate of 13.0 percent in 1993.[4] Economic progress was an important accomplishment of the Clinton years. As the former governor of Arkansas, Clinton understood the plight of everyday Americans and just how difficult it was for them to achieve normality. Normality, or the middle-class dream, was something very difficult to pin down. Scholars and pundits routinely tried to grasp what this meant in all practicality. For some it meant securing a list of possessions that could be easily measured through quantitative means: cars, homes, electronic devices, vacations, second homes, private schools for children or at least well-respected suburban public schools, and white-collar employment. Clinton understood that while the above measurements were certainly a part of the normal life, they were not all of it.

The normal life was also a state of mind. It was visceral and cultural as well as economic. It meant being able to not just secure economic gains but maintain the importance of family, religion, and social ties. People must believe that they are making progress while not losing the things that make them who they are. It must be believed that children will have opportunity and the likelihood of doing better than their parents. For some that means college educations and higher standards of living. For others that means that work must pay and that through hard work they can gain security. This is generally lost on pundits and politicians, who, because of their privileged status and high earning potential, lack understanding of the concerns of average Americans. As the son of a single mother and a dysfunctional home, Clinton needed no tutorials about the life of ordinary Americans.

Even more important than his grasp of ordinary hopes and wishes was Clinton's innate grasp that those hopes and wishes were universal. Blacks and whites held the same desires: progress, security, and respect. This separated Clinton from many politicians who focus on one group and neglect the other. It is in part what made him such a fascinating public figure. While most southern politicians focused on their white constituents, and at times fed their insecurities about economic and cultural change, and urban politicians pursued the interests of their constituents, Clinton knew that the two groups were not that far apart in terms of their respective dreams. The one group

Clinton neglected, perhaps for political reasons, was those unable to uplift themselves out of their present conditions.

While millions succeeded in gaining security for themselves, others struggled just to maintain their meager existence. More than 31 million people were considered poor in 2000.[5] Black poverty accounted for 22.1 percent. And white poverty accounted for 7.5 percent.[6] With 281,421,906 Americans in 2000, this was a large percentage of Americans living in poverty. A blind spot of President Clinton and all New Democrats was these Americans. The fact that United States was experiencing the greatest economic boom since the end of World War II and millions more were gaining economically belied the notion that Clinton's economic policies were doing enough for those at the bottom of the ladder. Further, it was often believed that those Americans desperately trying to survive were somehow suspect. Even Clinton himself talked frequently of the hardworking, deserving Americans. Essentially, this played into notion of "deserving" versus "undeserving" Americans. Those who worked hard and those who supposedly did not do enough to help themselves was often how politicians and policymakers divided up Americans.

Clinton Legacy in Motion: The Bush Years

The Clinton legacy was immediately seen in the George W. Bush presidency. Bush was the scion of one of the most prominent American families: Bush-Pierce. Born in New England and an alumnus of Yale and Harvard Business School, George W. Bush was a part of the American aristocracy. After receiving his MBA in the 1970s, Bush moved to Texas, where his family had lived and where he had deep roots within the business and political circles of the state. An average businessman, Bush had moderate success in the oil business. Moreover, the free-spirited and fun-loving Bush also developed a serious drinking habit. After his wife forced him to give up the bottle he became a born-again Christian. Also, he became increasingly active politically as he parlayed his experience in a failed congressional run in the late 1970s and as a primary advisor to his father during his victorious 1988 presidential campaign into valuable political capital as he increasingly focused on securing the governorship of Texas in 1994.

After Bush defeated the beloved and charismatic Texas governor Ann Richards in the midterm elections, Bush became a national figure. The elder Bush's defeat to Bill Clinton in 1992, combined with a lackluster field of candidates and Senator Robert Dole's embarrassing loss to Clinton in 1996, led political prognosticators to take a close look at George W. Bush for the 2000 Republican presidential nomination. In addition, while Bush was certainly conservative and evangelical, he also was open to minorities and sought ways to attract blacks and Latinos to the Republican Party.

Bush was also a product of the social revolution of the 1960s that increasingly saw minorities and women as equal to whites. In fact, Bush understood that much of the then current platform of the Republican Party would appeal to these groups. That appeal included low taxes, strong national defense, and the importance of faith in both private lives and the life of the nation. In fact, Bush sought out two prominent African Americans, retired chairman of the joint chiefs of staff General Colin Powell and Stanford provost and former member of the National Security Council Condoleezza Rice, to serve as secretary of state and national security advisor respectively. Further, Bush hired Karen Hughes, Alberto Gonzalez, Gale Norton, Margaret Spellings, Mel Martinez, Alphonso Jackson, Elaine Chao, Christine Todd Whitman, Carlos Gutierrez, Rod Paige, Ron Christie, and others to serve as key advisors and members of the presidential cabinet. President Bush went much further than just appointing people to high-ranking positions in his administration. He also touched on politics and policies that directly or indirectly impacted African Americans.

George W. Bush viewed minorities as a key component to his electoral coalition. Much like Richard M. Nixon in the late 1960s, Bush sought to attract key voting blocs from the Democratic base. George Gerstle, in an essay providing early historical analysis of the Bush years, noted, "The original vision of George W. Bush and Karl Rove, the new and permanent Republican electoral majority, was to emerge only in part from the relentless mobilization of conservatives and their moderate allies. It was also to emerge from the Republican

Party's success in peeling significant percentages of voters away from traditional Democratic constituencies, most notably Hispanics, but even to some degree African Americans."[7] Furthermore, Bush had secured 49 percent of the Hispanic vote and 27 percent of the African American in his 1998 reelection campaign in Texas.[8] If Bush could secure both voting blocs consistently, as Gerstle notes, "the party could declare its minority success and use it to establish what it most wanted, a permanent Republican majority."[9] By focusing on minorities to a greater extent than his recent Republican predecessors, he could, in effect, do what Bill Clinton had done so successfully during the 1990s: secure an electoral and governing coalition by bringing traditional and mainstream forces together with minority buy-in.

Much like Clinton, Bush was separating himself somewhat from the traditionally potent forces of his own party. Clinton had made his name in the 1980s and early 1990s by maintaining distance between himself and the liberal forces that controlled the Democratic Party. In the 1980s, Tip O'Neill, the Congressional Black Caucus, and women tended to dominate the party, along with white liberals in the House of Representatives. As mentioned earlier, Clinton had been a founding member of the Democratic Leadership Council, which fought to take the party back from the liberals that so annoyed wide swaths of the electorate. This meant maintaining the commitment to minorities but becoming more sensitive to the needs and concerns of the white middle class. Also, Clinton increasingly used values rhetoric that would appeal to everyone, including African Americans and the business class. Bush continued on this path in his roles as both party leader and president.

This was not an easy fight. Conservatives and culture warriors dominated the Republican Party. Since Reagan's first election in 1980 the Grand Old Party had become more and more a party that embraced the politics of resentment and backlash. White Americans who were uncomfortable with political and social change looked to Ronald Reagan, Pat Buchanan, and others to give voice to their discontent. At the end of the twentieth century, these forces controlled the Republican Party and exiled a great many moderates. While Bush had been a part of the conservative wing of the GOP, he had not been a part of that faction. But appealing to minorities who were distrustful of the GOP was not going to be easy.

There were major issues that Bush could not move away from: breaking affirmative action, destroying the welfare state as it stood at the end of the Clinton era, dealing with antagonism toward public education. Since Bush could not back away from these Republican positions he had to find ways that could break through the logjam. The faith-based initiative and the White House Office of Faith-Based and Neighborhood Partnerships were key components making progress on these fronts. Through the West Wing, Bush directed monies and services to the states and down to the people by using private actors instead of the government. The New Federalism of the Nixon era had been updated to include the private sector to a much greater extent than before.[10] Welfare benefits were a big target of this effort. Where Clinton had conceded, at least partially, to using block grants to the states to distribute monies and services, Bush brought in the evangelical community. Those in the evangelical community saw it as important to their heavenly missions to help the poor and dispossessed, even if sometimes that commitment was more rhetorical than actual.

Another major policy of the Bush years was the president's landmark domestic achievement: No Child Left Behind.[11] In the early 1980s policymakers and politicians became increasingly concerned with the state of education in the United States. Secretary of Education Terrel Bell created a new body to examine American education in 1981: The National Commission on Excellence in Education. The purpose of the commission was to investigate education, identify problems in schools, and make recommendations as to how to improve American education. On April 26, 1983, the commission issued its report: *A Nation At Risk: The Imperative for Educational Reform.*[12] The report named several areas for improvement: "1. Content, 2. Standards and Expectations, 3. Time, 4. Teaching, and 5. Leadership and Fiscal Support."[13] The result of this report was to stir up embers of reform throughout the United States. The Congress, states, and education officials began pouring over their respective educational systems looking for ways to improve them. As governor of Arkansas, Bill Clinton was a leader in pursuing educational reform.

Hillary Rodham Clinton was appointed by her husband to lead a committee to come up with ways to reform Arkansas's kindergarten through twelfth-grade system. As a result of her work, the committee recommended that higher standards had to become the norm. Moreover, all teachers had to pass basic competency tests in their areas of expertise. Education helped to push Bill Clinton into the national discussion for the first time.[14] And it fit well with DLC ideas about greater accountability for public schools. Furthermore, it was also in the mainstream of dialogue about education leveling the playing field between whites and blacks, poor and the affluent. Clinton went to great lengths to promote education reform.

As president, Clinton continued to pursue education as a top priority. Clinton pursued increased funding, reduced class sizes, increased teacher quality, and included computers in the classroom, and higher test scores resulted. In fact, increasing test scores was a key component of education reform. Equally important was expansion of charter schools. Churches, nonprofits, and others promoted the use of charter schools as an answer to failing public schools. These efforts were controversial as teacher unions and liberals complained that charter schools were not a real solution to the problem but a Trojan horse designed to further destroy public education. In 1994, Clinton signed into law the Improving America's Schools Act (IASA).[15] The law afforded poor and disadvantaged children greater educational assistance. Also, it supported drug-free schools and demanded that schools be accountable for their students' performance. Lastly, Clinton made sure that immigrants and bilingual education received greater attention and public funding. Appealing to African Americans and immigrants, especially Hispanics, served to raise Clinton's popularity among those demographic groups. It also helped to fulfill a major part of the DLC-centrist policy agenda: accountability, opportunity, and progress. Few asked whether demanding greater performance and accountability, without supporting reforms that would improve the domestic lives of the poorest and most vulnerable students, would be enough. In essence, reform efforts such as these served to improve public education marginally, allowed the upper middle class some relief, and appealed to reformers eager to do something. These efforts were not lost on Clinton's successor, who followed Clinton's lead in designing legislation aimed at improving kindergarten through twelfth-grade education.

In January 2001, President Bush announced his new legislation: No Child Left Behind. The act was passed by Congress and signed into law by Bush in January 2002. In addition to reauthorizing the Elementary and Secondary Education Act of 1965 (ESEA), the new law required that schools make yearly progress in achieving critical benchmarks in reading, math, science, and more.[16] Progress was determined by adequate yearly progress reports. Student outcomes, as determined by standardized tests, were a major element of the new law. Critics claimed that it damaged public education through standardized testing, unfunded mandates, and increased support for charter schools. But the law had the imprimatur of the "Lion of the Senate," who shepherded the bill through the Congress, Senator Edward M. Kennedy, the liberal icon from Massachusetts. While most liberals and conservatives disliked major portions of the law, it was a middle approach that appealed to a key component of the electorate: middle-class, educated taxpayers—the very same group Clinton and his centrist Democrats did so much to court. After passage of this landmark law, Bush pursued another policy directly aimed at Clinton's most faithful voting bloc, African Americans: housing.

On December 16, 2003, President Bush announced his support for what he called the "Ownership Society."[17] Homeownership was a major part of the American dream. For generations Americans— African Americans, Hispanics, and whites—eagerly pursued the dream of homeownership. In his 1944 "State of Union Address," President Franklin D. Roosevelt spoke of a "Second Bill of Rights," "under which a new basis of security and prosperity can be established for all regardless of station, race, or creed."[18] The fifth of these rights was "the right of every family to a decent home."[19] In the years after World War II, homeownership became a sacred aspect of the American experience. Federal agencies were dedicated to helping Americans become homeowners. Presidents and other politicians often used lofty rhetoric to exalt homeownership. President Clinton made owning a home one of the central themes of his years in office. Moreover, he empowered government entities, such as Fannie Mae and Freddy Mac, to assist more Americans in securing homes. Fannie

Mae and Freddy Mac were created during the Great Depression as a part of the New Deal.[20] Clinton saw this issue in economic and social and moral terms. In June 1995, Clinton announced his strategy for homeownership and proclaimed: "You want to reinforce family values in America, encourage two-parent households, get people to stay home? Make it easy for people to own their own homes and enjoy the rewards of family life and see their work rewarded. This is about more than money and sticks and boards and windows. This is about the way we live as a people and what kind of society we're going to have."[21] But along the way African Americans and other minorities were often unable to secure what Franklin Roosevelt claimed was a right.

Practices such as redlining, segregation, and racism often prevented these minorities from achieving the American dream. Equally important, there were real world consequences stemming from the lack of homeownership. Wealth in the United States has traditionally been created, in part, from the transfer of property from one generation to another. In addition, families in the second half of the twentieth century that owned homes could use their property to put kids through college and pay off bills, and they could use their homes as collateral to create their own businesses. Since the average American's home represented more than 50 percent of his or her wealth, owning a home was a key indicator of stability, wealth, and security.[22] The implications of not owning a home were often very serious. People did not generally live as well. Others we're reduced to poverty. Still others lived paycheck to paycheck. Families were not as secure as they would have been had they owned a home. With some exceptions, the middle class was defined by ownership. Lastly, for African Americans, the ability to purchase a home signaled respectability and success. As more and more African Americans secured this precious right in the 1970s, 1980s, and 1990s, they proved to be increasingly moderate, even conservative on matters of public policy. President Bush recognized it and moved aggressively to seize the growing African American professional class.

It was the politics of race and class that led President Bush to deliver his speech calling for an "ownership society." He, too, empowered Fannie and Freddy to make more home mortgages available to the public. Bush also, through various legislative and administrative actions, made it easier for African Americans and others to purchase homes. Unfortunately, this contributed greatly to the housing bubble, which sent the economy into a tailspin toward the end of his presidency. But the failure of lending institutions to exercise due caution and restraint, along with the failure to perform basic investigations into whether or not applicants for mortgages could actually repay the loan, does not negate the president's efforts to increase homeownership. In fact, it was an admirable aspect of his legacy, a legacy which he inherited from his predecessor, President Clinton.

When the economy began its drastic collapse in 2007–08, Bush moved to help homeowners stay in their houses. He signed into law the Mortgage Forgiveness Debt Relief Act of 2007.[23] This helped to protect Americans who lost their homes to foreclosure from having to pay taxes on their former homes. In addition, Bush created the HOPE NOW Alliance, which provided for mortgage companies and other lenders to partner with homeowners in an effort to prevent foreclosures. Homeowners were allowed to refinance their mortgages in an effort to save their homes from foreclosure. Bush, like Clinton before him, viewed homeownership as critical to the life of the nation. Without it the family would further deteriorate and wealth could not be built, and without new policies aimed at the African American professional class there could not be anything resembling a permanent Republican majority. In the end it was not Bush's housing policies or multiculturalism that were remembered, as important as those things were, it was his failure to respond to one of the greatest natural disasters in American history and the worst economic calamity since the Great Depression.

In August 2005, weather forecasters began predicting that a monster storm would strike the Gulf Coast. From Texas to Louisiana to Mississippi to Alabama, a massive hurricane, fueled by the warm waters of the Gulf of Mexico, was barreling in. They predicted a category 5 storm with huge surges. New Orleans was directly in its path. The city was majority African American. As the storm hit and the floodwaters topped the levees, hundreds of thousands of poor, black residents were left to die in the sewage, waste, filth, and animals that were covering the below-sea-level Crescent City.

The federal government's response to the disaster left something to be desired. Bush's congratulations to Federal Emergency Management Agency (FEMA) director Michael Brown served only to further alienate those who were suffering. Rap artist Kanye West's comment that President Bush did not care about black people seemed to resonate with many as the devastation took its toll. This, combined with the wars in Afghanistan and Iraq and the cratering economy that hit the African American community disproportionately, compared to whites, left many with the impression that Bush was just another Republican. Nothing could be further from the truth.

President Clinton greatly influenced President Bush, as demonstrated by Bush's commitment to diversity. Furthermore, Bush followed Clinton's path of appealing to Americans based on social class. He may have been a fierce party chief, but he was determined to secure large numbers of African Americans and others for the Republican Party as both a political and personal ambition. Gary Gerstle notes:

> It may be appropriate to see Bush as the Republican Bill Clinton. Bush was the GOP candidate who intended to lance the boil of the culture wars by putting forward a soft multiculturalism that merged diversity and patriotism. In the process of doing so, he, Clinton, and others would relieve the American body politic of the distress and distraction that the culture wars had caused.[24]

Finally, George W. Bush, by following Bill Clinton's example on matters of race and class, helped open the door for the election of the nation's actual first black president.

Confirmation of the Winds of Change: Obama's America

In February 2007, the United States was growing weary of the Bush administration. The wars were going badly. The economy was slowing down. The nation was preparing for another presidential election. The Democratic Party was led by Senator Hillary Rodham Clinton (D-NY). The former first lady appeared to be the frontrunner for the nomination. One of the most dynamic and experienced candidates in recent memory, Hillary Clinton was also one of the most polarizing figures in American politics. In Illinois, a freshman senator with a strange name, a megawatt smile, and tremendous success fundraising for the party jumped into the race. Barack Obama was an unlikely candidate for president. He was black. He was unknown in many quarters of the country. Obama had only been on the national stage for less than three years. But unlike other black politicians Obama had no ties to the civil rights community. He was not a preacher. He grew up in Hawaii and was raised by his white grandparents. Obama had earned undergraduate and law degrees from Columbia and Harvard, respectively. His wife had earned her undergraduate and law degrees from Princeton and Harvard, respectively. Lastly, Obama was born in 1961, at the tail end of the baby boomer generation and the beginning of Generation X.

Barack Obama's youth and vigor, combined with his freshness to the political scene, proved to be a potent mixture within the Democratic Party and beyond. Equally important, he seemed to be running a campaign eerily similar to a recent occupant of the Oval Office, Bill Clinton. Senator Obama claimed to be a fresh voice for the future of the nation. His disdain for the politics of the 1960s conjured up memories of Clinton's quiet indifference to the greatest generation. It was time for a change. And "change" was at the heart of the Obama message. Obama did to Hillary Clinton what Bill did to George H. W. Bush: simply overwhelmed her. His come-from-behind victory, after nearly two years of campaigning for the nomination, will be seen as an important moment in modern American political history.

After securing the nomination in the summer of 2008, Obama went on to face the aging senator and former POW John McCain. McCain was badly hurt by the economy, Bush and his administration's legacy, and his selection of Alaska governor Sarah Palin as his vice presidential running mate. In November 2008, after more than two centuries in existence, with a long history of the most unique and horrific form of slavery in history and a century of brutal, unyielding segregation/apartheid, the United States had elected a president who was half white, half black.

During the campaign and throughout the Obama presidency the relationship between Obama and Bill Clinton would remain strained at best. Clinton needed Obama to reestablish ties to the African

American community after those ties had been badly frayed during the 2008 primary fight. Obama needed Clinton to legitimize him in the eyes of culturally conservative voters. Furthermore, by this time, Clinton was something akin to a political king within the Democratic Party. Democratic insiders may have rejected Hillary Clinton, but Bill Clinton remained the most popular and powerful force within it. Ironically, however, the two men had much in common personally and politically.

Like Bill Clinton, President Obama entered office at a time of economic distress and rapid social change. In 2009, Obama took the oath of office as the forty-fourth president of the United States. Tens of millions watched on television as a young and dynamic new president strolled down Pennsylvania Avenue on his way to the White House. Sixteen years before, Clinton had taken that same stroll. Moreover, Obama brought to his new administration a number of former Clinton-era officials. These people included Rahm Emanuel, Larry Summers, John Podesta, Stephanie Cutter, Elena Kagan, Bill Daley, Rob Nabors, Janet Yellen, Leon Panetta, and Susan Rice, among many others. Obama actively sought to appoint and hire individuals that were not traditionally represented in the White House, the Cabinet, and the Judiciary. On the last point, Obama has paid particular attention to the makeup of America's federal courts. According to the *Huffington Post*, "more than 70 percent of Obama's confirmed judicial nominees during his first two years were 'non-traditional,' or nominees who were not white males. That far exceeds the percentages in the two-term administrations of Bill Clinton (48.1 percent) and George W. Bush (32.9 percent), according to Sheldon Goldman, author of the authoritative book *Picking Federal Judges*."[25] Two of Obama's nominees were Supreme Court justices Sonia Sotomayor and Elena Kagan. While Obama has been criticized for overseeing an insular, largely white West Wing, he has provided opportunities to African Americans and women to serve in high-ranking positions. These positions are important because they often set the stage for higher positions in future administrations and greater commercial opportunities outside of government. Clinton helped to create this path, and some of his appointments are now high-ranking officials in Obama's administration. This is somewhat unnerving to those unaccustomed to and resentful of the changing complexion of the US government. And through all this Obama has walked firmly in the footsteps of a man who recognized early on that America was changing—technologically, economically, politically, and, most importantly, ethnically.

Presidents Obama and Clinton could not be more different personally. Clinton was the stereotypical gregarious, back-slapping politician. Needy to a fault for attention, Clinton constantly sought out attention and human companionship. Wickedly smart and cocky, Clinton also bent himself to the cares of whomever he was speaking with at the moment. Obama is more introspective and contemplative. Comfortable in his own skin and lusting for the privacy of the home, the seminar room of a university, or his private study, Obama perhaps may have been suited for the life of a research professor at a university or a writer living in TriBeCa. Both men love books, ideas, debate, and competition, but their individual approaches to life are very different. It was not apparent that Obama would be a politician as an adult. In fact, those embers of ambition did not stir until his college years at Occidental and Columbia. Everyone believed from early childhood that Clinton would seek a career in politics. During the presidential campaign in 2008 Obama made snide remarks about Clinton and his record in office. Clearly, the men had different personalities that clashed, especially after Obama defeated Hillary Clinton and succeeded Bush in 2009. Despite these differences, however, the two men had similar policy agendas.

Arguably, the most important program of the Obama presidency has been health care reform. In March 2010, Congress passed and Obama signed into law the Patient Protection and Affordable Care Act of 2010.[26] This law is one of the most important domestic programs since the Great Society. The law prohibits pre-existing conditions, allows college-age young adults to stay on their parents' health insurance until the age of twenty-six, ends lifetime limits on coverage, requires that hospitals and insurers spend more on patient care, provides preventive care, and creates health care exchanges for Americans to choose health care plans that suit their needs.[27] The model for this legislation was an important Massachusetts law passed in the early 2000s by then governor Mitt Romney, Obama's nemesis in the 2012 presidential election. It includes both employer and individual mandates that everyone have insurance. But this was just one part of it. The other was Clinton's failed attempt to overhaul the nation's health care system in 1993–94.

In 1993, Clinton initiated his own health care plan. Hillary Clinton was charged with leading the effort. Meetings of the health care task force met in secret. Legislators were kept out of the loop. Experts were pushed out of the process. Management gurus, such as Ira Magaziner, were brought in to help. Even Democrats on Capitol Hill were excluded from the process. As the task force did its work, thousands of individuals from business, health care, insurance, and politics gathered to defeated the legislation. President Clinton failed to make clear the legislation's intent. He failed to secure buy-in from key stakeholders in politics, policy, and industry. The legislation died in 1994 and Clinton learned an important lesson: he had gone too far to the left and sidelined his own centrist–third way philosophy. Obama would not make the same mistake.

In 2009, White House chief of staff Rahm Emanuel and others pleaded with the president to not make health care reform the signature issue of his presidency. Journalist Jonathan Alter recounts, "Obama's own top people—from Rahm Emanuel and David Axelrod to Joe Biden—were unenthusiastic at first. They felt that a big reform package would overload the circuits."[28] Obama refused. Further, Obama proceeded to make it the most visible part of his agenda. Urged on by his party's liberal base and key members of Congress, such as cancer-stricken Senator Edward M. Kennedy, Obama pursued not single-payer or universal health care but the market-centric individual mandate with important new rules, regulations, and laws concerning reimbursement, coverage, and guaranteed monies to the states. They actively sought out the assistance of former Romney aides, health care executives, and others to craft one of the most important pieces of legislation since Medicare. In the process, Obama secured the support of mainstream liberals, many academics, average Americans, and, most importantly, the health care insurers and organizations that would financially benefit from the thirty million or so new health care consumers. It was a pro-business law.[29] The politics of race and class were very apparent as minorities and women were emotionally tied to the legislation's passage and subsequent survival at the Supreme

Court. Businessmen and women, the working class, the lower middle class, and others were drawn into the bill. Obama even used language that signaled its economic and national security importance. Alter presciently notes, "His strategic view was that the health care system could no longer be patched up, and that the recovery wouldn't last if it came without long-neglected structural changes. He believed that the health care status quo was unsustainable and would wreck the fiscal future of the country; it was almost a national security issue for him."[30]

Bringing in diverse voices and adopting a plan that he originally did not favor proved Obama's willingness to move to the center, to appeal to a broader cross section of the population in an effort to pass important legislation. It would not be last time Obama took a centrist position designed to appeal to moderates.

Obama was faced with the greatest economic calamity since the Great Depression when he took office. His immediate concern was to stop the economic hemorrhaging and fix the economy. To do this Obama brought in talented and accomplished barons of Wall Street and academe to think through the problem. The aforementioned individuals and many others, especially from the business and corporate worlds, descended on Washington to deliver advice. To the chagrin of many liberals, Obama sided with the pro-business-minded centrists. He refused to break up the big banks and financial institutions that did so much to create the crisis. Congress passed the $787 billion stimulus bill.[31] The bill provided for infrastructure needs, direct aid to states, health care, education, law enforcement, tax credits, transportation, and other needs. The bill did much to stabilize the economy, but it was designed to help the middle class survive. The very poor and the near poor were not considered as highly important, even though money was set aside for unemployment benefits. Businesses profited from the legislation as well. While the law was controversial, it was yet another example of the centrist politics of the president.

In several other areas President Obama also put money and effort. One of the most important was education. Like Clinton before him, Obama saw education as central to the health of the economy and the nation. President Obama supported high-quality education for all children; this included reforming education, implementing Race to the Top, "enhancing outcomes and results in early learning," supporting research and development, raising standards, emphasizing science, technology, engineering, and math (STEM), lowering the costs of higher education, and keeping teachers in the classroom.[32] The president's commitment to education was solid and unwavering; however, his overall focus on "lifting all boats" echoed the rhetoric of the Clinton years. Education reform was one thing, but deciding to not focus more intently on the needs of the poor effectively made Obama's education programs another middle-class entitlement. The poor would not benefit as much since they often lacked the support, tools, and money to take advantage of these programs. Those who were well prepared to take advantage of secondary education and had family resources most often were successful in their attempt to leap to higher education. Consequently, the United States is looking at a generation, perhaps two generations, of Americans who will not live as well as their parents. High employment will continue as fewer jobs are available, and the stain of long-term unemployment prevents millions from ever fulfilling their dreams. Lastly, it is also important to note that Wall Street, investors, and many others are enjoying record profits and the return of previously lost wealth.

Conclusion

The legacy of President Clinton is clearly seen in the work of his two immediate predecessors. George W. Bush and Barack Obama gave more attention to minorities and issues that mattered to them. They tried to seize upon the demographic, economic, and technological changes that gripped the United States. Moreover, both men understood the importance of appealing politically to a greater cross section of the country in efforts to both create governing coalitions and win over African Americans, Hispanics, and others to their respective political parties. Most political historians view the Bush years as the zenith of the rise of conservatism. Yet Bush went to great lengths to appeal to African Americans and Latinos. As Donald Critchlow has demonstrated, "George W. Bush's election in 2000 marked the triumph of the conservative ascendancy."[33] In spite of the conservative onslaught, key programs, while diminished, remained intact.

In fact, class became increasingly important as economic dynamics and political demands forced Clinton, Bush, and Obama to pursue centrist approaches to big, complex problems. Critchlow notes, "The New Deal political coalition had finally been defeated, but the Bush presidency revealed the enduring strength of the liberal welfare state that had been created under Franklin Roosevelt and expanded under Lyndon Johnson."[34] These commitments to race and class were not to be found in the administrations of G.H.W. Bush, Ronald Reagan, or Jimmy Carter. It was Bill Clinton who led the way. His focus on responsibility, accountability, and opportunity was echoed in Bush's muted response to shrill calls for affirmative action to be ended. His work was seen in Bush's dogged effort to reform the nation's immigration laws. Clinton's influence was clearly seen in Obama's moderate approach to fiscal policy. Clinton's example was on display as Obama, from 2007 to the present, chastised young black males to do right by their children. In fact, Clinton's legendary speech in Memphis in 1993 could be heard in Obama's remarks to black churches, businesses, and communities. Presidents Obama and Bush may be very different men, but Clinton made their political existence possible. Finally, Clinton prepared the road for the nation's actual first black president.

Conclusion

THE POLITICAL ATMOSPHERE had changed dramatically from 2001 to 2008. The housing implosion, credit crisis, and the demise of major financial institutions were creating the worst economic crisis since the Great Depression. The United States was embroiled in two wars abroad in Iraq and Afghanistan. The government surplus left for President George W. Bush in 2001 had long been eliminated by tax cuts, increases in the size of government, and the War on Terror. The 2000s had refocused America's attention from mere consumption and domestic issues to fear, anxiety, and frustration. Nearly eight years after the departure of one of the most popular and controversial presidents in recent memory, the 2008 presidential election was the talk of the nation.

While Republicans were in the doldrums, the Democrats captured the lion's share of the political and media attention. The primary campaign featured two Democratic heavyweights: Senator and former first lady Hillary Rodham Clinton (D-NY) and Senator Barack Obama (D-IL). Conventional wisdom dictated that the former first lady would crush the relatively new and untested Obama. The *Washington Times* noted in the spring of 2007 that Clinton held a favorability rating of 58 percent in February 2007, around the time of Senator Obama's announcement.[1] While the article also noted that Senator Clinton was losing some support, she maintained her lead over Senator Obama through most of 2007. Yet as the returns came in from Iowa on the night of January 3, 2008, the political world was shocked to learn that the young, black, junior senator from Illinois had convincingly won the Iowa caucuses. No one in Clinton's camp was more flummoxed than the titular head of the Democratic Party: former president William Jefferson Clinton.

New York Times reporter Patrick Healy noted on January 18, "Some Clinton advisors say the campaign is trying to rein him in somewhat, so that his outbursts become less of a factor to reporters, but his flashes of anger only seem to be growing. . . . Mr. Clinton told Dartmouth students that it was a 'fairy tale' for Mr. Obama to contend that he had been consistently against the war in Iraq. And in December he said that voters supporting Mr. Obama were willing to 'roll the dice' on the presidency."[2] Clinton's public behavior only got worse from there. As the campaign made its way toward the important South Carolina primary on January 19, something strange began happening: the former president, the "first black president," Bubba himself, was directly appealing to white South Carolinians, seemingly driving a wedge between white and black Democratic primary voters. His rhetoric angered Obama supporters. As Eugene Robinson noted after the primary, "forget about the Bill Clinton we've known for the past eight years. . . . [F]orget about the apostle of brotherhood and understanding whose most recent book is titled, simply, 'Giving.' That Bill Clinton has left the building."[3] His off-the-cuff remarks to a reporter in the wake of Obama's crushing victory in South Carolina put Clinton's dark side on display. Bill Clinton remarked to reporters, "Jesse Jackson won South Carolina in '84 and '88 [and] Jackson ran a good campaign. And Obama ran a good campaign here." In essence, Clinton implied that a good black candidate could win a state with a huge black population but had no chance on a national level. Longtime Clinton watcher and *Newsweek* reporter Jonathan Alter remarked, "It was a sign of his desperation, that he was trying to find any way he could to minimize Obama's victory in South Carolina."[4] How could Clinton engage in the same kind of subtle race baiting that was more associated with conservatives? Had he lost his political touch? The truth is more nuanced, more human, and more sophisticated.

Clinton's behavior in 2008 was a departure from his public reputation. As was clearly demonstrated in his time as an attorney general, a governor, and a president, Bill Clinton was, as Joe Klein titled in his book about him, "the natural."[5] His ability to empathize with average Americans about their concerns, fears, and dreams was special. He convinced people that he was on their side, disarming their skepticism and seducing them to his side. In the White House, Clinton was legendary for conducting long, winding, seminar-style sessions that both frustrated and exhausted his subordinates. The compulsion to delay decisions until the last moment was criticized by observers and insiders alike. These behavior traits showed his propensity for easily manipulated issues, such as crime and welfare. Those same traits, however, also masked his steely backbone on major issues, such as the deficit, Medicare, Social Security, and education. More than Al From or Bruce Reed, Clinton was the living embodiment of the New Democrat ethos.

President Clinton had a core set of principles that included education, opportunity, fairness, and effective governmental action on behalf the American people. These principles were rooted in the moderate/progressive agenda of the early twenty-first century. Protecting the environment, providing effective governmental service, increasing the security of the American people, and providing ladders of opportunity to the downtrodden were, in Clinton's judgment, the responsibility of the federal government. He promoted expertise, science-driven data and analysis, and a brand of elitism that emphasized formal education and empiricism. If critics charged him with a moral relativism, Clinton nonetheless dismissed traditional liberalism as outdated, frustrated, and stale. Douglas Brinkley noted, "He made liberalism shameful—you didn't want to be caught with the 'L' tattooed on your chest or you'd lose elections. . . . A real leader would've been able to grab hold of liberalism. . . . [H]e never did that after his health care effort sunk in 1993."[6]

As race remained a subtly volatile issue in American politics, Clinton was careful in how he went about his efforts for African Americans. That caution explains, in part, his relationships with high-achieving African Americans, such as Vernon Jordan, Marian Wright Edelman, Ron Brown, Togo West, Rodney Slater, and John Hope Franklin. None of these figures fit the stereotypical "black" label. They were educated, sophisticated, and accomplished. Ironically, many of Clinton's actions made his African American advisors uncomfortable as well. Clinton, in the White House interviews conducted by Taylor Branch, noted, "Like [Colin] Powell, black members of the White House staff were circumspect about overt racial awareness, let alone advocacy, considering it unprofessional."[7] These inclinations and behavior are representative of a community tired of political and racial strife, exhausted with prominent displays of victimization, battle weary after twelve years of fierce political combat with the Reagan and Bush administrations, and eager to proceed forward with a forward-thinking, racially progressive, truly colorblind man. Clinton maybe represented, as much as anyone one man possibly could, a post-racial utopia dreamed of by so many in the African American community. Clinton was arguably ahead of many members of the Congressional Black Caucus in recognizing the new dynamics within Black America.

African Americans represented less than 15 percent of the nation. Furthermore, two-thirds of the African American community could be categorized as middle or upper class; the black poor made up only a third of the population. Clinton's positions on issues such as crime, welfare, and affirmative action resonated with many blacks, so he could stake out controversial positions without too much fear of losing his most loyal voting bloc. At any rate, who were they going to support: George H. W. Bush, Bob Dole, Newt Gingrich, Trent Lott? As Clinton tried to present a new society that valued responsibility, opportunity, and community, it also reflected the president's unease with racially tinged issues. Sister Souljah or Lani Guinier could make Clinton uncomfortable and nervous.

The Sister Souljah incident demonstrated Clinton's discomfort with the more populist, militant aspects of the African American community. His acquiescence in the face of political opposition in the Lani Guinier nomination and the Racial Justice Act in 1994 revealed that Clinton was uncomfortable with the political blowback that could result from being pegged as a race liberal in the old mold.

President Clinton supported "workfare" over welfare, the Earned Income Tax Credit over social entitlement spending, and federal protection of basic worker rights over the policies of the Republican Party, thereby demonstrating both his New Democrat credentials and political dexterity. In doing so, he showed a commitment to working

Americans but not the welfare state. The president's vigorous support of affirmative action was rooted in his experiences as a New South Democrat. He appealed to the African American community through the church, communities, and values-oriented rhetoric that others mistook for patronization and opportunism. It worked in securing the support of African Americans over the life of his presidency and beyond.

This support for the president and, by extension, his policies was galvanized by certain actions taken by Clinton. For instance, the President's Initiative on Race showed that the president did care about improving race relations. To be sure, it was a missed opportunity for the nation and the Clinton administration, but Clinton did try to improve race relations, governmental behavior, and policy after the publication of the PIR's final report in the fall of 1998 and through the end of his presidency in 2001 by using its recommendations and maintaining contact with its distinguished chairman, Dr. John Hope Franklin.[8]

So what did the Clinton years mean for African Americans? Did their lives and opportunities improve because of the president? The answer is nuanced and complicated. Blacks did gain economically, but generally among the middle class, not the poor. After Clinton's welfare reform went into law in 1996, the black poor suffered in an unforgiving labor market.

The Clinton years saw African Americans gain more stature in the political realm than they had at any previous time since the Great Society. In fact, Clinton helped to stop the marginalization of African Americans begun in 1981 under President Ronald Reagan. The president was serious when he addressed blacks and promoted such issues at affirmative action, community, security, and mobility.

Yet Clinton's stances on welfare and crime policy had a negative impact upon the most vulnerable within the African American community. Clinton bought into fashion the more conservative arguments that welfare encouraged dependency and dysfunction. Poor blacks often became the guinea pigs for New Democratic and conservative policy proposals. In addition, blacks became more isolated, more desperate, and more likely to need assistance than before. The real impact of welfare reform was not fully seen or felt until the Great Recession of 2007–2009. In 2008, white male unemployment reached 13.9 percent. Black male unemployment, on the other hand, reached 20.5 percent.[9]

Welfare reform greatly contributed to both high unemployment and greater need for social services, namely, welfare.

Clinton's crime policies, while often benefiting the middle class, did little to address underlying issues such as joblessness, family dysfunction, and lack of opportunity. It fed a growing industry that profited off of the so-called prison industrial complex. The president further refused to push for a reduction in the crack–powder cocaine disparities in sentencing, an end to the questionable war on drugs, and greater resources for those trapped in the muck of America's underclass. Clinton's policies reflected the pro-growth programs of the Democratic Leadership Council. The president did expend tremendous amounts of energy encouraging economic development in urban areas, which both benefited African Americans and suggested new difficulties in an era when the United States more fully moved into a service-based, high-tech economy. At the very least, the 1990s demonstrated both the continued relevance of class and the precarious position of African Americans.

Bill Clinton left the White House on January 20, 2001. Many, black and white, were glad that the scandals, personal misbehavior, and investigations were over. While the country divided over his successor, he left an ambiguous legacy in the African American community. Virginia Sapiro and David T. Canon note, "The key for the Democratic Party's race politics is to mobilize its support among black citizens and get them to the polls without, at the same time, alienating white voters whose security within the Democratic ranks may be more fragile."[10] No other Democratic politician in the late twentieth century so successfully accomplished this as Bill Clinton. As Sapiro and Canon also note, "Clinton was of just the right generation and position to understand and use these features of contemporary politics with respect to race."[11] His ability to coalesce the disparate forces within the Democratic Party produced moderate, incremental change that was progressive for African Americans and the country.

Bill Clinton was not the first black president; no white man could ever be. But Clinton came the closest of anyone up to that time. He restored many blacks' faith in the federal government as the protector of vulnerable groups. His actions to bolster and protect affirmative action, education, and race relations and to bring African Americans into his White House, with a serious seat at the head table, allowed many to overlook his stances on crime and welfare. Moreover, his fierce fights against dedicated ideological opposition from Republicans on Capitol Hill no doubt prevented severe and draconian cuts to various programs of great interest to the African American community. It was, in fact, the reactionary Clinton—the one always fighting against those who would use policy to inflict damage on African Americans—that galvanized the support and appreciation of African Americans. This was their president, their leader. The incessant investigations and inquires and hearings by his opponents only strengthened his support. The president was able to transmit hope to a community battered by years of government neglect. Longtime Democratic Party operative Donna Brazile noted this peculiar situation when she noted, "He not only connected symbolically with African Americans but, after twelve years of Reagan and Bush, he appeared to be somebody that was on the side of African Americans. He not only understood our language and our songs, he understood our dreams and aspirations."[12] No other American president had such a deep, connective understanding of African Americans before. Even Robert F. Kennedy had to be dragged into the fight for equality by outside events before he would act. But Clinton naturally and instinctively felt sympathy and respect for African Americans.

As Dewayne Wickman noted, despite the views of those who take issues such as crime and welfare and Lani Guinier and use them to attack Clinton, "when viewed in the context of a broader array of issues—and the political backdrop of the 1990s—Clinton is catapulted onto the short list of the best presidents for African Americans."[13] The events of the 2008 presidential campaign showed Clinton at his worst: petty, race baiting, and rusty. His attacks on Barack Obama demonstrate the complexity and pragmatism of not only his life but his presidency. That ability to seemingly be the greatest friend of the African American since Abraham Lincoln and Lyndon Johnson while also being a shrewd, opportunistic operator reflects the mixed and disjointed nature of the Clinton years as they related to the salient issues of race and class. In the end, the Clinton presidency reflected the frustrations, hope, progress, and continuation of the politics of race and class in the United States in the 1990s.

NOTES

INTRODUCTION
"The First Black President?"

1. Toni Morrison, "The First Black President," *New Yorker*, October 5, 1998, 31.

2. Statistical Abstract of the United States, 2007, Bureau of the Census, US Department of Commerce, *Statistical Abstract of the United States* (Washington, DC, 2007).

3. Steve Gillon, *The Pact: Bill Clinton, Newt Gingrich, and the Rivalry That Defined a Generation* (New York: Oxford University Press, 2008), 213.

4. John F. Harris, *The Survivor: Bill Clinton White House* (New York: Random House, 2005), 156.

5. The Progressive Alternative, "What Is to Be Done?," *New Democrat*, January–February 1995, 22.

6. James T. Patterson, *Restless Giant: The United States from Watergate to Bush v. Gore* (New York: Oxford University Press, 2005), 247.

7. Haynes Johnson, *Divided We Fall: Gambling with History in the Nineties* (New York: W. W. Norton, 1994), 66.

8. Ibid., 397.

9. Jean Bethke Elshtain, "Issues and Themes: Spiral of Delegitimation of New Social Covenant," in *The Elections of 1992*, ed. Michael Nelson et al. (Washington, DC: Congressional Quarterly, 1993), 116.

10. Ross K. Baker, "The Presidential Nominations," in *The Election of 1992: Reports and Interpretations*, ed. Gerald M. Pomper et al. (Chatham: New Jersey, 1993), 52.

11. Ibid., 43.

12. Ibid., 57.

13. Jonathan Alter, Ginny Carroll, Howard Fineman, and Mary Talbot, "Substance vs. Sex," *Newsweek*, February 3, 1992, 18.

14. Jeffrey H. Birnbaum, "Clinton Bid to Avoid Vietnam May Prompt Fresh Scrutiny," *Wall Street Journal*, February 8, 1992.

15. David Maraniss, *First in His Class: The Biography of Bill Clinton* (New York: Simon & Schuster, 1995), 199.

16. Ibid., 184.

17. Jonathan Alter, "The Beast Is Always Hungry," *Newsweek*, February 17, 1992, 23.

18. Stephen J. Wayne, "Clinton's Legacy: The Clinton Persona," *Political Science and Politics* 32, no. 3 (September 1999): 559.

19. William Schneider, "The New Populism," *Political Psychology* 15, no. 4 (December 1994): 779.

20. Ibid., 779–80.

21. Joe Klein, The Natural: The Misunderstood Presidency of Bill Clinton (New York: Broadway Books, 2002), 25.

22. Richard Benedetto et al., "Clinton Endorsed," USA Today, April 22, 1992, 4A.

23. David Mills, "Sister Souljah's Call to Arms: The rapper says the riots were payback. Are you paying attention?," Washington Post, May 13, 1992, A29.

24. Gwen Ifill, "The 1992 Campaign: Democrat; Clinton at Jackson Meeting: Warmth, and Some Friction," New York Times, June 14, 1992, 30.

25. Ronald Walters, Freedom Is Not Enough: Black Voters, Black Candidates, and American Presidential Politics (New York: Rowman & Littlefield, 2005), 54.

26. Ibid., 54.

27. Joe Klein, "The Jesse Primary," Newsweek, June 22, 1992, 37.

28. Jack White, "Sister Souljah: Capitalist Tool," Time, June 29, 1992.

29. Chuck Philips, "'I Do Not Advocate . . . Murdering': 'Raptivist' Sister Souljah Disputes Clinton Charge," Los Angeles Times, June 17, 1992, Calendar, Part F, Entertainment Desk.

30. Roger Wilkins, quoted in Anthony Lewis, "Abroad at Home; Black and White," New York Times, June 18, 1992, A27.

31. Jesse Jackson and Sister Souljah, quoted in Jack E. White, "Sister Souljah: Capitalist Tool," Time, June 29, 1992, http://www.time.com/time/magazine/article/0,9171,1101920629-15999,00.html (accessed January 26, 2011).

32. "Manhattan Project, 1992," Newsweek, November 1, 1992, 40.

33. Ibid.

34. Marshall Frady, Jesse: The Life and Pilgrimage of Jesse Jackson (New York: Random House, 1996), 487.

35. Sean Wilentz, The Age of Reagan: A History, 1974–2008 (New York: HarperCollins Publishers, 2008).

36. Arthur M. Schlesinger Jr., The Vital Center (New York: Transaction Publishers, 2007).

37. Joseph E. Lowndes, From the New Deal to the New Right: Race and the Southern Origins of Modern Conservatism (New Haven: Yale University Press, 2008), 7.

38. Patrick Allitt, The Conservatives: Ideas and Personalities throughout American History (New Haven: Yale University Press, 2009), 5.

39. Lisa McGirr, Suburban Warriors: The Origins of the New American Right (Princeton: Princeton University Press, 2002).

40. Paul Pierson and Theda Skocpol, The Transformation of American Politics: Activist Government and the Rise of Conservatism (Princeton: Princeton University Press, 2007).

41. Adarand Constructors, Inc. v. Pena, 515 U.S. 200 (1995).

42. John Hope Franklin, interview with author, Durham, NC, August 14, 2007.

CHAPTER 1
The Democratic Leadership Council and African Americans

1. Judith Stein, Pivotal Decade: How the United States Traded Factories for Finance in the Seventies (New Haven: Yale University Press, 2010), 239.

2. Gil Troy, *Morning in America: How Ronald Reagan Invented the 1980s* (Princeton: Princeton University Press, 2005), 15.

3. Steven F. Lawson, Running for Freedom: Civil Rights and Black Politics in America since 1941, 3rd ed. (Malden, MA: Wiley-Blackwell, 2009), 3.

4. Ibid., 3.

5. Arthur M. Schlesinger Jr., *The Age of Jackson* (New York: Hachette Book Group, 1988); Arthur M. Schlesinger Jr., *The Crisis of the Old Order, 1919–1933: The Age of Roosevelt*, vol. 1 (New York: Houghton Mifflin Harcourt, 2003); Arthur M. Schlesinger Jr., *The Coming of the New Deal, 1922–1935: The Age of Roosevelt*, vol. 2 (New York: Houghton Mifflin Harcourt, 2003); Arthur M. Schlesinger Jr., *The Politics of Upheaval, 1935–1936: The Age of Roosevelt*, vol. 3 (New York: Houghton Mifflin Harcourt, 2003).

6. Maurice Isserman and Michael Kazin, *America Divided: The Civil War of the 1960s,* 3rd ed. (New York: Oxford University Press, 2008), 308.

7. Ibid.

8. Bruce Schulman and Julian Zelizer, eds., *Rightward Bound: Making America Conservative in the 1970s* (Cambridge: Harvard University Press, 2008).

9. Matthew Lassiter, "Inventing Family Values," in *Rightward Bound*, ed. Schulman and Zelizer, 27.

10. Brown v. Board of Education of Topeka, 347 U.S. 483 (1954).

11. Joseph Crespino, "Civil Rights and the Religious Right," in *Rightward Bound*, ed. Schulman and Zelizer, 105.

12. F. A. Hayek, *The Road to Serfdom* (Chicago: University of Chicago Press, 1944).

13. Milton Friedman and Anna Schwartz, *A Monetary History of the United States, 1867–1960* (Princeton: Princeton University Press, 1963).

14. Victor A. Canto, Douglas H. Joines, and Arthur B. Laffer, *Foundations of Supply-Side Economics—Theory and Evidence* (New York: Academic Press, 1982).

15. Donald T. Critchlow, *The Conservative Ascendancy: How the GOP Right Made Political History* (Cambridge: Harvard University Press, 2007).

16. Robert M. Collins, *Transforming America: Politics and Culture during the Reagan Years* (New York: Columbia University Press, 2007), 244.

17. Ibid.

18. Al From and Will Marshall, *Mandate for Change* (Washington, DC: The Progressive Policy Institute, 1993), xv.

19. Kenneth Baer, Reinventing Democrats: The Politics of Liberalism from Reagan to Clinton (Lawrence: University Press of Kansas, 2000), 39.

20. Ibid., 39–40.

21. Bill Clinton, *My Life* (New York: Alfred A. Knopf, 2004), 381.

22. Baer, Reinventing Democrats, 65.

23. Vesla Weaver, "Frontlash: Race and the Development of Punitive Crime Policy," *Studies in American Political Development* 21 (Fall 2007): 230–65. The concept of "frontlash" was developed by University of Virginia scholar Vesla Weaver, who argued that anger toward social change not only manifests itself through a backlash from the masses, but also comes from political elites responding to the changes. In her article, Weaver showed that despite the rights revolution of the 1960s, political elites were also putting into place a rigid criminal justice system that disproportionately impacted African Americans.

24. US representative Richard Gephardt, preface to *Winning in the Global Economy: The Economic Competition Index/Building a New Foundation for Economic Strength*, Democratic Leadership Council (Washington, DC: Democratic Leadership Council, 1995), i.

25. Woodrow Wilson, preface to his The New Freedom: A Call for the Emancipation of the Generous Energies of a People (New York: Doubleday, 1913), viii.

26. Democratic Leadership Council, *Winning in the Global Economy*, 7.

27. Baer, Reinventing Democrats, 166.

28. Ibid.

29. Governor Bill Clinton, interview by Lisa Myers, *Today Show*, NBC, May 6, 1991.

30. Collins, Transforming America, 76.

31. Walters, Freedom Is Not Enough.

32. Marshall Frady, *Jesse: The Life and Pilgrimage of Jesse Jackson* (New York: Random House, 1996), 390–91.

33. Baer, Reinventing Democrats, 108.

34. William Galston and Elaine Kamarck, *The Politics of Evasion: Democrats and the Presidency* (Washington, DC: Progressive Policy Institute, 1989), 3.

35. Manning Marable, Beyond Black and White: Transforming African-American Politics (New York: Verso, 1995), 81.

36. Ibid., 84.

37. Taylor Branch, *At Canaan's Edge: America in the King Years, 1965–1968* (New York: Simon & Schuster, 2006), 251.

38. Dr. Martin Luther King Jr., "Beyond Vietnam," in *A Call to Conscience: The Landmark Speeches of Dr. Martin Luther King, Jr.*, ed. Clayborne Carson and Kris Shepard (New York: Warner Books, 2001), 158.

39. Galston and Kamarck, "The Politics of Evasion," 17.

40. Democratic Leadership Council, *The New Orleans Declaration* (New Orleans: Fourth Annual DLC Convention, 1990), 2.

41. Arthur M. Schlesinger Jr., *The Disuniting of America: Reflections on a Multicultural Society* (New York: W. W. Norton, 1998), 49.

42. Thomas Edsall with Mary D. Edsall, *Chain Reaction: The Impact of Race, Rights, and Taxes on American Politics* (New York: W. W. Norton, 1991), 214.

43. Ibid.

44. Elaine Kamarck and Will Marshall, "Replacing Work with Welfare," in *The Mandate for Change*, ed. Will Marshall and Martin Schram (Washington, DC: The Progressive Policy Institute, 1993), 218.

45. Donna Shalala, phone interview by author, May 1, 2009.

46. Kamarck and Marshall, "Replacing Work with Welfare," 218.

47. Will Marshall, "Replacing Welfare with Work," Policy Briefing, *Progressive Policy Institute*, July 1994, 2.

48. Ibid., 5–6.

49. David C. Ruffin, "The DLC: Seeking a Party Shift to the Right," *Black Enterprise*, March 1987, 19.

50. Gideon v. Wainwright, 372 U.S. 335 (1963).

51. Ed Kilgore, "Safer Streets and Neighborhoods," in *Mandate for Change*, ed. Will Marshall and Martin Schram (Washington, DC: Progressive Policy Institute, 1993), 182.

52. Ibid., 184.

53. Michelle Alexander, The New Jim Crow: Mass Incarceration in the Age of Colorblind (New York: New Press, 2010).

54. Baer, Reinventing Democrats, 82.

55. Jon F. Hale, "The Making of New Democrats," *Political Science Quarterly* 110, no. 2, (Summer 1995): 216. Americans for Democratic Action is one of the oldest and most prominent lobbying groups in the modern Democratic Party. Founded by the likes of Arthur Schlesinger, Eleanor Roosevelt, John Kenneth Galbraith, and Hubert Humphrey, the ADA has been the premier advocate of liberal policies and politics since its founding in 1946. Furthermore, the ADA was known as a fierce defender of the Progressive tradition and the New Deal as well as a stalwart opponent of communism at home and abroad. The ADA annually publish voting records of members of Congress, detailing, on a scale of zero to one hundred, how liberal any particular member has been in the previous year.

56. Hale, "The Making of New Democrats," 216.

57. Baer, Reinventing Democrats, 82.

58. Ibid., 260.

59. Maynard Jackson, quoted in Jack W. Germond and Jules Witcover, "Democrats Press for Big Super Tuesday Turnout," *National Journal*, June 27, 1987, 1676.

60. Ibid.

61. R. H. Melton, "Wilder's Embrace of Jackson Stays a Long Arm's Length Away; Wilder Keeps Jesse Jackson—and Liberal Label—a Long Arm's Length Away," *Washington Post*, September 30, 1989, B1.

62. Ibid.

63. E. J. Dionne Jr., "Again Democrats Agonize over the Rules," *New York Times*, May 21, 1989, section 4, page 5.

64. Ibid.

65. Thomas B. Edsall, "Liberal Democrats Fragmented by Politics of War; Disputes over Gulf Distract Coalition from Focus of Strategy Meeting on Domestic Issues," *Washington Post*, January 27, 1991, A5.

66. Thomas B. Edsall, "Democrats Scramble to Win Black Support; Wilder's Withdrawal May Allow Party to Begin Resolving Racial Tensions before Convention," *Washington Post*, January 10, 1992, A4.

67. Ibid.

68. John E. Jacob, quoted in Frank McCoy, "Can Clinton's Urban Policies Really Work?: B.E.'s Economists Weigh the Value of Empowerment Zones and Community Banks in Revitalizing America's Cities," *Black Enterprise*, June 1994, 180.

69. William Julius Wilson, The Declining Significance of Race: Blacks and Changing American Institutions (Chicago: University of Chicago Press, 1980).

70. Paul Taylor, "Jackson Says Democrats Are Pushing Blacks Out," *Washington Post*, December 7, 1985, A15.

71. Ibid.

72. Donald P. Baker, "Robb Says Wilder Has Alienated Him; 'Very Difficult' to Support Governor Bid, He Asserts," *Washington Post*, December 3, 1986, B1.

73. Douglas Wilder, quoted in R. H. Melton, "While Trying to Close Rift, Wilder Repeats Criticisms; He Scores Robb's Letters and Calls Group 'Demeaning,'" *Washington Post*, December 5, 1986, B3.

74. Maynard Jackson, quoted in Taylor, "New Optimism for Democrats; Hopes for '88 Are Buoyed by Republicans' Crisis," *Washington Post*, December 12, 1986, A3.

75. Charles Robb, quoted in R. H. Melton, "Wilder Feud Tails Robb to Williamsburg Parley," *Washington Post*, December 11, 1986, A3.

76. John W. Mashek, "It's not all clear sailing despite the turnaround in party's fortunes; Democrats' own dilemma—Jackson," *U.S. News & World Report*, December 15, 1986, 34.

77. Charles Robb, quoted in Richard Benedetto, "Dems Scold Jackson for 'Divisiveness,'" *USA Today*, March 13, 1989, 4A.

78. Ibid.

79. J. Joseph Grandmaison, quoted in Thomas B. Edsall and David S. Broder, "Latest News about Jackson Pleases Democrats; Allies Say Becoming Mayor Would Be Asset; Others Look Forward to '92 Race without Him," *Washington Post*, April 30, 1989, A4.

80. Al From, quoted in Edsall and Broder, "Latest News about Jackson Pleases Democrats," A4.

81. "The Clinton Presidency: Historic Economic Growth: Smallest Welfare Rolls since 1969," http://clinton5.nara.gov/WH/Accomplishments/eightyears-03.html (accessed September 15, 2015).

82. Henry Reddy, quoted in Dan Balz, "Democrats Face Minority Skepticism; Blacks Ask Whether Moderate's Strategy Abandons Civil Rights," *Washington Post*, May 8, 1991, A7.

83. John F. Harris, "'Clean Our House of Racism,' Clinton Urges Nation," *Washington Post*, October 17, 1995, A1.

84. Democratic Leadership Council, *The New American Choice Resolution* (Cleveland, OH: Democratic Leadership Council, 1991), 2. This was a pamphlet released by the DLC on May 9, 1991.

85. William Schneider, "No Modesty, Please, We're the DLC," *National Journal*, December 12, 1998, 2962.

86. Ibid.

87. David A. Bositis, "1997 National Opinion Poll-Politics," Joint Center for Political and Economic Studies, March 1997.

88. Margaret Weir, "The Political Collapse of Bill Clinton's Third Way," in *New Labour and the Future of Progressive Politics*, ed. Stuart White and Susan Giaimo (New York: MacMillan, 2001), 137–48.

89. Walters, Freedom Is Not Enough, 143.

90. Bill Clinton, "Tribute to Al From," Andrew W. Mellon Auditorium, Washington, D.C., June 16, 2009, Democratic Leadership Council.

CHAPTER 2
Race and Class in the 1990s

1. Lou Cannon, *The Role of a Lifetime* (New York: Public Affairs, 2000), 520.

2. Voting Rights Act of 1965, Pub. L. 89–110.

3. Thomas J. Sugrue, *Not Even Past: Barack Obama and the Burden of Race* (Princeton: Princeton University Press, 2010), 66.

4. Thomas Sugrue, Sweet Land of Liberty: The Forgotten Struggle for Civil Rights in the North (New York: Random House, 2008), 521.

5. Eugene Robinson, *Disintegration: The Splintering of Black America* (New York: Doubleday, 2010).

6. Ibid., 76.

7. "We the Americans: Blacks," Bureau of the Census, Economics and Statistics Administration, US Department of Commerce, September 1993.

8. Mary Pattillo-McCoy, *Black Picket Fences: Privilege and Peril among the Black Middle Class* (Chicago: University of Chicago Press, 1999), 15.

9. "Table 296, Bachelor's degrees conferred by degree-granting institutions, by race/ethnicity and sex of student: Selected years, 1976–77 through 2008–09," *Digest of Education Statistics*, National Center for Education Statistics, September 2010.

10. "Table 299, Master's degrees conferred by degree-granting institutions, by race/ethnicity and sex of student: Selected years, 1976–77 through 2008–09," *Digest of Education Statistics*, National Center for Education Statistics, September 2010.

11. "Table 302, Doctor's degrees conferred by degree-granting institutions, by race/ethnicity and sex of student: Selected years, 1976–77 through 2008–09," *Digest of Education Statistics*, National Center for Education Statistics, September 2010.

12. "Table 305, First-Professional degrees conferred by degree-granting institutions, by race/ethnicity and sex of student: Selected years, 1976–77 through 2008–09," *Digest of Education Statistics*, National Center for Education Statistics, September 2010.

13. Thomas C. Holt, *Children of Fire: A History of African Americans* (New York: Hill and Wang, 2010), 353.

14. Ellis Cose, The Rage of a Privileged Class: Why Are Middle-Class Blacks Angry? Why Should America Care? (New York: HarperPerennial, 1993), 105.

15. Ibid., 105–6.

16. Bureau of the Census, "We the Americans: Blacks," Economics and Statistics Administration, US Department of Commerce, September 1993, 9.

17. Ibid.

18. Ibid.

19. William Julius Wilson, *The Declining Significance of Race: Blacks and Changing American Institutions* (Chicago: University of Chicago Press, 1978), 140.

20. Derrick Bell, Faces at the Bottom of the Well: The Permanence of Racism (New York: Basic Books, 1992), 163.

CHAPTER 3

The Politics of Racial Appointments:
The Nomination of Lani Guinier

1. Steven F. Lawson, Running for Freedom: Civil Rights and Black Politics in America since 1941, 3rd ed. (Malden, MA: Wiley-Blackwell, 2009), 280.

2. Editorial, "Lani Guinier: The Making of a Cause Celebre," *The Crisis*, August/September 1993, 23.

3. Civil Rights Act of 1957, Public Law 85–315.

4. Marshall Ingwerson, "Clinton Stresses Diversity, Fiscal Probity in Cabinet," *Christian Science Monitor*, December 14, 1992, 3.

5. John Hope Franklin and Evelyn Brooks Higginbotham, *From Slavery to Freedom: A History of African Americans* (New York: McGraw-Hill, 2011), 425.

6. Harvard Sitkoff, A New Deal for Blacks: The Emergence of Civil Rights as a National Issue—the Depression Decade, 1st ed. (New York: Oxford University Press, 2008).

7. Eric Porter, "Affirming and Disaffirming Actions: Remarking Race in the 1970s," in *America in the 70s*, ed. Beth Bailey and David Farber (Lawrence: University Press of Kansas, 2004), 66.

8. John Ehrman, "Domestic Politics and Issues," in *Debating the Reagan Presidency*, ed. John Ehrman and Michael W. Flamm (New York: Rowman & Littlefield, 2009), 9.

9. Isaiah J. Poole, "Appointments: Numbers or Substance," *Black Enterprise*, July 1981, 21.

10. Ibid.

11. Joseph E. Lowndes, From the New Deal to the New Right: Race and the Southern Origin of Modern Conservatism (New Haven: Yale University Press, 2009).

12. Isaiah J. Poole, "Who Is Ronald Reagan," *Black Enterprise*, February 1981, 27.

13. Clinton, *My Life*, 204.

14. Lani Guinier, Lift Every Voice: Turning a Civil Rights Setback into a New Vision of Social Justice (New York: Simon & Schuster, 1998), 53.

15. Curriculum vita of Lani Guinier, http://www.law.harvard.edu/faculty/guinier/cv.php (accessed November 10, 2015).

16. David S. Broder, "Diversity Was Paramount in Building the Cabinet," *Washington Post*, December 25, 1992, A1.

17. M. Rucci, "Bill Gives Jobs to Women, Blacks," *Courier Mail (Brisbane)*, December 26, 1992.

18. Joel Kotkin, "The Entitlement Trap; Why Pushing Group Rights Is a Danger to Diversity," *Washington Post*, February 7, 1993, C1.

19. David Gates, "White Male Paranoia," *Newsweek*, March 29, 1993, 48.

20. George Stephanopoulos, *All Too Human: A Political Education* (New York: Little, Brown, 1999). The author notes that appointing minorities was a way to appease liberals and others because of the administration's inability to pass legislation. However, the administration had not been in office six months, and thus the argument that it was simply a way of appeasing liberals seems disingenuous at best.

21. Nigel Hamilton, *Bill Clinton: Mastering the Presidency* (New York: Public Affairs, 2007), 134.

22. Taylor Branch, *The Clinton Tapes: Wrestling History with the President* (New York: Simon & Schuster, 2009), 69.

23. Clint Bolick, "Clinton's Quota Queen," *Wall Street Journal*, April 30, 1993, A12.

24. Ibid.

25. Ibid.

26. Ibid.

27. Neil A. Lewis, "May 2–8: Civil Rights Nominee; Lani Guinier's Agenda Provokes Old Enemies," *New York Times*, May 9, 1993, section 4, 2.

28. Jerry Seper, "Civil Rights Nominee May Be in Jeopardy: Guinier's Radical Writings Questioned," *Washington Times*, May 13, 1993, A1.

29. Tony Mauro, "Two Clinton Nominees Face Tough Sledding," *USA Today*, May 14, 1993, 2A.

30. Neil A. Lewis, "Lani Guinier's Agenda Provokes Old Enemies," *New York Times*, May 9, 1993, section 4, 2.

31. Michael Isikoff, "Confirmation Battle Looms over Guinier; Critics Target 'Extreme' Views in Law Review Articles by Justice Dept. Civil Rights Nominee," *Washington Post*, May 21, 1993, A23.

32. Ibid.

33. Ibid.

34. Laurel Leff, "From Legal Scholar to Quota Queen: What Happens When Politics Pulls the Press into the Groves of Academe," *Columbia Journalism Review* 32, no. 3 (September–October 1993): 36.

35. Ibid.

36. Paul A. Gigot, "Hillary's Choice on Civil Rights: Back to the Future," *Wall Street Journal*, May 7, 1993, A14.

37. Laurel Leff, "From Legal Scholar to Quota Queen," 36.

38. Ibid.

39. Michael Isikoff, "Power behind the Thrown Nominee: Activist with Score to Settle," *Washington Post*, June 6, 1993, A11.

40. Ibid.

41. Voting Rights Act of 1965, Public Law 89–110.

42. Earl Ofari Hutchinson, "Why Republican Rip the Voting Rights Act," *alternet.com*, June 28, 2006, http://www.alternet.org/story/38202/ (accessed February 3, 2011).

43. Krista Helfferich, "Note and Comment: The Stress, the Press, the Test, and the Mess with the Lani Guinier Smear: A Proposal for Executive Confirmation Reform," *Loyola of Los Angeles Law Review* 28 (1995): 1141.

44. Lani Guinier, "The Triumph of Tokenism: The Voting Rights Act and the Theory of Black Electoral Success," *Michigan Law Review* 89 (March 1991): 1154.

45. Lani Guinier, "No Two Seats: The Elusive Quest for Political Equality," *Virginia Law Review* 77 (November 1991): 1512.

46. Ibid., 1513.

47. Ibid., 1514.

48. Alexis de Tocqueville, *Democracy in America* (New York: Penguin Group, 2003).

49. Guinier, "The Triumph of Tokenism," 1154.

50. Lani Guinier, telephone interview with author, November 2007.

51. Mari Matsuda, quoted in Helfferich, "Note and Comment," 1157.

52. Robert Dole, quoted in Isikoff, "Confirmation Battle Looms over Guinier," A23.

53. Joe Biden, quoted in Neil A. Lewis, "Clinton Faces Battle over a Civil Rights Nominee," *New York Times*, May 21, 1993, Section B, 9.

54. Donald Baer, "The Trials of Lani Guinier," *U.S. News & World Report* 114, no. 22 (1993): 38.

55. Branch, *The Clinton Tapes*, 69.

56. Al From, "Guinier Had to Go. Now," *New York Times*, June 5, 1993, 21.

57. Al From, "Hey, Mom, What's a New Democrat?," *Washington Post*, June 6, 1998, C1.

58. Will Marshall, quoted in Michael Kelly, "Clinton Myth of Nonideological Politics Stumbles," *New York Times*, June 6, 1993.

59. Patrick J. Leahy, quoted in Isikoff, "Confirmation Battle Looms over Guinier," A23.

60. Dave McCurdy, quoted in Lally Weymouth, "Lani Guinier: Radical Justice," *Washington Post*, May 25, 1993, A19.

61. Lani Guinier, Lift Every Voice: Turning a Civil Rights Setback into a New Vision of Social Justice (New York: Simon & Schuster, 1998), 111.

62. Branch, *The Clinton Tapes*, 70.

63. Ricki Seidman, quoted in Guinier, *Lift Every Voice*, 111.

64. Guinier, *Lift Every Voice*, 112.

65. Ibid., 116.

66. Lani Guinier, interview with author, by telephone, November 27, 2007.

67. Guinier, *Lift Every Voice*, 118.

68. Branch, *The Clinton Tapes*, 69.

69. Guinier, *Lift Every Voice*, 121.

70. Public Papers of the Presidents of the United States: William J. Clinton, 1993–2001 (Washington, DC: Government Printing Office, 1993–2001), 1:808.

71. Ibid., 1:809.

72. Lani Guinier, The Tyranny of the Majority: Fundamental Fairness in Representative Democracy (New York: Free Press, 1994); Lani Guinier, Lift Every Voice: Turning a Civil Rights Setback into a New Vision of Social Justice (New York: Simon & Schuster, 1998); Lani Guinier, The Miner's Canary: Enlisting Race, Resisting Power, Transforming Democracy (Cambridge: Harvard University Press, 2002); Lani Guinier, Tyranny of the Meritocracy: How Wealth Became Merit, Class Became Race, and Higher Education Became a Gift from the Poor to the Rich (Boston: Beacon Press, 2011).

73. Editorial, "Slick Willie Rides Again?," *The Crisis*, August/September 1993, 3.

74. Eleanor Clift, "A Hard Right Turn," *Newsweek*, June 14, 1993, 26.

75. Kweisi Mfume, quoted in Editorial, "Lani Guinier: The Making of a Cause Celebre," *The Crisis*, August/September 1993, 52.

76. Clift, "A Hard Right Turn," 25.

CHAPTER 4
Responsibility and Accountability: The Politics of Crime

1. William J. Clinton, interview by Amy Goodman, *Democracy Now*, PBS, November 8, 2000.

2. William Julius Wilson, *When Work Disappears: The World of the New Urban Poor* (New York: Knopf Doubleday, 1997).

3. Elijah Anderson, *Streetwise: Race, Class, and Change in an Urban Community* (Chicago: University of Chicago Press, 1990).

4. Andrew Hacker, Two Nations: Black and White, Separate, Hostile, Unequal (New York: Scribner, 2003).

5. David B. Holian, "He's Stealing My Issues! Clinton's Crime Rhetoric and the Dynamics of Issue Ownership," *Political Behavior* 26, no. 2 (June 2004): 95.

6. Ishmael Reed, "The Black Pathology Biz," *The Nation*, February 12, 2002. Originally appeared in the November 12, 1989, issue of *The Nation*.

7. "Organizing Principles: Crime and Violence," Domestic Policy Council, Bruce Reed, Crime, Folder 9, Box 85, William J. Clinton Presidential Library (hereafter cited as WJCPL).

8. Maraniss, *First in His Class*, 434.

9. Martin Tolchin, "Study Says 53,000 Got Prison Furloughs in '87, and Few Did Harm," *New York Times*, October 12, 1988, special to the *New York Times*. The Contact Center, a nonprofit criminal information clearinghouse in Lincoln, Nebraska, conducted a study that showed that state and federal furlough programs were very successful in 1987.

10. General Election Presidential Debate, October 13, 1988, at the Pauley Pavillion, University of California at Los Angeles. Moderated by Bernard Shaw of CNN and sponsored by the Commission on Presidential Debates. Vice President George H. W. Bush (R) vs. Governor Michael Dukakis (D-MA).

11. Michael Schaller, *Right Turn: American Life in the Reagan-Bush Era, 1980–1992* (New York: Oxford University Press, 2006), 63.

12. Governor Bill Clinton, "Making Our Streets Safe," City Hall, July 23, 1992, Houston, TX, Domestic Policy Council, Bruce Reed, Folder 15, Box 85, WJCPL.

13. Kevin Kruse, *White Flight: Atlanta and the Making of Modern Conservatism* (Princeton: Princeton University Press, 2005).

14. Matthew Lassiter, *The Silent Majority: Suburban Politics in the Sunbelt South* (Princeton: Princeton University Press, 2006).

15. Wilson, When Work Disappears.

16. Travis L. Dixon, "Psychological Reactions to Crime News Portrayals of Black Criminals: Understanding the Moderating Roles of Prior News Viewing and Stereotype Endorsement," *Communication Monographs* 73, no. 2 (June 2006): 163.

17. "Organizing Principles: Crime and Violence," Domestic Policy Council, Bruce Reed, Crime, Folder 9, Box 85, WJCPL.

18. Memorandum for Circulation, from Rahm Emanuel and Michael Waldman, January 27, 1994, Domestic Policy Council, Bruce Reed, Crime, Folder 6, Box 79, WJCPL.

19. Crime and Violence Meeting, Roosevelt Room, November 15, 1993, Domestic

Policy Council, Bruce Reed, Crime, Folder 7, Box 79, WJCPL. According to this particular source, Midnight Basketball was "modeled after the National Midnight Basketball League, San Francisco's program, headquartered at the Ella Hill Hutch Community Center. . . . [It] uses basketball as a hook to encourage inner city young adults into a comprehensive service program." In addition, it provided monies for basketball courts and related activities to keep kids off the streets, off drugs, and out of trouble. The total cost of the bill was less than 1 percent of the $33 billion crime bill. Republicans lampooned it and the bill as welfare and more social programs.

20. Racial Justice Act of 1994, HR 4017, 103rd Cong., 2nd sess., *Congressional Record,* 140.

21. David C. Baldus, George G. Woodworth, and Charles A. Pulaski Jr., *Equal Justice and the Death Penalty: A Legal Empirical Analysis* (Boston: Northeastern University Press, 1990).

22. Justice Powell, writing for the Majority on the US Supreme Court on April 22, 1987, p. 319, McCleskey v. Kemp, 482 U.S. 279.

23. Senator Carol Moseley-Braun, May 19, 1994, Senate Floor, *Congressional Record,* p. S6112, Racial Justice Act.

24. Baldus, Woodworth, and Pulaski, *Equal Justice and the Death Penalty.* The authors studied verdicts, sentences, and executions in the State of Georgia over a ten-year period, 1969–1979. When *McCleskey v. Kemp* was in the courts, the authors' study and findings were used to demonstrate that McCleskey's sentence was unjust and that there were vast racial disparities in the sentencing of defendants in capital cases.

25. Anti-drug Abuse Act of 1988, 21 U.S.C. 848 (e)-(q).

26. "Title VII: Death Penalty and Other Criminal and Law Enforcement Matters—Subtitle A: Death Penalty," Anti-Drug Abuse Act of 1988.

27. Staff report by the Subcommittee on Civil and Constitutional Rights, Committee on the Judiciary, "Racial Disparities in Federal Death Penalty Prosecutions, 1988–1994," 103rd Congress, 2nd sess., March 1994.

28. Democrats controlled the Senate, 56 to 44, and the House, 256 to 177.

29. New York senator D'Amato, speaking for the Sense of the Senate Amendment No. 1685, on May 6, 1994, to the US Senate, S. amendment 1685, 103rd, 2nd sess., *Cong. Rec.* 140: S5371.

30. US representative John Stephen Horn of California, speaking in opposition to the Racial Justice Act on May 11, 1994, to the House of Representatives, H.R. 4092, 103rd Cong., 2nd sess., *Cong. Rec.* 140: H3272.

31. US representative Bill McCollum (R-FL), as quoted in *New York Times* editorial, "For Racial Justice Executions," *New York Times,* April 22, 1994, A26, New York edition.

32. General Accounting Office, Report on Death Penalty Sentencing: Research Indicates Pattern of Racial Disparities, February, 1990 (Washington, DC: US Government Printing Office, 1990).

33. Director Lowell Dodge, "Administration of Justice Issues, Speaking for Death Penalty Sentencing: Research Indicates Pattern of Racial Disparities before the Subcommittee on Civil and Constitutional Rights," Committee on the Judiciary, US House of Representatives, May 3, 1990.

34. Racial Justice Act of 1994.

35. Editorial, "Pull the Plug on This Crime Bill," *New York Times*, July 22, 1994, A26.

36. Kweisi Mfume, quoted in Gayle Pollard Terry, "The Driving Force behind the Black Caucus' Increasing Clout," *Los Angeles Times* interview with Kweisi Mfume, *Los Angeles Times*, August 21, 1994.

37. Darren Wheelock and Douglas Hartmann, "Midnight Basketball and the 1994 Crime Bill Debates," *Sociological Quarterly* 48 (2007): 317.

38. Donna Brazile, quoted in Dewayne Wickham, *Bill Clinton and Black America* (New York: Ballantine Books, 2002), 49.

39. Editorial, "The Silent White House," *New York Times*, July 15, 1994, A26, New York edition.

40. George Stephanopoulos, *All Too Human: A Political Education* (New York: Little, Brown, 1999), 294.

41. Taylor Branch, *The Clinton Tapes: Wrestling History with the President* (New York: Simon & Schuster, 2009), 174.

42. Katherine Q. Seelye, "White House Offers Compromise to Free Logjam on Crime Measure," *New York Times*, July 21, 1994, A20, New York edition.

43. General Accounting Office, Death Penalty Sentencing: Research Indicates Pattern of Racial Disparities, 6.

44. Charlie Rangel, quoted in Katherine Q. Seelye, "White House Offers Compromise to Free Logjam on Crime Measure," *New York Times*, July 21, 1994, A20, New York edition.

45. This is a procedural task that, if it had passed, would have proceeded to a vote on the actual bill.

46. Joe Biden, quoted in Harry A. Chernoff, Christopher M. Kelly, and John R. Kroger, "Essay: The Politics of Crime," *Harvard Journal on Legislation* 33, no. 527 (Summer 1996): 567. Kelly worked on the Domestic Policy Council in the Clinton White House and Kroger worked for the Clinton Transition Team and in the office of Speaker Thomas Foley.

47. Ibid.

48. Kweisi Mfume, quoted in Terry, "The Driving Force behind the Black Caucus' Increasing Clout."

49. Dr. John Hope Franklin, interview by author, Durham, North Carolina, August 14, 2007.

50. Legal Services for Prisoners with Children, "People of Color and the Prison Industrial Complex." They used the Statistical Abstract of the United States (1999), Sourcebook of Criminal Justice Statistics (1998), and others government sources to compile to the data.

51. Violent Crime Control and Law Enforcement Act of 1994, Public Law 103–322.

52. Michelle Alexander, The New Jim Crow: Mass Incarceration in the Age of Colorblindness (New York: New Press, 2010), 48–49.

53. Bill Clinton, "Remarks at a Town Meeting in Detroit, February 10, 1993," in *Public Papers of the Presidents of the United States: William J. Clinton*, 1:76.

54. Bill Clinton, "Remarks of President William J. Clinton to the Convocation of the Church of God in Christ," Memphis, TN, November 13, 1993, in *Public Papers of the Presidents of the United States: William J. Clinton*, 2:1986–91.

55. The Violent Crime Control and Law Enforcement Act of 1994, Public Law 103–322.

56. Higher Education Act of 1965, Public Law 89–329.

57. Title 20 United States Code, Higher Education Amendments of 1972

58. Alexander, *The New Jim Crow*, 93.

59. William J. Sabol and Heather Couture, *Bureau of Justice Statistics, Prison Inmates at Midyear 2007* (Washington, DC: US Department of Justice, 2008), 7.

60. US Commission on Civil Rights, Testimony of Bill Moffitt of the National Association of Criminal Defense Lawyers, July 12, 1996.

61. Ibid.

62. Branch, *The Clinton Tapes*, 534.

63. Alan Whyte and Jamie Baker, "Prison Labor on the Rise in US," International Committee of the Fourth International, May 8, 2000, http://www.wsws.org/articles/2000/may2000/pris-m08.shtml (accessed on January 31, 2011). The Federal Prison Industries is a government-created and -operated program that uses the labor of inmates to create everything from furniture to electronics. It is but one example of the use of convict labor in the United States.

64. Bill Clinton, "State of the Union Address," January 24, 1994, in *Public Papers of the Presidents of the United States: William J. Clinton*, 75.

65. "Memorandum for Circulation, from Rahm Emanuel and Michael Waldman, Subject: Proposed Communications Strategy and Schedule for Crime," January 27, 1994, Domestic Policy Council, Bruce Reed, Crime, Folder 6, Box 79, WJCPL.

66. It is also important to note that the National Rifle Association was still smarting over a humiliating defeat in 1993, when the Congress passed and President Clinton signed into law the Brady Bill in November 1993. The Brady bill restricted felons, mentally defective persons, and others from purchasing a gun. It also required background checks on prospective gun purchasers.

67. Christopher Kenny, Michael McBurnett, and David Bordua, "The Impact of Political Interests in the 1994 and 1996 Congressional Elections: The Role of the National Rifle Association," *British Journal of Political Science* 34, no. 2 (April 2004): 342–43.

68. As a result of the NRA's efforts, along with many others, the Republican Party was able to defeat dozens of House and Senate Democrats, including the Speaker of the House Tom Foley, and assume the majority of both houses of Congress for the first time in forty years.

69. Wheelock and Hartmann, "Midnight Basketball and the 1994 Crime Bill Debates," 319. Wheelock and Hartmann base this finding on the work in Holly Idelson's May 7, 1994, article, "Provisions: Anti-Crime Bills Compared," in the *Congressional Quarterly Weekly*, and Holly Idelson and David Masci's December 10, 1994, article, "Provisions: Crime Bill Provisions," in the *Congressional Quarterly Weekly*.

70. Wheelock and Hartmann, "Midnight Basketball and the 1994 Crime Bill Debates," 319.

71. Violent Crime Control and Law Enforcement Act of 1994, Public Law 103–322.

72. Steven F. Lawson, *Running for Freedom: Civil Rights and Black Politics since 1941*, 3rd ed. (Malden, MA: Wiley-Blackwell, 2009), 297.

73. Gwen Ifill, "The Nation: After Clinton's Sermon Blacks Are Looking for Action, Not Amens," *New York Times*, November 21, 1993, 43, New York edition.

74. Speech of Mayor David N. Dinkins, "Mobilizing to Fight Crime," as excerpted in the October 3, 1990, edition of the *New York Times*.

75. Bill Clinton, "Remarks of President Clinton at the National Association of Police Organizations," August 12, 1994, in *Public Papers of the Presidents of the United States: William J. Clinton*, 2:1464.

76. Ibid.

77. Ibid.

78. "Statement by African American Religious Leaders," August 16, 1994, Press Release, Folder 4, Box 1, Subject File, WJCPL.

79. Ibid. They also proclaimed their support for programs to end violence against women, limit assault weapons, put 100,000 police officers on the streets, and they supported the billions of dollars in funding for preventative programs.

80. US Commission on Civil Rights, *Revisiting Who Is Guarding the Guardians? A Report on Police Practices and Civil Rights in America* (Washington, DC: Government Printing Office, 2000), chap. 1, p. 2, http://www.usccr.gov/pubs/guard/main.htm (accessed November 10, 2016).

81. Letter from Mary Frances Berry, chair of the US Commission on Civil Rights, to President Clinton, February 23, 1999, Domestic Policy Council, Bruce Reed, Crime, Folder 3, Box 86, Police Misconduct, WJCPL.

82. Steven A. Holmes, "Blacks Relent on Crime Bill, but Not without Bitterness," *New York Times*, August 18, 1994, A1, New York edition.

83. Drug Policy Information Clearinghouse Fact Sheet, "Drug-Related Crime," Executive Office of the President, Office of National Drug Control Policy, March 2000, http://www.whitehousedrugpolicy.gov/publications/factsht/crime/index.html (accessed January 31, 2011).

84. *Incarceration Is Not an Equal Opportunity Punishment, Prison Policy Initiative*, Northampton, MA, 2005, http://www.prisonpolicy.org/articles/not_equal_opportunity.pdf (accessed November 10, 2015).

85. Ibid.

86. Elliott Currie, quoted in Ronald Kramer and Raymond Michalowski, "The Iron Fist and the Velvet Tongue: Crime Control Policies in the Clinton Administration," *Social Justice* 22 (Summer 1995): 87.

87. Ibid.

88. Becky Pettit and Bruce Western, "Mass Imprisonment and the Life Course: Race and Class Inequality in U.S. Incarceration," *American Sociological Review* 69, no. 2 (April 2004): 155.

89. Dorothy E. Roberts, "The Social and Moral Cost of Mass Incarceration in African American Communities," *Stanford Law Review* 56 (2004): 1275–76.

90. Census 2000 Summary File 1, https://www.census.gov/census2000/sumfile1.html (accessed November 10, 2015).

91. Lisa Thomas-Laury, "Crisis Facing Single Black Women," Special Report, WPVI-TV, Philadelphia, PA, March 1, 2010.

92. Ibid.

93. US Census Bureau, "America's Families and Living Arrangements: 2007," https://www.census.gov/prod/2009pubs/p20-561.pdf (accessed November 10, 2015).

94. National Organization for Women, "Violence Against Women in the United States: Statistics," http://www.now.org/issues/violence/stats.html (accessed March 22, 2010).

95. Bureau of Statistics, "Correctional Populations in the United States, 1998," Office of Justice Programs, US Department of Justice, Washington, DC.

96. Bureau of Justice Statistics Bulletin, "Prison Inmates at Midyear 2007," 7, http://www.bjs.gov/content/pub/pdf/pim07.pdf (accessed November 10, 2015).

97. Timothy Messer-Kruse, *Race Relations in the United States, 1980–2000* (Westport, CT: Greenwood Press, 2008), 132.

98. Roberts, "The Social and Moral Cost of Mass Incarceration in African American Communities," 1275.

99. Marc Mauer, "The Crisis of the Young African American Male and the Criminal Justice System," prepared for the US Commission on Civil Rights, April 15–16, 1999, in Washington, DC, p. 2.

100. "Do you think that police brutality and harassment of African Americans is a serious problem where you live?," Joint Center for Political and Economic Studies, www.jointcenter.org/DB/table/dataank/NOP/NOP_1996/Social/BRUTAL.htm. (accessed September 19, 2010).

101. "Contact between Police and the Public: Findings from the 2002 National Survey," Bureau of Justice Statistics, Office of Justice Programs, US Department of Justice, April 2005, p. 8.

102. "Police Use of Force: Collection of National Data," Bureau of Justice Statistics, Office of Justice Programs, US Department of Justice, p. 13.

103. Ibid.

104. February 23, 1999, letter from Mary Frances Berry to President Clinton, Domestic Policy Council, Bruce Reed, Crime, Folder 3, Box 3, WJCPL.

105. "Contacts between Police and the Public: Findings from the 1999 National Survey," Bureau of Justice Statistics, Office of Justice Programs, US Department of Justice, February 2001, p. 19.

106. "Chance of Going to Prison During Rest of Life," Bureau of Justice Statistics, Office of Justice Programs, US Department of Justice. http://www.ojp.usdoj.gov/bjs/pub/ascii/llgsfp.txt (accessed September 19, 2010).

107. "Sexual Victimization in Prisons and Jails Reported by Inmates, 2008–09," Bureau of Justice Statistics, Office of Justice Programs, US Department of Justice, 22.

108. Rose M. Brewer, "Imperiled Black Families and the Growth of the Prison Industrial Complex in the U.S.," Council on Crime and Justice, www.crimeandjustice.org/ (accessed September 27, 2010).

109. Marc Mauer, "Collateral Consequences of Criminal Convictions: Barriers to Reentry for the Formerly Incarcerated," testimony of Marc Mauer, Executive Director The Sentencing Project, prepared for House Judiciary Subcommittee on Crime, Terrorism, and Homeland Security, June 9, 2010, p. 5.

110. Roberts, "The Social and Moral Cost of Mass Incarceration in African American Communities," 1276.

111. Pettit and Western, "Mass Imprisonment and the Life Course," 151.

112. Devah Pager, "The Mark of a Criminal Record," *American Journal of Sociology* 108 (March 2003): 937.

113. Alexander, *The New Jim Crow*, 56.

114. Jeff Manza and Christopher Uggen, "Punishment and Democracy: Disenfranchisement of Nonincarcerated Felons in the United States," *American Political Science Association* 2 (September 2004): 502.

115. Lawson, *Running for Freedom*, 298–301.

116. Mauer, "Collateral Consequences of Criminal Convictions," 12–13.

117. Alexander, *The New Jim Crow,* 56.

118. Bruce Reed, "Who's Soft on Crime Now?," *Blueprint*, July 12, 2001, http://www.dlc.org/ndol_ci.cfm?kaid=119&subid=157&contentid=3534 (accessed February 1, 2011).

119. Vesla M. Weaver, "Frontlash: Race and the Development of Punitive Crime Policy," *Studies in American Political Development* 21 (Fall 2007): 230.

120. Ibid.

121. Randall Kennedy, "The Triumph of Robust Tokenism," *Atlantic Monthly*, February 2001, 51.

122. Alexander, *The New Jim Crow*, 57.

CHAPTER 5
"Mend It, Don't End It": The Politics of Affirmative Action

1. Regents of the University of California v. Bakke, 438 U.S. 265 (1978).

2. Democratic Leadership Council, *The New Orleans Declaration*, statement endorsed at the Fourth Annual DLC Conference, March 1, 1990.

3. Adarand Constructors, Inc. v. Pena, 515 U.S. 200 (1995).

4. President John F. Kennedy, Executive Order 10925, Section 201, Part II— Non Discrimination in Government Employment, March 6, 1961.

5. Kennedy, Executive Order 10925, Section 301, Part II—Non Discrimination in Government Employment, March 6, 1961.

6. Lyndon B. Johnson, "Commencement Address at Howard University," June 4, 1965, in *Public Papers of the Presidents of the United States: Lyndon B. Johnson* (Washington, DC: Government Printing Office, 1963–1969), vol. 2, entry 301, 635–40.

7. David C. Carter, The Music Has Gone Out of the Movement: Civil Rights and the Johnson Administration, 1965–1968 (Chapel Hill: University of North Carolina Press, 2009), 9.

8. Ibid.; Dan Carter, The Politics of Rage: George Wallace, the Origins of the New Conservatism, and the Transformation of America Politics (Baton Rouge: Louisiana State University Press, 2000); Rick Perlstein, Before the Storm: Barry Goldwater and the Unmaking of the American Consensus (New York: Nation Books, 2009).

9. David Carter, The Music Has Gone Out of the Movement, 135.

10. Maurice Isserman and Michael Kazin, *America Divided: The Civil War of the 1960s*, 3rd ed. (New York: Oxford University Press, 2008), 116–17.

11. David Carter, The Music Has Gone Out of the Movement, 135.

12. Christopher Edley Jr., *Not All Black and White: Affirmative Action and American Values* (New York: Hill and Wang, 1996), 52.

13. Sharon M. Collins, "The Making of the Black Middle Class," *Social Problems* 30, no. 4 (April 1983): 369.

14. Mary Pattillo-McCoy, *Black Picket Fences: Privilege and Peril among the Black Middle Class* (Chicago: University of Chicago Press, 1999), 6.

15. Justice Lewis Powell, Syllabus, Regents of the University of California v. Bakke, 438 U.S. 265, Supreme Court of the United States, Decided: June 28, 1978.

16. Syllabus, Fullilove v. Klutznick, 448 U.S. 448, Supreme Court of the United States, Decided: July 2, 1980. MBE stands for Minority Business Enterprise; a critical provision of the Public Works Employment Act of 1977, whose constitutionality was the principal target of the plaintiffs.

17. Chief Justice Warren Burger, Syllabus, Fullilove v. Klutznick.

18. "Certiorari" is a legal term meaning that the higher court sends a writ or order to the lower court to send all relevant materials to the Supreme Court for review. In granting certiorari, the Supreme Court sided with the plaintiffs and rejected the rationale of the Court of Appeals for the Sixth Circuit.

19. Syllabus, Wygant v. Jackson Board of Education, 476 U.S. 267, Supreme Court of the United States, Decided: May 19, 1986.

20. Ibid., Justice Powell.

21. Syllabus, City of Richmond v. J. A. Croson Co., 488 U.S. 469, Supreme Court of the United States, Decided: January 23, 1989.

22. Ibid., Justice O'Connor.

23. Brown v. Board of Education of Topeka, 347 U.S. 483 (1954).

24. Ira Katznelson, *When Affirmative Action Was White* (New York: W. W. Norton & Company, 2006), 152.

25. Edley, *Not All Black and White*, 84. Edley, currently dean of the Boalt School of Law at the University of California, Berkeley, was a central figure in the Clinton administration's affirmative action efforts.

26. Edley, Not All Black and White, 85.

27. Thomas Sowell, *Affirmative Action: An Empirical Study* (New Haven: Yale University Study, 2005).

28. Clarence Thomas, *My Grandfather's Son: A Memoir* (New York: Harper, 2007), 78–79.

29. Shelby Steele, The Content of Our Character: A New Vision of Race in America (New York: Harper, 1990).

30. Ibid., 124–25.

31. Stephen L. Carter, *Reflections of an Affirmative Action Baby* (New York: Basic Books, 1991).

32. John McWhorter, "Who Should Get into College?," *City Journal* 13, no. 2 (Spring 2003), http://www.city-journal.org/html/13_2_who_should_get.html (accessed November 10, 2015).

33. Hacker, *Two Nations*, 67.

34. E. J. Dionne, *Why Americans Hate Politics* (New York: Simon & Schuster, 2004).

35. Ward Connerly, quoted in Scott Jaschik, "Battle over Affirmative Action,"

chronicle.com, March 17, 1995, http://chronicle.com/article/Battle-Over-Affirmative-Action/85618/ (accessed January 26, 2011). Ward Connerly rose to prominence in the early 1990s as a prominent opponent of affirmative action and political ally of Californian Pete Wilson. He successfully led a ballot referendum banning the use of race in admissions and hiring throughout the state of California.

36. Roger Wilkins, "The River of Racism," *Chronicle of Higher Education*, March 27, 1995, http://chronicle.com/article/The-River-of-Racism/83547 (accessed November 10, 2015).

37. Affirmative Action, "Black/White Relations in the United States—1997," GALLUP Poll Social Audit program (Princeton: GALLUP News Service, 1997), 2.

38. Democratic Leadership Council, "The New American Choice Resolution," resolutions adopted at the DLC Convention, Cleveland, OH, May 1, 1991, 2.

39. Keynote Address of Gov. Bill Clinton to the DLC's Cleveland Convention, May 6, 1991.

40. Syllabus, Adarand Constructors, Inc. v. Pena, 515 U.S. 200, Supreme Court of the United States, Decided: June 12, 1995. In 1990 the Supreme Court ruled that the Federal Communications Commission's minority members give preference to policies that strongly encouraged minority ownership and participation in management in order to secure licenses for brand-new television and radio stations. Justice Brennan, writing for the court, held that the FCC policies "do not violate equal protection, since they bear the imprimatur of longstanding congressional support and direction and are substantially related to the achievement of the important governmental objective of broadcast diversity."

41. The Small Business Act, 15 U.S.C. §637 (a) and (d). Section A refers to "economically disadvantaged individuals and Section D refers to socially disadvantaged individuals.

42. Syllabus, Adarand Constructors, Inc. v. Pena, Justice Sandra Day O'Connor.

43. Ibid.

44. Bill Clinton, "The President's News Conference," March 3, 1995, in *Public Papers of the Presidents of the United States: William J. Clinton*, 1:293.

45. Letter to the president, July 19, 1995, from George Stephanopoulos and Christopher Edley, Affirmative Action Review, WJCPL.

46. Ibid.

47. Cabinet Affairs, "President Defends Affirmative Action, Calls for Reforms," Wednesday, July 19, 1995, Domestic Policy Council, Stephen Warnath, Civil Rights, Folder 3, Box 1, WJCPL.

48. Memorandum for the President, RE: Civil Rights Policy, January 28, 1994, from Alexis Herman, Domestic Policy Council, Stephen Warnath, Civil Rights Series, Folder 4, Box 11, WJCPL.

49. Ibid.

50. "Affirmative Action: No 'Widespread Abuse' in Job Cases, Few Reverse Bias Claims, Study Says," March 23, 1995, Bureau of National Affairs, Inc., Domestic Policy Council, Stephen Warnath, Civil Rights, Folder 5, Box 1, WJCPL.

51. Ibid. This study was conducted by Alfred W. Blumrosen, professor of law at Rutgers University, for the Labor Department, "How the Courts Are Handling Reverse Discrimination," March 23, 1995.

52. Section 3.1: "Review of the Empirical Literature, in Summary," Affirmative Action Review, July 19, 1995, WJCPL, http://clinton4.nara.gov/WH/EOP/OP/html/aa/aa03.html (accessed November 10, 2015).

53. Section 4.3: "Exclusion from Mainstream Opportunities: Continuing Disparities in Economic Status," Affirmative Action Review, July 19, 1995, WJCPL.

54. Federal Glass Ceiling Commission, *Good for Business: Making Full Use of the Nation's Human Capital* (March 1995). According to the Department of Labor website, "The term glass ceiling was popularized in a 1986 *Wall Street Journal* article describing the invisible barriers that women confront as they approach the top of the corporate hierarchy. The Federal Glass Ceiling Commission, a 21-member bipartisan body appointed by President Bush and Congressional leaders and chaired by the Secretary of Labor, was created by the Civil Rights Act of 1991. Its mandate was to identify the glass ceiling barriers that have blocked the advancement of minorities and women as well as the successful practices and policies that have led to the advancement of minority men and all women into decision-making positions in the private sector." www.dol.gov/oasam/programs/history/reich/reports/ceiling.htm (accessed May 28, 2010).

55. Section 3.2.1: "Effect on Earnings: Anti-Discrimination Policy, the Minority-White Earnings Gap," Affirmative Action Review, July 19, 1995, WJCPL.

56. US Department of Labor, "About OFFCP," , www.dol.gov/ofccp/mission.htm (accessed May 28, 2010).

57. Ibid.

58. Section 11.4: "Conclusions and Recommendations, Selected Other Federal Policies," Affirmative Action Review, July 19, 1995, WJCPL.

59. Ibid.

60. Bill Clinton, "Memorandum for Heads of Executive Departments and Agencies, Subject: Evaluation of Affirmative Action Programs," July 19, 1995, WJCPL.

61. Walter Dellinger, "Memorandum to General Counsels," from Assistant Attorney General/Office of Legal Counsel, June 28, 1995, WJCPL. A "general counsel" is the top lawyer at a government agency. For instance, the general counsel for the Department of Labor was required to make sure that affirmative action programs within the purview of the Labor Department are able to survive the "strict scrutiny standard" set in Adarand v. Pena.

62. Bill Clinton, "Remarks on Affirmative Action at the National Archives and Records Administration," July 19, 1995, in *Public Papers of the Presidents of the United States: William J. Clinton*, 2:1108.

63. Ibid.

64. Bill Clinton, "Remarks on Affirmative Action at the National Archives and Records Administration," July 19, 1995, in *Public Papers of the Presidents of the United States: William J. Clinton*, 2:1109.

65. Ibid.

66. Adarand Constructors, Inc. v. Pena, 515 U.S. 200 (1995).

67. Bill Clinton, "Remarks on Affirmative Action at the National Archives and Records Administration," 2:1113.

68. Section 6.5.2: "Recommendations, Office of Federal Contract Compliance Programs, Reviews of Federal Affirmative Action Programs," WJCPL.

69. Ibid.

70. Section 7.5.2: "Recommendations, Affirmative Action and Equal Opportunity in the Military, Reviews of Federal Affirmative Action Programs," WJCPL.

71. Section 9.5.2: "Conclusions and Recommendations, Federal Procurement Policies & AMP; Practices, Review of Federal Affirmative Action Programs," WJCPL.

72. Ibid.

73. Section 10.6.1: "Conclusions, Education and HHS Policies & AMP; Practices, Review of Federal Affirmative Action Programs," WJCPL. The Government Performance Results Act of 1993 was enacted to improve confidence in the federal government, report on progress and goals, improve public accountability by promoting quality, satisfaction, and results, and improve the internal management of the federal government.

74. Memorandum, Special Counsel Eddie Correia to Deputy Chief of Staff Sylvia Mathews, February 13, 1998, p. 1, Domestic Policy Council, Elena Kagan, Folder 2, Box 38, Race-Affirmative Action, WJCPL.

75. Ibid.

76. Hopwood v. Texas, 78 F.3d 932, 944 (5th Cir.), cert. denied, 116 S. Ct. 2581 (1996).

77. Bakke v. California, 438 U.S. 265, 312 (1978).

78. Richard Hayes, Office of Public Liaison, to Angus S. King, July 2, 1996, "Affirmative Action Question/Answer," Domestic Policy Council, Stephen Warnath, Folder 10, Box 1, Civil Rights, WJCPL.

79. Ibid.

80. Opinion of the Court, Justice O'Connor, Grutter v. Bollinger, 539 U.S. 306 (2003).

81. Piscataway School Board v. Taxman, 91 F. 3d 1547 (1996).

82. Ibid. No. 96-679, "In The Supreme Court Of The United States, October Term 1996, Piscataway Township Board of Education, Petitioner v. Sharon Taxman, On Writ of Certiorari To The United States Court of Appeals For The Third Circuit, Brief For The United States As Amicus Curiae, Walter Dellinger, Acting Solicitor General," p. 2.

83. Ibid.

84. Memorandum for the President, from Charles F. C. Ruff, Dawn Chirwa, and Bill Marshall, "Subject: 1. Board of Education of the Township of Piscataway v. Taxman and 2. Adarand v. Pena," June 4, 1997, Domestic Policy Council, Elena Kagan, Race—Affirmative Action, Folder 2, Box 38, p. 2, WJCPL.

85. Ibid.

86. Letter from Solicitor General Walter Dellinger to Attorney General Janet Reno, July 29, 1997, Domestic Policy Council, Elena Kagan, Race—Affirmative Action, Folder 2, Box 38, p. 2, WJCPL.

87. Ibid.

88. Ibid.

89. Bill Clinton, "Remarks at the University of California, San Diego," June 14, 1997, in *Public Papers of the Presidents of the United States: William J. Clinton*, 2:739.

90. Ibid.

91. Abigail Thernstrom and Bill Clinton, "Race Initiative Outreach Meeting

with Conservatives," December 19, 1997, in *Public Papers of the Presidents of the United States: William J. Clinton,* 2:1804.

92. William Galston and Elaine Kamarck, *The Politics of Evasion: Democrats and the Presidency* (Washington, DC: Progressive Policy Institute, 1989), 17.

93. Alan Wolfe, "Movin' On Up," *New Democrat,* July/August 1996, 22.

94. Ibid.

95. Ibid., 23.

96. Seymour Martin Lipset, "Two Americas, Two Systems," *New Democrat,* May/June 1995, 14.

97. Joel Kotkin, "The Hot Zone: Why Did the New Affirmative Action Debate Erupt in California," *New Democrat,* May/June 1995, 17.

98. Joe Klein, The Natural: The Misunderstood Presidency of Bill Clinton (New York: Broadway Brooks, 2003).

99. Randall Kennedy, "The Enduring Relevance of Affirmative Action," *prospect. com,* August 11, 2010, http://www.prospect.org/cs/articles?article=the_enduring_ relevance_of_affirmative_action (accessed January 26, 2011).

100. Equal Opportunity Act of 1995, S. 1085.

101. Illinois senator Paul Simon, speaking against S. 1085, Equal Opportunity Act, on July 27, 1995, 104th Cong., 1st sess., *Cong. Rec.* S10842.

102. California congressman Esteban Edward Torres, speaking against S. 1085, Equal Opportunity Act, on September 13, 1995, 104th Cong., 1st sess., *Cong. Rec.* E1769.

103. Georgia congressman John Lewis, speaking against S. 1085, Equal Opportunity Act, on June 13, 1995, 104th Cong., 1st sess., *Cong. Rec.,* H5779.

104. US Department of Labor, *Good for Business: Making Full Use of the Nation's Human Capital: The Environment Scan,* a fact-finding report of the Federal Glass Ceiling Commission, March 1995 (Washington: DC: Government Printing Office, 1995), 54–56.

105. Ibid.

CHAPTER 6

Welfare Reform: The New Democratic Ethos and African Americans

1. The Public Welfare Amendments Act of 1962, Public Law 87-543.

2. Kenneth J. Neubeck and Noel A. Cazenave, *Welfare Racism: Playing the Race Card against America's Poor* (New York: Routledge, 2001), v.

3. Personal Responsibility and Work Opportunity Reconciliation Act of 1996, Public Law 104–193.

4. Clinton, *My Life,* 329.

5. Ron Haskins, *Work over Welfare: The Inside Story of the 1996 Welfare Reform Law* (Washington, DC: Brookings Institution Press, 2006), 4.

6. Julian E. Zelizer, *Taxing America: Wilbur D. Mills, Congress, and the State, 1945–1975* (New York: Cambridge University Press, 1998), 13.

7. Robert C. Lieberman, *Shifting the Color Line: Race and the American Welfare State* (Cambridge: Harvard University Press, 1998), 64.

8. Jason DeParle, American Dream: Three Women, Ten Kids, and a Nation's Drive to End Welfare (New York: Penguin, 2004), 86.

9. Neubeck and Cazenave, *Welfare Racism,* vii.

10. Jill Quadagno, *The Color of Welfare: How Racism Undermined the War on Poverty* (New York: Oxford University Press, 1994), 197.

11. Haskins, Work over Welfare, 4.

12. Isserman and Kazin, *America Divided,* 114.

13. US Department of Labor, Office of Policy Planning and Research, *The Negro Family: The Case for National Action,* 89th Cong., 1st sess. (Washington, DC: US Department of Labor, 1965).

14. Ibid.

15. David Carter, The Music Has Gone Out of the Movement, 68.

16. Rick Perlstein, Nixonland: The Rise of a President and the Fracturing of America (New York: Scribner, 2008), 396.

17. Dean J. Kotlowski, *Nixon's Civil Rights: Politics, Principle, and Policy* (Cambridge: Harvard University Press, 2001), 22.

18. Joseph E. Lowndes, From the New Deal to the New Right: Race and the Southern Origins of Modern Conservatism (New Haven: Yale University Press, 2008), 123.

19. Barack Obama, The Audacity of Hope: Thoughts on Reclaiming the American Dream (New York: Three Rivers Press, 2006), 31.

20. Thomas Byrne Edsall and Mary D. Edsall, *Chain Reaction: The Impact of Race, Rights, and Taxes on American Politics.* (New York: W. W. Norton & Company, 1991), 192.

21. R. Kent Weaver, *Ending Welfare as We Know It* (Washington, DC: Brookings Institution Press, 2000), 70.

22. Ibid.

23. Charles Murray, *Losing Ground: American Social Policy, 1950–1980* (New York: Basic Books, 1984).

24. Neubeck and Cazenave, *Welfare Racism*, 133.

25. Kevin Phillips, *The Politics of Rich and Poor: Wealth and the American Electorate in the Reagan Aftermath* (New York: Random House, 1990). Kevin Phillips rose to national prominence with his highly influential work, *The Emerging Republican Majority* (New Rochelle, NY: Arlington House, 1969). It was a highly important book that foretold the rise of conservatism in America and was based on the use of race as a bludgeon to break white, working-class Americans' loyalty to the Democratic Party. By 1980, with Reagan at the head of the party, the GOP embraced racial politics as a way to win elections and maintain a strong southern base. Largely, the southern strategy of race-baiting cast minorities—particularly those on the dole—in unflattering moral terms. The Republican Party won every presidential election from 1968 to 2008 except for four, Carter in 1976, Clinton in 1992 and 1996, and Obama in 2008. The GOP won in 1968, 1972, 1980, 1984, 1988, 2000, 2004.

26. Peter Edelman, telephone interview with author, September 18, 2008.

27. Neubeck and Cazenave, *Welfare Racism,* 137.

28. Ibid. The authors note, "Welfare officials at times provided higher benefit levels to European-American recipients than to recipients of color. As more of the latter made up the welfare rolls, the ways in which welfare racism was expressed

shifted to meet the changing conditions. Racial state actors allowed the dollar value or purchasing power of benefits to progressively decline, and instituted new behavioral standards to discourage applications for aid and to pressure existing recipients off the rolls" (ibid., 137).

29. Weaver, Ending Welfare As We Know It, 26.

30. Murray, Losing Ground.

31. Haskins, *Work over Welfare*, 7.

32. Ibid.

33. "A Community of Self-Reliance: The New Consensus on Family and Welfare," working seminar, American Enterprise Institute, Washington, DC, 1987.

34. Lawrence M. Mead, Beyond Entitlement: The Social Obligations of Citizenship (New York: Free Press, 1986).

35. Margaret Weir, Review of Beyond Entitlement: The Social Obligations of Citizenship, by Lawrence M. Mead, American Journal of Sociology 93, no. 2 (September 1987): 495.

36. John McWhorter, Winning the Race: Beyond the Crisis in Black America (New York: Gotham, 1999), 13.

37. See Michael Takiff, A Complicated Man: The Life of Bill Clinton as Told by Those Who Know Him (New Haven: Yale University Press, 2010), 139.

38. David Kusnet, quoted in Takiff, *A Complicated Man*, 140–41.

39. Internal Revenue Code, US Code, Title 26, Section 32.

40. Tax Policy Center, "Earned Income Credit," The Encyclopedia of Taxation and Tax Policy, http://www.taxpolicycenter.org/publications/urprint. cfm?ID=10000524.html (accessed December 1, 2010).

41. Klein, *The Natural*, 56.

42. US House of Representatives, "Republican Contract with America," US House of Representatives, http://www.house.gov/house/Contract/CONTRACT. html (accessed June 28, 2009).

43. Ibid.

44. Mary Reintsma, *The Political Economy of Welfare Reform in the United States* (Northampton: MA: Edward Elgar, 2007), 121–22.

45. Elaine Kamarck, quoted in Takiff, *A Complicated Man*, 139.

46. Stan Greenberg, quoted in Takiff, *A Complicated Man*, 139.

47. Georgia representative John Lewis, speaking against the Personal Responsibility Act of 1995, on March 21, 1995, to the House of Representatives, H.R. 4, 104th Cong., 1st sess., *Cong. Rec.* 141, P. H3359.

48. California representative Maxine Waters, speaking against the Personal Responsibility Act of 1995, on March 22, 1995, to the House of Representatives, H.R. 4, 104th Cong., 1st sess., *Cong. Rec.* 141, P. H3543.

49. Jacob Weisberg, "Clintonism That Works," *New Yorker*, May 30, 1994, 15.

50. Evelyn Z. Brodkin, "Requiem for Welfare," *Dissent*, Winter 2003, http://www. dissentmagazine.org/article/?article=352 (accessed January 29, 2011).

51. Pennsylvania representative Robert Walker, speaking in favor of the Personal Responsibility Act of 1995, on March 23, 1995, to the House of Representatives, H.R. 4, 104th Cong., 1st sess., *Cong. Rec.* 141, P. H3598.

52. New York representative Charles Rangel, speaking against the Personal Responsibility Act of 1995, on March 24, 1995, to the House of Representatives, H.R. 4, 104th Cong., 1st sess., *Cong. Rec.* 141, P. H3738.

53. Ronald Brownstein, "Clinton's 'New Democrat' Agenda Reopens Racial Divisions, President's ideas on crime and welfare don't sit well with blacks in Congress. Liberals' dissatisfaction may be rising," *Los Angeles Times*, February 9, 1994, A5.

54. Sharon D. Wright, "Clinton and Racial Politics," in *The Postmodern Presidency: Bill Clinton's Legacy In U.S. Politics*, ed. Steven E. Schier (Pittsburgh: University of Pittsburgh Press, 2000), 229.

55. US Department of Commerce, Economic and Statistical Administration, Bureau of the Census, *Statistical Brief, Health Insurance Coverage—1993, SB/94-28*, 103rd Cong., 2d sess. (Washington, DC: US Department of Commerce, 1994).

56. DeParle, *American Dream,* 108–109.

57. Baer, Reinventing Democrats, 219.

58. Ibid.

59. Bill Clinton, "Remarks to the National Governors' Association," February 2, 1993, in *Public Papers of the Presidents of the United States: William J. Clinton,* 1:33–34.

60. "Table H-1: Poverty Status of Persons by Age, Race, Region, and Family Type, 1994," "Appendix H, Data on Poverty," Ways and Means Committee, in *Green Book* (Washington, DC: Government Printing Office, 1996).

61. US Department of Health and Human Services, Office of the Assistant Secretary for Planning and Evaluation, Figure 1, "TANF 'Leavers,' Applicants, and Caseload Studies: Preliminary Analysis of Racial Differences in Caseload Trends and Leaver Outcomes," Elizabeth Lower-Basch, December 2000, http://aspe.hhs.gov/hsp/leavers99/race.htm (accessed February 8, 2010).

62. Sarah Staveteig and Alyssa Wigton, "Racial and Ethnic Disparities: Key Findings from the National Survey of America's Families," in *New Federalism: National Survey of America's Families* (Washington, DC: Urban Institute, February 2000), 1.

63. Haskins, *Work over Welfare*, 82.

64. Peter Edelman, quoted in Takiff, *A Complicated Man*, 287.

65. Peter Edelman, interview by author, September 18, 2008.

66. Pennsylvania representative Chaka Fattah, speaking against the Personal Responsibility Act of 1995, on March 24, 1995, to the House of Representatives, H.R. 4, 104th Cong., 1st sess., *Cong. Rec.* 141, H3766.

67. Daniel Moynihan, quoted in Robert Pear, "Clinton Objects to Key Elements of Welfare Bill," *New York Times*, March 26, 1995, 1.

68. Bill Clinton, quoted in Pear, "Clinton Objects to Key Elements of Welfare Bill," 1.

69. Memorandum for the President, Subject: Block Granting Income Security Programs, January 19, 1995, Domestic Policy Council, Bruce Reed, Folder 2, Box 3, Block Grants, WJCPL.

70. Branch, *The Clinton Tapes*, 313.

71. Haskins, *Work over Welfare*, 268–69.

72. Ibid.

73. Executive Action on Work, Domestic Policy Council, Bruce Reed, Welfare Reform, Box 10, WJCPL.

74. Illinois senator Carol Moseley-Braun, speaking against the Personal Responsibility and Work Opportunity Reconciliation Act of 1996, on August 1, 1996, to the US Senate, H.R. 3734, 104th Cong., 2nd sess., *Cong. Rec.* 142, p. S9363.

75. Florida representative Carolyn Meeks, speaking against the Personal Responsibility and Work Opportunity Act of 1996, on July 18, 1996, to the House of Representatives, H.R. 3734, 104th Cong., 2nd sess., *Cong. Rec.* 142, p. H7788.

76. California representative Robert Matsui, speaking against the Personal Responsibility and Work Opportunity Reconciliation Act of 1996, on July 18, 1996, to the House of Representatives, H.R. 3734, 104th Cong., 2nd sess., *Cong. Rec.* 142, p. H7797.

77. New York representative Charles Rangel, speaking against the Personal Responsibility and Work Opportunity Reconciliation Act of 1996, on July 31 1996, to the House of Representatives, H.R. 3734, 104th Cong., 2nd sess., *Cong Rec.* 142, p. H9395.

78. South Carolina representative James Clyburn, speaking against the Personal Responsibility and Work Opportunity Reconciliation Act of 1996, on July 31, 1996, to the House of Representatives, H.R. 3734, 104th Cong., 2nd sess., *Cong. Rec.* 142, p. H9399.

79. Social Security Administration, "Vote Tallies, 1996 Welfare Amendments," Social Security Online, www.ssa.gov/history/tally1996.html (accessed November 20, 2010).

80. Personal Responsibility and Work Opportunity Reconciliation Act of 1996, Public Law 104-193, 104th Cong., 2d sess. (August 22, 1996).

81. US Commission on Civil Rights, *A Bridge to One America: The Civil Rights Performance of the Clinton Administration* (Washington, DC: Government Printing Office, 2001), 48.

82. Report of the Citizens' Commission on Civil Rights, *The Test of Our Progress: The Clinton Record on Civil Rights*, ed. Corrine Yu and William L. Taylor (Washington, DC: Citizens' Commission on Civil Rights, 1999), 122.

83. Lydia L. Blalock, Vicky R. Tiller, and Pamel A. Monroe, "'They Get You Out of Courage': Persistent Deep Poverty among Former Welfare-Reliant Women," *Family Relations* 53, no. 2 (2004): 128.

84. *Fact Sheet: The Gender Wage Gap*, Institute for Women's Policy Research, updated March 2010, prepared by Heidi Hartmann, Ariane Hegewisch, Hannah Liepmann, and Claudia Williams at the Institute for Women's Policy Research. According to the institute, women's median weekly earnings were just 80.2 percent of white males' weekly earnings. For African American women, they earned just 68.9 percent of white males' weekly earnings in 2009.

85. *Fact Sheet*, 123.

86. DeParle, *American Dream*, 331.

87. "Welfare Reform, National Association of Black Social Workers," position paper, National Association of Black Social Workers, August 2002.

88. Ibid.

89. Will Marshall, "Putting Work First: A Plan for Converting Welfare into an Employment System." *New Democrat*, January/February 1995, 44.

90. CNN, "In Focus: Challenges Ahead," http://us.cnn.com/ALLPOLITICS/1997/gen/resources/infocus/welfare/trends/challenges.html (accessed February 5, 2010)

91. Jeffrey B. Fannell, "The Welfare Workforce: The National Labor Perspective of the AFL-CIO," *St. John's Law Review* 761 (Summer 1999): 763.

92. Remarks by Secretary of Labor Robert B. Reich to the National Baptist Convention in San Diego, California, on June 21, 1995, Domestic Policy Council, Carol Rasco, Subject Files, Folder 22, Box 31, WJCPL.

93. Public Papers of the Presidents of the United States: William J. Clinton, 1:1328.

94. Arloc Sherman, Cheryl Amey, Barbara Duffield, Nancy Ebb, and Deborah Weinstein, *Welfare to What: Early Findings on Family Hardship and Well-Being*, report of the Children's Defense Fund and the National Coalition for the Homeless (Washington, DC: Children's Defense Fund, 1998), 8. This report was sponsored by the Kellogg Foundation, Ford Foundation, and the George Gund Foundation.

95. National Governors' Association survey, http://www.nga.org/files/live/sites/NGA/files/pdf/WELFARESURVEY0402.pdf (accessed November 10, 2015).

96. Sherman et al., *Welfare to What*, 28.

97. DeParle, *American Dream*, 321.

98. James Jennings, "Welfare Reform and Neighborhoods: Race and Civic Participation," *Annals of the American Academy of Political and Social Science* 577 (2001): 96.

99. Ibid., 97.

100. Blalock, Tiller, and Monroe, "'They Get You Out of Courage,'" 127.

101. Z. Fareen Parvez, "Women, Poverty, and Welfare Reform," *Sociologists for Women in Society*, August 15, 2002, 2.

102. Figure B, "Trend in TANF Families by Race/Ethnicity, FY 2002–FY 2006," Temporary Assistance for Needy Families Program (TANF), Eighth Annual Report to Congress, US Department of Health and Human Services, June 2009, p. 69.

103. Parvez, "Women, Poverty, and Welfare Reform," 2.

104. Ibid.

105. Peter Edelman, interview with author, September 18, 2008.

106. John Schmitt, "Inequality as Policy: The United States since 1979," Center for Economic and Policy Research, October 2009, 8.

107. Judith Stein, Pivotal Decade: How the United States Traded Factories for Finance in the Seventies (New Haven: Yale University Press, 2010).

108. Marcus D. Pohlmann, *Black Politics in Conservative America*, 2nd ed. (New York: Longman, 1999), 102.

109. "Welfare Reform," position paper, National Steering Committee, National Association of Black Social Workers, October 2002.

110. Reed A. Hoffman, "How Welfare Reform Changed America," *USA TODAY*, July 18, 2006, http://www.usatoday.com/news/nation/2006-07-17-welfare-reform-cover_x.htm (accessed March 16, 2010).

111. Weaver, Ending Welfare as We Know It, 26.

112. Ibid., 356.

113. Peter Edelman, "The Worst Thing Bill Clinton Has Done," *Atlantic*, March 1997, http://www.theatlantic.com/magazine/archive/1997/03/the-worst-thing-bill-clinton-has-done/376797/. He resigned his position in disgust over Clinton's support for and signing of the Personal Responsibility and Work Opportunity Reconciliation Act of 1996.

114. Bill Clinton, "Remarks at a Democratic Leadership Council Luncheon,"

December 11, 1996, in *Public Papers of the Presidents of the United States: William J. Clinton*, 1:2187.

115. The purpose of the empowerment zones/enterprise community program was to attract business to the inner city and, through its presence, revitalize those areas. Federal grants were awarded to each zone, and businesses were given tax credits and other benefits. Late in 1994, President Clinton made 105 areas, 72 urban areas and 33 rural areas, empowerment zones. It was established in 1993 under the Federal Omnibus Budget Reconciliation Act, Pub.L. 103-66, 107 Stat. 312.

116. George Stephanopoulos, quoted in Ann Devroy, "Clinton Aides: 'Something' Better Than Nothing," *Washington Post*, September 21, 1995, A6.

117. David Hess, "GOP Is Finally Scoring Points for Fall Election," *Philadelphia Inquirer*, April 13, 1996, A1.

118. Evelyn Brooks Higginbotham, telephone interview with author, March 11, 2010.

119. Donna Shalala, telephone interview with author, 2009.

120. William J. Clinton, "How We Ended Welfare Together," *New York Times*, August 22, 2006, 19.

CHAPTER 7

A Missed Opportunity:
President Clinton's Race Initiative, 1997–1998

1. Shelby Steele, *A Dream Deferred: The Second Betrayal of Black Freedom in America* (New York: HarperPerennial, 1998); Steele, *The Content of Our Character*; Cornel West, *Race Matters* (New York: Vintage Books, 2001); McWhorter, *Winning the Race*; Edley, *Not All Black and White*; Guinier, *Lift Every Voice*.

2. William Jefferson Clinton, "Transcript of President Clinton's Speech on Race Relations," delivered on October 17, 1995, to a meeting of the Liz Carpentar Distinguished Leadership in the Humanities and Sciences at the University of Texas, http://www.cnn.comm/US/9510/meamarch/10-16/clinton/update/transcript.html.

3. Bill Clinton, "Commencement Address at the University of California in La Jolla, California, June 14, 1997," in *Compilation of the Messages and Papers of the Presidents, 1997* (Washington, DC: Government Printing Office, 1997), 737.

4. Presidential Executive Order 13050, June 13, 1997.

5. Gunnar Myrdal, *The American Dilemma: The Negro Problem and Modern Democracy* (New York: Transaction Publishers, 1995).

6. Harold F. Gosnell, review of An American Dilemma: The Negro Problem and Modern Democracy, by Gunnar Myrdal, American Political Science Review 38, no. 5 (October 1944): 955.

7. Charles E. Wilson, committee chairman, To Secure These Rights: The Report of the President's Committee on Civil Rights (New York: Simon & Schuster, 1947).

8. Daniel Patrick Moynihan, *The Negro Family: The Case for National Action* (Washington, DC: Office of Policy Planning and Research, US Department of Labor, 1965).

9. Claire Jean Kim, "Clinton's Race Initiative: Recasting the American Dilemma," *Polity* 33, no. 2 (Winter 2000): 175–97.

10. Renee M. Smith, "The Public Presidency Hits the Wall: Clinton's Presidential Initiative on Race," *Presidential Studies Quarterly* 28, no. 4 (Fall 1998): 780–85.

11. John Hope Franklin, *Mirror to America: The Autobiography of John Hope Franklin* (New York: Farrar, Straus, and Giroux, 2005), 345.

12. California Constitution, Article I, § 31.

13. There were several cases that the courts considered. Here I list a few of them. Regents of the University of California v. Blakke, 430 U.S. 234 (1978), Fullilove v. Klutznick, 448 U.S. 448 (1980), Wygant v. Jackson Board of Education, 467 U.S. 267 (1986), Hopwood v. University of Texas Law School, 78 F. 3d 392 (5th Cir. 1996), and United States v. Fordice, 505 U.S. 717 (1992). Finally and arguably, the most important affirmative action case to reach the Supreme Court was Adarand Constructors, Inc. v. Pena, 515 U.S. 200 (1995).

14. Clinton, "Commencement Address at the University of California, San Diego, June 14, 1997," 741.

15. "Policy Dimension of the Race Initiative," p. 1, ABPIR-Meeting Notebooks, Box AB1, John Hope Franklin Papers, 1889–1998, Rare Book, Manuscript, and Special Collection Library, Duke University, Durham, NC (hereafter cited as JHFP).

16. Ibid., 3.

17. Franklin, *Mirror to America*, 345.

18. Steven A. Holmes, "Many Uncertain about President's Racial Effort," *nytimes.com*, June 16, 1997, http://www.nytimes.com/1997/06/16/us/many-uncertain-about-president-s-racial-effort.html?src=pm (accessed January 26, 2011).

19. Eric Pooley, "Fairness or Folly?," *time.com*, June 23, 1997, http://www.time.com/time/magazine/article/0,9171,986563-4,00.html (accessed January 26, 2011).

20. Smith, "The Public Presidency Hits the Wall: Clinton's Presidential Initiative on Race," 783.

21. Lassiter, The Silent Majority.

22. Lowndes, From the New Deal to the New Right.

23. Kruse, *White Flight*.

24. Letter from J. Alfred Smith Sr. of Allen Temple Baptist Church to Dr. Susan Johnson-Cook, July 11, 1997, Folder 1, Box 006, President's Initiative on Race, Correspondence Files, President's Advisory Board on Race, WJCPL.

25. Letter from Cheryl L. Hogan to President William J. Clinton, October 8, 1997, Folder 4, Box 007, President's Initiative on Race, Correspondence Files, President's Advisory Board on Race, WJCPL.

26. Ibid.

27. "Angry white man" was a term used by many in the media to describe the tension and resentment present in many white males during the 1990s. It relates to the frustration felt by some whites over affirmative action, welfare, and a perceived loss of status and opportunity. It also directly relates to the end of the manufacturing era and the beginning of the technology age.

28. Letter from Mr. Hills to President William J. Clinton, September 30, 1997, Folder 3, Box 006, President's Initiative on Race, Correspondence Files, President's Advisory Board on Race, WJCPL.

29. Letter from James A. Gibson to the Advisory Board, October 2, 1997, Folder 2, Box 006, President's Initiative on Race, Correspondence Files, President's Advisory Board on Race, WJCPL.

30. Response letter from Ms. P. Boyle to Executive Officer Randy D. Ayers, May 28, 1998, Folder 1, Box 22, President's Initiative on Race, Correspondence Files, President's Advisory Board on Race, WJCPL.

31. Letter from Ms. Iva G. Good Voice Flute to One America Executive Director Judith Winston, October 2, 1997, Folder 4, Box 022, President's Initiative on Race, Correspondence Files, President's Advisory Board on Race, WJCPL.

32. US Census Bureau, Census 2000, "Table DP-1. Profile of General Demographic Characteristics: 2000," https://www.census.gov/prod/cen2000/dp1/2khus.pdf (accessed November 10, 2015).

33. Immigration Act of 1924, Public Law 89-236; Immigration and Nationality Act of 1965, Public Law 89-236.

34. Center for Immigration Studies, "Three Decades of Mass Immigration: The Legacy of the 1965 Immigration Act," September 1995, p. 2, http://cis.org/1965ImmigrationAct-MassImmigration (accessed November 10, 2015).

35. Ibid.

36. Peter Baker, "With Outburst at Fairfax Forum, Race Initiative Finally Hits a Nerve," *Washington Post*, December 18, 1997, A-1, Box 64, Meetings, President's Advisory Board on Race, WJCPL.

37. Linda Chavez-Thompson, interview with author, by telephone, November 6, 2008.

38. This is in reference to the legendary *Washington Post* reporters Bob Woodward and Carl Bernstein, whose investigative reporting led to the resignation of President Richard M. Nixon in August 1974. They began reporting on and investigating the break-in of the Democratic National Committee Headquarters at the Watergate Hotel in Washington, D.C., in June 1972. They followed a trail that ultimately uncovered a wide array of abuses of power, corruption, and unethical/criminal acts on the part of Nixon and prominent members of the White House staff and administration.

39. Larry Sabato, S. Robert Lichter, and Mark Stencel, *Peepshow: Media and Politics in an Age of Scandal* (New York: Rowman & Littlefield, 2000).

40. Toby Harshaw was one of Steven Holmes's bosses at *New York Times*.

41. Letter from advisory board chairman, Dr. John Hope Franklin to Mr. Toby Harshaw of the *New York Times*, May 20, 1998, Folder 6, Box 022, Correspondence Files, President's Advisory Board on Race, WJCPL.

42. John Hope Franklin, "Some Activities of the Advisory Board to the President's Initiative on Race," Folder 6, Box 22, Correspondence Files, President's Advisory Board on Race, WJCPL.

43. John Hope Franklin, interview with author, Durham, NC, August 14, 2007.

44. Ibid.

45. Ibid.

46. Franklin, Mirror to America, 354.

47. PIR 3/22-3/26 Denver Advisory Board Press Clips, Folder 2, Box 064, Meetings, President's Advisory Board on Race, WJCPL.

48. Letter from Josephine Nieves, executive director of the National Association

of Social Workers, to President Bill Clinton, June 19, 1997, Folder 1, Box 10, PIR Correspondence/Outreach, President's Advisory Board on Race, WJCPL.

49. Letter from White House Director of Personnel/Assistant to the President Bob J. Nash to Josephine Nieves, June 19, 1997, Folder 1, Box 10, PIR Correspondence/Outreach, President's Advisory Board on Race, WJCPL.

50. California Constitution, Article I, § 31.

51. Clinton, "Commencement Address at the University of California in La Jolla, California, June 14, 1997," 737.

52. Franklin, Mirror to America, 349.

53. Linda Chavez-Thompson, telephone interview with author, November 6, 2008. She is referring to the President Clinton's legal troubles.

54. Ibid.

55. Schedules for President Clinton from June 1997 to October 1998, WJCPL.

56. John Hope Franklin, interview with author, Durham, NC, August 14, 2007.

57. Governor Tom Kean, interview with author, by telephone, December 16, 2008.

58. Ibid.

59. Franklin, interview with author.

60. "Interview with Tavis Smiley of Black Entertainment Television on August 4, 1997," in *Compilation of the Messages and Papers of the Presidents*, 1048. Tavis Smiley interviewed President Clinton.

61. David A. Bositis, "Joint Center for Political and Economic Studies 1997 National Opinion Poll: Race Relations," Joint Center for Political and Economic Studies, p. 1, ABPIR-Meeting notebooks, Box AB1, JHFP.

62. John Hope Franklin, interview with author, Durham, NC, August 14, 2007.

63. Smith, "The Public Presidency Hits the Wall: Clinton's Presidential Initiative on Race," 783.

64. "Why a Major Initiative on Race, and Why Now?," p.1, ABPIR-Meeting Notebooks, Policy Dimensions of the Race Initiative, July 17, 1997, Box AB1, JHFP.

65. The President's Initiative on Race examined many issues that are discussed at length in the Advisory Board's final report to the president in September 1998.

66. "What Are the Initiative's Goals and Methods?," p. 2, ABPIR-Meeting Notebooks, Policy Dimensions of the Race Initiative, July 17, 1997, Box AB1, JHFP.

67. Ibid., 6.

68. Governor Tom Kean, interview with author, by telephone, December 16, 2008.

CHAPTER 8

The Clinton Legacy: Bush, Policy, and Obama

1. Joint Statement of Lawrence H. Summers, Secretary of the Treasury, and Jacob J. Lew, Director of the Office of Management and Budget, on Budget Results for Fiscal Year 2000, October 24, 2000, http://www.treasury.gov/press-center/press-releases/Pages/ls968.aspx (accessed November 10, 2015).

2. Joint Statement of Lawrence H. Summers, Secretary of the Treasury, and

Jacob J. Lew, Director of the Office of Management and Budget, on Budget Results for Fiscal Year 2000, October 24, 2000, http://www.treasury.gov/press-center/press-releases/Pages/ls968.aspx (accessed November 10, 2015).

3. Bureau of Labor Statistics, "Labor Force Statistics from the Current Population Survey," Series Id:LNU03000006, Series title: "(Unadj) Unemployment Level—Black or African American," retrieved on November 27, 2012, http://data.bls.gov/timeseries/LNU03000006?include_graphs=false&output_type=column&years_option=all_years.

4. Ibid.

5. Poverty in the United States: 2000, Current Population Reports: Consumer Income, Joseph Dalaker, September 2001, p. 7, https://www.census.gov/prod/2002pubs/p60-219.pdf (accessed November 10, 2015).

6. Ibid.

7. Gary Gerstle, "Minorities, Multiculturalism, and the Presidency of George W. Bush," in *The Presidency of George W. Bush: A First Historical Assessment*, ed. Julian E. Zelizer (Princeton: Princeton University Press, 2010), 252.

8. Ibid.

9. Ibid.

10. Ibid.

11. No Child Left Behind Act of 2001, Public Law 107-110.

12. National Commission on Excellence in Education, *A Nation at Risk: The Imperative for Educational Reform* (Washington, DC: Government Printing Office, 1983).

13. Ibid.

14. Maraniss, *First in His Class*, 409–14.

15. Improving America's Schools Act of 1994, Public Law 103-382.

16. Elementary and Secondary Education Act of 1965, Public Law 89-10.

17. President George W. Bush, "Remarks on Signing the American Dream Down Payment Act," December 16, 2003, in *Public Papers of the Presidents of the United States: George W. Bush* (Washington, DC: Government Printing Office, 2001–2009), 2:1733.

18. Franklin D. Roosevelt, "State of the Union Message to Congress," January 11, 1944, http://www.fdrlibrary.marist.edu/archives/address_text.html (accessed November 10, 2015).

19. Ibid.

20. Federal National Mortgage Association (Fannie Mae) and the Federal Home Loan Mortgage Corporation (Freddie Mac).

21. Bill Clinton, "Remarks on National Home Ownership Strategy," June 5, 1995, in *Public Papers of the Presidents of the United States: William J. Clinton*, 1:806.

22. Brendan Greeley, "U.S. Homeowners Are Repeating Their Mistakes," *Bloomberg Businessweek*, February 14, 2013, http://www.bloomberg.com/bw/articles/2013-02-14/u-dot-s-dot-homeowners-are-repeating-their-mistakes.

23. The Mortgage Forgiveness Debt Relief Act of 2007, Public Law 110-142.

24. Gerstle, "Minorities, Multiculturalism, and the Presidency of George W. Bush," 261.

25. Jesse J. Holland, "Obama Judicial Nominations Set Record for Women, Minorities," *Huffington Post*, September 13, 2011.

26. The Patient Protection and Affordable Care Act of 2010, Public Law 111-148.

27. US Department of Health and Human Services, "About the Law, Health Care," http://www.hhs.gov/healthcare/rights (accessed December 12, 2013.

28. Jonathan Alter, *The Promise: President Obama, Year One* (New York: Simon & Schuster, 2010), 244.

29. This law was immediately attacked by conservatives, Republicans, and Tea Party members who despised the new president and feared that the new law would further deepen the nation in the fiscal muck.

30. Alter, *The Promise*, 246.

31. American Recovery and Reinvestment Act of 2009, Public Law 111-5.

32. Obama Administration Record on Education, www.whitehouse.gov/record (accessed December 12, 2013).

33. Donald Critchlow, *The Conservative Ascendancy: How the GOP Right Made Political History* (Cambridge: Harvard University Press, 2007), 286.

34. Ibid.

Conclusion

1. Donald Lambro, "Polls see Obama gaining as Hillary appears waning; Former first lady losing support of single women, liberals and independents," *Washington Times*, April 23, 2007, A1.

2. Patrick Healy, "Bill Clinton, Stumping and Simmering," *New York Times*, January 18, 2008, 17.

3. Eugene Robinson, "What's Gotten into Bill," *Washington Post*, January 22, 2008, A19.

4. Bill Clinton and Jonathan Alter, quoted in Takiff, *A Complicated Man*, 417.

5. Klein, *The Natural*.

6. Douglas Brinkley, quoted in Takiff, *A Complicated Man*, 100.

7. Branch, *The Clinton Tapes*, 535.

8. John Hope Franklin, interview with author, August 14, 2007.

9. "Work-Experience Unemployment Rate, 2008," TED: The Editor's Desk, January 6, 2010, US Bureau of Labor Statistics, http://data.bls.gov/cgi-bin/print.pl/opub/ted/2010/ted_20100106.htm (accessed January 29, 2011).

10. Virginia Sapiro and David T. Canon, "Race, Gender, and the Clinton Presidency," in *The Clinton Legacy*, ed. Colin Campbell and Bert A. Rockman (New York: Chatham House Publishers, 2000), 173.

11. Ibid., 174.

12. Donna Brazile, quoted in Wickham, *Bill Clinton and Black America*, 49–50.

13. Dewayne Wickman, quoted in Wickham, *Bill Clinton and Black America*, 235.

BIBLIOGRAPHY

ARCHIVAL SOURCES

Rare Book, Manuscript, and Special Collections Library, Duke University, Durham North Carolina.

The William J. Clinton Presidential Library, Little Rock, Arkansas.

Advisory Board on Race

Correspondence Series.

Meetings Series.

Miscellaneous Series.

PR/Media Series.

Programs and Forums Series.

Reports Series.

Domestic Policy Council
Carol Rasco, Subject File

Bruce Reed, Assistant to the President for Domestic Policy and Director, Subject File Series.

Bruce Reed, Crime Series.

Bruce Reed, Education Series.

Bruce Reed, Welfare Reform (1993–2001) Subject File.

Carol Rasco, Assistant to the President for Domestic Policy, Meetings, Trips, Events.

Cynthia Rice, Special Assistant to the President for Domestic Policy, Subject File Series.

Kendra Brooks, Assistant Director of Domestic Policy, Printed Materials Series.

Kendra Brooks, Correspondence.

Stephen Warnath, Senior Policy Analyst, Civil Rights Series.

African and African American Collections
The John Hope Franklin Papers

Advisory Board for the President's Initiative on Race (ABPIR) Series, 1972–1999.

Obama Administration Record on Education, www.whitehouse.gov/record.

American Enterprise Institute

"A Community of Self-Reliance: The New Consensus on Family and Welfare," 1987.

Center for Economic and Policy Research

Schmitt, John. "Inequality as Policy: The United States since 1979." October 2009.

Citizens' Commission on Civil Rights

Yu, Corrine, and William L. Taylor, eds. *The Test of Our Progress: The Clinton Record on Civil Rights.* Washington, DC: Citizens' Commission on Civil Rights, 1999.

Children's Defense Fund and National Coalition for the Homeless

Sherman, Arloc, Cheryl Amey, Barbara Duffield, Nancy Ebb, and Deborah Weinstein. *Welfare to What: Early Findings on Family Hardship and Well-Being.* Washington, DC: Children's Defense Fund, 1998.

Council on Crime and Justice

Brewer, Rose M. "Imperiled Black Families and the Growth Industrial Complex in the U.S." 2010.

Democratic Leadership Council

Clinton, Bill. "Al From Tribute to Al From," June 16, 2009.

"The New Orleans Declaration," March 1, 1990.

"The New American Choice Resolution," Cleveland, Ohio, May 1, 1991.

"Winning in the Global Economy: The Economic Competition Index/Building a New Foundation for Economic Strength," 1985.

Institute for Women's Policy Research

Fact Sheet: The Gender Wage Gap, 2010.

Joint Center for Political and Economic Studies

"1997 National Opinion Poll—Politics," March 1997.

"Do you think that police brutality and harassment of African Americans is a serious problem where you live," 1996.

Legal Services for Prisoners with Children

"People of Color and the Prison Industrial Complex," 1999.

National Association of Black Social Workers

Welfare Reform, position paper, August 2002.

National Commission on Excellence in Education

A Nation at Risk: The Imperative for Educational Reform, 1983.

National Organization of Women

Violence against Women in the United States: Statistics, 2010.

Prison Policy Initiative

"Incarceration Is Not an Equal Opportunity Punishment," 2005.

Progressive Policy Institute

Galston, William, and Elaine Kamarck. *The Politics of Evasion*. Washington, DC: Progressive Policy Institute, 1989.

Marshall, William. "Replacing Welfare with Work." Policy briefing, July 1994.

Tax Policy Center

"Earned Income Credit." *The Encyclopedia of Taxation and Tax Policy*, 2010.

The Urban Institute

Staveteig, Sarah, and Alyssa Wigton. "Racial and Ethnic Disparities: Key Findings from the National Survey of America's Families." In *New Federalism: National Survey of American Families*. Washington, DC: Urban Institute, 2000.

US GOVERNMENT PUBLICATIONS

103rd Congress. "Racial Disparities in Federal Death Penalty Prosecutions 1988–1994." Staff Report, Subcommittee on Civil and Constitutional Rights, Committee on the Judiciary, Second Session, March 1994.

111th Congress. Marc Mauer. "Collateral Consequences of Criminal Convictions: Barriers to Reentry for the Formerly Incarcerated." Testimony prepared for the House Judiciary Subcommittee on Crime and Terrorism, and Homeland, June 9, 2010.

Compilation of the Messages and Papers of the Presidents, 1995.

Congressional Record. Volumes 139–47 (1993–2001).

US Department of Commerce

Bureau of the Census. *Statistical Abstract of the United States.* Washington, DC: Government Printing Office, 2007.

Census 2000.

Dalaker, Joseph. "Poverty in the United States: 2000, Current Population Reports: Consumer Income," September 2001.

Statistical Brief, Health Insurance Coverage, 1993.

US Department of Health and Human Services

"About the Law, Health Care, Rights."

Report to Congress, June 2009.

"TANF 'Leavers', Applicants, and Caseload Studies: Preliminary Analysis of Racial Difference in Caseload Trends and Leaver Outlines," December 2000.

"Trends in TANF Families by Race/Ethnicity, FY 2002–FY2006," Eighth Annual US House of Representatives. *Green Book,* 1996.

US Department of Justice

Bureau of Justice Statistics.

Sourcebook of Criminal of Justice Statistics.

US Department of Labor

Good for Business: Making Full Use of the Nation's Human Capital, March 1995.

"Labor Force Statistics from the Current Population Survey," Series Id: LNU03000006.

The Negro Family: The Case for National Action, 1965.

"Work-Experience Unemployment Rate, 2008, Bureau of Labor Statistics."

Executive Office of the President, Office of National Drug Control Policy

Drug Policy Information Clearinghouse Fact Sheet, "Drug-Related Crime."

General Accounting Office. *Report on Death Penalty Sentencing: Research Indicates Pattern of Racial Disparities.* Washington, DC: Government Printing Office, 1990.

Public Papers of the Presidents of the United States: William J. Clinton, 1993–2001. Washington, DC: Government Printing Office, 1993.

Social Security Administration

Testimony, Director Lowell Dodge, Administration of Justice Issues, speaking for death penalty sentencing: "Research Indicates Pattern of Racial Disparities before the Subcommittee on Civil and Constitutional Rights," Committee on the Judiciary, May 3, 1990.

To Secure These Rights: The Report of the President's Committee on Civil Rights, 1947.

"Vote Tallies, 1996 Welfare Amendments."

US Commission on Civil Rights

A Bridge to One America: The Civil Rights Performance of the Clinton Administration. Washington, DC: Government Printing Office, 2001.

Mauer, Marc. "The Crisis of the Young African American Male and the Criminal Justice System." April 15–16, 1999.

"Revisiting Who Is Guarding the Guardians? A Report on Police Practices and Civil Rights in America," 2000.

The Test of Our Progress: The Clinton Record on Civil Rights. Washington, DC: Government Printing Office, 1999.

Testimony of Bill Moffitt of the National Association of Criminal Defense Lawyers, July 12, 1996.

US Department of Treasury

Joint Statement of Lawrence H. Summers, Secretary of the Treasury, and Jacob J. Lew, Director of the Office of Management and Budget. "Budget Results for Fiscal Year 2000." October 24, 2000.

ORAL INTERVIEWS

Blair, Jim, interview by author, Springdale, Arkansas, March 24, 2008.

Cashin, Sheryl, telephone interview by author, December 16, 2008.

Chavez-Thompson, Linda, telephone interview by author, November 6, 2008.

Clinton, Bill, interview by Lisa Myers, May 6, 1991, NBC's *Today Show*.

Clinton, Bill, interview by Amy Goodman, November 8, 2000, PBS's *Democracy Now*.

Connerly, Ward, telephone interview by author, November 18, 2008.

Edelman, Peter, telephone interview by author, September 18, 2008.

Edley Jr., Christopher, telephone interview by author, April 1, 2009.

Franklin, John Hope, interview by author, Durham, North Carolina, August 14, 2007.

Guinier, Lani, telephone interview by author, November 27, 2007.

Higginbotham, Evelyn Brooks, telephone interview by author, March 11, 2010.

Kean, Tom, telephone interview by author, December 16, 2008.

Shalala, Donna, telephone interview by author, May 1, 2009.

Steinberg, Arnold, telephone interview by author, December 18, 2008.

Winters, William, telephone interview by author, December 3, 2008.

JOURNAL ARTICLES

Blalock, Lydia L., Vicky R. Tiller, and Pamel A. Monroe. "'They Get You Out of Courage': Persistent Deep Poverty among Former Welfare-Reliant Women." *Family Relations* 53 (2004): 127–37.

Chernoff, Harry A., Christopher M. Kelly, and John R. Kroger. "Essay: The Politics of Crime." *Harvard Journal on Legislation* 527 (1996): 527–78.

Collins, Sharon M. "The Making of the Black Middle Class." *Social Problems* 30 (April 1983): 369–82.

Dixon, Travis L. "Psychological Reactions to Crime News Portrayals of Black Criminals: Understanding the Moderating Roles of Prior News Viewing and Stereotype Endorsement." *Communication Monographs* 73 (June 2006): 162–87.

Fannell, Jeffrey B. "The Welfare Workforce: The National Labor Perspective of the AFL-CIO." *St. John's Law Review* 73 (Summer 1999): 761–85.

Gosnell, Harold F. Review of *An American Dilemma: The Negro Problem and Modern Democracy*, by Gunnar Myrdal. *American Political Science Review* 38, no. 5 (October 1944): 955.

Guinier, Lani. "No Two Seats: The Elusive Quest for Political Equality." *Virginia Law Review* (November 1991): 1413–1514.

———. "The Triumph of Tokenism: The Voting Rights Act and the Theory of Black Electoral Success." *Michigan Law Review* 89 (March 1991): 1077–1154.

Hale, Jon F. "The Making of New Democrats." *Political Science Quarterly* 110 (Summer 1995): 207–32.

Helfferich, Krista. "Note and Comment: The Stress, the Press, the Test, and the Mess with the Lani Guinier Smear: A Proposal for Executive Confirmation Reform." *Loyola of Los Angeles Law Review* 28 (1995): 1139–41.

Holian, David B. "He's Stealing My Issues! Clinton's Crime Rhetoric and the Dynamics of Issue Ownership." *Political Behavior* 26 (June 2004): 95–124.

Jennings, James. "Welfare Reform and Neighborhoods: Race and Civic Participation." *Annals of the American Academy of Political and Social Science* 577 (2001): 94–106.

Kenny, Christopher, Michael McBurnett, and David Bordua. "The Impact of Political Interests in the 1994 and 1996 Congressional Elections: The Role of the National Rifle Association." *British Journal of Political Science* 23 (April 2004): 331–44.

Kim, Claire Jean. "Clinton's Race Initiative: Recasting the American Dilemma." *Polity* 33, no. 2 (Winter 2000): 175–97.

Kramer, Ronald, and Raymond Michalowski. "The Iron Fist and the Velvet Tongue:

Crime Control Policies in the Clinton Administration." *Social Justice* 22 (Summer 1995): 87–100.

Leff, Laurel. "From Legal Scholar to Quota Queen: What Happens When Politics Pulls the Press into the Groves of Academe." *Columbia Journalism Review* 32 (September–October 1993): 36–41.

Manza, Jeff, and Christopher Uggen. "Punishment and Democracy: Disenfranchisement of Nonincarcerated Felons in the United States." *American Political Science* 2 (September 2004): 491–502.

Pager, Devah. "The Mark of a Criminal Record." *American Journal of Sociology* 108 (March 2003): 937–75.

Parvez, Z. Fareen. "Women, Poverty, and Welfare Reform." *Sociologists for Women in Society,* August 15, 2002, 1–5.

Pettit, Becky, and Bruce Western. "Mass Imprisonment and the Life Course: Race and Class Inequality in U.S. Incarceration." *American Sociological Review* 69 (April 2004): 151–64.

Roberts, Dorothy E. "The Social and Moral Cost of Mass Incarceration in African American Communities." *Stanford Law Review* 56 (2004): 1271–1305.

Schneider, William. "The New Populism." *Political Psychology* 15 (December 1994): 779–84.

Smith, Renee M. "The Public Presidency Hits the Wall: Clinton's Presidential Initiative on Race." *Presidential Studies Quarterly* 28 (Fall 1998): 780–85.

Wayne, Stephen J. "Clinton's Legacy: The Clinton Persona." *Political Science and Politics* 32 (September 1999): 558–61.

Weaver, Vesla. "Frontlash: Race and the Development of Punitive Crime Policy." *Studies in American Political Development* 21 (Fall 2007): 230–65.

Weir, Margaret. "Review of *Beyond Entitlement: The Social Obligations of Citizenship*, by Lawrence M. Mead." *American Journal of Sociology* 93, no. 2 (September 1987): 495.

Wheelock, Darren, and Douglas Hartman. "Midnight Basketball and the 1994 Crime Bill Debates." *Sociological Quarterly* 48 (2007): 315–42.

BOOKS

Alexander, Michelle. *The New Jim Crow: Mass Incarceration in the Age of Colorblind.* New York: New Press, 2010.

Allitt, Patrick. *The Conservatives: Ideas and Personalities Throughout American History.* New Haven: Yale University Press, 2008.

Alter, Jonathan. *The Promise: President Obama, Year One.* New York: Simon & Schuster, 2010.

Anderson, Elijah. *Streetwise: Race, Class, and Change in an Urban Community.* Chicago: University of Chicago Press, 1990.

Baer, Kenneth. *Reinventing Democrats: The Politics of Liberalism from Reagan to Clinton.* Lawrence: University Press of Kansas, 2000.

Bailey, Beth, and Farber, David, eds. *America in the 70s.* Lawrence: University of Press of Kansas, 2004.

Baldus, David C., George G. Woodworth, and Charles A. Pulaski Jr. *Equal Justice and the Death Penalty: A Legal Empirical Analysis.* Boston: Northeastern University Press, 1990.

Ball, Howard. *The Bakke Case: Race, Education, and Affirmative Action.* Lawrence: University Press of Kansas, 2000.

Bell, Derrick. *Faces at the Bottom of the Well: The Permanence of Racism.* New York: Basic Books, 1992.

Branch, Taylor. *At Canaan's Edge: America in the King Years, 1965–1968.* New York: Simon & Schuster, 2006.

———. *The Clinton Tapes: Wrestling History with the President.* New York: Simon & Schuster, 2009.

Campbell, Colin, and Bert A. Rockman, eds. *The Clinton Legacy.* New York: Chatham House Publishers, 2000.

Cannon, Lou. *The Role of a Lifetime.* New York: Public Affairs, 2000.

Canto, Victor A., Douglas H. Joines, and Arthur B. Laffer. *Foundations of Supply-Side Economics—Theory and Evidence.* New York: Academic Press, 1982.

Carson, Clayborne, and Kris Shepard, eds. *A Call to Conscience: The Landmark Speeches of Dr. Martin Luther King, Jr.* New York: Warner Books, 2001.

Carter, Dan. *The Politics of Rage: George Wallace, the Origins of the New Conservatism, and the Transformation of American Politics.* Baton Rouge: Louisiana State University Press, 2000.

Carter, David C. *The Music Has Gone Out of the Movement: Civil Rights and the Johnson Administration, 1965–1968.* Chapel Hill: University of North Carolina Press, 2009.

Carter, Stephen L. *Reflections of an Affirmative Action Baby.* New York: Basic Books, 1991.

Clinton, Bill. *My Life.* New York: Alfred A. Knopf, 2004.

Collins, Robert M. *Transforming America: Politics and Culture during the Reagan Years.* New York: Columbia University Press, 2007.

Cose, Ellis. *The Rage of a Privileged Class: Why Are Middle-Class Blacks Angry? Why Should America Care?* New York: Harper Perennial, 1993.

Critchlow, Donald T. *The Conservative Ascendancy: How the GOP Right Made Political History.* Cambridge: Harvard University Press, 2007.

DeParle, Jason. *American Dream: Three Women, Ten Kids, and a Nation's Drive to End Welfare.* New York: Penguin, 2004.

Dionne, E. J. *Why Americans Hate Politics.* New York: Simon & Schuster, 2004.

Edley Jr., Christopher. *Not All Black and White: Affirmative Action and American Values*. New York: Hill and Wang, 1996.

Edsall, Thomas, and Mary D. Edsall. *Chain Reaction: The Impact of Race, Rights, and Taxes on American Politics*. New York: W. W. Norton, 1991.

Ehrman, John, and Michael W. Flamm, eds. *Debating the Reagan Presidency*. New York: Rowman & Littlefield, 2009.

Frady, Marshall. *Jesse: The Life and Pilgrimage of Jesse Jackson*. New York: Random House, 1996.

Franklin, John Hope. *Mirror to America: The Autobiography of John Hope Franklin*. New York: Farrar, Straus, Giroux, 2005.

Franklin, John Hope, and Evelyn Brooks Higginbotham. *From Slavery to Freedom: A History of African Americans*. New York: McGraw-Hill, 2011.

Friedman, Milton, and Anna Schwartz. *A Monetary History of the United States, 1867–1960*. Princeton: Princeton University Press, 1963.

From, Al, and Will Marshall. *Mandate for Change*. Washington, DC: Progressive Policy Institute, 1993.

Gillon, Steve, *The Pact: Bill Clinton, Newt Gingrich, and the Rivalry That Defined a Generation*. New York: Oxford University Press, 2008.

Guinier, Lani. *Lift Every Voice: Turning a Civil Rights Setback into a New Vision of Social Justice*. New York: Simon & Schuster, 1998.

———. *The Miner's Canary: Enlisting Race, Resisting Power, Transforming Democracy*. Cambridge: Harvard University Press, 2002.

———. *The Tyranny of the Majority: Fundamental Fairness in Representative Democracy*. New York: Free Press, 1994.

———. *Tyranny of the Meritocracy: How Wealth Became Merit, Class Became Race, and Higher Education Became a Gift from the Poor to the Rich*. Boston: Beacon Press, 2011.

Hacker, Andrew. *Two Nations: Black and White, Separate, Hostile, Unequal*. New York: Scribner, 2003.

Hamilton, Nigel. *Bill Clinton: Mastering the Presidency*. New York: Public Affairs, 2007.

Harris, John F. *The Survivor: Bill Clinton in the White House*. New York: Random House, 2005.

Haskins, Ron. *Work over Welfare: The Inside Story of the 1996 Welfare Reform Law*. Washington, DC: Brooking Institution Press, 2006.

Hayek, F. A. *The Road to Serfdom*. Chicago: University of Chicago Press, 1944.

Holt, Thomas C. *Children of Fire: A History of African Americans*. New York: Hill and Wang, 2010.

Isserman, Maurice, and Michael Kazin. *America Divided: The Civil War of the 1960s*, 3rd ed. New York: Oxford University Press, 2008.

Johnson, Haynes. *Divided We Fall: Gambling with History in the Nineties*. New York: W. W. Norton, 1994.

Katzelson, Ira. *When Affirmative Action Was White: An Untold History of Racial Inequality in Twentieth-Century America*. New York: W. W. Norton, 2005.

Klein, Joe. *The Natural: The Misunderstood Presidency of Bill Clinton*. New York: Broadway Books, 2002.

Kotlowksi, Dean J. *Nixon's Civil Rights: Politics, Principles, and Policy*. Cambridge: Harvard University Press, 2001.

Kruse, Kevin. *White Flight: Atlanta and the Making of Modern Conservative*. Princeton: Princeton University Press, 2005.

Lassiter, Matthew. *The Silent Majority: Suburban Politics in the Sunbelt South*. Princeton: Princeton University Press, 2006.

Lawson, Steven F. *Running for Freedom: Civil Rights and Black Politics in America since 1941*, 3rd ed. Malden, MA: Wiley-Blackwell, 2009.

Lieberman, Robert C. *Shifting the Color Line: Race and the American Welfare State*. Cambridge: Harvard University Press, 1998.

Lowndes, Joseph E. *From the New Deal to the New Right: Race and the Southern Origins of Modern Conservatism*. New Haven: Yale University Press, 2008.

Marable, Manning. *Beyond Black and White: Transforming African American Politics*. New York: Verso, 1995.

Maraniss, David. *First in His Class: The Biography of Bill Clinton*. New York: Simon & Schuster, 1995.

Marshall, Will, and Martin Schram. *The Mandate for Change*. Washington, DC: Progressive Policy Institute, 1993.

McWhorter, John. *Winning the Race: Beyond the Crisis in Black America*. New York: Gotham, 1999.

Mead, Lawrence M. *Beyond Entitlement: The Social Obligations of Citizenship*. New York: Free Press, 1986.

Messer-Kruse, Timothy. *Race Relations in the United States, 1980–2000*. Westport, CT: Greenwood Press, 2008.

Murray, Charles. *Losing Ground: American Social Policy, 1950–1980*. New York: Basic Books, 1984.

Myrdal, Gunnar. *The American Dilemma: The Negro Problem and Modern Democracy*. New York: Transaction Publishers, 1995.

Nelson, Michael, et al. *The Elections of 1992*. Washington, DC: Congressional Quarterly, 1993.

Neubeck, Kenneth J., and Noel A. Cazenave. *Welfare Racism: Playing the Race Card against America's Poor*. New York: Routledge, 2001.

Obama, Barack. *The Audacity of Hope: Thoughts on Reclaiming the American Dream*. New York: Three Rivers Press, 2006.

O'Neill, Timothy J. *The Politics of Equality: Friends and Foes in the Classroom of Litigation*. Middletown, CT: Wesleyan University Press, 1985.

Patterson, James T. *Restless Giant: The United States from Watergate to Bush v. Gore*. New York: Oxford University Press, 2005.

Pattillo-McCoy, Mary. *Black Picket Fences: Privilege and Peril among the Black Middle Class*. Chicago: University of Chicago Press, 1999.

Perlstein, Rick. *Before the Storm: Barry Goldwater and the Unmaking of the American Consensus*. New York: Nation Books, 2009.

———. *Nixonland: The Rise of a President and the Fracturing of America*. New York: Scribner, 2008.

Phillips, Kevin. *The Politics of Rich and Poor: Wealth and the American Electorate in the Reagan Aftermath*. New York: Random House, 1990.

Pierson, Paul, and Theda Skocpol. *The Transformation of American Politics: Activist Government and the Rise of Conservatism*. Princeton: Princeton University Press, 2007.

Pohlmann, Marcus D. *Black Politics in Conservative America*. 2nd ed. New York: Longman, 1999.

Pomper, Gerald M. *The Election of 1992: Reports and Interpretations*. Chatham, NJ: Chatham House Publishers, 1993.

Quadagno, Jill. *The Color of Welfare: How Racism Undermined the War on Poverty*. New York: Oxford University Press, 1994.

Reintsma, Mary. *The Political Economy of Welfare Reform in the United States*. Northampton, MA: Edward Elgar, 2007.

Robinson, Eugene. *Disintegration: The Splintering of Black America*. New York: Doubleday, 2010.

Sabato, Larry, S. Robert Lichter, and Mark Stencel. *Peepshow: Media and Politics in an Age of Scandal*. New York: Rowman & Littlefield, 2000.

Schaller, Michael. *Right Turn: American Life in the Reagan-Bush Era, 1980–1992*. New York: Oxford University Press, 2006.

Schier, Steven E., ed. *The Postmodern Presidency: Bill Clinton's Legacy in U.S. Politics*. Pittsburgh: University of Pittsburgh Press, 2000.

Schlesinger Jr., Arthur M. *The Age of Jackson*. New York: Hachette Book Group, 1988.

———. *The Coming of the New Deal, 1922–1935: The Age of Roosevelt*. Vol. 2. New York: Houghton Mifflin Harcourt, 2003.

———. *The Crisis of the Old Order, 1919–1933: The Age of Roosevelt*. Vol. 1. New York: Houghton Mifflin Harcourt, 2003.

———. *The Disuniting of America: Reflections on a Multicultural Society*. New York: W. W. Norton, 1998.

———. *The Politics of Upheaval, 1935–1936: The Age of Roosevelt*. Vol. 3. New York: Houghton Mifflin Harcourt, 2003.

———. *The Vital Center*. New York: Transaction Publishers, 2007.

Schulman, Bruce, and Julian E. Zelizer, eds. *Rightward Bound: Making America Conservative in the 1970s*. Cambridge: Harvard University Press, 2008.

Sitkoff, Harvard. *A New Deal for Blacks: The Emergence of Civil Rights as a National Issue—the Depression Decade*. New York: Oxford University Press, 2008.

Sowell, Thomas. *Affirmative Action: An Empirical Study*. New Haven: Yale University Press, 2005.

Steele, Shelby. *The Content of Our Character: A New Vision of Race in America*. New York: Harper, 1990.

———. *A Dream Deferred: The Second Betrayal of Black Freedom in America*. New York: Harper Perennial, 1998.

Stein, Judith. *Pivotal Decade: How the United States Traded Factories for Finance in the Seventies*. New Haven: Yale University Press, 2010.

Stephanopoulos, George. *All Too Human: A Political Education*. New York: Little, Brown, 1999.

Sugrue, Thomas J. *Not Even Past: Barack Obama and the Burden of Race*. Princeton: Princeton University Press, 2010.

———. *Sweet Land of Liberty: The Forgotten Struggle for Civil Rights in the North*. New York: Random House, 2008.

Takiff, Michael. *A Complicated Man: The Life of Bill Clinton as Told by Those Who Know Him*. New Haven: Yale University Press, 2010.

Thomas, Clarence. *My Grandfather's Son: A Memoir*. New York: Harper, 2007.

Tocqueville, Alexis de. *Democracy in America*. New York: Penguin Group, 2003.

Troy, Gil. *Morning in America: How Ronald Reagan Invented the 1980s*. Princeton: Princeton University Press, 2005.

Walters, Ronald W. *Freedom Is Not Enough: Black Voters, Black Candidates, and American Presidential Politics*. Lanham, MD: Rowman & Littlefield, 2005.

Weaver, R. Kent. *Ending Welfare as We Know It*. Washington, DC: Brookings Institution Press, 2000.

West, Cornel. *Race Matters*. New York: Vintage Books, 2001.

White, Stuart, and Susan Giaimo, eds. *New Labour and the Future of Progressive Politics*. New York: MacMillan, 2001.

Wickham, Dewayne. *Bill Clinton and Black America*. New York: Ballantine Books, 2002.

Wilentz, Sean. *The Age of Reagan: A History, 1974–2008*. New York: Harper Collins Publishers, 2008.

Wilson, William Julius. *The Declining Significance of Race: Blacks and Changing American Institutions*. Chicago: University of Chicago Press, 1980.

———. *When Work Disappears: The World of the New Urban Poor*. New York: Knopf Doubleday, 1997.

Wilson, Woodrow. *The New Freedom: A Call for the Emancipation of the Generous Energies of a People.* New York: Doubleday, 1913.

Zelizer, Julian E. *The Presidency of George W. Bush: A First Historical Assessment.* Princeton: Princeton University Press, 2010.

———. *Taxing America: Wilbur D. Mills, Congress, and the State, 1945–1975.* New York: Cambridge University Press, 1998.

NEWSPAPERS AND MAGAZINES

Atlantic Monthly.

Black Enterprise.

Bloomberg Businessweek.

Blueprint.

Christian Science Monitor.

Chronicle of Higher Education.

City Journal (New York).

Courier Mail (Brisbane, Australia).

Crisis.

Crises.

Dissent.

Huffington Post.

Los Angeles Times.

Nation.

National Journal.

New Democrat.

New Yorker.

New York Times.

Newsweek.

Philadelphia Inquirer.

Time.

USA Today.

Wall Street Journal.

Washington Post.

Washington Times.

U.S. News & World Report.

WEBSITES

www.alternet.com.

www.bls.gov.

www.cnn.com.

www.crimeandjustice.org.

www.dlc.org.

www.hhs.gov.

www.now.org.

www.nytimes.com.

www.prospect.com.

www.ssa.gov.

www.taxpolicycenter.org.

www.time.com.

www.washingtonpost.com.

www.whitehousedrugpolicy.gov.

www.wsws.org.

INDEX

A

Adarand Constructors, Inc. v. Pena (1995): decision, 148–49, 271n40; impact of, 17–18, 136, 153, 155, 157, 167; importance of, 281n13

AFDC. *See* Aid to Families with Dependent Children (AFDC, 1935)

affirmative action: advantages for women, 140, 164, 165; angry white male syndrome and, 165; backlash, 63; benefits to blacks, 53–54, 59, 119, 151–52; California Proposition 209, 207, 208, 217; Clinton administration's defense of, 155–163; Clinton's defense of, 18, 48, 133, 135–36, 151, 153–55, 165, 243; colorblind philosophy and, 143–48; descriptions of, 143, 145; disadvantages to blacks, 144–45; DLC's view of, 31, 35–36; history of, 136–140; legal challenges, 17–18, 135, 136, 140–43, 148–49, 159–161, 203, 207, 281n13; New Democratic philosophy concerning, 34–36, 135–36; opposition to, 135, 140, 144–46, 147, 151, 166, 203, 207, 225; President's Initiative on Race and, 217–18; Republican goals, 3; revision of, 159; supporters of, 135, 165–68; uneven distribution of benefits, 54

Affirmative Action Review (1995), 17, 149–153

Afghanistan, 236, 245

AFL-CIO, 195

African American elites: Clinton's appeal to, 65; federal appointments of, 69–70; influence and power of, 58–60; response to Reagan administration, 71–72; view of welfare, 182

African American middle class: appeal of Clinton, 4; appeal of DLC, 40, 41, 47; benefits of affirmative action, 164–66; class division within black community and, 29, 39, 41–42, 43, 51, 165–66; Clinton's appeal to, 65; complicity in fleecing of poor, 66; development of, 18, 43, 48, 53–54, 60–65, 139–140, 145, 152, 225; hardline crime policies and, 39; justification for social Darwinism, 57–58; political affiliation, 164–65; pressure to uplift lower class blacks, 62–65; response to Reagan administration, 71–72; support of 1994 crime bill, 113, 119; view of welfare, 180, 182, 183, 225

African American political leaders: centrism of, 63; disconnect with African Americans, 182–86; DLC and, 39–43, 51; political appointments of, 69–70; political strength of, 59; support of 1994 crime bill, 107; support of Clinton, 43–50; view of Reagan administration, 70–71; view of welfare, 201. *See also* Congressional Black Caucus (CBC); Jackson, Jesse; *specific African American politician*

African American religious leaders: influence of, 58; percentage of black professionals, 62; push for equality, 24; support of Clinton, 183; support of crime bill, 97, 120–21, 267n79

African Americans: 1994 crime bill and, 2, 17, 97, 111, 113–15, 118–131; affirmative action, 17–18, 34–36, 54,

135–168, 203; aspirations of, 227–28; backlash against gains of, 44, 51, 53, 63, 70; Bush administration and, 236; civil rights movement, 23, 24, 25; class division among, 16, 29, 41–42, 43, 51, 54–60, 62–66, 97, 102, 145, 164, 165–66, 182–83, 201–2, 204; Clinton's effect on household income, 2; Clinton's relationship with, 247–49; criteria for underclass, 198; Democrats, 164; disparity in earnings, 278n84; disparity in sentencing, 11, 103, 104–5, 106, 111, 115, 122–23, 125, 163, 250, 264n24; distrust of electoral concerns, 31; in DLC, 39–43; DLC's view of alignment with, 26–27; effects of deindustrialization, 44, 54–55, 60, 61, 64–65, 97, 119, 188, 195–96; exclusion from Social Security Act, 172; failed nomination of Guinier, 14, 16–17, 72, 75–91; family life, 123–25, 128–29, 174, 196, 198; federal intervention on behalf of, 29. *See also* Civil Rights Act (1964); Voting Rights Act (1965); hardline crime policies' impact on, 39, 95–97, 103, 105, 249, 250, 264n24; homeownership, 233–35; Hurricane Katrina and, 235–36; impact of War on Drugs, 57, 62, 115, 125–26; impact of welfare reform, 170, 193–200, 249–250; incarceration rate, 127–28, 129; income, 151; in inner cities, 101–2, 112; legacy of Clinton years, 19; negative image of, 65; New Deal benefits, 22; opposition to welfare, 180; percentage of population, 212; police brutality against, 10–11, 114, 121, 122, 126–27, 203, 221; political affiliation, 62, 229; political appointments of, 260n20; political diversity, 40–43, 49, 51, 71–72, 146; political strength, 83–86, 226; poverty levels, 64, 165, 188, 193, 228; President's Initiative on Race, 19, 203–23; Racial Justice Act and,

103–6; racial profiling, 122, 126–27, 163; reception of Great Society, 71; rightward shift of politics and, 15; Rodney King murder trial, 10–13; solidarity of, 55–56; support of Clinton, 2, 43–44; support of Gore, 2; suspicion of DLC, 44–50; unemployment rate, 4, 15, 129, 226, 227, 242, 249; view of Clinton, 1–4, 12–13, 49–50, 92–93; view of New Democrats and DLC, 36, 38; view of Reagan administration, 31–32; views of welfare, 18–19, 182–86; welfare equated with, 36, 169–170, 171–78, 200, 225; welfare programs' effects, 174–75; welfare recipients, 188. *See also* Congressional Black Caucus (CBC); *specific African American*

Aid to Dependent Children (ADC, 1935), 36

Aid to Families with Dependent Children (AFDC, 1935): abolition of, 173; African American recipients, 188; cuts in funding, 176; Democrats view of, 171, 172; failures of, 200; institution of, 169; penalty for work, 175; programs under, 170; reforms, 170, 181, 191; replacement of ADC, 37; restrictions proposed, 184

Alexander, Michelle, 112, 114, 129, 131

Alito, Samuel, 73

Allitt, Patrick, 15

Alter, Jonathan, 8, 240, 241, 246

American Civil Liberties Union, 115

American Dilemma, The (Myrdal), 205

American Enterprise Institute, 179

Americans for Democratic Action, 257n55

Anderson, Elijah, 97

angry white male syndrome, 165, 210–11, 212–13, 281n27

antibusing movements, 23, 26

anti-Communism, 25–26

Anti-Drug Abuse Act (1988), 105

anti-feminist women's groups, 14, 23

antiliberalism, 24–26
anti-statist fervor, 82–83
Asian Americans, 226
assault weapons ban, 97, 101, 103, 107, 117–18, 122, 267n79
assimilation: conservative clergy's view of, 24; of elite blacks, 60; impact on black community, 65; New Democratic philosophy concerning, 35–36; as requirement of integration, 56; white view of, 55
Atwater, Lee, 100
Audacity of Hope, The (Obama), 176
Axelrod, David, 240
Ayers, Randy, 211

B

backlash: in 1990s, 225; against affirmative action, 140–41; against civil rights gains, 24, 25–26, 29, 44, 51, 53, 63; against liberalism in 1970s, 23–24, 29, 70
Baer, Donald, 88
Baer, Kenneth: on Democratic coalition, 40; on DLC, 29, 33; on New Democrats, 27, 30–31; view of Clinton's personality, 187
Baird, Zoe, 74, 76, 87
Baker, Ross K., 6–7
Bakke, Allan, 17, 135, 140–41, 159
Bakke v. California (1978), 17, 135, 140–41, 159
balanced budget agreement, 190
Baldus study, 103, 104–5, 264n24
ballot initiatives, 167, 207, 208, 217
Balz, Dan, 47–48
Basic Opportunity Grant Program, 114
Begala, Paul, 11
Bell, Derrick, 65
Bell, Terrel, 231
Bernstein, Carl, 214, 282n38
Berry, Mary Frances, 121, 127
Beyond Entitlement (Mead), 179–180
Biden, Joe, 87–88, 91, 110, 240
big government, 14, 25, 32
big-tent strategy, 36, 45

black conservative movement, 72
Black Enterprise magazine, 71
black pathology: crime equated with, 62, 98, 102, 108, 162; as source of black problems, 50; welfare equated with, 174
Black Power, 70, 98
blacks. *See* African American elites; African American middle class; African American political leaders; African American religious leaders; African Americans; Congressional Black Caucus (CBC); *and specific African American*
Blalock, Lydia L., 193, 197
block grants: for crime prevention, 116; for welfare, 190, 191, 194, 231
Blueprint (Reed), 132
Blum, Barbara, 179
Blumrosen, Alfred W., 271n51
Blythe, Virginia, 8
Board of Carnegie Corporation, 205
Bolick, Clint, 76–77, 78, 79, 80–81
Bolton, John, 73
Booker, Cory, 51
Boothe, Demico, 127
Bordua, David, 118
Bork, Robert H., 72, 79, 81–82
Borking, 82
Bradley, Melvin, 71
Bradley Foundation, 179
Brady Bill (1993), 101, 102, 112, 266n66
Branch, Taylor: on balanced budget, 190; on death of Byrd, 115; discussion on crime bill, 109; on Guinier's nomination, 76, 88, 89–90, 91; on investigation of King, 35; on racial awareness of blacks in Clinton's administration, 248
Brazile, Donna, 108, 251
Breaux, John, 29
Brennan, William J., 271n40
Brewer, Rose M., 128
Brinkley, Douglas, 247
Broder, David S., 74
Brodkin, Evelyn Z., 184

Brookins, H. Hartford, 43
Brown, Hank, 166
Brown, Jerry, 6, 7
Brown, Jesse, 75
Brown, Michael, 236
Brown, Ronald: investigation of, 14; on
    Jackson's liberal politics, 42; nom-
    ination as secretary of commerce,
    75; relationship with Clinton, 247–
    48; upward trajectory of, 59–60;
    work with DLC, 40, 65
Brownstein, Ron, 185
Brown v. Board of Education of Topeka,
    24, 143
Bryan, William Jennings, 6
Buchanan, Patrick J., 5–6, 7, 230
Buckley, William F., Jr., 25
Bureau of Census, 186, 186–87
Bureau of Justice Statistics, 127–28
Burger, Warren, 141
Bush, George H. W.: 1988 election, 100–
    101; 1992 election, 9, 13; Buchanan's
    attack on, 5–6; colorblind philoso-
    phy of, 34; creation of Glass Ceiling
    Commission, 152, 272n54; domestic
    policy, 231; education reforms, 231,
    233; exploitation of fear of crime,
    98; lack of commitment to minori-
    ties, 243; minority appointments,
    72, 73; nomination of judges, 143;
    Racial Justice Act and, 105
Bush, George W.: 2000 election, 131,
    242; background of, 228–29; cen-
    trism of, 243; Clinton's influence
    on, 242; election of 2008, 245–46;
    housing reforms, 233, 234–35; issues
    of concern, 231; legacy of, 245;
    minority appointments, 229; race
    policy, 236; response to Katrina,
    235–36; strategy of, 229–231; view
    of minorities, 229–230
Bush, Jeb, 167
Bush administration, 112
Byrd, James, Jr., 115, 222

C

California Proposition 209, 207, 208, 217
campaign finance, 6
Canady, Charles, 162
Canon, David T., 250
Cantu, Norma, 77
capital punishment. *See* death penalty
Carter, David C., 137, 138, 174
Carter, Jimmy, 27, 70, 99, 243
Carter, Stephen L., 73, 145
Casey, Robert, 9
Cazenave, Noel A., 169–170, 173, 177–78
CBC. *See* Congressional Black Caucus
    (CBC)
centrism: of Clinton, 16, 49–52, 65–66,
    98–99, 243; of DLC, 46–47; of New
    Democrats, 2, 3–4, 26, 170
Cerda, Jose, 103
certiorari, 270n18
Chao, Elaine, 162, 229
charter schools, 232, 233
Chavez-Thompson, Linda, 206, 213,
    218, 219
Chernoff, Harry, 110
Chicago Tribune, 214
Chicanos, 138. *See also* Hispanic
    Americans
child care assistance, 196
Children's Defense Fund, 185
Children's Defense Fund/National
    Coalition for the Homeless
    report, 196
Chirwa, Dawn, 160
Christian Right, 14, 24
Cisneros, Henry, 14, 75
Citizens' Commission on Civil
    Rights, 193
City of Richmond v. Croson, 142
Civil Rights Act (1957), 68
Civil Rights Act (1964): adoption
    of, 137; benefits to women, 140;
    changes due to, 107; contribu-
    tion to growth of black middle
    class, 152; creation of Civil Rights
    Division, 68; creation of Federal
    Glass Ceiling Commission, 272n54;

crime policy following, 132; effect
on black community, 53, 182;
response to, 29, 143

Civil Rights Division of Department
of Justice, 67–68

civil rights movements: backlash
against, 24, 25–26, 29, 44, 51, 53,
63; failures of, 175; impact on
Democratic Party, 23; legislative successes of, 29, 59; New
Democratic philosophy concerning, 32–33; objectives of, 56; political focus on gains, 55

class: in 1990s, 53–66; American
attention to, 5; as dividing line in
America, 34–35; division among
blacks, 16, 29, 41–43, 43, 51, 54,
58–60, 62–66, 97, 102, 145, 164,
165–66, 182–83, 201–2, 204. *See also*
African American elites; African
American middle class

Clift, Eleanor, 93

Clinton, Bill: 1988 election, 33; 1992
election, 2, 7–8, 9–10, 11, 43–44, 170;
1994 State of the Union address,
117; 1996 election, 2; affair with
Flowers, 7, 12, 96; affirmative action
review, 149–153; African American
support of, 2; African American
view of, 1–4; antagonism toward,
51; appeal to black community, 65;
appointment of minorities, 69, 205;
approach to crime, 14, 95–99, 96,
101, 102–11, 112–13, 115–16, 120–21,
131–33; approach to crime and
criminals, 96; approach to social
policy, 98; association with Guinier,
72–73; attack on Sister Souljah,
11–14, 248; attacks on Obama,
246–47, 251; attempt to update
Social Security, 3; background of,
8–9, 227; Brady Bill, 266n66; cabinet of, 73–76; centrist position, 2,
3–4, 16, 49–52, 65–66, 98–99, 243;
colorblind philosophy of, 147–48;
core beliefs of, 27–28, 247; creation
of racial undercaste, 131; defense

of affirmative action, 18, 48, 133,
135–36, 151, 153–55, 159, 161–62, 165,
168; defense of DLC, 51–52; denunciation of colorblind philosophy,
147, 162; education reform, 231–32,
241–42; effect of 1994 elections,
3–4; establishment of DLC, 26;
establishment of New Democratic
philosophy, 31; FBI files, 217; as
first black president, 1–2, 20, 250;
founding on DLC, 16, 26, 29, 230;
framework of his Presidency, 14–16;
Guinier's nomination, 67, 76, 81, 88,
89–91, 92–93, 136, 248; health care
plan, 240; on homeownership, 233;
impeachment of, 217; legacy of, 19,
225–243, 250–51; Lewinsky scandal,
1, 49, 214, 216–17, 219; liberal support of, 49; loss of reelection bid in
Arkansas, 98–99; New Democratic
philosophy, 13–14, 27; Paula Jones
fiasco, 214, 217, 219; personality of,
8–9, 187, 239, 246–47, 251; plan to
update Social Security, 3; political power of, 131–33; position on
1994 crime bill, 51, 97; position on
welfare, 47, 180–81, 183; race initiative, 19, 161–62, 204–23, 236; race
relations speech, 204, 206–7; racial
influences on policies, 66; relationship with blacks, 26–27, 247–251;
relationship with Obama, 237–38;
relationship with Republicans,
3; separation from traditional
Democrats, 230; silence on Racial
Justice Act, 108–9; as standard
bearer for DLC, 43; strategy in
tough situations, 217; vision for
America, 91, 97, 98, 103; welfare
reform, 18, 38, 170, 171, 184–85,
186–193, 190, 192–93, 200–201, 202;
Whitewater scandal, 214, 217, 219

Clinton, Hillary Rodham: 2008 election, 236–37, 245–46; association
with Guinier, 73; education reform,
232; efforts on health care reform,
240; Guinier's nomination, 76, 88

Clinton, Roger, 8

Clinton, Roger, Jr., 9

Clinton administration: affirmative action review, 149–153; defense of affirmative action, 155–163; negotiations on Racial Justice Act, 109; tax policies, 226

Clyburn, Jim, 192

Cold War, end of, 5, 25–26

Collins, Robert M., 26, 32

Collins, Sharon, 139

colorblind philosophy: affirmative action and, 34–36, 48, 143–48, 151, 207; Clinton's denunciation of, 147, 162; Connerly's vision of, 208; definition of, 163; of DLC, 36, 143, 147; general acceptance of, 146, 147–48; Guinier's nomination and, 17, 72, 88; heart of, 163; integration and, 57; public push for, 209; welfare reform and, 178, 197

Coming of the New Deal, 1922-1935, The (Schlesinger), 22

Committee on Party Effectiveness (CPE), 27

community policing programs, 39, 101, 103, 113

computers, 66

Congressional Black Caucus (CBC): approach of, 106–7; domination of Democratic Party, 230; Guinier's nomination and, 67, 93; on opposition to affirmative action, 146; position on 1994 crime bill, 107–8, 110, 111, 119; position on welfare reform, 180, 183, 184–86, 191–92; power of, 59; support of Racial Justice Act, 105, 106–7, 109–10

Connerly, Ward: advocation of Proposition 209, 208; colorblind philosophy of, 34, 147; conflict with Franklin, 215; opposition to affirmative action, 162, 270–71n35

conservative activism, 15–16

conservative movement, 25

conservative political clubs, 14

conservatives: backlash against civil rights and liberalism, 24, 25–26, 53; colorblind philosophy of, 143; domination of Republican Party, 230; opposition to affirmative action, 166, 207; opposition to Racial Justice Act, 103–4; opposition to voting rights laws, 82–83; race and, 101–2; Racial Justice Act and, 106; response to social transformation of 1960s, 144; strategies for recapturing dominance, 15–16; view of affirmative action, 34; view of equal rights, 25; view of welfare, 170, 170–71, 177, 178. *See also* Republican Party; Republicans; *and specific conservative*

Content of Our Character, The (Steele), 145, 203

Coolidge, Calvin, 169

Correia, Eddie, 158–59

Cose, Ellis, 62–63

counterscheduling, 13

Cox, Archibald, 81

CPE (Committee on Party Effectiveness), 27

crack-cocaine epidemic, 102, 112, 119, 125–26

Crespino, Joseph, 24

crime: as black pathology, 62, 98, 102, 108, 162; Clinton's approach, 95–99, 101, 102–11, 120–21, 131–33; Dukakis's approach, 99–101; Justice Department shift in attention, 112; on national level, 99–101; political exploitation of fear of, 98; poverty and drug-abuse associated with, 112

crime bill (1994). *See* Violent Crime Control and Law Enforcement Act (1994)

crime initiatives, 14, 38–39. *See also* Violent Crime Control and Law Enforcement Act (1994)

criminal defendants: civil rights movement, 25; racial disparity in sentencing, 11, 103, 104–5, 106, 109, 115, 122–23, 125, 163, 250, 264n24; recidivism, 114, 123, 127, 198, 199; rights of, 38–39, 96–97, 129–130

criminal justice system: disenfranchisement of convicts, 129–130; disparity in sentencing, 11, 57, 103, 104–5, 106, 111, 115, 122–23, 125, 163, 250, 264n24; expansion of death penalty, 111, 115; Federal Prison Industries, 116, 266n63; furlough programs, 100, 263n9; impact on African Americans, 57, 62, 256n23; increase in prison population, 114, 122–23, 125–26; Miranda rights, 38–39; Pell Grants for inmates, 39, 114; preventative programs, 267n79; prison-industrial complex, 17, 39, 116, 129, 250; recidivism, 114, 123, 127, 198, 199; sexual violence in prisons, 127; Three Strikes law, 108, 113, 114–15; Truth in Sentencing Incentive Grants, 116. *See also* death penalty; prison-industrial complex; Violent Crime Control and Law Enforcement Act (1994)

Crisis (NAACP magazine), 68, 92

Crisis of the Old Order, 1919-1933, The (Schlesinger), 22

Critchlow, Donald, 25–26, 242–43

cumulative voting, 84–85

Cuomo, Mario, 7

Currie, Elliott, 123

Cutter, Stephanie, 238

D

Daley, Bill, 238

D'Amato, Alfonse, 105

Davis, Artur, 43, 51

Days, Drew, 73, 81

Dean, Howard, 41

death penalty: Clinton's view of, 95–97, 99, 108–9; expansion of, 97, 111, 115; racial disparity in sentencing, 103, 104–5, 106, 109, 111, 115, 264n24; Racial Justice Act and, 2, 103–8, 109, 131, 248; racial justice executive order, 109, 110–11

DeConcini, Dennis, 88

defense spending, 4, 30, 186

deficit spending, 25, 29–30

deindustrialization: angry white male syndrome and, 165; effect on blacks, 44, 60, 61, 64–65, 97, 119, 188, 195–96; effect on economy, 4; effect on white Americans, 54; Jackson's stand on, 32

Delay, Tom, 51

Dellinger, Walter, 153, 160, 161, 273n82

Democratic Leadership Council (DLC): African Americans in, 39–43; approach to affirmative action, 31–36, 35–36, 48, 147–48, 165, 166; approach to crime, 38–39; approach to welfare, 47, 176; big-tent strategy, 36, 45; blacks' suspicion of, 44–50; centrism of, 46–47, 51, 232; Clinton's reflection of, 2; colorblind philosophy of, 36, 143; core beliefs, 27–28; dealings with Jesse Jackson, 32–33, 45–46; electoral successes of, 50; founding of, 16, 26, 29, 230; ideas about education, 232; Jackson's criticism of, 31; market-based solutions, 29–31, 44, 63; nominees to Clinton cabinet, 75; platform of, 26; position on welfare, 18, 36–38, 47; President's Initiative on Race, 19; pro-growth policies, 250; purpose of, 48–49; Racial Justice Act and, 107; search for alternatives to Democratic Party, 50; search for alternatives to liberalism, 23; on third choice in 1994, 4; view of alignment with African Americans, 26–27, 32–33. *See also* New Democratic philosophy; New Democrats

Democratic National Committee, 29

Democratic Party: in 1960s, 22–23; 1984 election, 21–22; 2008 election, 236–37; black faction, 164; Clinton's takeover, 99; coalition formed by Roosevelt, 22; Committee on Party Effectiveness, 27; dominant players

in 1980s, 230; effect of Republican
takeover of Congress, 3, 181, 182,
186, 188–89, 210, 266n68; position
on affirmative action, 163–66;
refocusing of, 26, 42–43; rise of
New Democrats, 26–29; strategies
for recapturing dominance, 15–16.
See also Democratic Leadership
Council (DLC); New Democratic
philosophy; New Democrats; *and
specific Democrat*

Democrats: in 1960s, 22–23; 1980 election, 70; colorblind philosophy of,
143; exploitation of fear of crime,
98; FDR's consolidation of, 22–23;
New Deal/liberal consensus of,
14; passage of 1994 crime bill, 119;
Racial Justice Act and, 105, 106;
refocusing of, 98–99; response to
social transformation of 1960s, 144;
splintering of New Deal coalition,
139; view of Family Assistance
Plan, 175; view of welfare reform,
177, 184, 189. *See also* Democratic
Leadership Council (DLC); New
Democratic philosophy; New
Democrats; *and specific Democrat*

DeParle, Jason, 172, 187, 194, 196

Department of Defense, 156

Department of Education, 158

Department of Health and Human
Services, 158, 198

Department of Justice, 68, 111, 114,
116, 160

Department of Labor, 151, 272n61

deregulation, 2

Devroy, Ann, 201

Diallo, Amadou, 126

Dinkins, David N., 120

Dionne, E. J., 42, 146

direct-mailing campaigns, 14

Disintegration (Robinson), 55

Dissent (Brodkin), 184

Dixon, Travis L., 102

DLC. *See* Democratic Leadership
Council (DLC)

Dodge, Lowell, 106

Dole, Robert, 3, 51, 87, 166, 229

Domenici, Pete, 105

Domestic Policy Council, 51

domestic spending, 30

domestic violence, 97, 113, 124–25, 131,
267n79

Dream Deferred, A (Steele), 203

Drudge Report, 216

drug education, 39

drug interdiction, 163

Drug Kingpin Death Penalty, 39, 105

DuBois, W.E.B., 14, 58–59

Due Process Clause (5th Amendment),
141, 148

Dukakis, Michael, 13, 99–101

Duke, David, 213

E

Earned Income Tax Credit (EITC,
1976), 168, 181–82, 248

economic disparity, 34–35, 46

Economic Opportunity Act (1964), 174

economic policy: of 1980s, 25; of DLC,
29–31; Reagan administration
and, 14

economic security, 32

economy: in 1990s, 225; in 1993, 186; in
2001-2008, 245; Great Recession
(2007-2009), 202, 235, 236, 241, 245,
249; housing bubble, 235; progress
in 2000s, 226; recession (1970s),
36; recession (1992), 4–5, 186–87;
recession (2001-2002), 202; savings
and loan debacle (1980s), 6; under
second Bush administration, 236;
stagflation (1970s), 70, 176

Edelman, Marian Wright, 247

Edelman, Peter, 178, 189, 199, 200,
279n113

Edley, Christopher, Jr.: affirmative
action review, 18, 150, 270n25;
attack on affirmative action, 203;
on critics of race-conscious measures, 144; defense of affirmative
action, 155–58; on Nixon's racial
policy, 139

Edsall, Mary, 176
Edsall, Susan, 36
Edsall, Thomas B., 36, 42–43, 176
education: affirmative action programs,
17, 72, 140–43, 158; for blacks,
198, 199; budget cuts, 190; Bush
reforms, 231, 233; charter schools,
232, 233; Clinton reforms, 231–32,
241–42; effects of integration,
56; Elementary and Secondary
Education Act, 233; as essential
for middle class status, 61; funding for schools, 57, 64; integration
of schools, 24, 137–38; National
Commission on Excellence in
Education, 231–32; No Child Left
Behind, 231, 233; private schools,
24, 143; reforms of civil rights
movement, 29. *See also* affirmative
action; universities
Edwards, Don, 103
Ehrman, John, 70
EITC. *See* Earned Income Tax Credit
(EITC, 1976)
Elder, Larry, 180
Elders, Jocelyn, 14, 75
elections: of 1932, 22; of 1964, 26; of
1980, 14–15, 25, 26, 27, 70, 176; of
1984, 13, 16, 21–22, 26, 29, 31–32,
41, 46, 246; of 1988, 32–33, 41, 46,
99–101, 246; of 1992, 2, 4–11, 43–44,
46, 49, 170, 229; of 1994, 3–4, 181,
182, 186, 188, 210, 266n68; 1994
gubernatorial election in Texas,
229; of 1996, 2, 49, 229; of 2000, 2,
130–31; of 2004, 130–31; of 2008, 19,
66, 236, 245
Elementary and Secondary Education
Act (ESEA 1965), 233
Elshtain, Jean Bethke, 5
Emanuel, Rahm, 103, 238, 240
empowerment zones, 165, 201, 280n115
Enemy of the State (Voigt film), 5
energy crisis, 70
enterprise community program, 201,
280n115
equality: Johnson's position on, 136–38;

New Democratic philosophy on,
135–36. *See also* affirmative action
Equal Protection Clause (14th
Amendment), 85, 104, 141–42
ESEA (Elementary and Secondary
Education Act), 233
Espy, Mike, 14, 40, 43, 75
evangelical community, 231
Executive Order 10925 (1961), 136
Executive Order 11246, 152
Executive Order 13050 (1997), 205

F

fair deal, 25
fair housing laws, 29
Falwell, Jerry, 24
Family Assistance Plan (FAP 1971),
175, 181
Family Support Act (1988), 177
Fannell, Jeffrey B., 195
Fannie Mae, 233–34
FAP. *See* Family Assistance Plan
(FAP 1971)
Farrakhan, Louis, 48, 204
Fattah, Chaka, 189
FBI files, 217
Federal Bureau of Investigation, 116
Federal Emergency Management
Agency (FEMA), 236
Federal Glass Ceiling Commission,
167, 272n54
federal law enforcement, 101
Federal Omnibus Budget
Reconciliation Act (1993), 280n115
Federal Prison Industries (FPI), 116,
266n63
federal procurement policies, 157
Feinstein, Dianne, 33
felon disenfranchisement, 130–31
FEMA (Federal Emergency
Management Agency), 236
Ferraro, Geraldine, 33
Fields, Cleo, 122
Fifteenth Amendment, 144
Fifth Amendment, 141–42, 148
Flake, Floyd, 40

Fletcher, Arthur, 139
Flowers, Gennifer, 7, 12, 96
Foley, Tom, 266n68
forced busing, 16, 23, 26, 29, 70
Ford, Harold, 43
Ford administration, 70
Fourteenth Amendment: affirmative
    action and, 141, 159; enactment of,
    144; racial bias in sentencing and,
    104; voting rights and, 85
FPI (Federal Prison Industries), 116,
    266n63
Frady, Marshall, 13, 33
Franklin, John Hope: on Advisory
    Board function, 218; on Clinton's
    distraction from One America
    initiative, 19, 219; disagreement
    with Oh, 221; on gauging pulse of
    black community, 69; media cov-
    erage of race initiative and, 214–15;
    on President's Advisory Board on
    Race, 206, 207–8, 213, 214; relation-
    ship with Clinton, 247–48; view of
    race relations in 1990s, 220
Franks, Gary, 186
Freddy Mac, 233–34
Freedman's Bureau, 144
Friedman, Milton, 25
From, Al: appeal to biracial coalition,
    47; approach to crime, 38–39; DLC
    honoring of, 51–52; establishment
    of DLC, 26; on Guinier's nomina-
    tion, 88; on Jackson, 32–33; New
    Democratic philosophy, 27; per-
    sonality of, 247
From the New Deal to the New Right
    (Lowndes), 15, 71
frontlash, 29, 132, 256n23
Fullilove v. Klutznick (1979), 141, 142,
    148, 270n16, 281n13
furlough programs, 100, 263n9

G

Galbraith, John Kenneth, 257n55
Galston, William, 33, 35, 164
gang violence, 102, 112, 119

Gantt, Harvey, 42–43
Garvey, Marcus, 11
Gates, David, 75
gay rights, 23, 25
General Accounting Office, 106
general counsel, 272n61
Gephardt, Dick, 27, 29
Germond, Jack, 41
Gerstle, George, 229, 230, 236
Gideon v. Wainwright, 39
Gigot, Paul, 80
Gillon, Steve, 3
Gingrich, Newt, 3, 50–51
Ginsberg, Ruth Bader, 159
Glass Ceiling Commission, 152, 272n54
globalization: angry white male syn-
    drome and, 165; effect on black
    community, 44, 102, 164, 188, 195–
    96; effect on economy, 4; Jackson's
    stand on, 32; New Deal/liberal con-
    sensus and, 14
Goldman, Sheldon, 238
Goldwater, Barry, 25, 26, 138
Gonzalez, Alberto, 229
Gore, Al: 2000 election, 2, 131; African
    American support of, 2; defense
    of affirmative action, 162; meet-
    ing on welfare reform, 192; New
    Democratic philosophy of, 27, 29;
    presidential ambitions, 219–220
Gorton, Slade, 105
Government Performance and Results
    Act, 158, 273n73
government shutdowns, 190
governors, role in welfare reform, 187,
    190–91
Gradison, Bill, 182
Graham, Hugh Davis, 137
Grandmaison, J. Joseph, 46
Grassley, Chuck, 88
Gray, William, 27, 40, 41
Great Recession (2007-2009), 202, 235,
    236, 241, 245, 249
Great Society: approach to social
    policy, 98; division caused by, 23;
    failure of, 58, 118, 243; increase in
    welfare programs, 173; reception

of, 71; results of, 175–76; Vietnam and, 138

Greenberg, Stan, 183

Green Book, 188

Grutter v. Bollinger (2003), 160

Guinier, Lani: aftermath of nomination withdrawal, 91–93; appearance on *Nightline*, 89–90; association with Clinton, 72–73; background of, 68; defense of Voting Rights Act, 68, 77, 78, 81, 82–86; media attack on, 68, 76–81, 87, 88; meeting with Clinton, 90; New Democrats view of, 87–89; nomination of, 14, 16–17, 52, 72, 75–76, 75–91, 248; on racial dynamics, 203; termination of nomination, 67–68, 81, 89–91, 136; writings and ideas of, 81–87

gun restrictions, 39

H

Hacker, Andrew, 97, 146

Hale, John F., 40

Hamilton, Nigel, 76

Harding, Warren, 169

Harkins, Ron, 171

Harris, John F., 3, 48

Harshaw, Toby, 214

Hart, Gary, 32, 100

Hart-Cellar Immigration Act (1965), 212

Hartmann, Douglas, 108, 118

Haskins, Ron, 179, 189, 190–91, 192

Hatch, Orrin, 88

Hayek, F. A., 25

Hayes, Richard, 159

health care reform, 186–87, 239–241, 247. *See also* Patient Protection and Affordable Care Act (2010)

health insurance, 186–87. *See also* Medicaid; Medicare; Patient Protection and Affordable Care Act (2010)

Healy, Patrick, 246

Heflin, Howell, 88

Helfferich, Krista, 84

Heller, Walter, 138

Helms, Jesse, 42

Herman, Alexis, 75, 150–51

Hess, David, 201

"He's Stealing My Issues!" (Holian), 97–98

Higher Education Act (1965), 114

high finance, 66

Hill, Anita, 71

Hilley, John, 192

Hispanic Americans: civil rights movement, 25; education of, 232; percentage of population, 212; political affiliation, 229; welfare recipients, 198. *See also* Chicanos; Latinos

Holian, David B., 97–98

Holliday, George, 10

Holmes, Eugene, 8

Holmes, Steven A., 122, 208, 214–15

Holt, Thomas, 62

homeownership, 233–35

Hoover, Herbert, 169

Hoover, J. Edgar, 35

Hoover administration, 69

HOPE NOW Alliance, 235

Hopwood, Cheryl J., 159

Hopwood v. Texas (1996), 159–160, 281n13

Horn, Steven, 105–6

Horton, William R., 100

housing, 29, 129–130, 233–35

housing bubble, 235

Hoy, Robert, 212–13

Hubbell, Webster, 76, 87

Huffington Post, 238

Hughes, Karen, 229

Hutchinson, Earl Ofari, 82

I

IASA (Improving America's Schools Act), 232

Ifill, Gwen, 11, 120

illegitimacy, 177, 179, 180, 182

immigrants: cutting of welfare funds to, 188, 189, 191, 192; funding for education of, 232; incarceration of illegals, 113; increase in political power, 213; influx of, 212, 213

Improving America's Schools Act (IASA 1994), 232

industry, 4, 54–55. *See also* deindustrialization; globalization

inner cities: 1994 crime bill and, 112; concentration of black poor in, 173; crisis in, 54–55, 119; effects of deindustrialization, 44, 60, 61, 64–65, 97, 119, 188, 195–96; influx of business, 201, 280n115; violence and tension in, 175; white flight from, 101–2, 112, 119. *See also* deindustrialization; globalization

Innocence Project, 115

integration: impact on black community, 55–58, 65, 139–140, 182; of military, 156; of universities, 140; white benefits from, 56–57; white response to, 101–2, 112, 119, 143

Internal Revenue Service, 24

Internet, 66, 226

Iraq War, 236, 245

Isikoff, Michael, 79, 80–81

Isserman, Maurice, 23, 138, 173–74

J

Jackson, Alphonso, 229

Jackson, Jesse: 1984 and 1988 elections, 31–32, 31–33, 41, 46, 246; affirmative action and, 48; attack on welfare reform, 185; Clinton's attack on Sister Souljah and, 11–14; concerns about police brutality and racial profiling, 127; DLC's dealings with, 32–33, 45–46; support of Clinton, 43; view of DLC, 31, 44; Wilder's distancing from, 41–42

Jackson, Maynard, 40, 41, 45

Jacob, John E., 44

J. A. Croson Company, 142

Jefferson, William J., 40, 43

Jennings, James, 197

Jim Crow, 53, 55, 58, 63, 144, 173

John Birch Society, 32

Johnson, Haynes, 5

Johnson, Lyndon Baynes: 1964 election, 26; Civil Rights Act, 136–37; Great Society, 38, 138, 175, 243; investigation of King, 35; racial appointments, 70; speech on affirmative action, 137–38, 155, 163–64; Voting Rights Act, 83, 137; War on Poverty, 173

Johnson, Robert, 206

Johnson, Suzan D., 206

Johnson administration, 114

Johnson-Cook, Susan, 210

Johnson-Reed Immigration Act (1924), 212

Joint Center for Political and Economic Studies, 49

Jones, Paula, 214, 217, 219

Jordan, Vernon, 40, 54, 60, 247

Jordan, Vernon E., Jr., 48

Judicial Selection Monitoring Project, 78

Justice Department, 112, 116, 126

K

Kagan, Elena, 238

Kamarck, Elaine: on affirmative action, 35, 164; on transformation of liberalism, 33; on welfare, 37, 180, 183

Kantor, Mickey, 192

Katrina, 235–36

Katzenbach, Nicholas, 35

Katznelson, Ira, 144

Kazin, Michael, 23, 138, 173–74

Kean, Thomas, 206, 219–220, 223

Kefauver, Estes, 101

Kelly, Christopher M., 110, 265n46

Kelly, Guy, 216

Kelly, Walt, 5

Kennedy, Edward M., 81, 88, 91, 233, 240

Kennedy, John F., 69, 136, 138

Kennedy, Randall, 132, 166

Kennedy, Robert F., 70, 101, 251

Kennedy administration, 136

Kenny, Christopher, 117–18

Kerner Commission, 162

Kerry, John, 131
Keyes, Alan, 71
Kilgore, Ed, 39
Kim, Claire Jean, 206
King, Martin Luther, Jr.: assassination
   of, 98; civil rights work, 24; content
   of their character passage, 144,
   163; as go-between for blacks and
   whites, 58–59; political positions
   of, 34–35; view of Vietnam War,
   34–35, 138
King, Rodney, 10–11, 126, 203, 221
Klein, Joe, 9, 12, 165–66, 181–82, 247
Kohl, Herb, 88, 91
Koppel, Ted, 89
Kotkin, Joel, 74, 165
Kotlowksi, Dean, 175
Kramer, Ronald, 123
Kroger, John R., 110, 265n46
Kruse, Kevin, 101, 209
Ku Klux Klan, 29, 32, 213
Kusnet, David, 181

L

labor unions, 195
Laffer, Arthur, 25
La Raza, 167
Lassiter, Matthew, 23, 102, 209
Latinos, 125, 212, 213, 219, 226. *See also*
   Hispanic Americans
Lawson, Steven F., 22, 67, 119, 130
Leadership Conference, 167
Leahy, Patrick J., 88–89
Leff, Laurel, 79, 80
legacy of Clinton years, 225–243
Legal Services for Prisoners with
   Children, 111
Lew, Jacob, 226
Lewinsky, Monica, 1, 49, 214, 216–17, 219
Lewis, John: advise to Clinton, 48;
   affiliation with DLC, 40; defense
   of affirmative action, 167; endorse-
   ment of Clinton, 43; opposition to
   welfare reform, 183–84, 184; prag-
   matism of, 41; vote on crime bill,
   110, 122

liberalism: backlash against, 23–24,
   26, 29, 70; Clinton's impact on,
   247; creation of schism in society,
   22–24, 146; of Jackson, 32–33; New
   Democratic move away from,
   32–33, 37–38; Reagan administra-
   tion and, 14, 70–72; transformation
   of, 33
liberals: affirmative action and, 34, 146,
   166; Clinton as hero, 49; Racial
   Justice Act and, 106; view of
   Clinton, 93; view of welfare, 171, 178,
   185; view of welfare reform, 36, 187
Lieberman, Joseph I., 48, 49
Lieberman, Robert C., 172
Lift Every Voice (Guinier), 92, 203
Limbaugh, Rush, 209
Lipset, Seymour Martin, 165
Long, Gillis, 27
Long, Russell, 181
Los Angeles race riots (1992), 10–11
Los Angeles Times, 12
Losing Ground (Murray), 177, 179
Lott, Trent, 3
Louima, Abner, 126
Lower-Basch, Elizabeth, 188
Lowndes, Joseph E., 15, 71, 175, 209

M

Madison, James, 84
Magaziner, Ira, 240
mandatory sentencing laws, 39
Manza, Jeff, 130
Marable, Manning, 34
Maraniss, David, 7–8, 99
market-based solutions: black politicians' view of, 44, 51, 63; as
   conservative solution to domestic
   problems, 25; for distressed cities,
   168; effect on poor, 65–66; New
   Democratic philosophy, 29–31; to
   social problems, 63; for welfare,
   37–38, 189, 192
Marshall, Will, 26, 37–38, 88, 160, 194
Martin, Robert, 95
Martinez, Mel, 229

Mashek, John W., 45
Mason, George, 147
Matsuda, Mari, 87
Matsui, Robert, 192
Mauer, Marc, 126, 128, 130
Maximus, Inc., 194
McBrunett, Michael, 117–18
McCain, John, 237
McCleskey v. Kemp, 104, 105, 264n24
McClesky, Warren, 104
McCollum, Bill, 106, 108
McConnell, Mitch, 166
McCurdy, Dave, 89
McGirr, Lisa, 15
McWhorter, John, 145, 146, 180, 203
Mead, Lawrence, 179
media: on Clinton's cabinet, 74–75;
    Clinton's strategy concerning, 9;
    coverage of Affirmative Action
    Review and defense, 164; cover-
    age of Guinier's nomination, 68,
    76–81, 87, 88; coverage of Lewinsky
    scandal, 216–17; coverage of O. J.
    Simpson trial, 222; on crime, 98;
    portrayal of black criminal pathol-
    ogy, 62, 102; on President's Initiative
    on Race, 208–9, 214–16, 221; report-
    ing of Guinier's nomination, 17;
    reporting of Rodney King beating,
    221; on welfare programs, 173
Medicaid, 3, 190, 192
Medicare, 3, 190, 201
Meek, Kendrick, 51
Meeks, Carolyn, 191–92
Melton, R. H., 41–42
mend it, don't end it policy, 161, 165
Messer-Kruse, Timothy, 125
Metro Broadcasting, Inc. v. FCC, 148
Metzenbaum, Howard M., 88
Mfume, Kweisi, 67, 93, 107, 110, 111
Michalowski, Raymond, 123
Midnight Basketball League, 103, 118–
    19, 122, 263–64n19
military: ex-soldiers in police forces,
    103, 114; integration and affirmative
    action, 156, 166; Vietnam Veterans'
    Readjustment Assistance Act, 152

Miller, Tyisha, 126
Million Man March on Washington,
    D.C. (1995), 48, 204, 217
Mills, David, 10
Miner's Canary, The (Guinier), 92
Mineta, Norman, 75
minimum wage, 168
Mink, Patsy, 189
Minority Business Enterprise, 141,
    270n16
Minority Business Utilization Plan
    (Virginia), 142
Miranda rights, 38–39
Mitchell, George, 91
Mitchell, Mrs. Mitch, 162
Modern Conservatives, 14
Moffitt, Bill, 115
Mondale, Walter, 13, 21, 22, 27, 32, 33
*Monetary History of the United
    States, 1867-1960, The* (Friedman/
    Schwartz), 25
monetary policy, 25
Monica Lewinsky affair, 1, 49, 214,
    216–17, 219
Monroe, Pamela A., 193, 197
morality, 5–6
Morrison, Toni, 1–2
Mortgage Forgiveness Debt Relief Act
    (2007), 235
Moseley-Braun, Carol, 88, 104, 191
"Moving Ahead" (Wednesday Group),
    182
Moynihan, Daniel Patrick, 174–75,
    189, 206
Murray, Charles, 177, 179
Myrdal, Gunnar, 205, 206

N

NAACP: attack on welfare reform,
    185; concern about California
    Proposition 209, 207; Guinier's
    award, 91; on opposition to affir-
    mative action, 146, 167; support of
    Guinier's nomination, 67–68
Nabors, Rob, 238
NAFTA, 187

Nash, Bob J., 216
National Action Network, 185
National Association of Black Social
Workers, 194, 200
National Center for Education
Statistics, 61
National Commission on Excellence in
Education, 231–32
National Domestic Hotline, 113
National Endowment for the Arts, 6
National Governors Association, 196
National Organization of Women,
124–25, 185
National Review, 177
National Rifle Association (NRA),
117–18, 266n66, 266n68
National Urban League, 146
Nation At Risk, A (National
Commission on Excellence in
Education), 231–32
Nation of Islam, 48, 204
Native Americans: civil rights move-
ment, 25; One America and, 219;
President's Advisory Board on
Race and, 209, 211, 215–16
Negro Family, The (Moynihan), 174–75,
206
neighborhood activists, 14, 23
Neubeck, Kenneth J., 169–170, 173,
177–78
New Deal: African Americans' benefits,
22; approach to social policy, 98;
conservative opposition to, 25;
creation of Fannie Mae and Freddy
Mac, 234; end of, 243; increase
in welfare programs, 18; Reagan
administration and, 14, 15; Social
Security Act, 171
New Democrat, 4, 164, 194
New Democratic philosophy: abhor-
rence of quotas, 74; on affirmative
action, 34–36, 135–36, 164, 165;
blacks' view of, 2–3; centrism of, 3,
26; of Clinton, 13–14, 131; Clinton's
embodiment of, 2, 247; colorblindness, 143; on crime and criminals,
39, 96, 98, 115–16, 116, 133; on equal-

ity, 35–36; influences on, 15–16;
market-based solutions, 29–31, 168,
200; mission of, 225; pro-growth
policies, 46; on race, 204, 232; on
social policy, 109; toward the poor,
170; on welfare, 36–38, 47, 177, 180,
185, 202, 225. *See also* Democratic
Leadership Council (DLC)
New Democrats: 1994 elections, 3–4;
blacks' suspicion of, 44–50; centrism of, 2, 3–4, 26, 170; Committee
on Party Effectiveness, 27; core
beliefs, 27–28; election of 1988 and,
32–33; emergence of, 26; Guinier's
nomination, 87–89; New Orleans
Declaration, 135–36; use of affirmative action, 168; view of Clinton's
health care concerns, 187; view of
Jackson, 32–33
New Federalism model for welfare,
171, 231
New Freedom (Wilson), 30
New Jim Crow, The (Alexander), 133
New Left, 28
New Orleans, 235–36
New Orleans Declaration (1990),
135–36
New Right, 24–25
Newsweek, 7, 8, 13
New York Times: on 1992 election, 12;
on 1994 crime bill, 108; coverage
of Guinier's nomination, 78, 88; on
furlough programs, 100; on race
initiative, 214–15; on Racial Justice
Act, 106, 109
Nickles, Don, 166
Nieves, Josephine, 216
Nightline, 89–90
Nixon, Richard M.: exploitation of fear
of crime, 98; Family Assistance
Plan, 175; New Federalism model
for welfare, 171; racial policies of,
135, 138–39; strategy of, 229; use
of block grants, 116; Watergate, 6,
282n38
Nixon administration, 70, 175
No Child Left Behind (2002), 231, 233

normality, 227
Norton, Gale, 229
Not All Black and White (Edley, Jr.), 203
NOW, 167
NRA. *See* National Rifle Association (NRA)
Nunn, Sam, 27, 29
Nutter, Michael, 43

O

Obama, Barack: 2008 election, 236–37, 245–46; appointees, 238–39; ascendancy of, 19; background of, 237, 239; benefit from affirmative action, 54; centrism of, 51, 241, 243; Clinton's attacks on, 246–47, 251; Clinton's influence on, 19, 225, 236–242, 243; elections of, 66, 225; health care reform, 239–241, 285n29; personality of, 239; on Reagan's speaking ability, 176; relationship with Clinton, 237–38
O'Connor, Sandra Day, 142, 148–49
Office of Federal Contract Compliance Programs, 152, 156
Office of Management and Budget, 158
Office of National Drug Control Policy, 122–23
Oh, Angela, 206, 213, 221
O. J. Simpson trial, 222
Old-Age Insurance, 172
O'Leary, Hazel, 68, 75
Olin Foundation, 179
One America, 204–5, 210–11. *See also* President's Initiative on Race (PIR 1997)
O'Neill, Tip, 28–29, 230
one man, one vote system, 85–87
organized labor, 138
outsourcing, 4, 97, 102
Ownership Society, 233, 234–35

P

Pact: Bill Clinton, Newt Gingrich, and the Rivalry That Defined a Generation (Gillon), 3

Pager, Devah, 129, 130
Palin, Sarah, 237
Panetta, Leon, 109, 192, 238
Parvez, Z. Fareen, 198
Patient Protection and Affordable Care Act (2010), 239–241, 285n29
Patterson, James T., 4–5
Pattillo-McCoy, Mary, 61, 140
Paula Jones fiasco, 214, 217, 219
peace activism, 26, 138
Pell, Claiborne, 114
Pell grants: increases, 168, 202; for prisoners, 39, 114
Pena, Federico, 75
Perlstein, Rick, 175
Perot, Ross, 6–7
Personal Responsibility Act (1995), 189
Personal Responsibility and Work Opportunity Reconciliation Act (1996): consequences of, 18, 170, 193–200, 249–250; mission of, 182; passage of, 193
Pettit, Becky, 123, 129, 130
Philadelphia Plan, 135, 139. *See also* affirmative action programs
Phillips, Kevin, 178, 275n25
Picking Federal Judges (Goldman), 238
Pierce, Samuel, 71
Pierson, Paul, 15–16
PIR. *See* President's Initiative on Race (PIR 1997)
Piscataway Township Board of Education v. Taxman (1996), 160–61, 273n82
Pivotal Decade (Stein), 199
Podesta, John, 238
Pohlmann, Marcus D., 199
police brutality, 10–11, 114, 121, 122, 126–27, 203, 221
police force: as deterrent to crime, 112; ex-military in, 103, 114; increase presence on streets, 39, 97, 101, 114, 126, 267n79
political activism, 23–24, 25
political correctness, 209, 213
political culture: of 1950s and 1960s, 22–23, 24; of 1960s, 22–23, 25–26; of 1970s and 1980s, 23–24, 26, 36–37;

impact of black class division, 65–66

Politics of Rich and Poor, The (Phillips), 178

Politics of Upheaval, The (Schlesinger), 22

Polity, 206

Poole, Isaiah J., 72

Pooley, Eric, 208

Porter, Eric, 70

poverty: in black population, 64, 112, 188, 193, 228; race associate with, 193

poverty levels, 15

Powell, Colin, 54, 65, 71, 229, 248

Powell, Lewis, 104, 141, 142

presidential authority, 131

Presidential Committee on Equal Employment Opportunity, 136

Presidential Studies Quarterly, 206

President's Advisory Board on Race: hindrances to, 208–14, 221; institution of, 205; issues examined, 222; media coverage of, 208–9, 214–16, 221; members' contributions to failure, 220–23; members of, 206; mission of, 207–8, 218–19, 222; outreach meeting, 162

President's Initiative on Race (PIR 1997): Advisory Board's report, 283n65; components of, 207; failure of, 220–23, 222–23; institution of, 205, 206; limiting factors, 19, 204; media coverage of, 208–9, 214–16; public response to, 209–13; purpose of, 161–62, 206; results of, 249; White House hindrances, 217–220

prisoner rights, 38–39

prison-industrial complex, 17, 39, 116, 129, 250

prisons, 97, 111, 113, 116, 122–23, 125

privatization of services, 194

pro-business advocacy, 23

pro-business policies, 2, 240, 285n29

pro-family movement, 23–24

Progressive Policy Institute, 31

progressives: anger at retreat from civil rights gains, 50; criticism of, 46; in

New Deal coalition, 22; principles of, 30; view of crime bill, 111; view of DLC, 38; view of welfare reform, 169

proportionate interest representation, 86

Providence Journal-Bulletin, 216

Public Welfare Amendments (1962), 169, 170

Public Works Employment Act (1977), 141, 270n16

Q

Quadagno, Jill, 173

R

race: in 1970s and 1980s, 70; in 1990s, 11–14, 53–66, 104–5, 143–48, 163–66, 203, 209–13, 220–21; American attention to, 5; Clinton's approach to, 247; diversity of in US, 212; DLC's approach to, 35–36; failed nomination of Guinier, 14, 16–17; poverty associated with, 193; Racial Justice Act, 2, 103–8, 109, 131, 248; racial justice executive order, 109, 110–11; Victim's Rights Amendment, 103–4; welfare equated with, 36, 169–170, 171–78, 200, 225. *See also* affirmative action; African Americans; color-blind philosophy; criminal justice system; police brutality; racial profiling

race-baiting, 275n25

race initiative (1997-98), 93, 203–23. *See also* President's Advisory Board on Race; President's Initiative on Race (PIR 1997)

Race Initiative Advisory Board, 162

Race Initiative Outreach Meeting, 162

Race Matters (West), 203

race riots, 10–11, 70

Race to the Top, 241–42

racial animus: in 1990s, 170, 178, 209–13; within President's Advisory

Board on Race, 213; President's Initiative on Race increasing, 223; Reagan administration and, 14

racial backlash. *See* backlash

Racial Justice Act (1994), 2, 103–8, 109, 131, 248

racial justice executive order, 109, 110–11

racial profiling, 121, 122, 126–27, 163

racial reconciliation, 14, 19. *See also* race initiative (1997-1998); Race Initiative Advisory Board

racial solidarity, 55–56

Rage of a Privileged Class, The (Cose), 63

Rainbow Coalition, 185

Raines, Franklin, 179

Randolph, A. Phillip, 138

Rangel, Charles: defense of welfare, 185; on Racial Justice Act, 109; on violence in cities, 120; vote on 1994 crime bill, 110, 122; on welfare reform, 192

Rather, Dan, 21

Reagan, Ronald: 1980 election, 25, 27, 70; 1984 election, 21–22, 26; African American response to, 71–72; African Americans' view of, 31–32; approach to welfare, 176; colorblind philosophy of, 34; conservatism of, 209; criticism of civil rights measures, 53; Democratic response to, 26; economic policy, 25; end on New Deal/liberal consensus, 14; exploitation of fear of crime, 98; Guinier's attacks on his civil rights record, 81; influence of, 201; minority appointments, 70–71, 72, 73, 243; nomination of judges, 143; opposition to affirmative action, 42; popularity of, 230; racialization of welfare, 36; Racial Justice Act and, 105; realignment of US politics, 22–26, 27–28; view of Voting Rights Act, 82; view of welfare, 36, 178–79; War on Drugs, 39, 57, 62

Reagan administration: African Americans' view of, 31–32; backlash against civil rights gains, 53; black politicals' view of, 70–71; effect of tax cuts on economy, 4; impact on Democratic Party, 15–16; lack of minorities in, 69; pressure on middle class blacks, 63; reduction of funding to combat poverty, 112; unrest over welfare programs, 18; welfare reform, 179

recession (1970s), 36

recession (1992), 4–5, 186–87

recession (2001-2002), 202

Reconstruction (1960s), 59

Rector, Rickey Ray, 14, 95–96

Reddy, Henry, 47–48

redlining, 234

Reed, Bruce, 51, 103, 132, 247

Reed, Ishmael, 98

Reflections of an Affirmative Action Baby (Carter), 145

Regents of the University of California v. Bakke (1978), 17, 135, 140–41, 159, 281n13

regulatory reform, 65

Rehabilitation Act (1973), 152

Reich, Robert, 73, 195

Reinstma, Mary, 182

Reischauer, Robert, 179

religious zealotry, 23–24

Reno, Janet, 74, 87, 161

"Republican Contract with America" (1994), 182

Republican Party: appeal to Latinos and women, 229; colorblind philosophy of, 143; control of Congress, 3, 181, 182, 186, 188–89, 210, 266n68; dominant players in 1990s, 230; embracing of black conservatism, 72; political power between 2001 and 2007, 131; racial politics of, 275n25; seizure of New Deal coalition, 28–29

Republicans: approach to welfare, 169, 177, 178–79, 182; assumption of power in 1980, 176; challenges to affirmative action, 166, 203; as cover for Democrats, 49; exploitation of fear of crime, 98; impeachment of Clinton, 217; interference in President's Advisory Board on Race, 209; opposition to Clinton, 3; opposition to Racial Justice Act, 105–6, 107; position of race, 230; position on 1994 crime bill, 110, 119; view of welfare, 179–180; Wednesday Group, 182; welfare reform proposals, 184, 189–190. *See also specific Republican*

Reynolds, William Bradford, 78, 81
Rice, Condoleezza, 229
Rice, Susan, 238
Richards, Ann, 229
Richardson, Bill, 75
Rights Revolution, 137–38
Rivlin, Alice, 179
Road to Serfdom, The (Hayek), 25
Robb, Charles, 27, 41, 44, 45, 46
Roberts, Dorothy E., 123, 125, 129
Robertson, Pat, 24
Robinson, Eugene, 55, 58, 246
Rocky Mountain News, 214, 216
Rodney King murder trial, 10–11, 126, 203, 221
Romney, Mitt, 239
Roosevelt, Eleanor, 257n55
Roosevelt, Franklin Delano: on American Dream, 233; black cabinet of, 69; Democratic coalition forged by, 22–23; New Deal, 22, 38, 171, 243
Roosevelt administration, 171–73
Rove, Karl, 229
Rucci, M., 74
Ruff, Charles F. C., 160
Ruffin, David C., 38
Rusk, Dean, 35

S

Sabol, William L., 115
Sapiro, Virginia, 250
Satcher, David, 75

Savage, David, 79
savings and loan debacle (1980s), 6
SBA (Small Business Administration), 148–49, 157
Schaller, Michael, 100–101
Schlesinger, Arthur M., Jr., 15, 22, 35–36, 257n55
Schmitt, John, 199
Schmoke, Kurt, 40
Schneider, William, 9, 49
school desegregation, 24
Schulman, Bruce, 23
Schwartz, Anna, 25
Second Bill of Rights, 233
Second Reconstruction (1960s), 59, 141, 144
secularization, 23, 25–26
segregation, 58–59, 234
Seidman, Ricki, 90
sexual permissiveness, 23, 26
Shalala, Donna, 37, 190
Sharpton, Al, 127, 185
Shaw, Bernard, 100
Shelby, Richard, 166
Sherman, Arloc, 196
Shriver, Sargent, 173–74
Silent Majority, The (Lassiter), 102
Simon, Paul, 88, 166
Simpson, Alan, 88
Sister Souljah, 10–14, 248
Sitkoff, Harvard, 69
Skocpol, Theda, 15–16
Slater, Rodney, 75, 247
Small Business Act, 271n42
Small Business Administration (SBA), 148–49, 157
Smith, J. Alfred, Sr., 210
Smith, Renee M., 206, 208
social Darwinism, 57
Social Security Act (1935): Aid to Dependent Children, 36, 37, 169; cuts in funding, 3; exclusion of African Americans, 172; middle class' view of changes to, 201; passage of, 169, 171; provisions of, 171–72; purpose of, 18
social unrest, 14

Sotomayor, Sonia, 73, 238
Souls of Black Folk (DuBois), 14
Souter, David H., 159
Sowell, Thomas, 34, 144, 146, 180
Spellings, Margaret, 229
stagflation, 176
Starr, Kenneth, 216
Steele, Shelby, 145, 146, 180, 203
Stein, Judith, 21, 199
Stennis, John, 138
Stephanopoulos, George, 18, 109, 150, 155–58, 201
stimulus bill, 241
Streetwise (Anderson), 97
student loans, 168, 202
suburbanization, 101–2, 112, 119
Suburban Warriors (McGirr), 15
Sugrue, Thomas, 55
Summers, Lawrence, 226, 238

T

Taft, Robert, 25
TANF. *See* Temporary Aid for Needy Families (TANF)
taxation, 14, 46
tax cuts, 186
Taxman, Sharon, 160–61
Taylor, Paul, 44
technology sector, 226
Teele, Arthur, 71
televangelists, 15
Temporary Aid for Needy Families (TANF), 188, 191, 194, 195, 198
Thernstrom, Abigail, 34, 80–81, 82, 162, 163
Thernstrom, Stephen, 34, 162
Thirteenth Amendment, 144
Thomas, Clarence: on affirmative action, 72, 144, 145, 146; appointment to Supreme Court, 72, 79, 82; benefit from affirmative action, 54; black image and, 65; education of, 73; service in Reagan administration, 71; view of affirmative action, 72
Thomas-Laury, Lisa, 124
Three Strikes law, 108, 113, 114–15

Thurmond, Strom, 88
Tiller, Vicky R., 193, 197
Time, 12–13, 208, 214
Torres, Esteban Edward, 166–67
To Secure These Rights (Truman commission), 205
Troy, Gil, 21
Truman, Harry, 205
Truth in Sentencing Incentive Grants, 111, 113, 116
Twenty-Fourth Amendment, 82
Two Nations (Hacker), 97
Tyranny of the Majority, The (Guinier), 92
Tyranny of the Meritocracy (Guinier), 92

U

Uggen, Christopher, 130
Unemployment Insurance, 172
unemployment rate, 4, 15, 129, 226, 242, 249
United Negro Improvement Association, 11
United States Commission on Civil Rights, 193
United States Sentencing Commission, 125
United States v. Fordice, 281n13
universities: affirmative action programs, 158; California Proposition 209, 207; integration of, 56, 72, 137–38, 140; legal challenges to affirmative action, 135, 140–43, 159–160
Urban Institute, 188, 198
USA Today, 78, 200
US Commission on Civil Rights, 121
U. S. News and World Report, 88
US Supreme Court: decisions on affirmative action, 17–18, 135, 136, 140–43, 148–49, 159–160, 281n13; Miranda rights, 38–39

V

victims' rights, 38–39, 96–97, 99
Victim's Rights Amendment, 104

victims' rights laws, 39

Vietnam Veterans' Readjustment Assistance Act (1974), 152

Vietnam War: Clinton and, 7–8; failure of government in, 175; impact on Democratic Party, 23; King's position on, 35, 138

violence: conservative response to, 26; effect of liberal solutions, 175; Las Angles race riots, 10–11; pleas for help with, 62; in prisons, 128; in urban areas, 101, 112, 119–120; urban riots of 1970s, 70; against women, 97, 113, 124–25, 131, 267n79. *See also* police brutality

Violence Against Women Act (1994), 124–25, 131

Violent Crime Control and Law Enforcement Act (1994): African American support of, 119–122; Clinton's position on, 50, 187; Congressional Black Caucus's opposition to, 93, 109–11; effect on black Americans, 17, 97, 122–131, 249, 250; outcomes, 121, 131–32; passage of, 39, 97, 111, 117–19; provisions of, 97, 111, 112–16; Racial Justice Act, 2, 103–9, 131, 136; selling of, 65, 120–21

Voight, Jon, 5

voter referendums, 167, 207, 208, 217

Voting Rights Act (1965): adoption of, 137; effect on black community, 182; Guinier's defense of, 68, 77, 78, 81, 82–85; New Democrats concern about enforcement of, 87–88; provisions of, 82; Reagan's opposition to, 53; response to, 29

voting rights of convicts, 129–130

W

Walker, Bob, 185

Wall Street Journal, 7, 76–77, 79–80, 82, 177

Walters, Ronald W., 11, 32, 50

War on Drugs: Clinton's refusal to end, 250; impact on African Americans, 57, 62, 115, 125–26; Jackson's position on, 39

War on Poverty, 173, 175

War on Terror, 236, 245

Washington, Booker T., 58–59

Washington Post, 10, 80, 214

Washington Times, 78, 79, 177, 245

Watergate, 6, 27, 282n38

Waters, Maxine, 184

Watts, J. C., 54, 186

Wayne, Stephen J., 9

Weaver, R. Kent, 176, 178, 200

Weaver, Vesla, 132, 256n23

Weber, Vin, 182

Wednesday Group, 182

Weir, Margaret, 50, 180

Weisberg, Jacob, 184

welfare: backlash, 29; at beginning of 1992, 181–82; under Bush administration, 231; disparity in benefits, 275–76n28; history of, 169, 171–77; intellectual opposition in 1980s and 1990s, 177–180; New Democratic criticism of, 28; privatization of services, 194; racialization of, 36, 169–170, 171–78, 200, 225; repercussions of, 170; variance in benefits, 57. *See also* Great Society; New Deal; Personal Responsibility and Work Opportunity Reconciliation Act (1996)

welfare recipients: after 1996 welfare reform, 198, 200; civil rights movement, 25; denigration of, 170, 176, 177–78; increase between 1981-1992, 47

welfare reform: of 1988, 171, 179; in 1993-1995, 186–88; of 1995-1996, 188–193, 225; African American views of, 47, 182–86; of Clinton, 2, 184; Congressional Black Caucus's opposition to, 93; impact on African Americans, 193–200, 249–250; impact on President's Race Initiative, 210; of New Deal, 18; New Democratic philosophy, 36–38, 47, 225; policy and results of,

14; under Reagan, 176; Republican goals, 3; as Republican issue, 184; selling of, 65; shifts needed for, 38; support for, 201, 225–26; Welfare Reform Act, 50, 190. *See also* Personal Responsibility and Work Opportunity Reconciliation Act (1996)

Welfare Reform Act (1996), 50, 190

West, Cornel, 203

West, Kanye, 236

West, Togo, 75, 247

Western, Bruce, 123, 129, 130

Wheelock, Darren, 108, 118

When Work Disappears (Wilson), 97

white Americans: advantages in education, work, mobility, 152; angry white male syndrome, 165, 211–12, 212–13, 281n27; aspirations of, 227–28; benefits of integration, 56–57; Clinton's effect on household income, 2; DLC's approach to, 45, 48; effects of deindustrialization, 54–55; incarceration rate, 111, 123, 125; opposition to affirmative action, 146; opposition to Voting Rights Act, 83; poverty levels, 64, 228; reception of Great Society, 71; response to integration, 24, 101–2, 112, 119, 143; unemployment rate, 226, 242, 249; view of race relations, 209, 212–13; view of welfare, 182; welfare recipients, 198. *See also* backlash

White Citizens' Councils, 32

white flight, 101–2, 112, 119

White Flight (Kruse), 101, 209

White House Office of Faith-Based and Neighborhood Partnerships, 231

white privilege, 171–73

Whitewater scandal, 1, 214, 217, 219

Whitman, Christine Todd, 229

Wickman, Dewayne, 251

Wilder, Douglas, 40, 41–42, 44, 45, 112

Wilentz, Sean, 15

Wilkins, Roger, 12, 147

Williams, Debra, 160

Williams, Juan, 180

Williams, Walter, 180

Wilson, Pete, 270–71n35

Wilson, William Julius, 44, 64, 97, 102

Wilson, Woodrow, 30

winner-take-all system, 85–87

Winning in the Global Economy (Gephardt), 29

Winning the Race (McWhorter), 203

Winston, Judith, 220

Winter, William, 206

Wirth, Tim, 27

Witcover, Jules, 41

Wolfe, Alan, 164

women: affirmative action and, 164, 165; benefits of affirmative action, 140; domination of Democratic Party, 230; effect of 1996 welfare reform, 197–98; income, 151–52; reliance on Medicaid, 193; weekly earnings of, 278n84; welfare reforms and, 176–77

women's rights, 23, 25, 35–36

Wood, Kimba, 74, 76

Woodward, Bob, 214, 282n38

Woodward, C. Vann, 144

workfare program, 2, 171, 173–74, 248

Workforce Florida, 194

Wright, Sharon D., 186

Wygant v. Jackson Board of Education (1986), 141–42, 281n13

Y

Yellen, Janet, 238

Young, Andrew, 41

Z

Zelizer, Julian E., 23, 172

DARYL A. CARTER is associate professor of history at East Tennessee State University. He specializes in modern American political history and African American history.

9/16